In the
NAME *of*
JESUS

In the NAME *of* JESUS

Exorcism among Early Christians

Graham H. Twelftree

B
Baker Academic
Grand Rapids, Michigan

Published by Baker Academic
a division of Baker Publishing Group
P.O. Box 6287, Grand Rapids, MI 49516-6287
www.bakeracademic.com

Printed in the United States of America

Library of Congress Cataloging-in-Publication Data

Twelftree, Graham H.
    In the name of Jesus : exorcism among early Christians / Graham H. Twelftree.
        p.   cm.
    Includes bibliographical references and indexes.
    ISBN 10: 0-8010-2745-4 (pbk.)
    ISBN 978-0-8010-2745-1 (pbk.)
        1. Demoniac possession—Biblical teaching. 2. Spirit possession—Biblical teaching.
    3. Exorcism in the Bible. 4. Church history—Primitive and early church, ca. 30–600.
    I. Title.
    BS2545.D5T84   2007
    265'.9409015—dc22   2007016832

To
Catherine and Paul
and
those they have
married and made

Contents

Preface

M Y INTEREST IN exorcism among early Christians began in Nottingham with my doctoral studies under James D. G. Dunn. This is the third book that has its origins in that research. The first book, *Jesus the Exorcist: A Contribution to the Study of the Historical Jesus* (Tübingen: Mohr Siebeck; Peabody, MA: Hendrickson, 1993) was a thorough revision of the dissertation, focusing on Jesus as an exorcist: his methods, self-understanding, and how his audience would have perceived what he was doing. The second book, *Christ Triumphant: Exorcism Then and Now* (London: Hodder & Stoughton, 1985), though published first, due to the mysteries of the publishing world, took the discussion a stage further in trying to recover what the New Testament writers understood about Jesus as an exorcist and what place exorcism had in their churches. A considerable part of that book also sought to draw out present-day implications from that study.

In this book I want to look in more detail at what was sketched out rather inadequately and too briefly in the fourth chapter ("The Early Church") of *Christ Triumphant*. This will also enable me to explore what Q and the Synoptic Gospels are able to tell us about exorcism among the early Christians they represent. Further, I want to focus more carefully on the issues raised by reading the Fourth Gospel and the letters of Paul with questions relating to exorcism in mind. As I will explain, to help do that I have looked beyond the canon, as well as to second-century critics of Christianity.

Few students of the New Testament are able to examine the earliest documents of the church without sensing an obligation to consider the contemporary ramifications of what is discovered and discussed. Also, not least because of significant changes in my views on exorcism in the contemporary church, this book concludes with some brief contemporary corollaries of our study.

As this project comes to completion I am gratefully aware of the help I have received from others: Dale Allison, Hessel Baartse (who can do mysterious things with a computer), Edwin Broadhead, Peter Davids, Clayton Jefford,

John Kloppenborg, Roy Kotansky, Randall Pannell, Todd Penner, Mark Roberts, Oskar Skarsaune, John Christopher Thomas, Brandon Walker, David Wenham, Archie Wright, and particularly Clint Arnold and Paul Trebilco. The investment of time and energy to point out errors, blind spots, lack of balance and offer suggestions for a project not their own is a priceless gift. Of course, not one of these kind people can be held responsible for what follows, not least because, on occasion, I have had the temerity to ignore their advice! Other helpful advice along the way has come from a very patient Jim Kinney, editorial director at Baker Academic, and the final product has been greatly improved by the editorial work of Brian Bolger and his team. Thank you.

I am fortunate to be part of the Regent University School of Divinity and appreciate the considerable amount of my time that is made available for research; I thank the deans as well as my colleagues, especially Bob Sivigny, the Divinity librarian, and the interlibrary loans team, for their support of my work. I also gratefully acknowledge the support I received for this project from a Regent University faculty research grant. Thank you. Over the years, Natasha Zhurauliova (research assistant); Christopher Emerick (teaching assistant); Lelia Fry, Ian Hackmann, Alicia Pickett, Jeremy Smith, and Andrew Whitaker (graduate assistants); and Julia Jennette, Megan Lee, and Kathy Schultz (secretaries) have all been a great help to me. My sincere thanks. To my wife goes my greatest thanks and highest praise. She gives immense practical support and help (she calls it assisted living!), creating the tranquil and orderly home life that provides the time and atmosphere for research to be carried out. Thank you, Barbara. Indeed, our children (Catherine and Paul) and those they have married (Brenton and Jacqueline) and made (Lewis and Jonah), though scattered across the world, also contribute to a fun and encouraging family environment for me.

I have a special friend in the Adelaide hills of South Australia who is an orchardist. As one drives along the roads and tracks around and between the twenty thousand and more pear trees spread across the rolling hills, there appears to be neither reason nor order to the manner of planting. Then, as one moves along looking at the apparently disordered trees, at certain spots here and there are moments when one can look in almost any direction and see the perfectly straight rows of evenly spaced trees. There is reason and order after all; one just needed to be standing in the right place to see it. In looking at exorcism among early Christians, I have often felt as if I was looking at a disordered mass of material. But from time to time, when I assume I was—I hope—looking at the subject from the perspective of those who set it out, the order at last became apparent. This book is an attempt to chart both my journey through the apparent disorder as well as give the reader the opportunity to stand with me at the various points where the order is obvious and the reasons apparent.

Graham H. Twelftree
Regent University
August 2006

Abbreviations

AB	Anchor Bible
ABD	*Anchor Bible Dictionary*. Edited by D. N. Freedman. 6 vols. New York: Doubleday, 1922
ABR	*Australian Biblical Review*
ABRL	Anchor Bible Reference Library
ACW	Ancient Christian Writers. 1946–
Ad Demetr.	*Ad Demetrianus = To Demetrian*, by Cyprian
AGJU	Arbeiten zur Geschichte des antiken Judentums und des Urchristentums
AGSU	Arbeiten zur Geschichte des Spätjudentums und Urchristentums
Alex.	*Alexander (Pseudomantis) = Alexander the False Prophet*, by Lucian of Samosata
Alleg. Interp.	*Legum allegoriae = Allegorical Interpretation*, by Philo
AMB	Joseph Naveh and Shaul Shaked. *Amulets and Magic Bowls: Aramaic Incantations of Late Antiquity*. 3rd ed. Jerusalem: Magnes, 1998. Followed by page, bowl, or amulet number.
AMIB	J. B. Segal and Erica C. D. Hunter. *Catalogue of the Aramaic and Mandaic Incantation Bowls in the British Museum*. London: British Museum, 2000. Followed by page or bowl number.
An.	*De anima = The Soul*, by Tertullian
AnBib	Analecta biblica
ANCL	*Ante-Nicene Christian Library*. 24 vols. Edinburgh: T&T Clark, 1867–1872
Ann.	*Annales = Annals*, by Tacitus
ANRW II	*Aufstieg und Niedergang der römischen Welt: Geschichte und Kultur Roms im Spiegel der neueren Forschung*. Part 2, *Principat*. Edited by H. Temporini and W. Haase. Berlin and New York: de Gruyter, 1972–

11

Ant.	*Antiquitates judaicae = Jewish Antiquities,* by Josephus
ANTC	Abingdon New Testament Commentaries
Antr. nymph.	*De antro nympharum = On the Cave of the Nymphs,* by Porphyry
1 Apol.	*Apologia i = First Apology,* by Justin (Martyr)
2 Apol.	*Apologia ii = Second Apology,* by Justin (Martyr)
Apol.	*Apologia = Apology,* by Aristides
AR	*Archiv für Religionswissenschaft*
AUSS	*Andrews University Seminary Studies*
Autol.	*Ad Autolycum = To Autolycus,* by Theophilus of Antioch
b. B. Bat.	*Baba Batra = Bava Batra,* in the Babylonian Talmud
b. Ber.	*Berakot = Berakhot,* in the Babylonian Talmud
b. Me'il.	*Me'ilah,* in the Babylonian Talmud
b. Šabb.	*Šabbat = Shabbat,* in the Babylonian Talmud
b. Sanh.	*Sanhedrin,* in the Babylonian Talmud
b. Šebu.	*Šebu'ot = Shevu'ot,* in the Babylonian Talmud
b. Sukkah	*Sukkah,* in the Babylonian Talmud
b.	Babylonian Talmud
2 Bar.	*2 Baruch* (*Syriac Apocalypse*)
Barn.	*Barnabas*
BBR	*Bulletin for Biblical Research*
BDAG	Bauer, W., F. W. Danker, W. F. Arndt, and F. W. Gingrich. *Greek-English Lexicon of the New Testament and Other Early Christian Literature.* 3rd ed. Chicago: University of Chicago Press, 2000
BDF	Blass, F., A. Debrunner, and R. W. Funk. *A Greek Grammar of the New Testament and Other Early Christian Literature.* Chicago: University of Chicago Press, 1961
BETL	Bibliotheca ephemeridum theologicarum lovaniensium
BHT	Beiträge zur historischen Theologie
Bib	*Biblica*
BiBh	*Bible Bhashyam* (Kerala, India)
bis	two times (twice)
BJRL	*Bulletin of the John Rylands University Library of Manchester*
BJS	Brown Judaic Studies
BK	*Bibel und Kirche*
BNTC	Black's New Testament Commentaries
BR	*Biblical Research*
BSac	*Bibliotheca sacra*
BSNTS	*Bulletin of the Studiorum Novi Testamenti Societas*
BTB	*Biblical Theology Bulletin*
BWANT	Beiträge zur Wissenschaft vom Alten und Neuen Testament
Byz	The majority of Byzantine witnesses to the New Testament Greek text
BZ	*Biblische Zeitschrift*

BZNW	Beihefte zur Zeitschrift für die neutestamentliche Wissenschaft
C. Ap.	*Contra Apion* = *Against Apion*, by Josephus
CahRB	Cahiers de la Revue biblique
Cas.	*Casina* [a comedy named after its heroine], by Plautus
Cat.	*Catecheses* = *Catechetical Lectures*, by Cyril of Jerusalem
CBQ	*Catholic Biblical Quarterly*
Cels.	*Contra Celsum* = *Against Celsus*, by Origen
CH	*Church History*
Chm	*Churchman*
Chron.	*Chronicon* = *Chronicle*, by Eusebius
Civ.	*De civitate Dei* = *The City of God*, by Augustine
Claud.	*Divus Claudius* = *Divine Claudius*, by Suetonius
1 Clem.	*1 Clement*
CMB	Dan Levene. *A Corpus of Magic Bowls: Incantation Texts in Jewish Aramaic from Late Antiquity*. London, New York, and Bahrain: Kegan Paul, 2003. Followed by page or M number for bowl.
CNT	Commentaire du Nouveau Testament
Colloq	*Colloquium*
Comm. Dan.	*Commentarium in Danielem* = *Commentary on Daniel*, by Hippolytus
Comm. Jo.	*Commentarii in evangelium Joannis* = *Expositions of the Gospel of John*, by Origen
Conc	*Concilium: International Journal for Theology* (also in Dutch, French, German, Italian, Portuguese, Spanish)
CQ	*Classical Quarterly*
CQR	*Church Quarterly Review*
CTM	*Concordia Theological Monthly*
CTR	*Criswell Theological Review*
CurBS	*Currents in Research: Biblical Studies*
CurTM	*Currents in Theology and Mission*
CV	*Communio viatorum*
DDD	*Dictionary of Deities and Demons in the Bible*. Edited by K. van der Toorn, B. Becking, and P. W. van der Horst. Leiden: Brill, 1995
De Philosophia	*De Philosophia* = *Philosophy* (*Oratio 70*), by Dio Chrysostom
Decal.	*De decalogo* = *On the Decalogue*, by Philo
Def. orac.	*De defectu oraculorum* = *On the Obsolescence of Oracles*, by Plutarch
Demetr.	*Demetrius* = *Life of Demetrius*, by Plutarch
Dial.	*Dialogus cum Tryphone* = *Dialogue with Trypho*, by Justin
Diat.	*Diatessaron* = *[One] through Four* = *Gospel Harmony*, by Tatian
Diatr.	*Diatribae* (*Dissertationes*) = *Discourses/Lectures*, by Epictetus
Did.	*Didache*
Diogn.	*Ad Diognetum* = *Epistle to Diognetus*
DivThom	*Divus Thomas* [a journal]

DJD	Discoveries in the Judaean Desert
DJG	*Dictionary of Jesus and the Gospels*. Edited by J. B. Green and S. McKnight. Downers Grove, IL: InterVarsity, 1992
DPL	*Dictionary of Paul and His Letters*. Edited by G. F. Hawthorne and R. P. Martin. Downers Grove, IL: InterVarsity, 1993
DSS	Dead Sea Scrolls (from Qumran caves)
ÉBib	Études bibliques
Eccl. Rab.	*Ecclesiastes Rabbah* (a midrash)
Ecl.	*Eclogae/Bucolika = Eclogues/Bucolics*, by Virgil
ÉgT	*Église et théologie*
EKK	Evangelisch-katholischer Kommentar zum Neuen Testament
1 En.	*1 Enoch*
Enn.	*Enneades = Enneads = The Nines* [6 books, 9 chapters each], by Plotinus
Ep.	*Epistulae morales = Moral Epistles*, by Seneca
Eph.	*To the Ephesians*, by Ignatius
Epid.	*Epidemiae* (Ἐπιδημίαι) *= Epidemics*, by Hippocrates
Epist. 121	*Epistula 121 = Ad Algasiam = Epistle to Algasia*, by Jerome
Epitaph.	*Epitaphius (Oratio 60) = Funeral Oration*, by Demosthenes
EPTABul	*European Pentecostal Theological Association Bulletin*
2 Esd.	2 Esdras = 4 Ezra
EstBib	*Estudios bíblicos*
ET	English translation
ETL	*Ephemerides theologicae lovanienses*
ÉtudFranc	*Études franciscaines*
EvQ	*Evangelical Quarterly*
EvT	*Evangelische Theologie*
ExAud	*Ex auditu*
Exc.	*Excerpta ex Theodoto = Excerpts from Theodotus* [of Alexandria], via Clement of Alexandria
ExpTim	*Expository Times*
fasc.	Fascicle
FB	Forschung zur Bibel
Flacc.	*In Flaccum = Against Flaccus*, by Philo
frg.	fragment
FRLANT	Forschungen zur Religion und Literatur des Alten und Neuen Testaments
FTS	Frankfurter Theologische Studien
GBSup	Grazer Beiträge Supplement
GCS	Die griechische christliche Schriftsteller der ersten [drei] Jahrhunderte
Gen. Rab.	*Genesis Rabbah* (a midrash)
2 Glor.	*De Gloria ii (Oratio 67) = Popular Opinion*, by Dio Chrysostom

GMA	Roy Kotansky. *Greek Magical Amulets: The Inscribed Gold, Silver, Copper, and Bronze "Lamellae": Text and Commentary.* Part 1, *Published Texts of Known Provenance.* Abhandlungen der Nordrhein-Westfälischen Akademie der Wissenschaften. Sonderreihe Papyrologica Coloniensia 22.1. Opladen: Westdeutscher, 1994. Followed by part and text numbers.
GNS	Good News Studies
Gorg.	*Gorgias,* by Plato
GR	*Greece and Rome*
Hadr.	*Vita Hadriani = Life of Hadrian,* in *Scriptores historiae Augustae*
Haer.	*Adversus haereses = Against Heresies,* by Irenaeus
HALOT	Koehler, L., W. Baumgartner, and J. J. Stamm. *The Hebrew and Aramaic Lexicon of the Old Testament.* Translated and edited under the supervision of M. E. J. Richardson. 5 vols. Leiden and New York: Brill, 1994–2000
HAT	Handbuch zum Alten Testament
HBS	Herders biblische Studien
HDR	Harvard Dissertations in Religion
Her.	*Heroicus,* attributed to Philostratus (the Elder) of Lemnos
Herm.	*Shepherd of Hermas*
HHM	Harvard Historical Monographs
Hist. eccl.	*Historia ecclesiastica = Ecclesiastical History,* by Eusebius
Hist. Franc.	*Historia Francorum = History of the Franks,* by Gregory of Tours
Hist.	*Historiae = Histories,* by Tacitus
HNT	Handbuch zum Neuen Testament
Hom. 1 Cor.	*Homiliae in epistulam I ad Corinthios = Homilies on the First Epistle to the Corinthians,* by John Chrysostom
Hom.	*Homiliae = Homilies,* by Pseudo-Clement
HTKNT	Herders theologischer Kommentar zum Neuen Testament
HTR	*Harvard Theological Review*
HTS	Harvard Theological Studies
HUT	Hermeneutische Untersuchungen zur Theologie
HvTSt	*Hervormde teologiese studies*
IBC	Interpretation: A Bible Commentary for Teaching and Preaching
ICC	International Critical Commentary
Il.	*Ilias = Iliad,* by Homer
Int	*Interpretation*
ITQ	*Irish Theological Quarterly*
JAAR	*Journal of the American Academy of Religion*
JAC	*Jahrbuch für Antike und Christentum*
JBL	*Journal of Biblical Literature*
JEA	*Journal of Egyptian Archaeology*
JECS	*Journal of Early Christian Studies*
JEH	*Journal of Ecclesiastical History*

JHS	*Journal of Hellenic Studies*
JJS	*Journal of Jewish Studies*
JLS	Alcuin/GROW Joint Liturgical Studies
JPT	*Journal of Pentecostal Theology*
JPTSup	Journal of Pentecostal Theology: Supplement Series
JR	*Journal of Religion*
JRitSt	*Journal of Ritual Studies*
JRS	*Journal of Roman Studies*
JSHJ	*Journal for the Study of the Historical Jesus*
JSJ	*Journal for the Study of Judaism in the Persian, Hellenistic, and Roman Periods*
JSJSup	Supplements to the Journal for the Study of Judaism
JSNT	*Journal for the Study of the New Testament*
JSNTSup	Journal for the Study of the New Testament: Supplement Series
JSOTSup	Journal for the Study of the Old Testament: Supplement Series
JSPSup	Journal for the Study of the Pseudepigrapha: Supplement Series
JTS	*Journal of Theological Studies*
Jub.	*Jubilees*
J.W.	*Bellum judaicum* = *Jewish War*, by Josephus
KBANT	Kommentare und Beiträge zum Alten und Neuen Testament
KBW	Katholisches Bibelwerk Verlag
KEK	Kritisch-exegetischer Kommentar über das Neue Testament (Meyer-Kommentar)
L	material/source(s) represented only in Luke
L.A.B.	*Liber antiquitatum biblicarum*, by Pseudo-Philo
Lampe	G. W. H. Lampe. *A Patristic Greek Lexicon*. Oxford: Clarendon, 1961
Lange	Lange, Armin, Hermann Lichtenberger, and K. F. Diethard Römheld, eds. *Die Dämonen: Die Dämonologie der israelitisch-jüdischen und frühchristlichen Literatur im Kontext ihrer Umwelt / Demons = The Demonology of Israelite-Jewish and Early Christian Literature in the Context of Their Environment*. Tübingen: Mohr Siebeck, 2003
LCC	Library of Christian Classics. Philadelphia: Westminster, 1953–
LCL	Loeb Classical Library
Leg.	*Legatio pro Christianis* = *Embassy/Supplication for the Christians*, by Athenagoras
Legat.	*Legatio ad Gaium* = *On the Embassy to Gaius*, by Philo
Lev. Rab.	*Leviticus Rabbah* (a midrash)
Life	*Vita* = *The Life* [autobiography], by Josephus
LNTS	Library of New Testament Studies
LSJ	Liddell, H. G., R. Scott, H. S. Jones. *A Greek-English Lexicon*. 9th ed. with revised supplement. Oxford: Clarendon Press, 1996
LXX	Septuagint (the Greek Old Testament)
M	material/source(s) represented only in Matthew

Magn.	*To the Magnesians*, by Ignatius
Mart. Isa.	*Martyrdom and Ascension of Isaiah* 1–5
MdB	Le Monde de la Bible
Med.	*Meditationes* = *Meditations*, by Marcus Aurelius
Mem.	*Memorabilia*, by Xenophon
Menex.	*Menexenus*, by Plato
Midr. Tanḥ.	*Midrash Tanḥuma*
Mir. ausc.	*De mirabilibus auscultationibus* = *On Marvelous Things Heard*, by Pseudo-Aristotle
MM	Moulton, J. H., and G. Milligan. *The Vocabulary of the Greek Testament*. London, 1930. Repr., Peabody, MA: Hendrickson, 1997
Mos.	*De vita Mosis* = *On the Life of Moses*, by Philo
MSF	Joseph Naveh and Shaul Shaked. *Magic Spells and Formulae: Aramaic Incantations of Late Antiquity*. Jerusalem: Magnes, 1993. Followed by page or bowl (B) number.
MT	Masoretic Text (of the Old Testament)
NA[27]	Eberhard Nestle and Barbara and Kurt Aland, eds. *Novum Testamentum Graece*. 27th ed. Stuttgart: Deutsche Bibelgesellschaft, 1993
NAPSPMS	North American Patristic Society Patristic Monograph Series
Nat.	*Naturalis historia* = *Natural History*, by Pliny the Elder
Nat. an.	*De natura animalium* = *Nature of Animals*, by Aelian
Nat. d.	*De natura deorum* = *Summary of Traditions of Greek Mythology*, by Cornutus
NCB	New Century Bible
Neot	*Neotestamentica*
NHC	Nag Hammadi Codices
NHL	*Nag Hammadi Library in English*. Edited by J. M. Robinson. 4th rev. ed. Leiden: Brill, 1996
NIB	*New Interpreter's Bible*. 13 vols. Nashville: Abingdon, 1994–2004
NICNT	New International Commentary on the New Testament
NIDB	*New Interpreter's Dictionary of the Bible*. Edited by Katharine D. Sakenfeld et al. 6 vols. Nashville: Abingdon, forthcoming
NIGTC	New International Greek Testament Commentary
Noct. att.	*Noctes atticae* = *Attic Nights*, by Aulus Gellius
NovT	*Novum Testamentum*
NovTSup	Novum Testamentum Supplements
NRSV	New Revised Standard Version
NRTh	*La nouvelle revue théologique*
NT	New Testament
NTAbh	Neutestamentliche Abhundlungen
NTApoc[2]	Wilhelm Schneemelcher, ed. *New Testament Apocrypha*. Rev. ed. 2 vols. Cambridge, UK: J. Clarke; Louisville: Westminster John Knox, 1991–1992

NTD	Das New Testament Deutsch
NTS	*New Testament Studies*
Numen	*Numen: International Review for the History of Religions*
ÖBS	Österreichische biblische Studien
OCD	*Oxford Classical Dictionary*. Edited by S. Hornblower and A. Spawforth. 3rd ed. Oxford: Oxford University Press, 1996
OCP	*Orientalia christiana periodica*
Oct.	*Octavius*, by Minucius Felix
Od.	*Odyssea* = *Odyssey*, by Homer
ODCC³	*The Oxford Dictionary of the Christian Church*. Edited by F. L. Cross and E. A. Livingstone. 3rd ed. Oxford: Oxford University Press, 1997
Odes Sol.	*Odes of Solomon*
olim	formerly
Orat.	*Oratio = Address to the Greeks*, by Tatian
OT	Old Testament
P.Köln	*Kölner Papyri*. Edited by Bärbel Kramer, Michael Gronewald, et al. 10 vols. Abhandlungen der Nordrhein-Westfälischen Akademie der Wissenschaften: Sonderreihe, Papyrologica Coloniensia 7. Opladen: Westdeutscher Verlag, 1976–
P.Lond.	Greek Papyri in the British Museum. London.
P.Oslo	*Papyri Osloenses*. Edited by Samson Eitrem and Leiv Amundsen. 3 vols. Oslo: Norske Videnskaps-Akademi i Oslo, 1925–1936
P.Oxy.	*The Oxyrhynchus Papyri*. 69 vols. London: Egypt Exploration Society in Graeco-Roman Memoirs, 1898–
P.Petr.	*The Flinders Petrie Papyri*. Dublin. Royal Irish Academy, Cunningham Memoirs. Edited by J. P. Mahaffy and J. G. Smyly. 3 vols. 1891–1905
P.Stras.	*Griechische Papyrus der Kaiserlichen Universitäts- und Landesbibliothek zu Strassburg*. Edited by F. Preisigke. 9 vols. Leipzig, 1912–1989. No. 73 is in vol. 1.
Pan.	*Panarion (Adversus haereses) = Refutation of All Heresies*, by Epiphanius
Pecc. merit.	*De peccatorum meritis et remissione = Guilt and Remission of Sins*, by Augustine
Peregr.	*De morte Peregrini = The Passing of Peregrinus*, by Lucian of Samosata
Pesiq. Rab Kah.	*Pesiqta de Rab Kahana = Pesiqta of Rab Kahana*
PG	Patrologia graeca [= Patrologiae cursus completus: Series graeca]. Edited by J.-P. Migne. 162 vols. Paris, 1857–1886
PGM	*Papyri graecae magicae: Die griechischen Zauberpapyri*. Edited by K. Preisendanz. 3 vols. Leipzig and Berlin: Teubner, 1928–1941
Phil.	*To the Philippians*, by Polycarp
Philops.	*Philopseudes = The Lover of Lies*, by Lucian of Samosata

Phld.	*To the Philadelphians*, by Ignatius
PL	Patrologia Latina [= Patrologiae cursus completus: Series latina]. Edited by J.-P. Migne. 217 vols. Paris, 1844–1864
Plut.	*Plutus = The Rich Man*, by Aristophanes
PNTC	Pelican New Testament Commentaries
Pol.	*To Polycarp*, by Ignatius
Procat.	*Procatechesis = Introductory Catechetical Lecture*, by Cyril of Jerusalem
Prot.	*Protrepticus = Exhortation to the Greeks*, by Clement of Alexandria
PSB	*Princeton Seminary Bulletin*
Ps.-Phoc.	Pseudo-Phocylides
Pss. Sol.	*Psalms of Solomon*
PTS	Patristische Texte und Studien
PTSDSSP	*The Dead Sea Scrolls: Hebrew, Aramaic, and Greek Texts with the English Translations*. Edited by James H. Charlesworth. Princeton Theological Seminary Dead Sea Scrolls Project. 10 vols. (4A + 4B = one) plus two concordances are projected. Tübingen: Mohr Siebeck; Louisville: Westminster John Knox, 1991, 1994–
Puls.	*De pulsuum differentiis = On Differences of Pulses/Influences*, by Galen
Q	*Quelle*/source: material represented in Matthew and Luke, not in Mark
QD	Questiones disputatae
R.	Rabbi
Rab.	*Midrash Rabbah* (on various books of the Hebrew Bible)
RAr	*Revue archéologique*
RB	*Revue biblique*
3 *Regn.*	*De regno iii (Oratio 3) = Kingship 3*, by Dio Chrysostom
RelS	*Religious Studies*
RelSBul	*Religious Studies Bulletin*
Res.	*De resurrectione = On the Resurrection*, by Methodius of Olympus
ResQ	*Restoration Quarterly*
RevExp	*Review and Expositor*
RevQ	*Revue de Qumran*
RevScRel	*Revue des sciences religieuses*
RGRW	Religions in the Graeco-Roman World
RHR	*Revue de l'histoire des religions*
Rom.	*To the Romans*, by Ignatius
RSV	Revised Standard Version
RTAM	*Recerches de théologie ancienne et médiévale*
RTL	*Revue théologique de Louvain*
Sacr.	*De sacramentis = The Sacraments*, by Ambrose
SANT	Studien zum Alten und Neuen Testaments
SBB	Stuttgarter biblische Beiträge

SBEC	Studies in the Bible and Early Christianity
SBFLA	*Studii biblici Franciscani liber annus*
SBLDS	Society of Biblical Literature Dissertation Series
SBLMS	Society of Biblical Literature Monograph Series
SBLSP	Society of Biblical Literature Seminar Papers
SBM	Stuttgarter biblische Monographien
SBS	Stuttgarter Bibelstudien
SBT	Studies in Biblical Theology
SC	Sources chrétiennes. Paris: Cerf, 1943–
ScEs	*Science et esprit*
SCM	Student Christian Movement Press
SE	*Studia evangelica I, II, II* (= TU 73 [1959], etc.)
SecCen	*Second Century*
SISTSym	Spiritan International School of Theology Symposium Series
SJT	*Scottish Journal of Theology*
Smyrn.	*To the Smyrnaeans*, by Ignatius
SNTSMS	Society for New Testament Studies Monograph Series
SNTSU	Studien zum Neuen Testament und seiner Umwelt (series)
SNTW	Studies of the New Testament and Its World
SO	Symbolae osloenses
Soph.	*Sophista = Sophist*, by Plato
SP	Sacra pagina
Spec.	*De specialibus legibus = On the Special Laws*, by Philo
SR	Studies in Religion
ST	*Studia theologica*
STDJ	Studies on the Texts of the Desert of Judah
StLit	*Studia liturgica*
StMiss	*Studia missionalia*
StPatr	*Studia patristica*. Edited by Elizabeth A. Livingstone. Papers from the Conferences on Patristic Studies at Oxford. Vols. 13 and 16, part 2, Berlin: Akademie-Verlag, 1975 and 1985. Vols. 21 and 26, Louvain: Peeters, 1989 and 1993
StPB	Studia post-biblica
Strom.	*Stromata = Miscellanies*, by Clement of Alexandria
StudOr	Studia orientalia
SUNT	Studien zur Umwelt des Neuen Testaments
SVTP	Studia in Veteris Testamenti pseudepigraphica
T. Sol.	*Testament of Solomon*
TAPA	*Transactions of the American Philological Association*
TBT	*The Bible Today*
TD	ἀληθὴς λόγος = *True Doctrine*, by Celsus

TDNT	*Theological Dictionary of the New Testament*. Edited by G. Kittel and G. Friedrich. Translated by G. W. Bromiley. 10 vols. Grand Rapids: Eerdmans, 1964–1976
Them	*Themelios*
THKNT	Theologischer Handkommentar zum Neuen Testament
Tim.	*Timaeus*, by Plato
TJ	*Trinity Journal*
TLG	*Thesaurus linguae graecae: Canon of Greek Authors and Works.* Edited by L. Berkowitz and K. A. Squitier. 3rd ed. Oxford: Oxford University Press, 1990
TPI	Trinity Press International
TQ	*Theologische Quartalschrift*
Trad. ap.	*Apostolic Tradition*, attributed to Hippolytus
Trall.	*To the Trallians*, by Ignatius
Trim. Prot.	*Trimorphic Protennoia = The Three-Formed [Divine] First Thought*, NHC XIII,1
tris	three times (thrice)
TS	*Theological Studies*
TThSt	Trierer theologische Studien
TTZ	*Trierer theologische Zeitschrift*
TU	Texte und Untersuchungen
Tusc.	*Tusculanae disputations = Disputations at Tusculum*, by Cicero
TynBul	*Tyndale Bulletin*
TZ	*Theologische Zeitschrift*
UNT	Untersuchungen zum Neuen Testament
USQR	*Union Seminary Quarterly Review*
VC	*Vigiliae christianae*
VCSup	Supplements to Vigiliae christianae
VD	*Verbum domini*
Vesp.	*Vespae = Wasps*, by Aristophanes
Vir. ill.	*De viris illustribus = On Illustrious Men*, by Jerome
Vit. Apoll.	*Vita Apollonii = Life of Apollonius of Tyana*, by Flavius Philostratus
VTSup	Vetus Testamentum Supplements
WBC	Word Biblical Commentary
WC	Westminster Commentaries
WTJ	*Westminster Theological Journal*
WUNT	Wissenschaftliche Untersuchungen zum Neuen Testament
WW	*Word and World*
y. 'Erub.	*'Erubin*, in the Jerusalem Talmud
y. Šabb.	*Šabbat = Shabbat*, in the Jerusalem Talmud
y.	Jerusalem Talmud
YClS	*Yale Classical Studies*
ZAC	*Zeitschrift für Antikes Christentum / Journal of Ancient Christianity*

ZAW	*Zeitschrift für die alttestamentliche Wissenschaft*
ZKG	*Zeitschrift für Kirchengeschichte*
ZNT	*Zeitschrift für Neues Testament*
ZNW	*Zeitschrift für die neutestamentliche Wissenschaft und die Kunde der älteren Kirche*
ZRGG	*Zeitschrift für Religions- und Geistesgeschichte*
ZTK	*Zeitschrift für Theologie und Kirche*
ZWT	*Zeitschrift für wissenschaftliche Theologie*

Part **1**

Jesus and the
Problem of Exorcism

1

The Problem of Exorcism

IN RECENT YEARS interest in exorcism in the New Testament has been increasing.[1] However, for most students of the New Testament, there are at least two significant problems in relation to exorcism. The fundamental problem is the premise on which exorcism is based: that malevolent spiritual beings exist and that they can invade, control, and observably impair the health of an individual who, in turn, can be cured through someone purportedly forcing the spiritual beings to leave.[2] For the vast majority of biblical scholars and theologians this is tantamount to belief in such entities as elves, dragons, or a

---

1. Most recently see the monographs by Eric Eve, *The Jewish Context of Jesus' Miracles* (JSNTSup 231; London and New York: Sheffield Academic, 2002); Todd E. Klutz, *The Exorcism Stories in Luke-Acts: A Sociostylistic Reading* (SNTSMS 129; Cambridge: Cambridge University Press, 2004); Eric Sorensen, *Possession and Exorcism in the New Testament and Early Christianity* (WUNT 2.157; Tübingen: Mohr Siebeck, 2002); Peter G. Bolt, *Jesus' Defeat of Death: Persuading Mark's Early Readers* (SNTSMS 125; Cambridge and New York: Cambridge University Press, 2003); Clinton Wahlen, *Jesus and the Impurity of Spirits in the Synoptic Gospels* (WUNT 2.185; Tübingen: Mohr Siebeck, 2004); as well as Ronald A. Piper, "Jesus and the Conflict of Powers in Q: Two Q Miracle Stories," in *The Sayings Source Q and the Historical Jesus* (ed. A. Lindemann; BETL 158; Louvain: Leuven University Press, 2001), 317–49; and their bibliographies.

2. Although the term ἐξορκιστής ("exorcist," from the verb ἐξορκίζω, "command," "compel," "adjure," or "oath," only in the NT at Matt. 26:63) occurs once in the NT (Acts 19:13), the earliest known occurrence of the word (cf. LSJ 598; BDAG 351), it was probably reasonably well known (see Josephus, *Ant.* 8.45) and can be taken as a fair description of what the NT writers thought Jesus and his followers were doing in expelling demons and unclean or evil spirits. For further discussion on the definition of exorcism, see Graham H. Twelftree, *Jesus the Exorcist: A Contribution to the Study of the Historical Jesus* (WUNT 2.54; Tübingen: Mohr Siebeck; Peabody, MA: Hendrickson, 1993), 13, including those cited and, more recently, Sorensen, *Possession*, 1–2.

flat earth.[3] Nevertheless, for the historian to deem possession and exorcism in the ancient world a problem of, for example, "crowd psychology" and so place it "off limits"[4] is to miss what was, for most people,[5] including early Christians, a significant aspect of their *Weltanschauung*.[6] Therefore, despite our difficulty with exorcism, for the sake of historical inquiry, it is important to suspend judgment on the reality of the demonic[7] and approach the subject in terms of the cultural milieu of the text.[8]

1.1 Setting the Scene

Notwithstanding, the issue that has given rise to this study—the second significant problem with exorcism—is the place and practice of exorcism among early Christians. In the modern study of early Christianity the prevailing view has been that exorcism played a significant role in the success of early Christianity. For example, many years ago Adolf von Harnack said, "It was as exorcisers that Christians went out into the great world, and *exorcism formed one very powerful method of their mission and propaganda*."[9] More recently, in seeking to explain the extraordinary and unparalleled success of early Christianity, Ramsay MacMullen has maintained not only that miracles were the primary engine for producing conversions in the ancient world, but also that exorcism was "possibly the most highly rated activity of the early Christian church."[10] Citing Justin, Tertullian, Cyprian, and Eusebius, he concludes that,

3. E.g., Walter Wink, *Naming the Powers: The Language of Power in the New Testament* (Philadelphia: Fortress, 1984), 4. Cf. Hans Hübner, *An Philemon, an die Kolosser, an die Epheser* (HNT 12; Tübingen: Mohr Siebeck, 1997), 267–68. See the discussion in Graham H. Twelftree, *Christ Triumphant: Exorcism Then and Now* (London: Hodder & Stoughton, 1985), 12–14.

4. See the discussion by Peter Brown, *The Cult of the Saints: Its Rise and Function in Latin Christianity* (Chicago: Phoenix / University of Chicago Press; London: SCM, 1982), 107–8.

5. Exceptions can be found in the skepticism of, e.g., Lucian, *Philops*. 29–40; Marcus Aurelius, *Med.*, preface 6; and Plotinus, *Enn.* 2.9.14. See the discussion by Craig S. Keener, *The Gospel of John: A Commentary* (2 vols.; Peabody, MA: Hendrickson, 2003), 1:261–63.

6. On first-century skepticism and credulity, see F. Gerald Downing, "Access to Other Cultures, Past and Present (on the Myth of the Cultural Gap)," *Modern Churchman* 21 (1977–78): 28–42; John Barton, "Reflections on Cultural Relativism," *Theology* 82 (1979): 103–9, 191–99; F. Gerald Downing, "Magic and Scepticism in and around the First Christian Century," in *Magic in the Biblical World: From the Rod of Aaron to the Ring of Solomon* (ed. Todd E. Klutz; London and New York: T&T Clark, 2003), 86–99.

7. For our inquiry being of more than antiquarian interest and, arguably, having implications for a contemporary debate about possession and exorcism, see the discussion in Twelftree, *Christ Triumphant*, chaps. 5–6.

8. Cf. Ralph Brucker, "Die Wunder der Apostel," *ZNT* 4 (2001): 32–45, esp. 32.

9. Adolf von Harnack, *The Expansion of Christianity in the First Three Centuries* (2 vols.; 1904–5; repr., New York: Arno, 1972), 1:160, emphasis his.

10. Ramsay MacMullen, *Christianizing the Roman Empire (A.D. 100–400)* (New Haven and London: Yale University Press, 1984), 27 (cf. 108), relying on Brown, *Cult of the Saints*,

although the institution of exorcism had taproots in Judaism and was of little account otherwise, "in Christianity it found an extraordinary flowering" and was essential in its growth.[11] Similarly, it has been Bernd Kollmann's main objective to show that healing miracles, notably exorcism, were critical for early Christians' success in winning many people to the faith.[12]

---

108. MacMullen, *Christianizing*, and S. Vernon McCasland, *By the Finger of God: Demon Possession and Exorcism in Early Christianity in the Light of Modern Views of Mental Illness* (New York: Macmillan, 1951), 104, who held a similar view, are followed by Amanda Porterfield, *Healing in the History of Christianity* (Oxford: Oxford University Press, 2005), 63. See also, e.g., Albrecht Oepke, "ἰάομαι . . . ," *TDNT* 3:214: "The unparalleled missionary vigor of Christianity in the first centuries derives not least of all from the bold supremacy, continually confirmed by striking experiences, with which the new religion brought freedom to those who were enslaved by demons and destiny (Εἰμαρμένη)."

11. MacMullen, *Christianizing*, 27–28.

12. Bernd Kollmann, *Jesus und die Christen als Wundertäter: Studien zu Magie, Medizin und Schamanismus in Antike und Christentum* (FRLANT 170; Göttingen: Vandenhoeck & Ruprecht, 1996), e.g., 375–80. Also, Christine Trevett, *Montanism: Gender, Authority and the New Prophecy* (Cambridge: Cambridge University Press, 1996), 157: "Exorcism was well established in Christianity and widely used" (citing Justin, *Dial.* 55; *2 Apol.* 6; Origen, *Cels.* 1.6, 25, 46; 3.24). See also Leslie W. Barnard, *The First and Second Apologies: St. Justin Martyr* (ACW 56; New York and Mahwah, NJ: Paulist Press, 1997), 191n34, citing Justin, *Dial.* 30; 49; 76; 85; Irenaeus, *Haer.* 2.32.4ff.; Tertullian, *Apologeticus* 23; 27; 32; 37; Cyprian, *Ad Demetr.* 15; Origen, *Cels.* 1; 46; 67; Augustine, *Civ.* 22.8. Making the same point, Reidar Hvalvik, "In Word and Deed: The Expansion of the Church in the Pre-Constantinian Era," in *The Mission of the Early Church to Jews and Gentiles* (ed. Jostein Ådna and Hans Kvalbein; WUNT 1.127; Tübingen: Mohr Siebeck, 2000), 283–84, adds Theophilus, *Autol.* 2.8; Eusebius, *Hist. eccl.* 3.37.3; 5.3.14; and *Acts of John* 38–42. Also, Sorensen, *Possession*, takes exorcism to be everywhere significant for early Christians. More generally, and at a more popular level—relying on Raphael Frost, *Christian Healing: A Consideration of the Place of Spiritual Healing in the Church of Today in the Light of the Doctrine and Practice of the Ante-Nicene Church* (London: Mowbray, 1954)—Morton T. Kelsey, *Healing and Christianity in Ancient Thought and Modern Times* (New York: Harper & Row, 1973), 128, supposes that the practice of healing described in the New Testament continued without interruption for the next two centuries.

Notably for us, in his essay on "Miracles and Early Christian Apologetic," Geoffrey Lampe (1912–1980) argued that, in early Christian writings that defended the faith and commended it to unbelievers, not only was the dominant miracle exorcism but also miracle was used in two ways: to introduce an argument in the most direct way by performing one, as in the case of John in the *Acts of John*; and by preachers to make an appeal to a miracle performed by another person in support of that person's authority, character, and doctrine (e.g., *Acts of Paul*). Lampe also argued that, sometimes, in the face of opposition, appeal to miracle took the form of a competition along the lines of that between Moses and the Egyptian magicians, as with Peter and Simon Magus in the *Acts of Peter*. Lampe says: "All this belongs essentially to the realm of popular fiction." However, attempting to save the integrity of great Christian writers, Lampe adds: "Serious authors pay little attention to all this." G. W. H. Lampe, "Miracles and Early Christian Apologetic," in *Miracles: Cambridge Studies in Their Philosophy and History* (ed. C. F. D. Moule; London: Mowbray, 1965), 205–18, quoting 206. However, Lampe does mention that Eusebius reproduces the legend of Abgar, king of Edessa, corresponding with Jesus about his healing (*Hist. eccl.* 1.13). Origen says of the apostles of Jesus: "Without miracles and wonders they would not have persuaded those who heard new doctrines and new teaching to leave their

Nevertheless, there have been a few voices, such as those of Kenneth Grayston and Ernest Best, suggesting that there was not much interest in exorcism among early Christians.[13] Also, F. Gerald Downing asserted, "Tales of miracles seemed to the evangelists to be worth repeating among the committed; they had little impact outside."[14] Further, in taking into account the Fourth Gospel, Frederick E. Brenk put it plainly: "The subsequent history of the Church shows a great reluctance to see demons in individuals or to practice exorcism."[15] Therefore, in light of this range of views, it is reasonable to heed H. K. Nielsen's call for more light to be shed on this relatively neglected area of research: the role that exorcism played in the early church.[16]

Part of the reason for this difference of opinion on the role of exorcism in the early church could be inherent in the New Testament canon itself. For, in seeking to shed more light on the place and practice of exorcism among early Christians, we are confronted with apparent significant anomalies embedded in the literary legacy of the early church. To begin with, there is a disjunct between the various ways Jesus' involvement in exorcism is portrayed. On the one hand, even though the Synoptic Gospels are not agreed on the precise place of exorcism in his ministry, they portray Jesus not only as spending a great deal of time performing exorcisms—as well as other healings—but also Matthew and Luke further report that he saw his exorcisms encapsulating his mission as no other aspect of his ministry was able.[17]

On the other hand, when we turn to the letters of Paul, the Christian writings closest in time to Jesus and his first followers, they appear to tell us nothing about Jesus being an exorcist. We are bound, then, to ask both about the accuracy of the Synoptic portrait of Jesus as well as whether Paul's apparent silence simply has to do with the difference in the two kinds of literature that Paul and the Synoptic Gospel writers were producing, or whether there are some other more fundamental explanations. More puzzling, and the point at which this problem of exorcism is most acute, is this question: Why do we hear nothing whatsoever from the canonical Johannine literature about exorcism or Jesus being an exorcist?

traditional religion and to accept the apostles' teaching at the risk of their lives" (*Cels.* 1.46). Also, of his own time Origen says that the name of Jesus has been "seen to have expelled countless daemons from souls and bodies, and to have had great effect on those people from whom they were expelled" (1.25; cf. 3.24). In this study we will not only want to test Lampe's conclusions but also to move beyond the literature to the level of historicity.

13. Ernest Best, "Exorcism in the New Testament and Today," *Biblical Theology* [Belfast] 27 (1977): 1–9; Kenneth Grayston, "Exorcism in the New Testament," *Epworth Review* 2 (1975): 94.

14. Downing, "Magic and Scepticism," 98.

15. Frederick E. Brenk, "The Exorcism at Philippoi in Acts 16.11–40: Divine Possession or Diabolical Inspiration," *Filología Neotestamentaria* 13 (2000): 21.

16. H. K. Nielsen, review of Kollmann, *Jesus und die Christen,* in *JTS* 48 (1997): 595.

17. E.g., esp. Matt. 12:28 ‖ Luke 11:20. Cf. Twelftree, *Exorcist,* §29.

The puzzle of this divergence of perspective on Jesus' ministry—not to say contradiction—continues to be played out in the different portrayals of what Jesus is said to require of his followers. The Synoptic Gospel writers have Jesus commissioning his followers to be exorcists while the Johannine tradition is completely silent on the matter. Paul, as well, at least on a prima facie reading, also appears to say nothing about exorcism in his own ministry nor among that of his readers. The problem of this diversity is further exacerbated when we take into account that, in telling the story of the first followers of Jesus, the Synoptic Gospel writers, especially Mark, wished to portray the disciples as model exorcists for their readers to follow in ministry.[18] In short, some writers in the New Testament suggest that exorcism is to be part of Christian ministry; others do not. Hence, I have two principal aims in this study. My chief aim is to determine the place as well as to describe the practice of exorcism among early Christians reflected in the New Testament documents. Secondarily, I will attempt to explain the variety of approaches to exorcism in the New Testament canon. Then, acknowledging the narrow basis of this study, I anticipate being able to make some brief comments about the role of the traditions about Jesus in shaping the theology and practice of early Christianity.

1.2 This Study

Solving the problem of the place of exorcism among early Christians is potentially important for a whole cadre of reasons. (1) Being able to describe the place of exorcism among early Christians contributes to our understanding of the nature of early Christianity, including what turns out to be its various understandings of its mission. In turn, (2) a careful study of what was thought and practiced in relation to exorcism among early Christians draws attention to aspects of significant early theological diversity. Further, (3) given the argued place of exorcism in the ministry of Jesus,[19] our project can provide a case study for understanding the various ways early Christians viewed and handled the traditions that had initially developed around Jesus and what part these traditions had in forming early theology and practice. This leads us (4) to inquire in what way, if at all, Jesus functioned—or intended to function—as a model for early Christian ministry, particularly in relation to conducting exorcism. Answering this question will require setting out what models or options were available for those early Christians who were interested in exorcism.

---

18. See §5.1 below. (I retain the convention of designating the Gospel audience as "readers," acknowledging that they were probably initially hearers, but also recognizing that, probably almost immediately, they were readers or included readers.)

19. See Twelftree, *Exorcist*.

From the work of those who have gone before us, we already have some hypotheses to hand that might explain the interest in and role of exorcism among early Christians. It could be that (1) interest in exorcism, along with miracles in general, diminished over time. In a 1965 essay Maurice Wiles contended that it was not long after the close of the New Testament that the apologetic appeal to outward miracles diminished. This was because, he argued, the early miracles were appropriate to the start of a great spiritual movement, only necessary to give rise to a faith, making further miracles unnecessary.[20] More recently, John Dominic Crossan has said, "Miracles were, at a very early stage, being washed out of the tradition and, when retained, were being very carefully interpreted."[21] Alternatively, (2) the variation we see in the interest in exorcism in the New Testament may be accounted for in terms of cultural variations across time and place. For example, relying on the work of Eric Sorensen, it may be possible to show that part of an attempt by early Christians to adapt to the cultural sensitivities of a Greco-Roman culture—where exorcism was an unconventional and peripheral occult activity, only "in the eddies of the cultural mainstream"[22]— explains the varying interest in exorcism. Sorensen argues this is particularly noteworthy in the continuation of exorcism in the westward expansion of early Christianity. Or, (3) it could be that the diverse attitudes toward exorcism had theological roots that we might be able to detect and describe through a close examination of the New Testament documents.

Another proposed role for exorcism is (4) its association with baptism, which Elizabeth Ann Leeper argued was a fundamental factor in the development of the church as an institution.[23] In two studies that arose out of her 1991 Duke University PhD dissertation, Leeper examined the role played by exorcism in early Christianity.[24] She says that, for modern historians, exorcism among early Christians is usually taken to be associated "within the context of baptism, where it formed an essential part of the catechumenate and baptismal preparation."[25] While this link may be obvious later, we need

20. Maurice F. Wiles, "Miracles in the Early Church," in Moule, *Miracles*, 221–34, esp. 221–25.

21. John Dominic Crossan, *The Historical Jesus: The Life of a Mediterranean Jewish Peasant* (North Blackburn, Victoria: Collins Dove / HarperCollins, 1993), 310.

22. Sorensen, *Possession*, 9.

23. Elizabeth A. Leeper, "From Alexandria to Rome: The Valentinian Connection to the Incorporation of Exorcism as a Prebaptismal Rite," *VC* 44 (1990): 6–24; Elizabeth A. Leeper, "Exorcism in Early Christianity" (PhD diss., Duke University, 1991). Not cited by Leeper is John Bowman, "Exorcism and Baptism," in *A Tribute to Arthur Vööbus: Studies in Early Christian Literature and Its Environment, Primarily in the Syrian East* (ed. Robert H. Fischer; Chicago: Lutheran School of Theology at Chicago, 1977), 249–63, who deals primarily with Theodore of Mopsuestia (ca. 350–428 CE).

24. Leeper, "Exorcism"; also see Leeper, "Alexandria," 6–24; Elizabeth Ann Leeper, "The Role of Exorcism in Early Christianity," *StPatr* 26 (1993): 59–62.

25. Leeper, "Role," 59, citing Thomas M. Finn, "Ritual Process and the Survival of Early Christianity," *JRitSt* 3 (1989): 69–89; see esp. 74–76.

to note how far and in what way this relationship had been established in the first two Christian centuries.

1.3 Scope and Hazards

This is unequivocally a study of New Testament texts, expecting them to yield at least some evidence to help solve the puzzles surrounding exorcism among early Christians. Nevertheless, in order not to torture the texts to say more than the authors intended,[26] we will be looking for assistance beyond the horizons of the canon.

In order to balance the need for the advantage gained from taking into account literature written some distance in time from the material in the canon over against the need to keep manageable the amount of material to be discussed, as well as to remain as close as possible in time and culture to the origins of the New Testament traditions, two limits have been set on the material to be taken into account. First, I have set the terminus ad quem for the scope of this study at 200 CE. This involves leaving aside Tertullian from consideration. Though born well within our period (probably ca. 170 CE), he was not converted until near the end of the century (ca. 195 or 196 CE) and did not begin writing until between then and the turn of the century.[27] Though this is unfortunate, it conveniently confines our study to the period when early Christians remained primarily in a Greek milieu. For Tertullian was the first theologian to write in Latin, the first Western Christian to give us an extended theology, and the writer who "liberated" Christian thought from its Greek origins.[28] Notwithstanding, Tertullian will still be of considerable interest in helping us understand exorcism among the Montanists of the late second century (see §11.8 below).

Secondly, not only in order to keep the amount of material discussed within reasonable bounds, but also because our interest is in what came to be orthodox Christianity, I have taken into account only that which is generally considered orthodox or from mainstream early Christianity. Although our results would be little changed, discussion of second-century gnostic documents will have to wait for a possible future study.

It is anticipated that, looking back as through a lens along the already diverging trajectories of their interpretations, we may be able to detect subtleties in the New Testament texts, as well as discern implications of these writings

---

26. This colorful and apposite image comes from Anthony N. S. Lane, "Did the Apostolic Church Baptise Babies? A Seismological Approach," *TynBul* 55 (2004): 109.

27. See Timothy D. Barnes, *Tertullian: A Historical and Literary Study* (Oxford: Clarendon, 1985), chap. 5, "Chronology."

28. Cf. Eric F. Osborn, *Tertullian, First Theologian of the West* (Cambridge: Cambridge University Press, 1997), xiii.

that would otherwise be imperceptible or appear insignificant to us in viewing the New Testament documents unaided. Or, to change the metaphor, as we survey an increased amount of material over time, we may be able to hear, as through an amplifier, signals that would be too faint for our senses in listening only to signals from the New Testament.[29]

Obviously, in turning to later sources to help interpret New Testament writings, we open ourselves to the potential hazard of using the increased distance in time to give us the illegitimate advantage of historical hindsight.[30] That is, without careful and convincing argument, we might be tempted to fill gaps in our knowledge by using information only known at a later time. In other words, we might read back into the New Testament conclusions drawn from material of a later time regarding practices and theologies relating to exorcism. Rather, resisting these temptations, we can reasonably use reported developments or outcomes, as well as evidence from later times, to help look back with new sensitivity to detect aspects, details, or implications of earlier reports that might otherwise escape our attention.[31]

1.4 Plan of Attack

My plan is, first, to set out a brief general description of exorcism and exorcists in the period, including that associated with Jesus. This will enable us to see more clearly not only how Jesus would have been perceived as an exorcist by his followers and early Christians, but also to see the options that were available to Christians who sought to perform exorcisms (chap. 2). This will provide a context of understanding, as well as points for comparison, to help us see more clearly not only the distinctive features of the practice of exorcism among early Christians, but also to see those points held in common with others. Then, in chronological order in part 2, beginning with the letters of Paul, I will carefully scrutinize New Testament documents so that each writer's view on the place and practice of exorcism among early Christians can be seen clearly (chaps. 3–9). The conclusions to these chapters are

29. Cf. Graham N. Stanton, "Other Early Christian Writings: 'Didache,' Ignatius, 'Barnabas,' Justin Martyr," in *Early Christian Thought in Its Jewish Context* (ed. John Barclay and John Sweet; Cambridge: Cambridge University Press, 1996), 174, who says that the second-century Christian writings "often spell out explicitly what is only implicit in New Testament writings; careful study of them often leads to fresh insights into the more familiar New Testament writings."

30. See the discussion by John Cannon, "The Historian at Work," in *The Historian at Work* (ed. John Cannon; London: George Allen & Unwin, 1980), 9–11.

31. Recognizing this hazard, Graham N. Stanton, "Jesus of Nazareth: A False Prophet Who Deceived God's People?" in *Jesus of Nazareth: Lord and Christ; Essays on the Historical Jesus and New Testament Christology* (ed. Joel B. Green and Max Turner; Grand Rapids: Eerdmans; Carlisle, UK: Paternoster, 1994), 164–80, esp. 165–66, uses a similar method in assessing whether or not Jesus was accused of being a magician.

particularly important[32] for they carry the results of our inquiry, results that will contribute to answering the major questions driving this study.

In part 3, I turn to the second century. In the first two chapters (10–11) I will examine the Apostolic Fathers, along with apologists and the longer ending of Mark—again in as near to chronological order as is possible given our imprecise knowledge. This will enable us to gather insight into what the more immediate inheritors of the traditions associated with Jesus thought about exorcism. Then, still in the second century, chapter 12 looks through the spectacles of critics of Christianity, including three of the most significant critics: Celsus, Lucian of Samosata, and Galen. It is anticipated that, through this set of historical lenses (the Apostolic Fathers and other early Christian writers, and the somewhat less focused critics of Christianity), I will be able to bring into sharper relief what we have seen in the New Testament texts. First, then, we turn to setting out a description of exorcism and exorcists that the Christians of the first two centuries would have known.

32. See §§3.6; 4.11; 5.10; 6.4; 7.8; 8.4; and 9.11 below.

2

Jesus and Other Exorcists

THE SYNOPTIC GOSPELS portray the disciples as obediently emulating Jesus in their exorcisms.[1] Yet where their methods and those of the early Christians are clear, they do not appear to be modeled on those of Jesus.[2] Keeping in mind that Jesus was not the only exorcist operating or known in the world of his early followers, this raises the question as to the origin of their methods and how important Jesus was in establishing the methods of early Christian exorcism. Therefore, the purpose of this chapter is to set out the options or models available to early followers of Jesus—before and after Easter—for conducting exorcism. Later, this will enable us to ascertain how important Jesus was as a model and also how far and in what way they emulated him in their exorcisms (see §13.4 below). Toward the end of this chapter, we will discuss what Jesus intended for his followers in relation to exorcism.

A survey of the literary remains of the period shows that there was probably a range of kinds of exorcisms and exorcists that would have been known to the early Christians. This range expressed the varying understandings of the relative importance of the exorcist, the power-authority, and the rites (including words) that were used to apply or bring into play sufficient spiritual force to evict the offending spiritual entity.[3] Taking soundings at three points along this range helps us to locate and see how Jesus was understood.

1. Cf. Matt. 10:1; Mark 3:15; 6:7, 13; 9:18, 28–29; Luke 9:1.
2. See Mark 9:29; Luke 10:17; Acts 16:18; 19:12.
3. What follows builds on and develops Graham H. Twelftree, *Jesus the Exorcist: A Contribution to the Study of the Historical Jesus* (WUNT 2.54; Tübingen: Mohr Siebeck; Peabody, MA: Hendrickson, 1993), §3.

2.1 Magical Exorcisms

To begin with, it needs to be stated clearly and categorically that my use of the words "magic" and "magician," along with related expressions, is not pejorative. These words are used neutrally, as terms of convenience to describe particular kinds of ideas, materials, people, and activities—including exorcists and approaches to exorcism—known in the ancient world.[4]

That is, at one end of a spectrum of kinds of exorcisms and exorcists are those thought to be successful because of what was said and done rather than because of who performed them. From its sheer volume, as well as chronological and geographical range,[5] this material probably reflects the most commonly known form of exorcism across the world of late antiquity, including first-century Palestine.[6]

Therefore we are obliged to give it pride of place in attempting to understand what early Christians would have known about exorcism. There are a number of sources that help us in this exercise: Qumran texts, stories from Tobit and from Josephus, the New Testament stories of the unknown exorcist and the sons of Sceva, the magical papyri, comments by Justin Martyr, and perhaps the notion of the *geṭ* in the magical bowls.[7]

a. The Qumran hymn 11Q5 (11QPsᵃ) 27.9–10 states that David was responsible for composing four songs for making music over "the stricken" or

---

4. Though not limited to exorcism, these phenomena are illustrated in the magical papyri. See, e.g., the collection in Hans Dieter Betz, *The Greek Magical Papyri in Translation Including the Demotic Spells*, vol. 1, *Texts* (2nd ed.; Chicago and London: University of Chicago Press, 1992). On the problem of defining magic, see, e.g., A. F. Segal, "Hellenistic Magic: Some Questions of Definition," in *Studies in Gnosticism and Hellenistic Religions: Presented to Gilles Quispel on the Occasion of His 65th Birthday* (ed. R. van den Broek and M. J. Vermaseren; Études préliminaires aux religions orientales dans l'Empire romain 91; Leiden: Brill, 1981), 349–75; John G. Gager, "A New Translation of Ancient Greek and Demotic Papyri, Sometimes Called Magical," *JR* 67 (1987): 80; and John G. Gager, "Introduction," in *Curse Tablets and Binding Spells from the Ancient World* (ed. John G. Gager; New York and Oxford: Oxford University Press, 1992), 3–41, esp. 24–25; and C. A. Hoffman, "Fiat Magia," in *Magic and Ritual in the Ancient World* (ed. Paul Mirecki and Marvin W. Meyer; Religions in the Graeco-Roman World 141; Leiden: Brill, 1995), 179–94.

5. See the material collected in, e.g., Robert W. Daniel and Franco Maltomini, *Supplementum Magicum* (2 vols.; Abhandlungen der Rheinisch-Westfälischen Akademie der Wissenschaften; Sonderreihe, Papyrologica Coloniensia 16.1/2; Opladen: Westdeutscher, 1990–1992); Betz, *Greek Magical Papyri*; Joseph Naveh and Shaul Shaked, *Magic Spells and Formulae: Aramaic Incantations of Late Antiquity* (Jerusalem: Magnes, 1993); *GMA*.

6. For solid evidence of such material in Palestine at the time of Jesus and his early followers, see the discussion by Esther Eshel, "Genres of Magical Texts in the Dead Sea Scrolls," in Lange, 395–415.

7. Further, and in more detail on what follows in this section, see Graham H. Twelftree, "Jesus the Exorcist and Ancient Magic," in *A Kind of Magic: Understanding Magic in the New Testament and Its Religious Environment* (ed. Michael Labahn and Bert Jan Lietaert Peerbolte; European Studies on Christian Origins; LNTS 306; London and New York: T&T Clark, 2007), 57–86.

"demon possessed."[8] Although we have no copies of these songs, assuming they were consistent in perspective with Qumran's apotropaic psalms,[9] it is reasonable to expect that these exorcisms would be conducted by a maskil (*maśkîl*) or scribe. Perhaps in a public worship setting,[10] as part of the adjuration he declared (hymnlike) the splendor and protection of God and his angels in order to reassure those involved, as well as to frighten and subdue the spirits. These exorcisms could also be expected to involve hurling abuse at the spirit and, probably, adjuring the spirit by God.[11] Alternatively, the exorcist could ask God to send a powerful angel (cf. 11Q11 4.5), causing the spirit to be dispatched to the great abyss (11Q11 4.7–9). Witnesses might have responded by saying, "Amen, Amen" (cf. 4Q511 4; 11Q11 5.14). In any case, what is important is not the identity of the exorcist but what is said, which involved frightening away the demon or co-opting a spiritual power to dispatch it.

b. Tobit[12] tells the story of a certain Sarah possessed by the demon Asmodeus. The text says that in a fit of jealousy the demon killed her seven successive husbands (Tob. 3:8; 6:13). Tobias, the new husband, is instructed, on entering the bridal chamber, to "take some of the fish's liver and heart, and put them on the embers of the incense. An odor will be given off; the demon will smell it and flee, and will never be seen near her any more" (6:17–18). On carrying out the instructions, "when the demon smelled the odor it fled to upper Egypt, and the angel bound it" (8:3, my translation). The author may not have considered this an exorcism—the removal of a spiritual being from within a person—but simply the defeating and chasing away of a troublesome spirit. Nevertheless, as this same technique of fumigation was later used as a

8. The term הפגועים was used both in the Qumran documents and in later literature of those possessed or tormented by evil spirits. See James A. Sanders, *The Psalms Scroll of Qumran Cave 11 (11QPsᵃ)* (DJD 4; Oxford: Clarendon, 1965), 93, citing *y. Šabb.* 6.8b; *y. ʿErub.* 10.26c; *b. Šebu.* 15b. See also 11Q11 4.2; and Marcus Jastrow, *A Dictionary of the Targumim: The Talmud Babli and Yerushalemi, and the Midrashic Literature* (New York: Pardes, 1950), 1135.

9. See 11Q11; 4Q510; 4Q511; 6Q18. For a thorough discussion of these texts, note Bilha Nitzan, "Hymns from Qumran—4Q510–4Q511," in *The Dead Sea Scrolls: Forty Years of Research* (ed. Devorah Dimant and Uriel Rappaport; STDJ 10; Leiden: Brill, 1992), 53–63. Eshel, "Genres," 395–415, takes 11Q11 to be exorcistic rather than apotropaic.

10. See 4Q511 frg. 63 4.1–3, on which see Philip S. Alexander, "'Wrestling against Wickedness in High Places': Magic in the World View of the Qumran Community," in *The Scrolls and the Scriptures: Qumran Fifty Years After* (ed. Stanley E. Porter and Craig A. Evans; JSPSup 26; Sheffield: Sheffield Academic, 1997), 321.

11. It is unlikely the tetragrammaton was used. Cf., e.g., 4Q511 frg. 35; 8Q5 1; 11Q11 3.1–12; on which see Joseph M. Baumgarten, "On the Nature of the Seductress, in 4Q184," *RevQ* 15 (1991): 136; Eshel, "Genres," 401–2, 404.

12. Tobit is probably of Palestinian origin and from the third or, more likely, second century BCE. See Merten Rabenau, *Studien zum Buch Tobit* (Berlin: de Gruyter, 1994), 175–90; Joseph A. Fitzmyer, *Tobit* (Commentaries on Early Jewish Literature; Berlin and New York: de Gruyter, 2003), 50–54.

method of exorcism (see f. below), it is likely that Tobit reflects a method of exorcism with which the early Christians would have been familiar.

It is notable that the instructions to Tobit also involved the direction, "Now when you are about to go to bed with her, both of you must first stand up and pray, imploring the Lord of heaven that mercy and safety may be granted to you" (Tob. 6:18). This does not seem to be part of the method proper of subjugating the unwanted spirit; more likely, it was a means of protection from subsequent demonic attack since they are said "to pray and implore that they might be kept safe" (8:5).[13]

c. From Josephus (ca. 37–ca. 100 CE) comes the well-known story of Eleazar, a Jew. The story, which can be expected to reflect what would have been known about exorcism by the early Christians, is told as an example of the exorcisms Josephus has seen him conduct, which depended on traditional "poetic songs" (τὰς ἐπῳδάς) and "methods" (τρόποι, *Ant.* 8.45–49; cf. *J.W.* 7.180–185). From this vocabulary, as well as the story itself, it can be deduced that it was customary for such healers to have in their keeping artifacts and also texts that included instructions on how they were to be used, along with directions for accompanying activity. As Eleazar is not called an exorcist, or even a healer, such activity presumably formed only part of his professional life. Josephus says that he exorcises a demon without the use of words, putting a ring to the nose of the sufferer; as the man smelled the roots in it, he drew out the demon.[14] Only when the man had fallen down, after the demon had left, does Eleazar turn to using the poems or songs, for he "adjured [ὥρκου] the demon never to come back into him, speaking Solomon's name and reciting the poems [or songs, τὰς ἐπῳδάς], which he had composed" (*Ant.* 8.47). Here the identity of the probably professional person who performs the exorcism is not important. What is important are the words and methods used by Eleazar to oath or adjure the demon out.

d. In the New Testament there is the story of the unknown exorcist about whom John reports to Jesus: "Teacher, we saw someone casting out demons in your name, and we tried to stop him, because he was not following us" (Mark 9:38 ‖ Luke 9:49). Similarly, Luke tells of seven sons of Sceva (Acts 19:13–19). These door-to-door exorcists are reported to use the name of Jesus in their incantations: "I adjure you by the Jesus whom Paul proclaims" (19:13). For our purposes, what is to be noted is that, at least from the perspective of the sons of Sceva in the story, success was not thought to depend

---

13. Cf. Luke 11:24–26; Josephus, *Ant.* 8.46–49; PGM IV. 1227–1264 (on which see below).

14. H. St. J. Thackeray and Ralph Marcus, *Josephus* (9 vols.; LCL; Cambridge, MA: Harvard University Press; London: Heinemann, 1926–1965), 5:597, note that T. Reinach plausibly conjectures that the root under the seal of the ring was the *baaras* plant described in Josephus, *J.W.* 7.180–185. If this is the poisonous, strong-smelling *Mandragora officinarum* (mandrake), the demon was probably thought to be drawn out by the smell. Cf. Song 7:13.

on their identity but on what was said in order to engage a particular source of power-authority.[15]

e. Although we have already noted that performing magical exorcisms was not confined to the practitioners reflected in the magical papyri, it is from this wealth of material that we gain most of our information about these exorcisms and exorcists that would have been familiar to the early Christians. Therefore, this material merits particular attention.[16] Some clear examples of these magical exorcisms are found in *PGM* IV and V. The former text, *PGM* IV, is a 3,274-line handbook for preternatural therapists, which includes two highly composite sections devoted to exorcism (IV. 1227–1264, 3007–3086). *PGM* V is a shorter manual containing another composite exorcistic text (V. 96–172). This kind of material provided professionals with the texts to be recited as well as directions for the accompanying rituals to be carried out. A discussion of one of these texts, *PGM* IV. 1227–1264, will be sufficient to understand the approach taken to exorcism.

In *PGM* IV. 1227–1264 exorcism is understood to be a power-encounter in that the exorcist acts out a dominance in speaking "over" (ἐπί) the person's head,[17] standing behind the sufferer (IV. 1228–1230), as well as using an olive branch whip during the exorcism (IV. 1248–1252). After the instructions for the preparation for the exorcism, the text directs the practitioner to say (in Coptic): "Hail, God of Abraham; hail, God of Isaac; hail, God of Jacob; Jesus Chrestos,[18] the Holy Spirit, the Son of the Father, who is above the Seven, who is within the Seven. Bring Iao Sabaoth; may your power issue forth from NN, until you drive away this unclean demon satan,[19] who is in him" (IV. 1231–1239). The rationale behind this amalgamated spell of Jewish, Christian, and pagan ideas is that a demon is expected to come out of a person because the power of a god comes to drive it away (IV. 1239; see also IV. 3025). This indicates that the exorcist is not presuming to function in his own power or any power he may have imbibed from the god; the power-authority itself is called up and asked to perform the exorcism.

15. The negative response of the spirit/man, "Who are you?" and the ensuing violence show a conflicting, more charismatic, view that depends on the identity of the exorcist. See below.

16. Here I summarize some of the more detailed treatment in Twelftree, "Ancient Magic."

17. Cf. J. D. M. Derrett, "Getting on Top of a Demon (Luke 4:39)," *EvQ* 65 (1993): 99–109.

18. Bentley Layton, *The Gnostic Treatise on Resurrection from Nag Hammadi* (HDR 12; Missoula, MT: Scholars Press, 1979), 44–45, says that even though "Christos" (Christ) and "Chrēstos" (excellent) were pronounced the same, in Coptic manuscripts of the classical period, the words were not generally confused, even though this was not the case among pagans. In this particular case we can only suppose that, though it is clear from the context that the name "Jesus Christ" is intended, the confusion must have come about from pagan Copts taking up the term.

19. A similar use of "*satan*" as an individual or class of demon, rather than the Christian archdemon, is found in 4Q213a 1.17 and 11Q5 19.15–16; see Michael E. Stone and Jonas C. Greenfield, "The Prayer of Levi," *JBL* 112 (1993): 262–65.

However, before this Coptic interpolation (*PGM* IV. 1231–1239), the earlier version of the text embodied a different and more charismatic view of exorcism. The exorcist began his rite in the first person: "I conjure [or 'oath'] you [ἐξορκίζω σε], demon, whoever you are, by this god . . . [*voces magicae*] come out . . . and stand away" (IV. 1239–1241). Even though it is the strength or authority of the gods named that is being used, the exorcist himself is still important in performing the exorcism. Thus, the text continues, "Come out, demon, since I bind [δεσμεύω] you" (IV. 1245–1246). In other words, the forceful expulsion of the demon from the person is expected to be successful because the practitioner is using the god as the means of eviction. After the expulsion of the demon, *PGM* IV. 1227–1264 ends by instructing the practitioner to hang around the person a phylactery on which are seven lines of magical words, ending with "protect him, NN" (IV. 1252–1262). Thus, amulets were expected not only to drive out demons (cf. XXXVI. 275–283) but, in this case, also to provide ongoing protection, presumably from the threat of the demon returning (cf. IV. 1244; Josephus, *Ant.* 8.47).

f. Hints as to what may have been known about exorcism by the early Christians also comes from two comments by Justin Martyr (ca. 100–ca. 165). In one of them he reports that both Jews and Gentiles "make use of craft [τῇ τέχνῃ] when they exorcise . . . and employ fumigations and incantations."[20] Although he does not tell us how this works, a later story—associated with Yoḥanan ben Zakkai—says, "People bring roots and smoke them under him and sprinkle water on the spirit and it flees" (*Pesiq. Rab Kah.* 4.5).[21] Although this story is likely to be fictional,[22] the method of exorcism may reflect actual practice for, at least from Josephus, we know of the supposed power of smell in removing a demon (*Ant.* 8.47; cf. n. 14 above). In another comment, Justin also admits that the Jews have had some success when they exorcised "in [the name of] the God of Abraham, and the God of Isaac, and the God of Jacob" (*Dial.* 85.3). As this simple method is attested in a number of places, it was probably well and widely known.[23] Once again, the factors understood to be critical in an exorcism are what was said and done, not the person performing the healing.

g. Of less certain value in setting out what early Christians knew and the options they had for conducting exorcisms is the notion of the *geṭ* from the magical bowls.[24] For, in the period of interest to us, the bowls seem to have

20. Justin, *Dial.* 85.3; cf. Tob. 6:7–8; 8:2–3; 4Q196 frg. 11 1.8–9; 4Q197 frg. 3 1.13–14.

21. The earliest version we have of this story is from the sixth or seventh century CE. See Jacob Neusner, *Pesiqta de Rab Kahana: An Analytical Translation* (2 vols.; BJS 122–23; Atlanta: Scholars Press, 1987), 1:65.

22. See Jacob Neusner, *Development of a Legend: Studies on the Traditions concerning Yohanan ben Zakkai* (StPB 16; Leiden: Brill, 1970), 167, 182.

23. See *PGM* IV; cf. Origen, *Cels.* 1.24–25; 4.33–34.

24. Jacob Neusner, *A History of the Jews in Babylonia* (vol. 5; StPB 15; Leiden: Brill, 1970), 227, says he does "not know of any case of the occurrence of this magical *Geṭ* outside of the bowls." For more detail on what follows, see Twelftree, "Ancient Magic."

temporarily fallen out of use.[25] Nevertheless, the ideas involved in the various kinds of letters of dismissal or bills of divorce (the magical *geṭ*[26]) written in the bowls[27]—understood to be issued to unwanted spirits in order to remove or keep them away—may have been known in Palestine in the first century. That is, the notion of the *geṭ* may be evident in Tobit 3:17.[28] There, in the fourth century CE Codex Sinaiticus, Sarah, who is about to marry, is to be "set free [λῦσαι] from the wicked demon Asmodeus," λῦσαι being a word sometimes used for divorce.[29] A Qumran document from the Herodian period saying that "the demon was 'in love' with Sarah" (4Q197 frg. 4 2.9)[30] enhances the idea of a magical *geṭ* being involved and, therefore, known in the New Testament era. As the concept implies, the *geṭ* seems to have been used to banish or ban an unwanted spiritual being from troubling a person. Also, in dealing with the removal of evil spirits,[31] it is not only assumed that a person is troubled because they are possessed but also because their place of residence could be inhabited by a demon. Hence, in getting rid of, or gaining protection from, an evil spirit, attention could also be focused on

25. William Stewart McCullough, *Jewish and Mandaean Incantation Bowls in the Royal Ontario Museum* (Near and Middle East Series 5; Toronto: University of Toronto Press, 1967), xiv–xv.

26. For the various types of divorce formulas occurring in the bowls, see Rebecca Lesses, "Exe(o)rcising Power: Women as Sorceresses, Exorcists, and Demonesses in Babylonian Jewish Society in Late Antiquity," *JAAR* 69 (2001): 343–75. Shaul Shaked, "The Poetics of Spells, Language, and Structure in Aramaic Incantations of Late Antiquity," in *Mesopotamian Magic: Textual, Historical, and Interpretative Perspectives* (ed. Tzvi Abusch and Karel van der Toorn; Ancient Magic and Divination 1; Groningen: Styx, 1999), 173–96, esp. 176, takes the *geṭ* to be a metaphor so that it is an act of sympathetic magic. See the discussions by Levene, *CMB*, 18–21, 58–62. See also Baruch A. Levine, "The Language of the Magical Bowls," appendix in Jacob Neusner, *Jews in Babylonia*, 5:349–50; and Cyrus H. Gordon, "The Aramaic Incantation Bowls in Historic Perspective," in *Minha le-Nahum: Biblical and Other Studies Presented to Nahum M. Sarna in Honour of His 70th Birthday* (ed. Marc Brettler and Michael Fishbane; JSOTSup 154; Sheffield: JSOT Press, 1993), 142–46, esp. 143.

27. E.g., *AMB* B5; *AMIB* 013A; *CMB* M50/M59; M103/M119.

28. On the dating of Tobit, see n. 12 above.

29. Paul E. Dion, "Raphaël l'exorciste," *Bib* 57 (1976): 399–413, esp. 407–8, argues that Tob. 3:17 describes the equivalent of a magical *geṭ* found in the bowls. See also Dan Levene, "'A Happy Thought of the Magicians,' The Magical *Geṭ*," in *Shlomo: Studies in Epigraphy, Iconography, History, and Archaeology in Honor of Shlomo Moussaieff* (ed. Robert Deutsch; Tel Aviv: Archaeological Center Publication, 2003), 183–84.

30. See Fitzmyer, *Tobit*, 215; Carey A. Moore, *Tobit* (AB 40A; New York: Doubleday, 1996), 158. On the dating of 4Q197 see DJD XIV p. 41.

31. *CMB* 2: two of the twenty Jewish Aramaic bowls Levene transcribes and discusses offered protection against curses and oaths in general, two were for protection against the malicious magic of named enemies, two others were dispensed for the protection of unborn or young babies, three more relate to healing specific sicknesses, seven were intended for general protection against demons and other agents, and only another four were also for general protection and include the notion of the *geṭ* against the evil spirits (*CMB* M50; M59; M103; M119).

the house or a particular room.[32] This probably explains why most bowls have been found buried upside down—perhaps as "demon traps"[33]—under the floors of homes.[34]

As this discussion of the bowls has indicated, there is magical material which assumes that an evil spiritual entity can trouble a person from the outside rather than through having infiltrated and taken up residence in the person. Thus the spirit is not expelled but caused to flee (e.g., Tob. 6:1–8:3; L.A.B. 60). Other texts deal with controlling demons (e.g., PGM I. 96–132; III. 1–164) or with protecting people from them as well as from magical powers.[35] There are also texts dealing with the expulsion of fevers or other diseases rather than of demons (e.g., GMA I.56). This variety of ways to control unwanted spiritual beings—all sharing the notion that what was important was not the "exorcist" but what was said and done—will help us in gaining a sense of perspective on how Jesus and the early Christians dealt with the demonic.

2.2 The Exorcists of Ancient Magic

Although, as is quite clear, the well and widely known magical techniques we have been surveying could be used by anyone (cf. Tob. 6:7–9; 8:1–3; Justin, Dial. 85.2–3), there were also in the period of Jesus and the early Christians professional practitioners (cf. Ant. 8.45–49)[36] or, as in the case among the Qumran people, designated practitioners. Further, as the material attests, they were more than exorcists.[37] What was collected in PGM IV shows that these individuals were called upon to help people find a lover, restrain anger, get rid of a friend, produce a trance, gain control of a god, acquire business and customers, and cause sickness, for example, as well as to remove demons. Often

32. E.g., AMB B1; B8; AMIB 015A; 016A; 020A; 023A; 027A; 048A.VI; 068A; CMB M50; M131; M142; MSF B14; B15. In CMB M155, perhaps in the name of Christ (see CMB, pp. 112, 115), the daughter of Lilith is commanded to "carry away the evil spirit from the belly of . . ."; and AMIB 029A and 013A, where the evil spirits are instructed to leave the clients as well as the home; cf. AMB B5; B10; MSF B15; B16.

33. Cf. E. A. Wallis Budge, "Babylonian Terra-Cotta Devil-Traps," in E. A. Wallis Budge, Amulets and Talismans (New Hyde Park, NY: University Books, 1961), 283–90.

34. There is no agreement as to the praxis associated with the bowls. See Gordon, "Bowls," 142–46, esp. 142–43; Hannu Juusola, Linguistic Peculiarities in the Aramaic Magic Bowl Texts (StudOr 86; Helsinki: Finnish Oriental Society, 1999), 4–9.

35. See 4Q510; 4Q511; also 11Q11; PGM I. 195–222; IV. 86–87; IV. 2145–2240; VII. 579–590; CXIV. 1–14; GMA, part 1, §§38, 52, 67.

36. That professionals rather than individual amateurs are responsible for many magical papyri, see Twelftree, "Ancient Magic."

37. The term "exorcist" does not appear, even in relation to Eleazar (Josephus, Ant. 8.46), though it is used in Acts 19:13 of the seven sons of Sceva. On the earliest uses of the term, see Roy Kotansky, "Greek Exorcistic Amulets," in Ancient Magic and Ritual Power (ed. Marvin W. Meyer and Paul Mirecki; RGRW 129; New York and Leiden: Brill, 1995), 249n14.

peripatetic,[38] these professionals were so highly regarded that their services were sought in the highest places (cf. Josephus, *Ant.* 8.46).

The texts give evidence of the exorcists collecting, amalgamating, and preserving a library of texts. They would also have had at their disposal the equipment necessary for copying out texts as a whole or in part (e.g., *PGM* IV. 1252–1261) for patients or colleagues (cf. *PGM* IV. 2006–2014). Some of the exorcists, at least on occasion, needed only a text for the incantations. Nevertheless, at least most of them also had on hand a wide range of materials, including rings, vegetable matter, materials for incense, cords and sheets of papyrus and metal. We can also assume they possessed such containers and utensils that facilitated the preparation of their prescriptions.

Even though considerable preparation may have been involved, such as collecting and preparing materials and wearing an amulet or ring,[39] at base, the practices of exorcism reflected in the earlier papyri traditions—that could conceivably reflect what was known by the early Christians—were relatively simple in conception and in practice. As we have seen, to drive a spirit from its habitat the exorcist could engage a god or power-authority (sometimes called an "assistant"[40]) or, himself, use the spiritual being as a power-source (e.g., *PGM* IV. 1240, 3019). Alternatively, this power source could be transferred or linked to an object (such as a ring or phylactery) in order to drive out a demon (e.g., *PGM* XII. 266, 281–282; cf. XXXVI. 275–83), or the object could be given to the patient for ongoing protection (e.g., *PGM* IV. 1252–1261).[41] The rationale was that the mere presence of supranatural power was sufficient to cause a demon to depart or stay away. Sometimes exorcisms were performed through carrying out an activity, unaccompanied by words, since actions as much as words were thought able to contain and convey spiritual power (e.g., Josephus, *Ant.* 8.46–47).

Particularly interesting when considering exorcism among the early Christians is the likelihood that some exorcists of ancient magic did not work alone but had apprentices, perhaps from among their family members.[42] It is probable that, at least in some cases, these exorcists were bilingual: their collecting of new spells crossed language as well as religious boundaries (e.g., *PGM* IV. 1227–1264, 3020). Yet, strikingly, most of the material remains of ancient magic

38. See Walter Burkert, *The Orientalizing Revolution: Near Eastern Influence on Greek Culture in the Early Archaic Age* (Revealing Antiquity 5; Cambridge, MA, and London: Harvard University Press, 1992), 41–46.

39. Cf. *PGM* IV. 2145–2240; XII. 270–350; XXXVI. 275–283.

40. On the inadequacy of "assistant" as the usual translation for πάρεδρος (cf. LSJ, "πάρεδρ—"), see Twelftree, "Ancient Magic."

41. Cf. Douglas L. Penney and Michael O. Wise, "By the Power of Beelzebub: An Aramaic Incantation Formula from Qumran (4Q560)," *JBL* 113 (1994): 630 and 630n12.

42. See Burkert, *Orientalizing Revolution*, 44–46. Cf. Matt. 12:27 ‖ Luke 11:19; Acts 19:13–14. Contrast John P. Meier, *A Marginal Jew* (3 vols.; New York: Doubleday, 1991–2001), 2:549: "The magician did not usually operate within a fairly stable circle of disciples or believers."

are "Jewish" or, in the case of the magical papyri, under such Jewish influence it is reasonable to suppose that they have their origins among Jews of some kind.[43] Hence, these records of ancient magic are extremely important in taking into account what the early Christians knew about exorcism and exorcists.

2.3 Charismatic Magicians

If the magical exorcisms we have been discussing were thought to be effective because of what was said and done, slightly further along the spectrum in this period were other exorcisms conducted by those we could term charismatic magicians. That is, these magico-charismatic exorcisms were thought to be successful because they combined the knowledge and art of the magicians with the personal force of the practitioner or healer. For example, in the story of Abraham in the *Genesis Apocryphon* from Qumran, the identity of the exorcist is important, for the point of the story is to glorify Abraham. However, in this case Abraham uses prayer, presumably to engage the help of the Most High God, who is said to have sent a spirit to scourge the Pharaoh and his household. Abraham is asked to pray for him and his house so that the evil spirit could be expelled. "I prayed that [he might be] cured and laid my hands upon his [hea]d. The plague was removed from him; the evil [spirit] was banished [from him], and he recovered" (1QapGen 20.28–29). Here both the person as well as the enlisted outside help are important.

Also, Josephus tells a story of David (1 Sam. 16; *Ant.* 6.166–169) in a way that describes him as a charismatic magician. Josephus says that Saul "was beset by strange disorders and evil spirits which caused him such suffocation and strangling that the physicians could devise no other remedy save to order search to be made for one with power to charm away spirits and to play upon the harp, and, whensoever the evil spirit should assail and torment Saul, to have him stand over the king and strike the strings and chant his songs." David was found to be such a person so that Saul's "illness was charmed away" by David and "the sight of the boy and his presence gave him [Saul] pleasure" (6.168–169). Here it is not only David's presence but also his playing the lyre that was considered important in removing an evil spirit from Saul and restoring him to full health.

2.4 Charismatic Exorcists

With what we could term the charismatic exorcists, we come to the other end of the spectrum of exorcists from those reflected in, for example, the magical papyri. In contrast to the so-called magical exorcists, success for the charismatics depended entirely on the personal or charismatic force of the exorcist, not on

---

43. See Morton Smith, "The Jewish Elements in the Magical Papyri," SBLSP 25 (1986): 456, on the difficulty of distinguishing characteristically Jewish elements in the magical papyri.

what was said or done, or on any outside source of power-authority. Among historical figures thought to be successful in controlling or exorcising demons in this way, we have an example in the rabbinic literature. In a story concerning Simeon ben Yose, a fourth-generation Tannaitic rabbi, a demon, Ben Temalion, enters the emperor's daughter. To bring about a cure, Rabbi Simeon is said simply to call out to the demon, "Ben Temalion, get out! Ben Temalion, get out!" (*b. Me'il.* 17b).[44] The resulting successful exorcism is portrayed as depending entirely on the charismatic force of the exorcist.

Similarly, writing early in the third century, Flavius Philostratus (ca. 170–ca. 245 CE) tells of a young lad who interrupts Apollonius of Tyana while he is speaking in the king's portico in Athens.[45] The lad is said to be cured of demon possession when Apollonius reprimands the demon and orders it to quit the youth (Philostratus, *Vit. Apoll.* 4.20).[46] Also to be taken into account here is the Syrian from Palestine about whom Lucian of Samosata (born ca. 120 CE) writes: for a large fee, the Syrian would restore the possessed to health. Standing beside the man, he would ask the spirit about his entry into the person. The spirit would answer, sometimes in a foreign language. In order to drive out the spirit, the Syrian would adjure and, if necessary, threaten it (*Philops.* 16).

Even though at first sight these stories may be considered to some extent reminiscent of those of Jesus, it is notable that they are all significantly later than the time of the first followers of Jesus and the early Christians. Therefore, this method of exorcism where, as Peter Brown put it, "the holy man was thought of as having taken into his person, skills that had previously been preserved by society at large," probably developed and flowered later than the time of the earliest followers of Jesus.[47] The significance of this is not to be underestimated as we seek to understand what early Christians knew about exorcism. With this in mind we turn now to describing what the first followers of Jesus would have known about him as an exorcist.

2.5 Jesus as an Exorcist

Having previously set out elsewhere what I consider to be a reasonable sketch of the historical Jesus as an exorcist, all that is required here is a sum-

---

44. See the discussion in Markham J. Geller, "Jesus' Theurgic Powers: Parallels in the Talmud and Incantation Bowls," *JJS* 28 (1977): 141–42.

45. Apollonius probably lived from 40 CE to about 120 CE, not 4 or 3 BCE to 97 CE as Flavius Philostratus claims. See Maria Dzielska, *Apollonius of Tyana in Legend and History* (Problemi e ricerche di storia antica 10; Rome: "L'erma" di Bretschneider, 1986), 32–38, 186.

46. For a discussion of the historical value of the story, see Twelftree, *Exorcist*, 23–27. Further, see E. L. Bowie, "Apollonius of Tyana: Tradition and Reality," *ANRW* II.16.2 (1978): 1652–99; and Dzielska, *Apollonius.*

47. Peter Brown, "The Rise and Function of the Holy Man in Late Antiquity," *JRS* 61 (1971): 100.

mary outline.[48] For that outline the following points are pertinent for what the followers of Jesus would have known about him as an exorcist:

a. Not only does the conducting of miracles appear to dominate the activity of the historical Jesus;[49] the exorcisms in particular loom large as one of the most obvious and important aspects of his ministry (cf., e.g., Matt. 12:28 ∥ Luke 11:20).[50] We know of no other healer in antiquity for whom this was true.

b. Exorcisms conducted by Jesus are portrayed as what could be called power-encounters. Thus, in the story of the healing of the demoniac in the Capernaum synagogue, the man screams out when he confronts Jesus (Mark 1:24). On seeing Jesus, the Gadarene demoniac runs, falls on his knees in front of Jesus, and shouts out (5:6–7). In Mark 9:20, on seeing Jesus the demon throws the boy into a convulsion.[51]

c. In his exorcisms Jesus is reported to have availed himself of standard formulas or incantations used by the exorcists of ancient magic. In Mark 1:25 Jesus says to the demon, "Be silent" (Φιμώθητι) or, more accurately, "Be bound."[52] In Mark 1:25; 5:8; and 9:25 Jesus is reported as saying to the demon, "Come out" (ἔξελθε).[53] Further, as part of the preternatural battle in Mark 5:9, Jesus follows a convention in asking the name of the demon.[54] Also, in the story of the so-called epileptic boy, Jesus adopts the practice of forbidding a demon to return to the person (Mark 9:25).[55]

d. In one of the reports Jesus took up the practice of transferring demons from the sufferer to an object, in this case to a herd of pigs (Mark 5:12–14). In antiquity, such demonically charged objects—a pebble or piece of wood or a pot or some water thought to contain the demons—could be thrown away or destroyed to effect and perhaps signify the demon's departure from the situation.[56]

---

48. See Graham H. Twelftree, *Christ Triumphant: Exorcism Then and Now* (London: Hodder & Stoughton, 1985), 57–71; Graham H. Twelftree, "ΕΙ ΔΕ . . . ΕΓΩ . . . ΕΚΒΑΛΛΩ ΤΑ ΔΑΙΜΟΝΙΑ! . . . [Luke 11:19]," in *The Miracles of Jesus* (ed. David Wenham and Craig Blomberg; Gospel Perspectives 6; Sheffield: JSOT Press, 1986), 368–92; and Twelftree, *Exorcist.*

49. Meier, *Marginal Jew,* vol. 2, part 3, esp. 970.

50. See Graham H. Twelftree, "The Miracles of Jesus: Marginal or Mainstream?" *JSHJ* 1 (2003): 104–24.

51. In Mark 7:24–30, the story of the Syrophoenician woman's daughter, Jesus does not meet the sufferer.

52. Cf. P.Lond. 121.396, 967; *PGM* IX. 9; XXXVI. 164, on which see Samson Eitrem, *Some Notes on Demonology in the New Testament* (2nd ed.; SO, fasc. suppl. 20; Oslo: Universitetsforlaget, 1966), 38; also on דמם, דמם see *HALOT* 1:338; and Jastrow, *Dictionary,* 488.

53. See *PGM* IV. 1239–1241, 1242–1249; Lucian, *Philops.* 11; 16; Philostratus, *Vit. Apoll.* 4.20.

54. See *T. Sol.* 2:1; 3:6; 4:3–4; 5:1; *PGM* IV. 1017–1019, 3037–3079; V. 247–303. Cf. Philostratus, *Vit. Apoll.* 4.20.

55. Cf. Josephus, *Ant.* 8.46–49; Philostratus, *Vit. Apoll.* 4.20; *PGM* IV. 1254, 3024–3025.

56. See P.Oslo 1:256–65; also, Count Goblet d'Alviella, *Lectures on the Origin and Growth of the Conception of God* (The Hibbert Lectures, 1891; London and Edinburgh: Williams & Nor-

e. The violence found in exorcism stories from Josephus (*Ant.* 8.49) and Philostratus (*Vit. Apoll.* 4.20) and implied in the magical papyri (IV. 1248–1252) is also apparent in those associated with Jesus (Mark 1:26; 9:26).

f. It is suggested that Jesus' methods of exorcism are nearer those of Apollonius (Philostratus, *Vit. Apoll.* 4.20) or that of a first-century Jewish charismatic than an exorcist in the magical tradition.[57] That is, without aid he was able to order unwanted spiritual beings out of a person. However, we have just seen that Jesus used standard magical formulas as well as, on one occasion, a herd of pigs in transferring demons from a person to a body of water. Also, even though during an exorcism Jesus makes no mention of his power-authority,[58] seeing him simply as a charismatic ignores the import of him saying that he casts out demons "by the Spirit [or finger] of God" (Matt. 12:28 ‖ Luke 11:20).[59] This is evidence that he understood he was not operating unaided—relying only on his personal force or presence—but was also using a power-authority, the Spirit or finger of God. Also, in the previous verse ("If I by Beelzebul cast out demons, by whom do your sons cast them out?" Matt. 12:27 ‖ Luke 11:19, my translation), Jesus places himself on a level with other healers[60] and uncritically takes up the assumption that he is using a power-authority for his exorcisms. In these sayings—the most explicit concerning his methods of exorcism—it is clear that he shares the same view of exorcism as some of those involved in ancient magic: using a power-authority to perform an exorcism. It is not that Jesus or others among his contemporaries coerced their spiritual supporters, but as reflected in the magical papyri, they assumed the right to use, at will, their chosen power-authorities. Further on this point, it is to be noted that even though the commands and methods of the exorcisms of ancient magic may not have been generally as clipped as those attributed to Jesus,[61] he shared with some traditions of ancient magic a simple understanding of exorcism:[62] a

gate, 1892), 88–89; Martin P. Nilsson, *A History of Greek Religion* (2nd ed.; Oxford: Clarendon, 1949), 85–86.

57. Cf., e.g., Geza Vermes, *Jesus the Jew* (London: SCM, 2001), 50, 60; cf. 195.

58. At least from Mark's perspective, there is the assumption that the source of Jesus' power-authority is known by the demons; cf. Mark 1:24.

59. See also Mark 3:28–30. Cf. *AMB* 57 (amulet 4.31–32): "I adjure you, by his right hand and the might of his holiness"; fifth or possibly fourth century CE, from Aleppo.

60. Matt. 12:27 ‖ Luke 11:19. See the discussion in Graham H. Twelftree, *Jesus the Miracle Worker: A Historical and Theological Study* (Downers Grove, IL: InterVarsity, 1999), 266–68; and Twelftree, *Exorcist*, 106–10.

61. Not fully appreciated by David E. Aune, "Magic in Early Christianity," *ANRW* II.23.2 (1980): 1532.

62. Contra, e.g., Vincent Taylor, *The Gospel according to St. Mark* (London: Macmillan, 1952), 171; Meier, *Marginal Jew*, 2:548. Meier also overplays the difference between the exorcisms of Jesus and those reflected in the magical papyri (2:550, 571n65).

command (given on the assumption that it was backed by a power-authority) could dislodge an unwanted spiritual being from a person.[63]

Yet, over against the traditions preserved in the materials of ancient magic there are some distinctive features of Jesus as an exorcist:[64]

a. There is no evidence that Jesus collected, maintained, or (apart from the episode of the pigs) used artifacts or a library of incantations.

b. Also, apart from exorcism Jesus expressed no interest in the control of, and protection from, unwanted demons, as frequently found in ancient magic.[65]

c. Further, though Jesus may have addressed a storm as if it were demonic (Mark 4:39),[66] he did not appear to rebuke sickness, reserving exorcistic language and technique for the removal of demons.

d. Also, Jesus showed no interest in exorcising buildings or places.

e. Although the early church, particularly as reflected by Luke, was keen to accentuate the prayer life of Jesus,[67] at no point did any of the traditions seek to attach the practice of prayer to Jesus' exorcistic technique.

f. We have already noted that, even though Jesus acknowledged a specific power-authority, according to the reports, during an exorcism he did not mention his source of power-authority. Concomitantly, it does not seem that Jesus used the formula "I bind you." That is, as part of his technique he did not "charge," "adjure," or "bind" the demons by another power-authority. At least in this, Jesus would have appeared to function like Apollonius and some of the rabbis, apparently neither publicly acknowledging his source of power nor using the accompanying "I bind you" formula. Instead, Jesus used the emphatic "I," for which I can find no parallel in any other incantation or exorcism story in the ancient world. It seems reasonable to conclude, therefore, that, in light of his statement that he was operating by the power-authority of the Spirit or finger of God, Jesus was particularly confident in his ability to use or even be identified with that power source. Thus, along with no declaration of his source of power-authority, Jesus deliberately draws attention to himself and his own resources in his ability to expel the demon. Hence, in his approach to exorcism, Jesus is best described as what we have termed a charismatic magician.

g. Given the common occurrence of exorcisms like his, as well as Jews not habitually looking for miracles as eschatological signs, it is most astounding that Jesus should make the unique claim that his particular exorcisms

---

63. Mark 9:25 is about the same length as, or slightly longer than, the incantation used by the Jews as reported by Justin, *Dial.* 85.3. Cf. e.g., *PGM* IV. 1227–1264. Also see the comments on incantations from Qumran by Eshel, "Genres," 405.

64. More fully on this paragraph, see Twelftree, "Ancient Magic."

65. On the story of the returning spirit, see §§4.10 and 7.6 below.

66. See Paul J. Achtemeier, "Person and Deed: Jesus and the Storm-Tossed Sea," *Int* 16 (1962): 175–76.

67. See Peter T. O'Brien, "Prayer in Luke-Acts," *TynBul* 24 (1973): 111–27.

were not only the vanguard of his battle with Satan, but concomitantly the coming or operation of the kingdom of God itself.[68] Given also that under critical examination, the gap between exorcists of ancient magic and Jesus the exorcist narrows, the audacity of this claim for his activity stands out all the more starkly.[69] It is these conclusions, including that Jesus as an exorcist appears to have been a charismatic magician, that are important as we turn to examine Jesus' intentions for his followers in relation to exorcism.

2.6 Jesus and His Followers as Exorcists

One of the ongoing points of contention in the study of the historical Jesus is whether or not, before Easter, he sent out followers on mission. Of particular interest for our study is the attendant question as to whether or not Jesus directed or intended his followers to conduct exorcisms.[70] George Caird, for example, was able to say of the pre-Easter situation: "The mission charge is better attested than any other part of the gospel record."[71] F. W. Beare, on the other hand, concluded a study of the mission charge by saying, "If there were indeed such a mission, we have so little information about it that it is not worth while to argue for or against its historicity."[72]

It is reasonable to conclude that the four reports we have of the disciples being sent on mission probably arose from Mark 6:7–13 (followed by Luke 9:1–6) and Q (Luke 10:1–12), with Matthew 10:1–15 conflating them.[73] It is also reasonable to argue that this material might have had its origins during the period of Jesus' ministry rather than in the early church. First, elements of the material fit a Palestinian milieu: the wholly negative character of Luke 10:4 ("Carry no purse, no bag, no sandals"); not greeting anyone on the road (10:4); the personification of peace (10:6); and shaking the dust off their feet (10:11).

Secondly, the disciples are charged with proclaiming the kingdom of God rather than Jesus, as might be expected if this charge had originated in the church after Easter. More broadly, two other factors incline us toward concluding that the followers of Jesus were also involved in mission in the lifetime of Jesus. That is, if, as is most probable, Jesus created the Twelve—a symbolic

---

68. Matt. 12:28 ‖ Luke 11:20; cf. Luke 9:1–2 ‖ Matt. 10:6–8; Mark 3:21–30. See Twelftree, "Marginal or Mainstream?" 120.

69. So, and in more detail, Twelftree, "Ancient Magic."

70. For an earlier discussion of this issue, see Twelftree, *Exorcist*, 122–27.

71. George B. Caird, "Uncomfortable Words II: Shake off the Dust from Your Feet (Mk 6[11])," *ExpTim* 81 (1969–70): 41.

72. Francis W. Beare, "The Mission of the Disciples and the Mission Charge: Matthew 10 and Parallels," *JBL* 89 (1970): 13.

73. Cf. F. C. Hahn, *Mission in the New Testament* (London: SCM, 1965), 41–46; Joachim Jeremias, *New Testament Theology* (London: SCM, 1971), 231.

action inaugurating the eschatological regathering of the twelve tribes of the people of God—the very notion of mission inheres in their institution.[74] Also, if, as is most probable, Jesus understood and portrayed himself as on an itinerant mission from God (as the eschatological prophet to win Israel), it could be expected that his followers would also take up such a notion of mission. Or, with Meier, to put it another way: "If the very existence of the Twelve was meant to symbolize the beginning of the eschatological regathering of Israel, who else would be better suited for a mission to Israel that would initiate, however symbolically, such a regathering?"[75] To this can be added the intriguing and probably historically reliable promise of Jesus to Simon—the leader of the Twelve—and Andrew ("I will make you fish for people" [Mark 1:17]). From the evidence we have, this promise could only have been fulfilled in such a mission.[76] Yet further support for the historicity of missionary work by the disciples during Jesus' ministry comes in how unlikely it is that such a notion would have been transferred into the Gospels after Easter. For there is no evidence in the New Testament that the Twelve, as a group, were involved in any organized post-Easter mission in Galilee or further afield in Israel. Instead, the Twelve appear to remain in Jerusalem.[77]

Even if it is quite probable that Jesus sent out his followers on mission, it is quite another thing to recover details of any mission charge. In particular, were the disciples charged with performing exorcisms? Our difficulty in giving a positive answer to this question arises because only one source says that Jesus "gave them authority over the unclean spirits" (Mark 6:7; followed by Matt. 10:8 and Luke 9:1). We can probably conclude that Mark is responsible for this reference to exorcism: he is deeply interested in exorcism (see chap. 5 below); he has most probably already added the idea of exorcism to the purpose of Jesus choosing the Twelve (Mark 3:15[78]), and the vocabulary and style of 6:7 suggest that Mark has created it.[79] The other source of possible information about a mission charge only mentions healing the sick (Q, Luke 10:9). However, given that in the story of the return of the Seventy(-two) Luke goes on to assume that exorcism was part of their brief (Luke 10:17),

74. See the discussion by Meier, *Marginal Jew*, 3:148–54. Cf. Scot McKnight, "Jesus and the Twelve," *BBR* 11 (2001): 203–31; John P. Meier, "Jesus, the Twelve, and the Restoration of Israel," in *Restoration: Old Testament, Jewish, and Christian Perspectives* (ed. James M. Scott; JSJSup 72; Leiden: Brill, 2001), 365–404.

75. Meier, *Marginal Jew*, 3:158.

76. See the discussion in Meier, *Marginal Jew*, 3:159–62.

77. So C. Kingsley Barrett, *The Signs of an Apostle* (London: Epworth, 1970), 31–32; and Robert H. Gundry, *Mark* (Grand Rapids: Eerdmans, 1993), 307; followed by Meier, *Marginal Jew*, 3:158.

78. See Robert A. Guelich, *Mark 1–8:26* (WBC 34A; Dallas: Word Books, 1989), 159–60, and works cited.

79. See the details in Taylor, *Mark*, 303; and those listed by E. J. Pryke, *Redaction Style in the Marcan Gospel* (SNTSMS 33; Cambridge: Cambridge University Press, 1978), 14.

it is highly unlikely that he would have dropped a reference to it if it had been in his tradition of the charge. Thus we arrive at the conclusion that we have no direct evidence that Jesus charged his followers with performing exorcisms.

Notwithstanding, even though the disciples probably received no such direct charge, other evidence leads us to conclude that there is every probability that the disciples included exorcism in their pre-Easter mission. First, there is good reason to suppose that Jesus told his followers to announce the coming of the kingdom of God (Luke 10:9), which is the theme of his own preaching and yet not taken up by the post-Easter community. In turn, given that, for Jesus, the kingdom of God and exorcism were intrinsically related, we could expect that his followers would assume the same relationship, as did at least Q, Matthew, and Luke (Matt. 12:28 ‖ Luke 11:20). Further, there is evidence independent of the mission charge that the disciples were involved in exorcism. That is, the story of the unknown exorcist (Mark 9:38–39 ‖ Luke 9:49–50), which arguably has its origins in the ministry of the historical Jesus,[80] assumes that the followers of Jesus were also involved in exorcism: "Teacher, we saw someone casting out demons in your name, and we tried to stop him, because he was not following us" (Mark 9:38). In this it is not the performing of exorcisms that distinguishes this person from the followers of Jesus but his relationship to the group. Also, the report of the return of the Seventy(-two)—also likely to be generally historically reliable[81]—assumes that the followers of Jesus were involved in exorcism ("Even the demons submit to us!" [Luke 10:17]).

The result of this discussion of the pre-Easter mission of Jesus' followers is that he does not seem to have spelled out his expectations in terms of them being exorcists. Nevertheless, in that the disciples are told to announce the arrival of the kingdom of God (which Jesus saw uniquely expressed in exorcism), it is reasonable that his followers took that charge to imply performing exorcisms.

2.7 "In the name of . . ."

Given the distinct probability that Jesus' pre-Easter followers took up exorcism, we are able to take this discussion at least one important step further and establish their method. We have two independent witnesses to their method of casting out demons "in the name of" Jesus: Mark 9:38, which assumes that the disciples were using the same method as the unknown exorcist,

80. See Twelftree, *Exorcist*, 40–43.
81. See Twelftree, *Exorcist*, 125–26. Historically less certain are the elements in the story of the healing of the so-called epileptic boy, which includes the idea that the disciples were attempting an exorcism (see Mark 9:14–29 and the discussion in Twelftree, *Exorcism*, 93–97).

and the story of the return of the Seventy(-two) in Luke 10:17, which also reports this method (see §6.2 below). Although we have noted that there is a good case to be made for the reliability of these two reports, we still have to consider the view, put long ago by Rudolf Bultmann, that "the use of the ὄνομα [of] Jesus in the exorcism of demons could hardly have antedated its use in the Church."[82] Over against Bultmann, two related points form a strong case for the historicity of this method of exorcism by the pre-Easter followers of Jesus.[83]

First, although the ἐν ὀνόματι formula is reported to have been well used after Easter for healing and exorcism,[84] it is not particularly Christian.[85] Thus, its appearance in pre-Easter stories is unlikely to be a simple retrojection of later Christian practices. Secondly, since it was not a particularly Christian method, if the first followers of Jesus had used another method—most naturally the magico-charismatic method of Jesus—it would be reasonable to assume that subsequent followers of Jesus would (also) have been keen to take up that approach. Since they did not emulate his method—and Luke does not even portray Paul, a significant hero, as using this method (Acts 16:18;[86] cf. 3:6)—we can suppose that the early Christians (by relying on Jesus' name) saw themselves as much more dependent on a declared outside power-authority than did Jesus. In subsequent chapters we will discuss the methods the early Christians adopted after Easter.

2.8 Conclusions

The purpose of this chapter has been to set out the options likely to have been available for early Christians who conducted exorcisms. This will enable us to gain a better grasp of what we see of exorcism in the New Testament, to ascertain how significant Jesus was as a model for the first followers, and to determine how far and in what way their successors emulated him (see chap. 13 below).

From what we have seen so far, it could hardly be concluded that Jesus had a monopoly on exorcism. To the contrary, exorcism would appear to have been a very common approach to healing, especially among Jews, so that we are already predisposed to cast doubt on MacMullen's statement that "in

82. Rudolf Bultmann, *The History of the Synoptic Tradition* (Oxford: Blackwell, 1963), 25. More recently see Eduard Schweizer, *Good News according to Mark* (London: SPCK, 1971), 194–95.

83. Cf. C. E. B. Cranfield, *The Gospel according to Saint Mark* (Cambridge: Cambridge University Press, 1966), 310.

84. Cf. Mark 16:17; Luke in Acts 3:6, 16; 4:7, 10, 30; 16:18; 19:13; James 5:14.

85. See G. Adolf Deissmann, *Bible Studies* (1901; repr., Peabody, MA: Hendrickson, 1988), 196–98; and Twelftree, *Exorcist*, 41. See also §8.4 below on James 5:14.

86. See Twelftree, *Christ Triumphant*, 112–13.

Christianity it [exorcism] found an extraordinary flowering."[87] We have seen that there was a range of kinds of exorcists in antiquity, from the magicians (where what was said and done was critical) to the charismatic magicians (whose presence combined with what was said and done was thought to be effective), through to the charismatics who relied entirely on their personal force for success.

Although most of the evidence relating to magical exorcisms comes from the second and following centuries CE, we have seen that the method was probably well and widely established before the time of Jesus and his first followers. Also, our evidence from the case of the Abraham of the *Genesis Apocryphon* and the story of David in Josephus also suggests that, in the period the first Christians were conducting exorcisms, the methods of exorcism adopted by charismatic magicians had already developed and probably would have been known to the early followers of Jesus. However, even given an untidy development of exorcism along this suggested spectrum of possibilities, the charismatic type had probably not emerged in time to be a model for the early Christians, probably flourishing only well after the time of the origins and early development of the Jesus traditions.

Considering both our description of Jesus as an exorcist and the range of kinds of exorcisms and exorcists known to the early Christians, they are most likely to have considered his approach to be nearest what we have called the charismatic magician. That is, his approach relied on both the rationale shared with the exorcists of ancient magic[88] (a dependence on an outside power-authority) as well as the force of his personal presence.

In the time before Easter, apart from being charged with announcing the coming of the kingdom of God, it is fairly certain that Jesus' first followers received no specific directions for conducting exorcisms. However, given the nexus Jesus established between exorcism and the coming of the kingdom of God, it is not surprising that the pre-Easter mission on which Jesus sent his followers involved exorcism. The method resorted to by these exorcists was not, however, the magico-charismatic practice they were familiar with from Jesus. Instead, they adopted a somewhat more magical approach, which depended not so much on their personal force as on engaging an outside power-authority. However, the most significant difference between the method of the first followers of Jesus and the magical exorcisms known at the time is both the high level of confidence reported of the followers of Jesus as well as the extreme brevity of their method, both of which are not generally seen in the magical literature.

87. Ramsay MacMullen, *Christianizing the Roman Empire (A.D. 100–400)* (New Haven and London: Yale University Press, 1984), 28.

88. Contra Howard Clark Kee, "Magic and Messiah," in *Religion, Science, and Magic: In Concert and in Conflict* (ed. Jacob Neusner, Ernest S. Frerichs, and Paul Virgil McCracken Flesher; New York and Oxford: Oxford University Press, 1989), 121–41, esp. 139.

For the succeeding generation(s) of early Christians, direct incentive from the Jesus tradition to be involved in exorcism could only come from the single statement in Mark 6:7, which was tied to the pre-Easter situation. Secondarily, however, as reflected in their received traditions, they could look both to Jesus as well as to his initial followers as models for their activity. This, we will see, was the approach of the Synoptic writers. Indeed, we look in vain for evidence that Jesus asked or expected his followers to be exorcists after Easter. This can hardly be surprising. If Jesus anticipated his own vindication after death, which is likely,[89] and if the expectation was not for an individual resurrection[90] but a soon-to-follow general resurrection,[91] it means, to follow James Dunn, that "the possibility is quite strong that Jesus saw the climax to his mission as the climax to God's eschatological purpose . . . the kingdom would come."[92] There would, then, be no need, no point, to encouraging exorcism! However, the obvious continued interest in exorcism among a large number of early Christians can probably be taken to indicate that they thought they remained in a similar situation to that of Jesus—the kingdom or powerful presence of God continued to break in, as during the ministry of Jesus.

89. Such expectation is likely in view of the postmortem, especially postmartyrdom expectations of a pious Jew. See, e.g., Isa. 26:19; Dan. 12:1–3; 2 Esd. 7:26–44; 1 En. 22–27; 92–105; Jub. 23:11–31; 2 Bar. 21:23; 30:1–5; Josephus, J.W. 2.154, 165–166; Ant. 18.14, 16, 18; on which see C. F. Evans, Resurrection and the New Testament (SBT 2.12; London: SCM, 1970), 14–30.

90. See N. T. Wright, The Resurrection of the Son of God (Minneapolis: Fortress, 2003), 205–6.

91. See Dan. 12:1–3; Isa. 26:19; on the expected soon-to-follow resurrection, see Craig A. Evans, "Did Jesus Predict His Death and Resurrection?" in Resurrection (ed. Stanley E. Porter, Michael A. Hayes, and David Tombs; JSNTSup 186; Sheffield: Sheffield Academic, 1999), 96.

92. James D. G. Dunn, Jesus Remembered (Christianity in the Making 1; Grand Rapids: Eerdmans, 2003), 824.

Part 2

The First Century

3

Paul

Turning to the letters of Paul, our earliest Christian documents, the anomaly surrounding exorcism among early Christians is immediately obvious. We have just seen how fundamental and significant exorcism was for Jesus, both for his understanding of his ministry as well as for that of his followers. Yet, writing a mere generation later, Paul has neither a clear reference to Jesus being an exorcist, nor an unmistakable statement that he, a self-confessed follower of Jesus, performed exorcisms. Further, Paul does not appear to mention exorcism as part of his expectations for members of his churches. Also, Paul has little to say about demons or evil spirits, at least in the way that is familiar to us from the Synoptic Gospels. The problem of Paul's view and practice regarding exorcism is compounded when we note that the book of Acts portrays Paul as a successful exorcist.

In light of this apparent conflict between Paul and Jesus and, as we will see, the Synoptic Gospels as well as the portrait of Paul in Acts, our task in this chapter is to attempt to explain this disconnect. Is it that Paul knew nothing of Jesus as a miracle-worker or exorcist? Or, perhaps it can be shown that Paul knew about miracles and exorcism in Jesus' ministry but, for reasons we would need to suggest, chose to ignore it or set it aside from his own ministry and from what he expected in his churches. Alternatively, as I will attempt to show, it could be that Paul knew Jesus to have been an exorcist, that Paul himself was an exorcist, and that he expected those in his churches to per-

1. This chapter is to be seen as a significant correction of parts of Graham H. Twelftree, *Christ Triumphant: Exorcism Then and Now* (London: Hodder & Stoughton, 1985), 90–94.

form such healings. Thus, is the disconnect between Paul and Jesus (and the Gospels and Acts) superficial—more to do with our prima facie misreading of Paul—or is it due to the subject of his writing and its apostolic nature?

If, through a careful reading of Paul's letters, we can demonstrate that Paul was an exorcist, we will want to be able to show what part exorcism may have played in his ministry. We will also want to try to uncover what he expected of his churches in relation to exorcism. Hence, we begin with a discussion of Paul's vocabulary and ideas about the demonic with a view to seeing whether the disconnect between Paul and the Gospel writers is fundamentally different so that we could not expect him to take up exorcism in his ministry.

3.1 Paul and the Demonic

Perhaps contrary to our expectations from reading the Gospels and Acts, Paul has almost nothing to say about unclean or evil spirits or demons. In the undisputed Pauline letters demons are mentioned in only one place, 1 Corinthians 10:20: "But that which they (the pagans) sacrifice is to demons and not to God" (my translation; cf. 10:21; 1 Tim. 4:1). Paul is taking up the belief— reflected in the Septuagint and elsewhere in the New Testament at Revelation 9:20—that the gods of the Gentiles are demons and that non-Jewish sacrifices are authorized by demons.[2] But, unlike his contemporary Greeks, Paul did not even attribute his catalog of troubles in 2 Corinthians 11:24–27 to sinister beings of the unseen world. Only in 2 Corinthians 12:7 does he attribute evil, a thorn in the flesh, to a messenger (ἄγγελος) of Satan.

However, even with such a tenuous association of Satan and demons with human suffering of some kind, we should not be too quick to conclude that Paul was far removed from the Synoptic tradition in his understanding of the negative capabilities of the unseen world in relation to human health. To begin with, there are a number of passages in which Paul shows how real he believes the unseen evil powers of Satan to be: 1 Corinthians 5:5; 7:5; 2 Corinthians 2:10–11; 11:14–15; 1 Thessalonians 2:18 (cf. 2 Thess. 2:9). Notwithstanding, much of what we can glean of Paul's ideas about evil spiritual beings is contained in his notion of "principalities and powers."[3]

---

2. See Deut. 32:17; Pss. 96:5 (95:5 LXX); 106:37 (105:37 LXX); *1 En.* 19:1; *Jub.* 1:11.

3. Further, see George B. Caird, *Principalities and Powers: A Study in Pauline Theology* (Oxford: Clarendon, 1956); Heinrich Schlier, *Principalities and Powers in the New Testament* (QD 3; Freiburg and New York: Herder; Edinburgh: Nelson, 1961); Hendrikus Berkhof, *Christ and the Powers* (Scottdale, PA: Herald, 1962); Wesley Carr, *Angels and Principalities: The Background, Meaning, and Development of the Pauline Phrase "hai archai kai hai exousiai"* (SNTSMS 42; Cambridge: Cambridge University Press, 1981); Walter Wink, *Naming the Powers* (Philadelphia: Fortress, 1984); Bayo Obijole, "St. Paul's Concept of Principalities and Powers," *BiBh* 15 (1989): 25–39; Clinton E. Arnold, *Powers of Darkness: Principalities and Powers in Paul's Letters* (Downers Grove, IL: InterVarsity, 1992).

The most obvious meaning of Paul's "principalities and powers" language is that it is at one with the Jewish idea that, behind the pagan world order, there were the supernatural motivating powers.[4] However, this by no means exhausts the content of Paul's use of "principalities and powers," in relation to which Romans 8:38–39 is of particular interest.[5] In the context of listing potential barriers between God and people, the word "rulers" (ἀρχαί) being tied to "angels" (ἄγγελοι) in the phrase "nor angels nor rulers" (οὔτε ἄγγελοι οὔτε ἀρχαί) suggests both that the "rulers" are probably not intended to refer to civil authorities but to evil opposing spiritual beings, and that, reciprocally, the "angels" (ἄγγελοι) are also sinister and rebellious beings in league with Satan.[6] For, as we have just noted, in 2 Corinthians 12:7, Paul also expresses the view that an "angel" (ἄγγελος) of Satan is responsible for harming his body (cf. Col. 2:18). Thus, not unlike the Synoptic traditions associated with exorcism, Paul has a notion of evil spiritual beings afflicting the body and being a potential spiritual barrier.[7]

In 1 Corinthians 15:24–25 Paul says, "Then comes the end, when he [Christ] hands over the kingdom to God the Father, after he has destroyed every rule and every authority and power" (πᾶσαν ἀρχὴν καὶ πᾶσαν ἐξουσίαν καὶ δύναμιν). Here it is not clear exactly how Paul envisages these entities save that they are preternatural enemies to be defeated before the kingdom can be handed over to God. In the post-Pauline Colossians 2:15 the triumph over the rulers and authorities takes place in relation to the cross, as it does in the Fourth Gospel.[8] That is not Paul's view here in 1 Corinthians 15:24–25.[9] Instead, like Jesus and the Synoptic evangelists, Paul has linked the destruction of Satan's

4. Deut. 32:8; Isa. 24:21–22; Dan. 10:13, 20; 1 Cor. 2:6–8.

5. Cf. 1 Cor. 15:24–25. See also Gal. 4:3, 9 (τὰ στοιχεῖα τοῦ κόσμου), on which see Clinton E. Arnold, "Returning to the Domain of the Powers: *Stoicheia* as Evil Spirits in Galatians 4:3,9," *NovT* 38 (1996): 55–76. We can leave aside from consideration Eph. 3:10; 6:12; Col. 2:8–15 (see n. 8 below), whose Pauline authorship is in question. On Eph. 6:12 see Clinton E. Arnold, "The 'Exorcism' of Ephesians 6.12 in Recent Research: A Critique of Wesley Carr's View of the Role of Evil Powers in First-Century AD Belief," *JSNT* 30 (1987): 71–87. See also Eduard Schweizer, "Die 'Elemente der Welt' Gal 4, 3. 9; Kol 2, 8. 20," in *Verborum Veritas: Festschrift für Gustav Stählin zum 70. Geburtstag* (ed. Otto Böcher and Klaus Haacker; Wuppertal: Brockhaus, 1970), 245–59.

6. See the discussions by James D. G. Dunn, *Romans 1–8* (2 vols.; WBC 38A; Dallas: Word Books, 1988), 1:506–7; and Arnold, *Powers*, 119–20.

7. This is captured in the term "unclean" (ἀκάθαρτος) spirits, especially in Mark's Gospel. See Mark 1:23, 26, 27; 3:11, 30; 5:2, 8, 12, 13; 6:7; 7:25; 9:25; otherwise in the NT at Matt. 10:1; 12:43; Luke 4:36; 6:18; 8:29; 9:42; 11:24; Acts 5:16; 8:7; Rev. 16:13; 18:2.

8. See John 12:31; 13:2; 14:30; 16:11. In Col. 2:8–15, especially verses 14–15, the writer portrays a consequence of the cross event. The unseen rulers and powers, which would otherwise enslave people, are disarmed and publicly displayed as a victorious emperor would display his spoils in a victory march. See Peter T. O'Brien, *Colossians, Philemon* (WBC 44; Waco: Word Books, 1982), 128–29.

9. As I mistakenly thought in Twelftree, *Christ Triumphant*, 91–92.

emissaries with the coming of the kingdom of God (Mark 3:20–27 ‖ Matt. 12:22–30 ‖ Luke 11:14–23). However, for Paul, that destruction takes place at the end of time (cf. 1 Cor. 15:24). Not surprisingly, then, in the Romans 8:38–39 passage we have been discussing, the assumption is that whatever the cross event (and the intercession of Christ Jesus) meant in relation to evil spiritual beings, Paul assumes that they are still active and potentially harmful, though now they are not able to effect a final separation between God and his people.

The upshot of our brief discussion of Paul and the demonic is that, despite the brevity and, at least for us, the cryptic nature of his comments, it is more than reasonable to suppose that Paul's notions and those found in the Synoptic Gospels are not sufficiently dissimilar to be able to conclude that his lack of references to exorcism is due to his too-different cosmology. Put positively, Paul's demonology and the ongoing threat he sees from spiritual beings is such that we would not be surprised to find—perhaps would expect to find—reference to exorcism in his writings.

3.2 Paul and the Miracles of Jesus

If we have been able to show that Paul's language and interests do not preclude him from talking of demon possession and exorcism, we next need to inquire what, if anything, he knew about Jesus and his miracles, particularly the exorcisms. This is an important exercise for, as we will see, he portrays himself as a servant of Jesus and as reflecting his ministry. Therefore, if Paul knew that Jesus performed exorcisms, he is also likely to have carried out such healings, unless we can find reasons why Paul would want to ignore knowledge of Jesus being an exorcist.

This is not the place for a full discussion of either the relationship between Jesus and Paul or of what Paul knew about Jesus.[10] The only clear things Paul tells us about the earthly Jesus is that he was sent by God (Gal. 4:4); that he was a Jew born in the line of David (Rom. 1:3; 9:5); that he had brothers, including James (1 Cor. 9:5; Gal. 1:19); that he lived under the law (Gal. 4:4); and that on the night he was betrayed he shared a meal at which he spoke particular words to those present (1 Cor. 11:23–25). Also, in 2 Corinthians 8:9 Paul says that although Jesus was rich he became poor (cf. Phil.

---

10. See S. G. Wilson, "From Jesus to Paul: The Contours and Consequences of a Debate," in *From Jesus to Paul: Studies in Honour of Francis Wright Beare* (ed. Peter Richardson and John C. Hurd; Waterloo, ON: Wilfrid Laurier University Press, 1984), 1–21; Alexander J. M. Wedderburn, ed., *Paul and Jesus: Collected Essays* (JSNTSup 37; Sheffield: JSOT Press, 1989); David Wenham, *Paul: Follower of Jesus or Founder of Christianity?* (Grand Rapids and Cambridge, UK: Eerdmans, 1995).

2:6–8).[11] Notably, Paul is particularly interested in Jesus' death on a cross,[12] which he says Jesus faced voluntarily (Gal. 2:20) and, in turn, is grounds for inferring his humility (Phil. 2:7–8). Although Nicholaus Walter may not be strictly accurate, therefore, to say that "we can detect no hint that Paul knew of the narrative tradition about Jesus," his assessment appears not far wide of the mark.[13] For, apart from the scant information we have just noted, Paul mentions nothing about the Gospels' stories of Jesus' baptism, his temptation, the disputes with religious leaders, his transfiguration, or the incident in the temple, nor is there mention of Jesus' exorcisms in particular, or his miracles in general.

However, a brief examination of two oft-cited references in Paul in relation to what he knew about Jesus[14] slightly but significantly alters Walter's conclusion, at least in relation to the miracles.

a. In the most important passage for us, Romans 15:18–19, Paul gives a summary of his own ministry as "what Christ has accomplished through me . . . by word and deed, in the power of signs and wonders, in the power of the Spirit" (my translation). Here Paul portrays himself as the representative and revealer of Jesus Christ. To anticipate something of our more detailed discussion of this passage below (§3.3a), this assumes not only that Paul's ministry included miracles, but also that this ministry was a reflection of or, perhaps it is not inaccurate to say, was modeled on the ministry of Jesus. Therefore, from this verse it is more than reasonable to conclude that Paul knows at least of the tradition that Jesus conducted miracles, and we can infer that Paul considered himself to have conducted miracles with Jesus as his model.[15] Whether or not these miracles included exorcism, we cannot tell, though it is highly likely. In turn, whatever we conclude about Paul and exorcism, it has to be done on this basis.

b. Another statement of Paul's that may lend credence to the idea that he knew of Jesus as a miracle-worker and, hence, provided a model for his ministry is 1 Corinthians 4:20. Paul ends the first major section of 1 Corinthians with this verse, in which he contrasts the gospel of eloquent wisdom

11. For a discussion of the possible interpretations of Jesus being "rich" (πλούσιος) and then "poor" (πτωχεύω) in 2 Cor. 8:9, see Margaret E. Thrall, *The Second Epistle to the Corinthians* (vol. 2; ICC; Edinburgh: T&T Clark, 2000), 532–34.

12. See, e.g., 1 Cor. 1:23; 2:2; Gal. 3:1, 13; Phil. 2:8.

13. Nicholaus Walter, "Paul and the Early Christian Tradition," in Wedderburn, *Paul and Jesus*, 60.

14. See esp., e.g., Wenham, *Paul*, 3–8.

15. This is entirely consistent with the broader theme in Paul of his desire to imitate Jesus. See 1 Cor. 4:16–17; 11:1; cf. 1 Thess. 1:6; 2:14. See the discussions by Willis Peter de Boer, *The Imitation of Paul: An Exegetical Study* (Kampen: J. H. Kok, 1962), esp. chap. 5; Robert G. Hamerton-Kelly, "A Girardian Interpretation of Paul: Rivalry, Mimesis and Victimage in the Corinthian Correspondence," *Semeia* 33 (1985): 65–81, esp. 69–73; Elizabeth Anne Castelli, *Imitating Paul: A Discourse of Power* (Louisville: Westminster John Knox, 1991), chap. 4.

proclaimed by his opponents with his own gospel of the power of God centered on the cross (1 Cor. 1:10–4:21). In this final verse of the section, he says that "the kingdom of God is not [or consists not[16]] in talk [λόγος] but in power [δύναμις]" (my translation). A number of aspects of this verse are important to us.

First, Chrysostom took δύναμις to refer to miraculous power (*Hom. 1 Cor.* 14.2).[17] However, Wolfgang Schrage dismisses such interpretation on the grounds that δύναμις derives its meaning from being put over against λόγος so that power refers to the ability to carry an act through effectively.[18] Yet, in 1 Corinthians 2:4 Paul has already contrasted his message and preaching of "a demonstration of the Spirit and of power" with "plausible words of wisdom." With the reappearance together of λόγος and δύναμις, and their being contrasted in this summary verse, we can be fairly confident that Paul has some form of powerful work of the Spirit in mind in using δύναμις. In view of what we are about to see below on the use of δύναμις by Paul and others, it is reasonable to assume—and it is not out of place here to understand—that he is talking about miracles as an important aspect of his ministry.

Secondly, the antithetical descriptions of the kingdom of God (Rom. 14:17; 1 Cor. 4:20)[19] are unparalleled in the Gospels and, therefore, more likely to be his creation than to have their origin in the Jesus tradition.[20] However, in view of the close association in 1 Corinthians 4:20 between the kingdom of God and miracles, which is also found in the Synoptic Gospels, especially of exorcism (Matt. 12:28 ‖ Luke 11:20), we could probably conclude that Paul may be reflecting a knowledge of the miracles of Jesus.[21]

16. The sentence lacks a verb, though Greek sentences often assume the verb "to be" (ἐστιν). See Anthony C. Thiselton, *The First Epistle to the Corinthians* (NIGTC; Grand Rapids and Cambridge, UK: Eerdmans; Carlisle, UK: Paternoster, 2000), 377.

17. Also, Thomas C. Edwards, *A Commentary on the First Epistle to the Corinthians* (2nd ed.; London: Hodder & Stoughton, 1885), 118, cites Theophilus, *Autol.* (ca. 180 CE) as taking δύναμιν as "the power of doing miracles."

18. Wolfgang Schrage, *Der erste Brief an die Korinther* (vol. 1; EKK 7.1; Neukirchen-Vluyn: Neukirchener Verlag; Zürich and Düsseldorf: Benzinger, 1991), 362–63; followed by Thiselton, *First Corinthians*, 377, who cites Edwards, *First Corinthians*, 118; and Cyril H. Powell, *The Biblical Concept of Power* (London: Epworth, 1963), 117–29.

19. The term occurs in Paul only in Rom. 14:17; 1 Cor. 4:20; 6:9, 10; 15:24, 50; Gal. 5:21 (cf. 1 Thess. 2:12; also see Eph. 5:5; Col. 1:13; 4:11; 2 Thess. 1:5; cf. 2 Tim. 4:1, 18); yet its casual use, including here, implies that it was part of Paul's thinking. So Gordon D. Fee, *The First Epistle to the Corinthians* (NICNT; Grand Rapids: Eerdmans, 1987), 192; followed by Thiselton, *First Corinthians*, 377.

20. Cf. Günter Haufe, "Reich Gottes bei Paulus und in der Jesustradition," *NTS* 31 (1985): 467–72, esp. 469–70. See also Gary Steven Shogren, "'Is the Kingdom of God about Eating and Drinking or Isn't It?' (Romans 14:17)," *NovT* 42 (2000): 238, and the works he cites in n. 1. For the idea of inheriting the kingdom of God in 1 Cor. 6:9–10, Paul may be dependent on Exod. 19 and Deut. 1. See Brian S. Rosner, "The Origin and Meaning of 1 Corinthians 6,9–11 in Context," *BZ* 40 (1996): 251–52.

21. Cf. Wenham, *Paul*, e.g., 73.

Thirdly, "power" (δύναμις) was used in the Gospels for miracles[22] and was associated with healing,[23] notably exorcism.[24] Fourthly, the plural "powers" (δυνάμεις) was also used for miracles of Jesus in the Gospels,[25] and there was a close association between "powers" or miracles and the kingdom of God in the Synoptic Gospels,[26] especially the unique association Jesus drew with his exorcisms (see chap. 2, n. 68). Therefore, in 1 Corinthians 4:20 it is possible that Paul may be reflecting a knowledge of the miracles of Jesus, including his exorcisms, in a way that was perhaps embedded in earliest Christianity. However, the nature of our evidence here yields no more than possibilities.

There are other passages that can be considered in assessing Paul's knowledge of the tradition about Jesus the miracle-worker. In 1 Corinthians 13:2 Paul mentions "faith so as to move mountains." At first it seems reasonable to suppose that this is an echo of Jesus' saying about miracle-working faith (Mark 11:23),[27] which Paul is assuming to be part of the knowledge base of his readers. However, when we take into account that Paul may be picking up a proverbial saying about great teachers being able to uproot or remove mountains,[28] the connection between a saying attributed to Jesus and what Paul says here may be a common Jewish proverbial heritage rather than a shared view of Jesus' miracles. Likewise, we will need to leave aside 2 Thessalonians 2:9–10: "The coming of the lawless one is apparent in the working of Satan, who uses all power, signs, lying wonders, and every kind of wicked deception." These verses are potentially useful, for the point that the lawless one conducts deceptive "powerful signs and wonders" has most force if writer and reader are assuming that Satan's archrival, Jesus, had miraculous powers.[29] However, there is considerable doubt about whether or not Paul is responsible for this letter.[30]

---

22. Used for Jesus in Mark 6:5 and for the unknown exorcist in 9:39.

23. Mentioned for Jesus in Mark 5:30 ‖ Luke 8:46; Luke 5:17; 6:19.

24. For Jesus: Luke 4:36; 6:18–19; for the Twelve: 9:1; for the Seventy(-two): 10:19–20.

25. Matt. 7:22 (δυνάμεις are probably miracles distinct from casting out demons); 11:20–21 ‖ Luke 10:13; Matt. 11:23; Mark 6:2 ‖ Matt. 13:54; Matt. 13:58; Luke 19:37. Of miracles of John the Baptist see Mark 6:14 ‖ Matt. 14:2.

26. See Luke 9:2 ‖ Matt. 10:7–8. See also Acts 8:12–13.

27. Cf. Fee, *First Corinthians*, 632n32; Wenham, *Paul*, 81–83.

28. See John Lightfoot, *A Commentary on the New Testament from the Talmud and Hebraica: Matthew—I Corinthians* (vol. 2; 1859; repr., Grand Rapids: Baker, 1979), 282–83; and Hans Conzelmann, *1 Corinthians* (Hermeneia; Philadelphia: Fortress, 1975), 222 and n. 38.

29. Cf. Wenham, *Paul*, 351n39.

30. See the summary discussions by Edgar M. Krentz, "2 Thessalonians," *ABD* 6:518–22. For Pauline authorship see, e.g., Abraham J. Malherbe, *The Letters to the Thessalonians* (AB 32B; New York: Doubleday, 2000), 349–75; and against Pauline authorship, e.g., Raymond F. Collins, *Letters That Paul Did Not Write: The Epistles to the Hebrews and the Pauline Pseudepigrapha* (GNS 28; Wilmington, DE: Glazier, 1988), 209–41.

In examining even what little evidence we have that Paul knew the miracles of Jesus,[31] we have been able to modify significantly, even if slightly, Nicholaus Walter's judgment that we have no hint that Paul knew of narrative traditions about Jesus. From Romans 15:18–19 it is more than reasonable to conclude that Paul knew of the tradition, even if not the details, that Jesus conducted miracles, and that he saw himself as reflecting, perhaps modeling, Jesus' miracle-working ministry. Although there is no mention of exorcism, or any other particular miracles, it is probably reasonable to assume that they formed part of what Paul understood to be miracles in Jesus' ministry as well as his own. A discussion of 1 Corinthians 4:20 gave rise to the possibility that Paul was talking about miracles as an important part of his ministry. Further, through the particular language of this verse, Paul may be reflecting a knowledge of the miracles of Jesus, including his exorcisms, in a way that was perhaps an established part of Christianity. These important even if slender conclusions oblige us to pursue the point further.

3.3 Paul the Exorcist?

In light of the picture Luke gives in Acts of Paul being a powerful miracle-worker, including a successful exorcist (cf. §6.3c–d below), we need to look more widely across Paul's letters to see if there are hints that he conducted miracles, particularly exorcisms. The most sure-footed way forward in providing evidence of this is in taking account of his use of the phrase "(both) signs and wonders" (σημείων [τε] καὶ τεράτων)—which we have already noted in Romans 15:18–19[32]—and the words "power" and "powers" (δύναμις and δυνάμεις).

The term "signs and wonders" is first known to us in Polybius (*Historiae* 3.112.18) and refers to the superstitious rites of the Romans (cf. Plutarch, *Alexander* 75.1).[33] In the Septuagint the phrase is generally confined to

---

31. Wenham, *Paul*, 351–52, suggests that Phil. 1:8 ("I long for you with all the deep yearnings [σπλάγχνοις] of Christ" [my translation]) may be another hint that Paul knows the miracle tradition of Jesus since the word "yearning" or "compassion" is also used of Jesus' attitude, sometimes in relation to those seeking healing (cf. Matt. 9:36; 14:14 ‖ Mark 6:34; Matt. 15:32 ‖ Mark 8:2; Matt. 20:34). However, Paul's use of the term is sufficiently distinctive (he uses only the noun, σπλάγχνον—2 Cor. 6:12; 7:15; Phil. 1:8; 2:1; Philem. 7, 12, 20; cf. Col. 3:12—and none of the uses has any obvious connection with the miraculous) to make it highly unlikely that Paul's use is influenced by the miracle stories of Jesus. Further, on Paul's distinctive use of σπλάγχνον, see Helmut Koester, "σπλάγχνον . . . ," *TDNT* 7:555–56.

32. See also 2 Cor. 12:12. The phrase "signs and wonders" also occurs in 2 Thess. 2:9, on which see above.

33. Molly Whittaker, "'Signs and Wonders': The Pagan Background," *SE* 5 (TU 103; Berlin: Akadamie-Verlag, 1968): 155–58. Further, see Graham H. Twelftree, "Signs, Wonders, Miracles," *DPL* 875; and more generally Twelftree, "Signs and Wonders," in *New Dictionary of Biblical Theology*

the wonders associated with Moses' leading God's people to freedom, and Philo only takes up the phrase as a traditional description of miracles in Egypt (e.g., *Spec.* 2.218).[34] However, Josephus almost completely avoids the term for the exodus events, probably because he does not want them to be associated negatively with charlatans of Egypt (cf. *Ant.* 2.284; 4.43).[35] Indeed, in the New Testament the phrase is often used with a negative ring.[36] Yet so strong was the association between the phrase "signs and wonders" and the salvation-history events of the exodus that Paul is not only happy to employ the phrase but also to use it in describing a fundamental aspect of his ministry. Also, in light of the strong association between "signs and wonders" and the miracle stories of the exodus tradition, the conclusion cannot be avoided that Paul intended this phrase to refer to miracles in his ministry. In turn, and significantly, in using the phrase "signs and wonders" rather than the simple "powers" (δυνάμεις), Paul is able to convey the point that he considers the miracles he performs are not mere wonders but salvific events through which God brings freedom to his people. We have already seen the likelihood that Paul would have had exorcism in mind.

a. In using the term "signs and wonders" in Romans 15:18–19, Paul says: "For I will not venture to speak of anything except what Christ has accomplished through me to win obedience from the Gentiles, by word and deed, in the power of signs and wonders, in the power of the Spirit of God" (my translation). The relationship between the phrase "word and deed" and the remainder of this quotation is not immediately clear. Cranfield notes that it has been suggested that "word and deed" is related chiastically to what follows so that "word" is explicated by "the power of the Spirit of God" and "deed" by "the power of signs and wonders."[37] However, in that "deed" is never otherwise used by Paul to refer to a miraculous work, Cranfield is probably right to maintain that it is better to understand "deed" here generally as "action" so that "word and deed" describe Paul's ministry in general. Notwithstanding, in light of the two phrases that follow, it is likely that "deed" is intended at least to include the notion of the miraculous.

The two phrases that follow "word and deed" (λόγῳ καὶ ἔργῳ) are constructed in parallel:

(ed. T. D. Alexander and Brian S. Rosner; Leicester, UK, and Downers Grove, IL: InterVarsity, 2000), 775–81.

34. Further, see Karl H. Rengstorf, "σημεῖον . . . ," *TDNT* 7:221.

35. Rengstorf, "σημεῖον . . . ," *TDNT* 7:224.

36. See Mark 13:22 ‖ Matt. 24:24; 2 Thess. 2:9; cf. Rev. 13:13–14; 16:14; 19:20. See also Dunn, *Romans 1–8*, 2:863.

37. C. E. B. Cranfield, *Epistle to the Romans* (2 vols.; ICC; Edinburgh: T&T Clark, 1975–1979), 2:758–59, citing J. A. Bengel, R. Cornely, O. Michel, F.-J. Leenhardt, M. Black, and K. H. Rengstorf.

in the power of signs and wonders [ἐν δυνάμει σημείων καὶ τεράτων],
in the power of the Spirit [of God] [ἐν δυνάμει πνεύματος (θεοῦ)].[38]

This suggests not only that they are a hendiadys, each nuancing the meaning of the other, but also that together they inform the meaning of "word and deed." In this way Paul's ministry is being characterized as in some way—depending on how "in the power of" (ἐν δυνάμει) is understood—to involve miracles as well as the Spirit. Keeping in mind both uses of ἐν δυνάμει here, as well as its wider use in his letters,[39] where it is used in relation either to miracles (Rom. 15:19; 1 Cor. 2:5) or to the resurrection (1 Cor. 15:43) or, also in contrast to speech (1 Cor. 4:20), Paul is probably saying not so much that his ministry was attested by signs and wonders,[40] but that his ministry was conducted on the basis of, or strength of, the miracles (or Spirit). In other words, it is not so much that the miracles proved his ministry of words but that his ministry arose out of the miraculous or, to follow Paul here and put it another way, out of the power of the Spirit. The importance of this point is not to be lost: just as Jesus' ministry is arguably miracle based,[41] so also was Paul's.

b. Paul's other use of the phrase "signs and wonders" occurs in 2 Corinthians 12:12. He says, "The signs [τὰ μὲν σημεῖα] of an apostle [τοῦ ἀποστόλου] were performed [κατειργάσθη] among [ἐν] you with [ἐν] utmost patience, signs and wonders and powers [σημείοις τε καὶ τέρασιν καὶ δυνάμεσιν]" (my translation). Here Paul is defending his apostleship before the Corinthians for it seems that Paul's opponents may have denied that he was able to perform miracles (cf. 2 Cor. 10:1, 10; 11:15) and accused him of being ill (2 Cor. 12:7–10).

Although Paul's grammar does not tell us how this sentence is to be connected to what he has just said (in 2 Cor. 12:11) about not being inferior to the "super" or "elite apostles" (ὑπερλίαν ἀποστόλων), he is probably explaining why he is not inferior to them. He begins by saying, "At least"[42] or "On the one hand" (τὰ μέν) signs were performed among them. If Paul means a contrast it is not completed, though it is obvious from the context: the Corinthians paid no attention.[43] In using the article in "the apostle" (τοῦ

---

38. On the uncertain status of θεοῦ in the text, see Bruce M. Metzger, *A Textual Commentary on the Greek New Testament* (2nd ed.; New York: American Bible Society, 1994), 473.

39. The phrase ἐν δυνάμει occurs in Paul at Rom. 1:4; 15:13, 19 (bis); 1 Cor. 2:5; 4:20; 15:43; 2 Cor. 6:7; 1 Thess. 1:5; cf. Col. 1:29; 2 Thess. 1:11.

40. Cranfield, *Romans*, 2:759.

41. See Graham H. Twelftree, "The Miracles of Jesus: Marginal or Mainstream?" *JSHJ* 1 (2003): 104–24.

42. Taking the restrictive sense of μέν occurring alone. See Archibald T. Robertson, *A New Short Grammar of the Greek Testament* (1908; 10th ed., Grand Rapids: Baker, 1977), §472 (d).

43. See BDAG, "μέν," §2.a; also E. Bernard Allo, *Saint Paul: Seconde épître aux Corinthiens* (2nd ed.; ÉBib; Paris: J. Gabalda, 1956), 325; Thrall, *Second Corinthians*, 2:837n507.

ἀποστόλου, 12:12), the issue here is the general concept of apostleship.[44] As Paul is responding to criticism, he has probably taken up the phrase "signs of an apostle," perhaps directly from the Corinthians[45] or, indirectly through them, from his opponents.[46]

By "signs [σημεῖα] of an apostle" Paul probably means "indications" or "confirmations," and encompasses what he goes on to say.[47] Although the passive verb "performed" or "accomplished" (κατειργάσθη) indicates that Paul considers the signs to have been the work of God,[48] just what these signs were is not immediately clear. To begin with, the aorist tense of κατειργάσθη suggests that Paul is probably considering that they were performed at a specific time, perhaps at his initial visit to the Corinthians, when the church was founded.[49] These signs of an apostle could include Paul's "utmost patience" (ἐν πάσῃ ὑπομονῇ).[50] However, ὑπομονή ("patience" or "endurance") is unlikely to be his description of the way he performed the miracles[51] but of his ministry, or a general characteristic of it (as it is in 2 Cor. 6:4; cf. 1:6). This is particularly appropriate in 2 Corinthians in the context of portraying his apostleship as one of strength in weakness (12:5–10). Thus, in concert with the theme of the context here (12:5–10), Paul is conveying the idea that the miracles he is about to mention have arisen not out of a triumphalist ministry but out of one of weakness and patiently enduring suffering. In any case, the successive use of "in" (ἐν ὑμῖν ἐν πάσῃ ὑπομονῇ) ties the idea of patience to what has preceded,[52] and qualifying patience with "utmost" (πᾶς) separates it from what follows in that none of the three following nouns ("signs," "wonders," "powers") is qualified. Further, the words "signs" and "wonders" are habitually tied to each other in the New Testament and strongly tied to each other here by τε καί, a connection common in Paul,[53] which explains the repetition in 12:12 of the word "signs."

44. Thrall, *Second Corinthians*, 2:837; citing Heinrich A. W. Meyer, *Critical and Exegetical Handbook to the Epistles to the Corinthians* (ICC; Edinburgh: T&T Clark, 1879), 2:484.

45. So C. Kingsley Barrett, *A Commentary on the Second Epistle to the Corinthians* (BNTC; London: Black, 1973), 320–21.

46. Stefan Schreiber, *Paulus als Wundertäter: Redaktionsgeschichtliche Untersuchungen zur Apostelgeschichte und den authentischen Paulusbriefen* (BZNW 79; Berlin and New York: de Gruyter, 1996), 217–18; Thrall, *Second Corinthians*, 2:837–38.

47. On the range of meanings of σημεῖον, see BDAG.

48. Cf. Alfred Plummer, *A Critical and Exegetical Commentary on the Second Epistle of St Paul to the Corinthians* (ICC; Edinburgh: T&T Clark, 1915), 358.

49. Cf. Victor P. Furnish, *II Corinthians* (AB 32A; Garden City, NY: Doubleday, 1984), 553.

50. E. Käsemann, "Die Legitimität des Apostels: Eine Untersuchung zu II Korinther 10–13," *ZNW* 41 (1942): 33–71; and the discussion in Thrall, *Second Corinthians*, 2:838.

51. So Thrall, *Second Corinthians*, 2:839.

52. Thrall (*Second Corinthians*), 2:838n512 observes that in 2 Cor. 12:12 the "reading ἐν σημείοις (א² D² Ψ [2495] 𝔐 vgᶜˡ) looks secondary."

53. See Rom. 1:12, 14 (bis), 27; 3:9; 10:12; 1 Cor. 1:24, 30; 2 Cor. 12:12.

All this means that Paul is saying the signs of an apostle that were performed were "both signs and wonders and powers" (σημείοις τε καὶ τέρασιν καὶ δυνάμεσιν). In view of the use of the term "signs and wonders" in the Septuagint (see above) and the two words being found frequently together in early Christian literature,[54] it is probably reading too much into the phrases to try to find particular meaning in each word,[55] especially since Paul has them in the traditional order of "signs and wonders" rather than the less frequent "wonders and signs," known only in Acts in the New Testament.[56]

If, from what we have seen so far, "signs and wonders" is a phrase Paul uses for miracles, the puzzle is why here he adds "and powers" (καὶ δυνάμεσιν), a word in the plural that for Paul, as well as for others, also means miracles (cf. 1 Cor. 12:10, 28–29; Gal. 3:5).[57] Calvin's suggestion that δυνάμεις indicated that Paul considered the miracles to be examples of divine power[58] is reasonable in light of what we have seen of Paul's use of δύναμις in Romans 15:19. Further, the addition of "and powers" with its sense of divine origins would counterbalance any negative connotations that might be conveyed in the phrase "signs and wonders" (see above).

Although, as elsewhere, here in 2 Corinthians 12:12 Paul does not specify the nature of the miracles,[59] from our discussion so far it appears more than reasonable to assume that Paul probably had in mind miracles that included exorcism.[60] However, at this stage in our discussion, we cannot be certain (see below). What we can conclude with some confidence is that these miracles were (taking into account what we saw in Rom. 15:18–19) not only the grounds of his ministry but also authenticating marks of his apostleship.[61] It bears making clear that while Victor Furnish is right to say that Paul obviously "shares the widespread ancient belief . . . that certain manifestations of divine power will accompany the propagation of any valid religious truth,"[62] this is only part, and perhaps even the lesser part, of Paul's understanding of miracle in relation to his ministry. From what we saw in Romans 15:18–19 and what we are about to see in 1 Thessalonians 1:5, the miracles were a fundamental aspect of the ministry, no less important than the words. Thus, in 1 Corinthians 4:20 it is notable that Paul says, not that the kingdom of God is attended by power, but that it consists in both word and power (see above).

---

54. Schreiber, *Paulus als Wundertäter*, 219.

55. Ralph P. Martin, *2 Corinthians* (WBC 40; Waco: Word Books, 1986), 437.

56. Acts 2:22, 43; 6:8; 7:36.

57. See BDAG, "δύναμις," §3; cf. §1b.

58. John Calvin, *The Second Epistle of Paul the Apostle to the Corinthians and the Epistles to Timothy, Titus and Philemon* (Grand Rapids: Eerdmans, 1964), 164.

59. Also see Barrett, *Second Epistle to the Corinthians*, 321–22.

60. Cf. Jean Héring, *The Second Epistle of Saint Paul to the Corinthians* (London: Epworth, 1976), 95.

61. So Thrall, *Second Corinthians*, 2:839.

62. Furnish, *II Corinthians*, 555.

Through examining these two passages where the phrase "signs and won-ders" occurs, it is reasonable to maintain that Paul has miracles in mind rather than, as Ernst Käsemann suggests, his sufferings. We have also firmly established that Paul conducted miracles, though not, as Käsemann also maintains, of only secondary importance.[63] Rather, we have been able to settle that *miracles were a fundamental part of his ministry*. We turn now to two other passages where the miraculous is most probably in view, beginning with Paul's earliest letter.

c. In 1 Thessalonians 1:5 Paul says that "our message of the gospel came to you not in word only, but also in power and in the Holy Spirit and with full conviction [καὶ ἐν[64] πληροφορίᾳ[65] πολλῇ]." Taking the most difficult reading (that Paul did not include the ἐν), which destroys the neat parallelism between the three latter components of the verse (power, Holy Spirit, and full convic-tion), the final clause is separated out from the other two so that "in power" and "in Holy Spirit" remain in parallel with each other and together become the counterbalance to "word" in the description of the coming of the gospel.

This description of his work among the Thessalonians as including more than mere words is an echo of a pattern also known among the philosophers, who speak about the need for a philosopher's words and deeds to conform to each other.[66] However, the pattern Paul has in mind is not the balance of his words with his life or deeds in general. Instead, in recalling his presentation of the gospel, he balances his words or speech (λόγος), on one side, with "power" and "the Holy Spirit" on the other, in a way we also find in 1 Corinthians 2:4 (see below) and 4:20 (see above). D. E. H. Whiteley urged that this "power," which is set over against Paul's words, referred not to the power to work miracles but to "the power to work the 'miracle' of causing the heathen to believe."[67] Support for this view might be found in Paul saying that his mes-sage came "with full conviction" (καὶ [ἐν][68] πληροφορίᾳ πολλῇ); that is, full conviction was the result in Paul's hearers. However, at this point Paul is still recalling the nature and means of the coming of the gospel, rather than the impact of his message on the Thessalonians. Paul does not turn to describe the response of the Thessalonians until the next verse (1 Thess. 1:6), where he writes of them becoming "imitators" of him and receiving "the word with joy inspired by the Holy Spirit." Therefore, the "full conviction" that Paul is talking about in the coming of the gospel is not the "deep inward persuasion"

---

63. Käsemann, "Die Legitimität des Apostels," 33–71.

64. On the status of ἐν in the text, see NA[27] 531. See also below.

65. For the noun πληροφορία see also Col. 2:2; Heb. 6:11; 10:22; and later *1 Clem.* 42.3; for the verb πληροφορέω see Luke 1:1; Rom. 4:21; 14:5; Col. 4:12; 2 Tim. 4:5, 17.

66. See Seneca, *Ep.* 108.35–37; Dio Chrysostom, *De philosophia* (*Or. 70*) 6; Lucian, *Peregr.* 19; cited by Abraham J. Malherbe, *Paul and the Thessalonians: The Philosophic Tradition of Pastoral Care* (Philadelphia: Fortress, 1987), 58.

67. D. E. H. Whiteley, *Thessalonians* (Oxford: Oxford University Press, 1969), 36. So also Wil-liam Neil, *The Epistle of Paul to the Thessalonians* (London: Hodder & Stoughton, 1950), 17.

68. See n. 64 above.

in the hearts of the hearers, as F. F. Bruce concluded,[69] but as the Geneva New Testament of 1557 put it, the "muche certaintie of persuasion,"[70] or the confidence with which Paul presented the gospel.[71]

The phrase "but also in power" (καὶ ἐν δυνάμει) could be contrasting mere ineffective human words with the Spirit-infused speech that becomes the vehicle of God's powerful word.[72] However, Paul is not offering a description of the words with which he came but is contrasting his words (μόνον ἀλλὰ καί, "not only but also") with "power" and "the Holy Spirit." From what we have seen so far in our discussion of Paul, it is highly likely that he is describing miracles here. The phrase καὶ ἐν δυνάμει ("and in power") in parallel with the next phrase, καὶ ἐν πνεύματι ἁγίῳ ("and in the Holy Spirit"), may be part of a hendiadys: two phrases expressing a single idea, so that whatever "power" means, it is to be understood as having a divine origin. That is, he is not drawing attention to himself or to his own accomplishments but to God's work in the miracles.[73] Power understood as miracles fits this interpretation. We can only say more after we have examined other passages.

d. In 1 Corinthians 2:4–5 Paul says, "My speech [ὁ λόγος μου] and my proclamation [καὶ τὸ κήρυγμά μου] were not with plausible words of wisdom, but with a demonstration [ἀποδείξει] of the Spirit and of power [δυνάμεως], so that your faith might rest not on human wisdom but on the power of God." As we have just seen in 1 Thessalonians 1:5, here Paul is again contrasting his speech and proclamation—once again a pair that is probably a hendiadys—with Spirit and power in some way. Although grammatically there is nothing other than the conjunction καί ("and") to suggest Spirit and power are to be taken as a hendiadys, Paul's dealing with these two terms in 1 Thessalonians 1:5 (see above) predisposes us to take them as such.

Paul says that "Spirit" and "power" function as a "demonstration" (ἀπόδειξις, only here in the New Testament) of his message. In Greek rhetoric an ἀπόδειξις was a technical term for a compelling conclusion to be drawn from a reasoned argument (e.g., Plato, *Tim.* 40E; 4 Macc. 3:19). On a number of counts it is probable that Paul is referring not only to a possible transforming encounter with God as the demonstration of his message, but also to miracles involved in his presentation of the gospel as a demonstration or proof of authenticity of his gospel (cf. 2 Cor. 12:9–10; 1 Thess. 1:9). First, here in 1 Corinthians 2 Paul is contrasting his weakness, fear, and spoken word with the demonstration of the gospel. Secondly, as we have seen in Romans 15:19, the power of the

---

69. F. F. Bruce, *1 & 2 Thessalonians* (Waco: Word Books, 1982), 14.

70. Cited by George Milligan, *St. Paul's Epistles to the Thessalonians* (London: Macmillan, 1908), 9.

71. Cf. also I. Howard Marshall, *1 and 2 Thessalonians* (Grand Rapids: Eerdmans; London: Marshall, Morgan & Scott, 1983), 54.

72. Noted in Marshall, *1 and 2 Thessalonians*, 53.

73. Cf. Malherbe, *Paul and the Thessalonians*, 58.

Spirit is parallel with the power of signs and wonders. Thirdly, when the Galatians received Paul's message (as we will see below), they experienced "miracles" (δυνάμεις, Gal. 3:5). Fourthly, in 1 Thessalonians 1:5, perhaps defending himself against a charge of not demonstrating the efficacy of his message, Paul says that his message came not only in word but also in power and in the Holy Spirit and in full conviction or assurance (see above).

Our examination of these four passages (Rom. 15:18–19; 2 Cor. 12:12; and also more briefly, 1 Thess. 1:5 and 1 Cor. 2:4–5) confirms our earlier conclusion that Paul knows Jesus conducted miracles and, in modeling Jesus (cf. Rom. 15:18–19), conducted miracles himself, most likely including exorcism. These passages also show us that Paul considered his miracles to be salvific events not so much authenticating his ministry—though they did that—but primarily giving rise to a ministry that could be described as of "word and deed."

3.4 Paul and Acts

There is an obvious difficulty in attempting to use Acts to help us understand Paul: we are dealing with a secondary source written by someone who was not a companion of Paul for more than a brief period, if at all. The differences between the portrait of Paul in Acts and the one that we get from his own pen are well known, perhaps sometimes exaggerated,[74] at other times played down.[75] One of the differences in portrayal involves the very area of our study. As well as general references to performing healings (Acts 14:3; 15:12; 28:9), in Acts there are stories of Paul blinding Elymas the sorcerer (13:9–12), healing the cripple at Lystra (14:8–10), his clothing being powerful in healing (19:11–12), his driving out a demon (16:16–18), raising the dead (20:9–12), and curing the father of Publius of fever and dysentery (28:7–9). As we have seen, Paul's testimony is that his ministry is not merely accompanied by miracles, but that it is also one of word and deed; yet we certainly do not get the picture of a man performing miracles with the frequency and in the way Luke suggests. Therefore, our use of Acts to understand the place of miracles, including exorcism, in Paul's ministry needs to be most circumspect.

Of particular interest to us is a story in Acts, which portrays Paul as an exorcist (Acts 16:16–18). In telling the story of the arrival of the gospel in Europe, Luke selects three quite different stories of the power of the gospel in Macedonia: the conversion of Lydia (16:13–15), the exorcism of a spirit from a slave girl (16:16–18), and the conversion of a jailer (16:19–40). In the second story Paul and his companions are followed by a slave girl who had a

---

74. E.g., Philipp Vielhauer, "On the 'Paulinism' of Acts," in *Studies in Luke-Acts* (ed. L. E. Keck and J. L. Martyn; London: SPCK, 1968), 33–50.

75. E.g., I. Howard Marshall, *The Acts of the Apostles* (Leicester, UK: Inter-Varsity, 1980), 42–44.

spirit of divination (πνεῦμα πύθωνα, 16:16). Exasperated at the girl's crying out over many days, Paul exorcised the spirit (16:18).

Ernst Haenchen lists a number of points that tell against the story's historical veracity.[76] First, the story is not logically tied to the context in which it now stands. However, of itself this does not impinge upon the historicity of an account. Secondly, Haenchen says that nobody can be indicted for driving out an evil spirit. However, Paul and Silas are not indicted specifically for the exorcism but for causing a public disturbance and for advocating un-Roman practices (Acts 16:20–21). These charges were couched in an anti-Jewish sentiment (cf. 18:2, 12–17). Haenchen also says that people would be careful not to arrest a powerful exorcist for fear of being harmed. Against this is the classic precedent of Jesus, the powerful exorcist, being arrested, tried, and crucified.[77]

As well as Haenchen's case against the historicity of this story not standing up against examination, there are a number of factors which tell in favor of the basic historicity of the story. First, the report forms part of the "we-passages."[78] The discussion of the "we-passages" has given rise to a range of theories. The passages could be a creation of the author; they could be the diary or notes of the author, or of another person taken up by the author; or as Colin Hemer has convincingly shown, they may reflect the author being an eyewitness to the particular stories.[79] If this is right, it is to be expected that the style would be Lukan. Secondly, the way in which Paul is portrayed makes it likely that this report does reflect an actual incident in Paul's life. That is, as Paul is a key figure and hero of Acts, it is unlikely that, in the course of trying to enhance Paul's reputation, Luke would create a story in which Paul's healing ministry was motivated by annoyance (διαπονέομαι, Acts 16:18).

Also, even though a wealth of evidence in the way this story is written indicates that Luke tells it in his own words, rather than simply copying it from any tradition,[80] he has included some details that are better understood as being authentic rather than from Luke's creative hand. In the cry of the girl, Paul and his associates are called servants of the Most High God—not a designation in which the early church showed much interest.[81] These men

76. Ernst Haenchen, "The Book of Acts as Source Material for the History of Early Christianity," in Keck and Martyn, *Studies in Luke-Acts*, 273.

77. Twelftree, "Marginal or Mainstream?" 113–14.

78. Acts 16:10–17; 20:5–15; 21:1–18; 27:1–28:16. The reference in Acts 11:28 is to be excluded as secondary. See Metzger, *Commentary*, 344.

79. Colin J. Hemer, *The Book of Acts in the Setting of Hellenistic History* (WUNT 49; Tübingen: Mohr Siebeck, 1989), 213–34. See also F. F. Bruce, *The Book of the Acts* (NICNT; Grand Rapids: Eerdmans, 1954), 328 and n. 22; and Martin Hengel, *Acts and the History of Earliest Christianity* (London: SCM, 1979), 66.

80. Twelftree, *Christ Triumphant*, 93n12.

81. Graham H. Twelftree, *Jesus the Exorcist: A Contribution to the Study of the Historical Jesus* (WUNT 2.54; Tübingen: Mohr Siebeck; Peabody, MA: Hendrickson, 1993), 82. Cf. Paul R. Trebilco, "Paul and Silas—'Servants of the Most High God' (Acts 16.16–18)," *JSNT* 36 (1989): 51–73.

are said to "proclaim to you a way of salvation." Only here does Luke use the phrase "*a* way of salvation." In every other case where Luke describes the Christian life as a "way," he calls it "*the* way of the Lord" (Acts 18:25) or "*the* way [of God]" (18:26)[82] or simply "*the* Way."[83] The exception is Acts 2:28, an exact quotation of Psalm 16 (15 LXX):11, which does not have the article with the plural "ways." In other words, here in Acts 16:17, the absence of an article before "salvation" suggests that Luke is not attempting to make the words of the girl in this report conform to his own theological interests. From this discussion of Acts 16:16–18, we can conclude that behind this report there is most probably an exorcism by Paul, which Luke saw and reported in his own words.

There is one more possible hint in Acts that Paul may have been an exorcist. In Acts 19:13 some Jews attempt an exorcism with the incantation "I exorcise you by the Jesus whom Paul preaches" (my translation). It is well known that in the use of an individual's name as a power-authority for an exorcism there is evidence that the individual had a reputation as an exorcist.[84] Although the power-authority here is Jesus, it is possible that a reputation in exorcism using the name of Jesus (Acts 16:18) is witnessed to here. On its own this would not be sufficient to show that Paul was an exorcist. At best it is corroborating evidence for what we have found in the story of the healing of the slave girl.

3.5 Exorcism in Paul's Churches

Having established that Paul probably conducted exorcisms, we must go on to ask whether he expected his readers to perform exorcisms. There are two places in his letters where the reader might detect his views: Galatians 3:5 and, less obviously, in 1 Corinthians 12.

In Galatians 3:5 Paul summarizes his argument of 3:1–4 about the basis of receiving the Spirit by repeating a question to his readers (cf. 3:2): "So then, is he supplying you [ὁ οὖν ἐπιχορηγῶν ὑμῖν] with the Spirit and working powers [ἐνεργῶν δυνάμεις] in you through works of the law or through the hearing of faith?" (my translation). The phrase "working powers" (ἐνεργῶν δυνάμεις) is probably equivalent to "powers" (δυνάμεις), for a similar phrase, "workings of powers" (ἐνεργήματα δυνάμεων) in 1 Corinthians 12:10 is paralleled a few verses later by "powers" (δυνάμεις, 12:28–29). From what we have seen both of Paul's use of δυνάμεις in other places, as well as its acknowledged use for miracles (see above), we are disposed toward translating it in Galatians

---

82. On the uncertain status of τοῦ θεοῦ in the text see Bruce M. Metzger, *A Textual Commentary on the Greek New Testament* (2nd ed.; New York: American Bible Society, 1994), 414.

83. Acts 9:2; 19:9, 23; 22:4; 24:14, 22.

84. See Twelftree, *Exorcist*, 139–40.

3:5 as "miracles."[85] There is nothing in the text to stand in the way of this conclusion. From the nonparallel construction of the statement "supplying you [ἐπιχορηγῶν ὑμῖν] with the Spirit and working powers in you [ἐνεργῶν δυνάμεις ἐν ὑμῖν]," we cannot draw the conclusion that the supplying of the Spirit is equivalent to the working of the miracles. Rather, the statement is best read as if the working of miracles is a distinct expression or manifestation of the ongoing supply of the Spirit.

In saying that these miracles are being worked "in [ἐν] you," Paul could mean that miracles are taking place or being seen among the Galatians.[86] More likely, he is referring to the capacity to perform miracles since 1 Corinthians 12:6 (and 10; cf. Matt. 14:2) probably reflects this understanding. There Paul is writing about the charismata: "God who activates all of them in [ἐν] everyone" (1 Cor. 12:6).[87] So, it is not that the Galatians are able to witness powers but that they are able to perform miracles to which Paul is drawing attention (cf. 1 Cor. 12:10). The present participles "supplying" (ἐπιχορηγῶν) and "working" (ἐνεργῶν) show that Paul understands the experience of the miracles to be present and ongoing among the Christians. However, in that he is recapitulating a discussion of the nature of the beginning of their Christian experience, this description would apply also to the initial experience of the Galatians, when the gospel came to them (cf. Gal. 3:2–3). From this we can see that Paul expects the performing of miracles to be a continuing ability among those in his churches.

What these miracles are is not agreed. Walter Schmithals thinks Paul is referring to ecstatic productions of the Spirit[88] and Franz Mussner that they are charismatic gifts.[89] But these suggestions are unlikely to be correct for, in 1 Corinthians ἐνεργήματα δυνάμεων (workings of powers) appears as one of a number of the ecstatic phenomena or charismatic gifts (1 Cor. 12:8–10, 28–29). Further, in both 1 Corinthians 12:9–10 and 28 "gifts of healing" (χαρίσματα ἰαμάτων) are distinguished from "workings of powers" (ἐνεργήματα δυνάμεων, 12:9–10) as well as "powers" (δυνάμεις, 12:28). Yet since they are listed next to each other, it is probably reasonable to assume that they are similar "gifts." The patristic writers Ambrose and Cyril of Alexandria suggest that Paul has in mind the casting out of demons.[90] A number

---

85. So also, e.g., J. B. Lightfoot, *Saint Paul's Epistle to the Galatians* (London: Macmillan, 1881), 136; Hans Dieter Betz, *Galatians* (Philadelphia: Fortress, 1979), 135n78, citing Mark 6:14; Matt. 14:2; also 1 Cor. 12:10, 28–29; 2 Cor. 12:12; 2 Thess. 2:9; Acts 2:22; Richard N. Longenecker, *Galatians* (WBC 41; Dallas: Word Books, 1990), 105; James D. G. Dunn, *The Epistle to the Galatians* (London: Black; Peabody, MA: Hendrickson, 1993), 158.

86. Cf. Frank J. Matera, *Galatians* (Collegeville, MN: Glazier / Liturgical Press, 1992), 113.

87. Cf. Lightfoot, *Galatians*, 136.

88. Walter Schmithals, *Paul and the Gnostics* (Nashville and New York: Abingdon, 1972), 47.

89. Franz Mussner, *Der Galaterbrief* (3rd ed.; HTKNT 9; Freiburg: Herder, 1977), 208.

90. See Thiselton, *First Corinthians*, 953, citing Ambrose, *Opera: In Ep. 1 ad Cor.*, 151D (PL 17:211, 259); Cyril of Alexandria, *Fragmenta: In Ep. 1 ad Cor.*, in *Sancti patris nostri*

of more recent writers have offered the same interpretation.[91] However, as with Helmut Thielicke's interpretation, which takes the gift to be "authority over the powers,"[92] there is no evidence upon which to base this conclusion. All that is reasonable to say is, with Gordon Fee, that it "most likely covers all the other kinds of supernatural activities beyond the healing of the sick,"[93] which, on the strength of our discussion so far, could have been thought to include exorcism.

However, there is good reason to suppose that Paul was *not* thinking of exorcism in enumerating the charismata, for their function, at least for Paul, probably precluded exorcism. In both major lists Paul has the Christian community (the body) in mind rather than those outside it. As a prelude to one list, Paul says in Romans 12:5, "Though many, we are one body in Christ, and each parts of *one another*" (my translation, emphasis added). In a similar fashion Paul says as an introduction to the charismata in 1 Corinthians 12:7: "To each is given the manifestation of the Spirit *for the common good*" (emphasis added). This makes plain that the charismata are given (and are to be used) for the benefit or, more properly, edification or upbuilding of the church.[94] In neither place is there any thought of those outside in relation to the charismata. This perspective is clarified when we take into account that, for Paul, people are seen in relation to either Christ or Satan, to the Holy Spirit or the spirit of evil (1 Cor. 5:5; 2 Cor. 6:15; Gal. 5:16–26). In turn, for Paul, the Christian has passed from Satan to Christ, from darkness to light.[95] Seen in this way, it would be inconceivable for Paul to require those in his churches to use exorcism within its own community; "What accord has Christ with Satan?" (2 Cor. 6:15, my translation). From Paul's perspective, exorcism would be needed only as the church confronted those outside the Christian community, those understood still to be in a particularly severe grip of Satan.[96]

Cyrilli archiepiscopi Alexandrini (ed. P. E. Pusey; 7 vols.; Brussels: Culture et civilization, 1965), 3:288.

91. E.g., Christian Wolff, *Der erste Brief des Paulus an die Korinther* (Leipzig: Evangelische Verlagsanstalt, 1969), 291; James D. G. Dunn, *Jesus and the Spirit* (London: SCM, 1975), 210.

92. Helmut Thielicke, *The Evangelical Faith* (3 vols.; Grand Rapids: Eerdmans, 1974–1982), 3:79.

93. Fee, *First Corinthians*, 594; similarly Walter Rebell, *Alles ist möglich dem, der glaubt: Glaubensvollmacht im frühen Christentum* (Munich: Kaiser, 1979), 115, who without evidence includes nature miracles, as does Dunn, *Jesus and the Spirit*, 210.

94. 1 Cor. 12:7; 14:1–5, 12, 17, 26.

95. See 2 Cor. 6:14–15; cf. Rom. 13:12; 2 Cor. 4:6. See also Col. 1:13. While Paul considers the Christian's status and security to be this clear, he does recognize the difficulties of this certainty being worked out in everyday experience. Note Rom. 7:14–25, on which see James D. G. Dunn, "Rom 7, 14–24 in the Theology of Paul," *TZ* 31 (1975): 257–73.

96. On a first reading, what Paul says in 2 Cor. 7:1 could be thought to refer to exorcism: "Let us cleanse ourselves from every defilement of flesh and spirit." The debate over the authorship of this passage and the problem of the relationship of the passage to the surrounding material need not detain us; see, e.g., Stephen J. Hultgren, "2 Cor 6.14–7.1 and Rev. 21.3–8: Evidence

Corroborating evidence that this is Paul's perspective on the charismata is seen in his omission of evangelism from the lists. Like exorcism, evangelism is not an expression of God's grace that is needed within the body of Christ. Exorcism is a function of the church in relation to the outside world, and in that connection Paul mentions evangelism (e.g., Rom. 10:15; 2 Cor. 8:18).[97]

Insofar as Paul expected members of his churches to emulate him, we can assume that he expected them to perform exorcisms. However, in light of the function of charismata being for the common good of the members of the body, we should not be surprised that he does not mention exorcism among them. Without any evidence to the contrary, we are obliged to conclude that, in Paul's mind, exorcism was not one of the charismata. In Matthew we will see that there is probably a different perspective (see §7.8 below).

3.6 Conclusions

In this chapter we have begun to solve the puzzle that, although the Synoptic Gospels give us strong evidence that Jesus and his first followers were successful exorcists, Paul (writing a little more than two decades after Easter) appears to say nothing about the subject. It is not that Paul's cosmology is significantly different from the Synoptic evangelists as to preclude his taking up the subject. His "principalities and powers" language, though enigmatic, shows not only that he has widened the demonic beyond the scope of certain types of illness to include even the evil of human designs. It also shows that he supposes there to be such an ongoing threat from spiritual beings that we would expect to find—perhaps would be surprised not to find—reference to exorcism in his writings. Indeed, from our discussion of Romans 15:18–19, it is more than reasonable to conclude that Paul knew Jesus conducted miracles and that, modeling that ministry, he himself also had a miracle-working ministry. Then, the language of 1 Corinthians 4:20 gives us the possibility of going on to conclude that Paul not only saw miracles as an important part of his ministry, but that exorcism also was perhaps an established part of Christianity, including his own ministry. Although these important conclusions have a slender

---

for the Ephesian Redaction of 2 Corinthians," NTS 49 (2003): 39–56, esp. 40–44; and the outline discussion by Furnish, II Corinthians, 378–83. The emphatic position of ταύτας ("these" promises) at the beginning of the verse shows that the cleansing of defilement has to do with the immediate context (2 Cor. 6:14–7:1). It is not any defilement arising from invading spiritual beings that concerns the author, but defilement arising from Christians associating with unbelievers (ἄπιστοι, 6:14). If Paul is the author, he probably has in mind a wide range of associations including marriage with an unbeliever (cf. 1 Cor. 7:12–15) as well as, perhaps, knowingly eating meat offered to idols (10:27–28) and, possibly, the use of non-Christian courts (6:1–8). See also the comments by Thrall, Second Corinthians, 2:473.

97. The later Pauline literature has a different perspective, mentioning evangelists. See Eph. 4:11; 2 Tim. 4:5. See also Acts 21:8; cf. 8:4–5, 12, 35, 40.

base, they can most probably be corroborated by a story in Acts 16:16–18, which portrays Paul as an exorcist and shows that he used the name of Jesus Christ as his power-authority to drive out the demon.

In using the language of "signs and wonders," which we argued is likely to have included exorcism, we see something of Paul's understanding of the function of exorcism: salvific events through which God brings freedom to people. In this we see a similar perspective to Jesus. Another side of this perspective is seen in Paul's discussion of sinister powers having the potential to separate people from God (Rom. 8:38–39). From Galatians 3:5 we have been able to see that Paul expected those in his church to continue performing miracles. Given the nature of his ministry, these are most likely to have included exorcism, though there is no thought of exorcism in Paul's discussion of the charismata for use within the church.

If performing miracles, including exorcisms, is to be seen as important in Paul's ministry, the explanation of his lack of overt interest in the subject in his letters is probably to be found in the epistolic and occasional nature of his writing and, for the purposes of his discussion, what he saw as the internal focus or use of the charismata. That is, in dealing with internal matters in his letters—not often touching on the church in relation to the outside world—it is not surprising that his references to exorcism should be cryptic to us, though perhaps clear to those who had experienced his ministry and were involved in a word-and-deed ministry in the world.

4

Q

O UR TASK IN this chapter is to discover what Q can tell us about exorcism among early Christians. In the two-source theory for solving the Synoptic Problem, along with Mark, Q is taken to be the other major source Matthew and Luke used in producing their Gospels.[1] More specifically, Q is agreed to be the material common to Matthew and Luke that is not found in Mark, though it probably also included other material; for example, the Beelzebul controversy,[2] and perhaps late in its redaction, the temptation stories.[3] Although most scholars are inclined to accept Q, debate about, for

---

1. For initial access into the immense literature on Q, see Frans Neirynck, "Recent Developments in the Study of Q," in *Logia: Les paroles de Jésus—The Sayings of Jesus* (ed. Joël Delobel; Louvain: Leuven University Press, 1982), 29–75; Ronald A. Piper, ed., *The Gospel Behind the Gospels: Current Studies on Q* (Leiden: Brill, 1995); Christopher M. Tuckett, *Q and the History of Early Christianity: Studies on Q* (Edinburgh: T&T Clark, 1996); and John S. Kloppenborg Verbin, *Excavating Q: The History and Setting of the Sayings Gospel* (Edinburgh: T&T Clark, 2000). For a recent critique and literature on the Q hypothesis, see Mark Goodacre, *The Case Against Q* (Harrisburg, PA: TPI, 2002).

2. On the status in Q of the various verses of the Beelzebul controversy, see the discussion by John S. Kloppenborg, *Q Parallels: Synopsis, Critical Notes, and Concordance* (Sonoma, CA: Polebridge, 1988), 92.

3. Against, e.g., A. W. Argyle, "The Accounts of the Temptation of Jesus in Relation to the Q-Hypothesis," *ExpTim* 64 (1952–1953): 382; and Dieter Lührmann, *Die Redaktion der Logienquelle* (Neukirchen-Vluyn: Neukirchener Verlag, 1969), 56, that the temptation narrative was part of Q, see John S. Kloppenborg, *The Formation of Q: Trajectories in Ancient Wisdom Collections* (Philadelphia: Fortress, 1987), 322–24. That the Temptation story is to be attributed to a late redaction of Q, see John S. Kloppenborg, "The Sayings Gospel Q: Literary and Stratigraphic

example, the extent, language, and unity of this written or oral source continues unabated.[4]

In light of the debates relating to Q, there could be doubtful wisdom in us proceeding without due caution, if at all, especially in attempting to recover an aspect of the theology of a document of unknown extent. In a lively exchange on Q in *Expository Times*, Cyril Rodd has said that, as "doubt must be expressed as to the possibility of recovering such a document," to claim "that the theology of the document can be systematically presented is to enter the realms of fantasy."[5] However, Christopher Tuckett was right to respond that we can discuss the theology of what material *is* there. In any case, he noted that, "a similar lack of certain 'knowledge' applies in the case of almost all historical and textual work."[6] Further, if, in being keen to take up the details of his sources, Matthew used about 90 percent of Mark, it is not unreasonable to assume that he took up a similar amount from Q so that our reconstruction of it is not much less extensive than it might originally have been.[7] Therefore, deferring to the majority, in this chapter I will assume it is not foolhardy to set out at least a provisional theology of Q as it relates to exorcism among early Christians. In doing so I will also assume that the Q used by Matthew and Luke was a single document written in Greek and that it was primarily a collection of sayings with some narrative material, especially early in the document and that, like the *Gospel of Thomas*, it ended without a passion narrative. Notwithstanding, it is also quite probable that Q had a complex history. For example, some distinguish two stages in the formation of Q,[8] others three,[9] and some four.[10] However, in order to keep speculation to

Problems," in *Symbols and Strata: Essays on the Sayings Gospel Q* (ed. Risto Uro; Helsinki: Finnish Exegetical Society; Göttingen: Vandenhoeck & Ruprecht, 1996), 10–11. See also the discussion by Christopher M. Tuckett, "The Temptation Narrative in Q," in *The Four Gospels, 1992: Festschrift Frans Neirynck* (ed. F. van Segbroeck et al.; 3 vols.; Louvain: Leuven University Press, 1992), 1:479–83.

4. See, e.g., John S. Kloppenborg, "The Sayings Gospel Q: Recent Opinion on the People behind the Document," *CurBS* 1 (1993): 9–34; Goodacre, *Case*; Peter M. Head and P. J. Williams, "Q Review," *TynBul* 54 (2003): 119–44; John S. Kloppenborg, "On Dispensing with Q? Goodacre on the Relation of Luke to Matthew," *NTS* 49 (2003): 210–36.

5. C. S. Rodd, "The End of the Theology of Q," *ExpTim* 113 (2001): 5.

6. Christopher M. Tuckett, "The Search for a Theology of Q: A Dead End?" *ExpTim* 113 (2002): 292.

7. Cf. Tuckett, "Dead End?" 293.

8. E.g., Siegfried Schulz, *Q: Die Spruchquelle der Evangelisten* (Zürich: Theologischer Verlag, 1972). I. Howard Marshall, *The Gospel of Luke* (Exeter, UK: Paternoster, 1978), e.g., 702, entertains the idea of there being two recensions of Q.

9. E.g., Kloppenborg, *Formation of Q*. For a report on the positive reception of Kloppenborg's various proposals as well as a critique of them, see Dale C. Allison Jr., *The Jesus Tradition in Q* (Harrisburg, PA: TPI, 1997), 3, esp. n. 16.

10. E.g., Heinz Schürmann, *Traditionsgeschichtliche Untersuchungen zu den synoptischen Evangelien* (Düsseldorf: Patmos, 1968). On the view of four stages initially proposed by Wilhelm

a minimum, our attention will be focused on the final stage of the redaction of Q to which, in any case, it is suggested that references to the devil, Satan, Beelzebul, evil spirits, and exorcism are to be assigned.[11]

4.1 The First Readers of Q

Although we should allow for later additions after 70 CE,[12] the date of the publication of Q should probably be placed before the start of the war in 66 CE. For, in contrast to Q generally portraying the coming One as arriving in judgment (e.g., Luke 17:22–37), in 13:35b the future of Jerusalem in relation to the coming One is hopeful and joyful, with no hint of any trouble ahead.[13]

Given that the only place names in Q other than Jerusalem are Chorazin, Bethsaida, and Capernaum, which are contrasted with the nearby western Syrian cities of Tyre and Sidon (Luke 7:1; 10:13–15),[14] it is reasonable to accept the general consensus that Q originated among people familiar with the area to the north and west of the Sea of Galilee.[15] The strength of this view is apparent when we notice that, although the passage of woes in which Chorazin, Bethsaida, and Capernaum are addressed (10:13–15) is probably secondary—in that it now interrupts the missionary discourse (cf. 10:12 and 13)—it coheres well with the interests of Q. That is, the passage deals with outsiders, miracles, rejection, and the possible positive response of the Gentiles (Tyre and Sidon) as a foil for the lack of belief among the Jews (Chorazin and Bethsaida).[16]

Assuming that the redactor was producing his document because he considered it valuable for his readers, we can suppose he has brought in this unit

---

Bussmann, see John S. Kloppenborg, "Tradition and Redaction in the Synoptic Sayings Source," *CBQ* 46 (1984): 35–36.

11. Cf. Ronald A. Piper, "Jesus and the Conflict of Powers in Q: Two Q Miracle Stories," in *The Sayings Source Q and the Historical Jesus* (ed. A. Lindemann; BETL 158; Louvain: Leuven University Press, 2001), 317–49, esp. 320–21n14.

12. Later additions are probably the temptation story (Luke 4:1–13) and two glosses (11:43c and 16:17). See Kloppenborg, *Excavating Q*, 87.

13. See Dale C. Allison Jr., "Matt. 23:39 = Luke 13:35b as a Conditional Prophecy," *JSNT* 18 (1983): 75–76. The attempt by Gerd Theissen, *The Gospels in Context: Social and Political History in the Synoptic Tradition* (Minneapolis: Fortress, 1991), 221–34, to date Q in the 40s has received disabling criticism. See Matti Myllykoski, "The Social History of Q and the Jewish War," in *Symbols and Strata: Essays on the Sayings Gospel Q* (ed. Risto Uro; Göttingen: Vandenhoeck & Ruprecht, 1996), 143–99; Kloppenborg, *Excavating Q*, 82–84.

14. The mention of Sodom in Luke 17:29 is intended to be historical (cf. Gen. 18:16–19:28) and in Luke 10:12 it is eschatological.

15. See the discussion in Tuckett, *History*, 102–3; Jonathan L. Reed, "The Social Map of Q," in *Conflict and Invention: Literary, Rhetorical, and Social Studies on the Sayings Gospel Q* (ed. John S. Kloppenborg; Valley Forge, PA: TPI, 1996), 17–36; Milton C. Moreland, "Q and the Economics of Early Roman Galilee," in Lindemann, *The Sayings Source Q and the Historical Jesus*, 561–75.

16. See Allison, *Jesus Tradition*, 35.

because it would apply to his readers living around the north and west of the Sea of Galilee.[17] We may be able to bring the first readers of Q into sharper focus when we take into account that there is an urban temper of mind in Q.[18] For example, while there is a tendency to use the second-person form of address, the impersonal passive ("they") is only used for agrarian activities, as in 6:44 where the writer says, "*They* do not gather figs from thorns" (my translation; cf. Luke 14:35).[19]

If it is correct to assume that the material in Q was collected not least because of its relevance to the first readers, their general situation is easily reconstructed.[20] We have just seen that there is evidence to suppose that the readers are urban dwellers. From the conservative attitude to the law (e.g., Luke 16:18) and the attacks on scribes and Pharisees for not keeping the law (11:37–52),[21] it would seem that Q reflects the perspective of conservative Jewish Christians in frequent conflict with other Jews. In bringing detail to this sketch it is notable that the teaching of Jesus in Q opens with Jesus addressing his disciples as poor, hungry, weeping, excluded, and reviled (6:17, 20–22). Though some of these may also be understood as referring to spiritual qualities, later, in an extended passage, the readers' material poverty is addressed directly in that they are urged not to be anxious in light of God's care (12:22–31, cf. 33–34).[22] The picture emerging of a people relatively low on the socio-economic scale is enhanced when we take into account that the criticisms directed to the Pharisees (11:39, 42–44) were directed against a ruling elite[23] (over against which the readers identified themselves), not just religious authorities, and

17. Cf. Reed, "Social Map of Q," 17–36, who suggests that Capernaum, Bethsaida, Chorazin, and Nazara function as real towns in Q's world, and that Jerusalem and Tyre and Sidon are on the near horizon of Q's world. Sodom and Nineveh are on the outer edges of Q's horizon, both having been destroyed.

18. Cf. Moreland, "Economics," 561–75, esp. 574.

19. So Reed, "Social Map of Q," 25–28, esp. 26.

20. Caution is required here for, as Raymond E. Brown, "Johannine Ecclesiology—the Community's Origins," *Int* 31 (1977): 380, says: "*Primarily*, the Gospels tell us how an evangelist conceived of and presented Jesus to a Christian community in the last third of the first century, a presentation that indirectly gives us an insight into that community's life at the time when the Gospel was written" (his emphasis).

21. Cf. John S. Kloppenborg, "Nomos and Ethos in Q," in *Gospel Origins and Christian Beginnings: In Honor of James M. Robinson* (ed. James E. Goehring, Jack T. Sanders, and Charles W. Hedrick, in collaboration with Hans Dieter Betz; Sonoma, CA: Polebridge, 1990), 35–48.

22. There is corroborating evidence in Santiago Guijarro, "Domestic Space, Family Relationships and the Social Location of the Q People," *JSNT* 27 (2004): 72–74, noting that the Q people show signs of closeness to the courtyard or simple house (Luke 6:47–49; 10:5–7; 11:33; 12:3; 15:8–9; cf. 12:53; 14:26; 16:18; 17:27), that homelessness is a way of life for the followers of Jesus (9:57–60; cf. 10:7; 12:3; 14:26), and also that the Q people are distant from the references to large families living in palaces (7:1–10; 11:17) or large houses (7:1–10; 12:39, 42–46; 13:2; 14:16–23; 19:12–26).

23. See Josephus, *J.W.* 1.111–114, 571; 2.411; Josephus, *Ant.* 13.408–410, 423; and on the Pharisees' influence in Galilee in particular, see Josephus, *Life* 189–198; Anthony J. Saldarini, *Pharisees, Scribes and Sadducees in Palestinian Society* (Grand Rapids: Eerdmans, 1988), 291–97;

that all the figures Q mentions from Israel's history—Solomon, the Queen of the South, Jonah, Noah, and Lot—are claimed by Q in a contest with the representatives of ruling institutions.[24] The readers also appear to be facing considerable suffering and persecution since in the opening section of teaching they are charged with, for example, loving their enemies and praying for those who abuse them (6:27–28, cf. 29–32). Later in the text Jesus tells them not to fear those who can kill the body (12:4) or be anxious about what to say when they are brought before the synagogues (12:11). Conceivably, some of this suffering involved family divisions (12:51–53; 14:26).

To this sad picture can be added a further note that the mission of the readers—perhaps undertaken reluctantly (cf. Luke 10:2)—probably involved wandering preachers and healers (10:9),[25] who were generally being rejected[26] or suffering real harm (10:3). Most of the evidence as to whether or not this is a Jewish or a Gentile focused mission is inconclusive.[27] However, the negative references to the Gentiles in 6:33 ("If you do good to those who do good to you, what credit is that to you? For even the Gentiles[28] do the same") and 12:30 ("It is the Gentiles . . . who seek these things" [my translation]) make it unlikely that Q is reflecting any interest in a Gentile mission. Therefore, the theory of mission that may best fit the evidence is not to suppose that Q is involved in a concerted Gentile mission.[29] Rather, noting the story of the centurion in Luke 7:1–10, readers are probably being encouraged in their mission to Jews (cf. 10:12–15).[30]

4.2 Q and the Miraculous

What Q tells us about exorcism among early Christians is to be seen against the background of a considerable interest in miracles and the miraculous and

---

Anthony J. Saldarini, "Political and Social Roles of the Pharisees and Scribes in Galilee," SBLSP 27 (1988): 200–209, esp. 204–6.

24. So John S. Kloppenborg, "The Formation of Q Revisited: A Response to Richard Horsley," SBLSP 28 (1989): 211–12.

25. The suggestion by Leif E. Vaage, *Galilean Upstarts: Jesus' First Followers according to Q* (Valley Forge, PA: TPI, 1994), 34–36, that the "weak" (ἀσθενεῖς) to be healed (θεραπεύετε) were morally weak is probably to be rejected since Q shows an interest in physical healing (Luke 7:1–10, 22; 10:13–15; 11:14; cf. §4.2 below), and ἀσθενής is primarily used by NT writers for physical sickness. See BDAG, "ἀσθενής," 142–43.

26. See Luke 9:57–60; 10:8–16; 11:16, 29–32.

27. See the summary of the debates in Tuckett, *History*, 393–94.

28. As is almost universally agreed, οἱ ἐθνικοί (Matt. 5:47) rather than οἱ ἁμαρτωλοί (Luke 6:33) is to be taken as reflecting the text of Q. See, e.g., W. D. Davies and Dale C. Allison Jr., *The Gospel according to Saint Matthew* (ICC; 3 vols.; Edinburgh: T&T Clark, 1988–1997), 1:559.

29. As does Paul D. Meyer, "The Gentile Mission in Q," *JBL* 89 (1970): 405–17.

30. Cf. Kloppenborg, "Formation of Q Revisited," 209–10. For a detailed discussion of Luke 7:1–10, see David Catchpole, *The Quest for Q* (Edinburgh: T&T Clark, 1993), 280–308.

in light of the nature of the document itself. The importance of thaumaturgical traditions in Q has been demonstrated by Ronald A. Piper.[31] He has drawn
attention to the importance of the two miracle stories—the healing of the
centurion's servant (Luke 7:1–10) and the exorcism of the demon from a
mute person (11:14)—both of which are used to introduce significant blocks
of sayings material. The material following the story of the centurion's servant includes the programmatic statement about the blind recovering their
sight, the lame walking, the lepers being cleansed, the deaf hearing, and the
dead being raised, as well as the poor being given good news (Luke 7:22).
The material following the brief exorcism story is a lengthy discussion of
Jesus' uniqueness and authority as well as the significance of his exorcisms
(11:15–26, esp. 20). Q's considerable thaumaturgical interest is also evident
in a number of passing references to healing (10:9, 13; 17:6).

The perception of Q has been governed by it being seen as predominantly
sayings material. However, it is far from accurate to understand the *Gattung*
(genre) of Q as "*logoi sophōn*" or "sayings of the sages"[32] or "the Sayings Gospel."[33] Even though Q is dominated by sayings of Jesus, the initial material
about John the Baptist, the inclusion of the temptation stories, the presence
of the miracle stories, the thaumaturgical interests, and the apparent purpose-
ful arrangement of Q strongly suggest that such designations of Q must be
left behind in favor of acknowledging that, while it is not a "Gospel,"[34] it is
more than a collection of sayings. As it stands, this proto-Gospel gives clear
evidence that its albeit elusive message[35] could not be conveyed by sayings
alone, or even by mere reference to the actions of Jesus, and that its material
has been organized intentionally.[36]

4.3 Jesus the Teacher

We can begin to elucidate some of the details of what Q might tell us
about exorcism among early Christians. First we note that there is not only

31. Piper, "Jesus and the Conflict," 317–49.

32. See James M. Robinson, "*LOGOI SOPHON*: On the Gattung of Q," in *Trajectories through Early Christianity* (ed. James M. Robinson and Helmut Koester; Philadelphia: Fortress, 1971), 71–113, esp. 73–74.

33. Cf., e.g., John S. Kloppenborg, ed., *The Shape of Q: Signal Essays on the Sayings Gospel* (Minneapolis: Fortress, 1994); and John S. Kloppenborg, ed., *Conflict and Invention: Literary, Rhetorical, and Social Studies on the Sayings Gospel Q* (Valley Forge, PA: TPI, 1995).

34. Cf. Kloppenborg, *Formation of* Q, 262.

35. See the discussion by Graham N. Stanton, "On the Christology of Q," in *Christ and Spirit in the New Testament: Studies in Honour of Charles Francis Digby Moule* (ed. Barnabas Lindars and Stephen S. Smalley; Cambridge: Cambridge University Press, 1973), 41–42.

36. Cf. James M. Robinson, "The Sayings Gospel Q," in van Segbroeck et al., *The Four Gospels*, 1:361–88.

an injunction to emulate Jesus generally (Luke 14:27), but also, immediately before the instruction to go out on mission without material support (10:2a–4), readers are told about Jesus' austere lifestyle (9:57–60). We can assume, then, that those responsible for Q understood that their portrait of Jesus was important in shaping early Christians attitudes, including those toward exorcism.

We have just seen that thaumaturgical themes, including exorcism, are important to Q, like Matthew, who will also take up this view (see §7.2 below). Nevertheless, through the large amount of sayings material, Jesus is portrayed first and foremost as a teacher, not as a miracle-worker or an exorcist. Thus, assuming that Luke 4:16–18 (which includes mention of Jesus healing the blind) is not part of Q,[37] the first activity discussed or attributed to Jesus after his temptation is not a miracle, or reference to miracles, but his teaching of his followers (Luke 6:12a, 17). It is not until after the long section of teaching (6:12–7:1) that there is a miracle story, that of the healing of the centurion's servant (7:2–10). Thus, we can already see that the relatively low importance of exorcism for Q is unlikely to be attributed to it being primarily a collection of sayings.

4.4 An Exorcism Story? (Luke 7:1–10)

Given that Q's first readers were predominantly from among poor conservative Jewish Christians, this story of a centurion seeking help from Jesus may well represent a model mission situation. It is possible that the importance of exorcism is already obvious here in Q's first miracle story being written up as an exorcism (Luke 7:1–10). Siegfried Schulz observed that, in this story, Jesus is portrayed as being involved in a chain of command (which he takes to be God-Jesus-demons) implying that Jesus only need speak to the demon, and it will flee.[38] From this, Piper has developed the argument that, based on the dominant popular view that regarded illness as an invasion of hostile foreign elements,[39] Q phrases this story in terms reminiscent of, even if not explicitly, an exorcism.[40] As an example of this in early Christianity, Piper rightly notes that Luke reworks the story of the healing of Simon's mother-in-law so that it

37. In arguing for Luke 4:16–18 as part of Q, Christopher M. Tuckett in his "Luke 4, Isaiah and Q," in Delobel, *Logia*, 343–54, and in his Q *and the History of Early Christianity: Studies on* Q (Edinburgh: T&T Clark, 1996), 226–37, has not found support from others. See Shawn Carruth and James M. Robinson, Q *4:1–13, 16: The Temptations of Jesus-Nazara* (Louvain: Peeters, 1996); James M. Robinson, Paul Hoffmann, and John S. Kloppenborg, eds.; Milton C. Moreland, managing ed., *The Critical Edition of* Q (Hermeneia; Minneapolis: Fortress, 2000), 42.

38. Schulz, Q, 243; on which see also Catchpole, *Quest*, 300.

39. Piper, "Jesus and the Conflict," esp. 322; relying on Dale B. Martin, *The Corinthian Body* (New Haven and London: Yale University Press, 1995), 140–62, esp. 143.

40. Piper, "Jesus and the Conflict," esp. 324.

becomes an exorcism story (Luke 4:38–39; cf. Mark 1:29–31).[41] To this could be added Luke's story of the crippled woman who is described as "having a spirit of sickness" or infirmity (γυνὴ πνεῦμα ἔξουσα ἀσθενείας, Luke 13:11, my translation) rather than being demon possessed (cf. 8:27, 36). Also, in a summary, Luke describes those troubled with unclean spirits being "cured" (ἐθεραπεύοντο, 6:18; cf. 7:21) rather than as demons coming out of people (cf. 4:35 and 8:33).

However, even though there could be a blurring of the boundaries between healing and exorcism, as is most clear with Luke,[42] there is nothing in the story of the healing of the centurion's servant, other than the idea of the chain of command, to suggest that Q (or Luke, for that matter) was telling this story reminiscent of an exorcism story. On the other hand, there are examples of Jesus speaking to a sick person or to body parts to effect a healing so that Jesus' chain of command need not be understood as directed toward a demon. For example, in Matthew 9:29 Jesus addresses the blind men, "According to your faith let it be done to you" (cf. 8:13; 15:28). In Mark 1:41 Jesus speaks to the leper, "Be made clean!" and in Mark 7:34 Jesus appears to be speaking to the ears of a deaf man in saying, "Be opened!" In other words, it is just as reasonable to suppose that Jesus' chain of command portrayed in Q could be directed toward the person or the sickness or the body part as to a demon.

Further, in making a distinction between those who were thought to be sick and those who were demon possessed,[43] the Gospel writers show they do not assume all sickness is to be attributed to demons.[44] There may be evidence that those responsible for Q also considered such a distinction could be made. In his answer to John the Baptist, Jesus says that John is to be told of a number of sicknesses that are being healed (Luke 7:22) without any mention of the demonic, while in Luke 11:14 a demon is said to be the cause of a person being sick, in this case to be mute. In short, the Gospel writers (and perhaps also Q) assume a distinction could be made between demonic and other kinds of sickness. And with only the concept of the chain of command, which we have argued could be expected to be directed toward a person or a body part as well as the demonic, it is unlikely that we can conclude with any confidence that Q has phrased this story in terms reminiscent of, even if not explicitly, an exorcism.

Our discussion of the story of the healing of the centurion's servant leads us to the position that it is not to be read in any way as dealing with the demonic. Therefore, a report of Jesus being an exorcist does not come in Q

41. Piper, *Jesus and the Conflict*, 322.

42. See Graham H. Twelftree, *Jesus the Miracle Worker: A Historical and Theological Study* (Downers Grove, IL: InterVarsity, 1999), 147–48, 176; cf. §6.2 below..

43. E.g., Mark 1:32–34 ‖ Matt. 8:16 ‖ Luke 4:40–41; Mark 3:10–11 ‖ Luke 6:18–19.

44. Cf. John Christopher Thomas, *The Devil, Disease, and Deliverance: Origins of Illness in New Testament Thought* (JPTSup 13; Sheffield: Sheffield Academic, 1998), esp. 297–305.

until Luke 11:14, with Jesus "casting out a demon that was mute."[45] This is well after the initial portrait of Jesus as a teacher has been established, which forms the background to the mission charge (Luke 10:1–12). From this it is apparent that, for the Jesus of Q, whose mission is to be emulated, exorcism has a relatively low priority.

4.5 The Place of Exorcism

In Q, this relatively low priority of exorcism in the ministry of Jesus needs explanation not only in light of its high priority in Mark, the other early Gospel, and what can be established for the historical Jesus, but also in light of Q's general interest in miracles and the miraculous. When we note that the relatively small showing of exorcism is in tension with other material in Q, we can see that the low profile of exorcism is probably the result of a deliberate downplaying of this aspect of Jesus' ministry. That is, the theme of the kingdom of God is very important to Q[46]—including its present fulfillment (e.g., Luke 10:9; 11:20; 16:16)—and it is strongly tied to exorcism in 11:20 ("But if by the finger [or Spirit] of God I cast out demons, then the kingdom of God has come upon you," my translation). This strong and clear connection between exorcism and the present aspect of the kingdom of God could reasonably be expected to give rise to a portrayal of exorcism as an important, if not the most important, aspect of the ministry of Jesus. Yet, exorcism is only mentioned relatively late in the portrait of Jesus and, as we will see, only implied in the ministry of his followers. This all suggests that there has been a deliberate downplaying of exorcism rather than an amplification of the theme of the kingdom of God, in which case it would not be connected with exorcism.

The explanation for this demotion of the importance of exorcism in the portrayal of Jesus' ministry may be found, in part, in noting that, along with an interest in the miracles and the miraculous, there also comes a cautious tone in Q. This is seen probably most clearly early in Q, in the temptations, which establish the ministry of Jesus—and by implication, those of his followers—as taking place in a dualistic cosmological framework.[47] In the first temptation the devil says to Jesus: "If you are the Son of God, command this stone to become a loaf of bread" (Luke 4:3).[48] In calling on Jesus to satisfy

45. Piper's case that, for Q, this exorcism is rather like a healing because, atypically, a dumb man speaks is not convincing for, at least on the basis of other evangelists, a demonized person could exhibit symptoms of other sicknesses (Matt. 9:32–33; Mark 9:17). See Piper, "Jesus and the Conflict," 321.

46. See Luke 6:20; 7:28; 9:2; 10:9; 11:2, 20; 12:31; 13:18, 20, 28, 29; 16:16.

47. So Piper, "Jesus and the Conflict," 343.

48. Further on this paragraph, see also Graham H. Twelftree, "Temptation of Jesus," *DJG* 823.

his hunger (Luke 4:2) by turning stones into bread, the devil is portrayed as appealing to Jesus' power as Son of God. This could be intended as a temptation to repeat the miracle of manna being provided in the wilderness,[49] or to perform a sign expected of the messianic age in order to win over people (cf. John 6:1–40). Or perhaps, depending on the conditional "if" for this interpretation, the devil is to be seen as attempting to raise doubt about Jesus' miraculous powers and, hence, his divine sonship.

However, Jesus' reply, "Not on bread alone shall a person live" (Luke 4:4, my translation), is almost exactly that of Deuteronomy 8:3, which alludes to the Israelites being in the wilderness as a father disciples his son. For this reason Q is probably conveying the idea that Jesus is being tempted to assert his independence from God by performing a miracle for his own benefit, rather than being under authority (cf. Luke 7:8) and trusting God as a son for all his needs (cf. Deut. 28:1–14; Pss. 33:18–19; 34:10). Thus the temptations in Q not only establish the legitimacy of Jesus,[50] nor are they only dealing with the accusation of Jesus' relationship with "evil,"[51] but they also set out a key aspect of his modus operandi. This involves Jesus having a cautious attitude toward miraculous power in his ministry and, given the interest in Jesus being emulated, would probably also be intended to convey a similar message of due caution to the readers in relation to their performing miracles. Added to this is the point that, in his physical need—hunger—Jesus is being portrayed in the same way that we concluded Q's readers are to be described (see §4.1 above). In such a condition the readers would be tempted to rely on the storehouses of wealth—miraculous or material—rather than on God's supplying their subsistence, as they are being encouraged to do through the paradigm of Jesus.

Further insight into the deliberate demotion of exorcism in Q's portrayal of Jesus' ministry may also be gained by reading the statement in Luke 11:19 ("If I cast out demons by Beelzebul, by whom do your children cast them out?" my translation) against the background of what I have suggested is the difficulty, if not failure, of the mission of the followers of Jesus represented in Q. That is, for Christians who may, like Jesus, have been accused of operating under the aegis of Satan (cf. Luke 11:15) and who were facing rejection from other Jews (10:13–14) who were also successfully conducting exorcisms (11:19), it would have been an easy matter to play down the importance of exorcism. It is not surprising, then, that the commission for mission to the followers of Jesus includes teaching and healing but no mention of exorcism (cf. 10:8–9).[52] Notwithstanding, it was not that the final redactors of Q set

49. See Exod. 16:13–21; 2 Bar. 29:1–8; Josephus, Ant. 20.168–172.

50. Cf. Kloppenborg, Formation of Q, 256–62.

51. Cf. Piper, "Jesus and the Conflict," 341.

52. As John S. Kloppenborg pointed out to me in private correspondence, it is notable that the side of wisdom that includes τέχνη, the ability to do things, including exorcism (cf. T. Sol.), is a side of wisdom that is for the most part missing in Q.

aside exorcism altogether. The significant length of its treatment in the Beelzebul controversy (11:14–26) is testimony to its probable ongoing, even if
arguably limited, use among the Christians addressed by Q.

4.6 The Mission Charge (Luke 10:1–11)

There is probably also some evidence of Q's interest in exorcism to be
found in the material devoted to the mission of the followers of Jesus (Luke
10:1–11). The mission charge is prefaced with the statement about the harvest
being plentiful (10:2). The image of mission as a harvest draws on the idea in
the Septuagint of the eschatological gathering of God's people.[53] When we
discuss Q's Beelzebul controversy material, we will see not only the connection that Jesus makes between his exorcism and the eschaton, but also that
exorcism is described as a gathering, as in a harvest. It is more than reasonable to suppose that readers would draw the conclusion that exorcism was
understood to be part of the mission of the followers of Jesus.

This supposition is confirmed when we also note that the mission pericope
contains the charge to say, "The kingdom of God has come near . . ." (Luke
10:9). The strong connection between the kingdom of God and exorcism,
which we will presently note in Q, further enhanced the probability that exorcism was implied—and would have been assumed by the first readers—to be
part of the task of the followers of Jesus. From this we can see that, although
exorcism is being played down in the ministry of Jesus and his followers, it
was still most probably seen as part of the means of eschatological harvest.

4.7 Luke 11:20

In that the followers of Jesus are expected to emulate the ministry of Jesus,
what Q says not only about his general approach to miracles and exorcism but
also about his method of exorcism can be taken as instructive as to how his
followers may have carried out exorcism. Q's understanding of Jesus' method
of exorcism is encapsulated in an important saying in the Beelzebul controversy: "But if it is by the finger of God that I cast out demons, then has come
upon you the kingdom of God" (Luke 11:20, my translation; cf. 11:14).

Before we can unpack what the publishers of Q may have had in mind here
in Luke 11:20, we have to resolve the problem of its wording. The issue on
which a great deal of our interpretation depends and on which, therefore, it
is difficult to be objective is whether or not Q used the word "finger" (Luke

53. Cf. Isa. 27:12–13; Joel 3:13 (4:13 LXX). See the discussion in Friedrich Hauck, "Θερισμός,"
TDNT 3:133; Marshall, *Luke*, 416; John Nolland, *Luke 9:21–18:34* (WBC 35B; Dallas: Word
Books), 550–51.

11:20) or "Spirit" (Matt. 12:28) in identifying Jesus' source of power-authority.[54] At first, in view of Luke's interest in the Spirit and his apparent lack of interest in "finger,"[55] it seems unlikely that he would exchange "Spirit" for "finger."[56] However, a closer look at the text seems to lead to a different conclusion.

Looking first at what Matthew has, it is noticeable that he uses the phrase "the kingdom of God" here rather than "the kingdom of heaven," as we would expect. For, in only one other place does he not change the phrase to "kingdom of heaven" (Matt. 19:24).[57] This habit of Matthew's leads to the impression that, if the phrase "kingdom of God" appears here in 12:28, he may not have changed the remainder of the text either. This impression is firmed up when we take into account the fact that it is unlikely that Matthew would have dropped the word "finger" and introduced the word "Spirit." Such an exchange would have heightened an unwelcome parallel between Jesus and the enthusiasts against whom he has written earlier (7:22–23).[58] To this we can add the point that, if "finger" was in Matthew's source, he is likely to have valued its presence in contributing to his portrait of Jesus as the new Moses (cf. Exod. 8:19).[59]

Yet, at this point, on the other hand, we can note that Luke also has an interest—and probably a stronger interest than Matthew—in Moses and especially the new exodus,[60] so that Luke would have a greater reason than Matthew to want "finger" in his text. Indeed, we do not have to look far to see that Luke

54. For an earlier version of the remainder of this point, see Graham H. Twelftree, *Jesus the Exorcist: A Contribution to the Study of the Historical Jesus* (WUNT 2.54; Tübingen: Mohr Siebeck, 1993), 108. For a recent survey of the debate on the wording of Q, see David T. Williams, "Why the Finger?" *ExpTim* 115 (2003): 45–49, esp. 45–46.

55. The other two uses of "finger" come from his sources: Luke 11:46 is from Q (∥ Matt. 23:4; see Moreland, *Critical Edition of Q*, 114–15), and Luke 16:24 is probably taken up from L (see Joachim Jeremias, *The Parables of Jesus* [London: SCM, 1972], 182–83).

56. Cf., e.g., Luke Timothy Johnson, *The Gospel of Luke* (Collegeville, MN: Glazier, 1991), 181.

57. See Matt. 4:17 ∥ Mark 1:14–15; Matt. 5:3 ∥ Luke 6:20; [Matt. 8:11 ∥ Luke 13:28]; Matt. 10:7 ∥ Luke 9:2; Matt. 11:11–12 ∥ Luke 7:28; Matt. 13:11 ∥ Mark 4:11; Matt. 13:31 ∥ Mark 4:30; Matt. 13:33 ∥ Luke 13:20; Matt. 19:14 ∥ Mark 10:14; Matt. 19:23 ∥ Mark 10:23.

58. Cf. James D. G. Dunn, *Jesus and the Spirit* (London: SCM, 1975), 373n22, who notes the parallel between Matt. 7:22 and 12:28.

59. Cf. Dale C. Allison Jr., *The New Moses: A Matthean Typology* (Edinburgh: T&T Clark, 1993); and note the critical review by Jack D. Kingsbury in *JBL* 115 (1996): 356–58. See also Dale C. Allison Jr., *The Intertextual Jesus: Scripture in Q* (Harrisburg, PA: TPI, 2000), 53–57.

60. Note C. F. Evans, "The Central Section of St. Luke's Gospel," in *Studies in the Gospels: Essays in Memory of R. H. Lightfoot* (ed. D. E. Nineham; Oxford: Blackwell, 1967), 37–53, arguing that Luke "has selected and ordered his material [in the central section of his Gospel] with a view to presenting it as a Christian Deuteronomy" (42). David P. Moessner, *Lord of the Banquet: The Literary and Theological Significance of the Lukan Travel Narrative* (Minneapolis: Fortress, 1989), goes further to argue that Jesus is presented as "the Prophet like Moses" (cf. 70). See also Allison, *Moses*, 98–100, for what is called "the remarkable parallels throughout Luke-Acts between Jesus and Moses" (98).

is most likely to have preferred "finger" rather than "Spirit" in his text. That is, as we will see, Luke lost little if anything from what he saw conveyed in his source through the word "Spirit." Changing to the word "finger" enabled him to bring out a parallel between the Exodus miracles[61] and those of Jesus in a way not possible in the word "Spirit." That Luke is able to pass up using the word "Spirit," despite his predilection for the subject, is also clear from him having done so at 20:42 and, perhaps, at 21:15.[62]

Therefore, acknowledging the strength of (but not persuaded by) the counterarguments, I take it that Matthew's "Spirit" has preserved the wording of Q in this case. Notwithstanding, the words "Spirit" and "finger" point to a common stock of ideas that help us understand what Q considered to be taking place in exorcism.[63] On the one hand, the phrase "finger of God" is used in the Old Testament to refer to the activity of God. For example, Exodus 31:18 says it is the finger of God that wrote on the tablets of stone (cf. Exod. 8:19; Deut. 9:10; Ps. 8:3). Similarly, in the Qumran *War Scroll*, God is said to raise his *hand* against Satan (1QM 18.1–15).

On the other hand, in the Old Testament a reference to the activity of the Spirit also referred to the activity of God. In Ezekiel 11:5 the "spirit of the Lord" falls on Ezekiel, and he is addressed by the Lord. What is interesting in our present discussion is that in Ezekiel 8:1 it is "the hand of the Lord" that falls on Ezekiel to bring about the vision. Thus, in Ezekiel we have an instance where "hand" and "spirit" are used synonymously. In turn, we need to take into account that, in the Old Testament, the "finger of God" is a variant of the "hand of God," with no alteration of meaning (cf. 1 Chron. 28:11–19).[64]

All this helps us to see that Q probably understood Jesus to be performing his exorcisms "by" or "in" (ἐν) God as an instrument of power. However, from what we have just seen concerning the use of "the Spirit" in the Old Testament, we need to nuance this conclusion by suggesting that it is not that Q is claiming that Jesus is simply using God as a source of power for his exorcisms, but that, in Jesus, God himself is performing the exorcisms.

Having settled as best we can the wording of Luke 11:20, and drawing attention to the most important implications, our next step in unpacking what Q understood to be taking place in an exorcism is to inquire about Q's understanding of the relationship between exorcism and the coming of the

61. Cf. Exod. 7:4–5; 8:19; 9:3, 15.

62. See Dunn, *Jesus and the Spirit*, 46; and also Marshall, *Luke*, 747; Joseph A. Fitzmyer, *The Gospel of Luke (X–XXIV)* (AB 28B; Garden City, NY: Doubleday, 1985), 1340.

63. If Q used the word "finger," we learn that interest in designating Jesus' power-authority as the Spirit is not yet evident in early Christianity.

64. See also Robert W. Wall, "'The Finger of God': Deuteronomy 9.10 and Luke 11.20," *NTS* 33 (1987): 144–50; J.-M. Van Cangh, "'Par l'esprit de Dieu—par le doigt de Dieu': Mt 12,28 par. Lc 11,20," in Delobel, *Logia*, 337–42; Chrys C. Caragounis, "Kingdom of God, Son of Man and Jesus' Self-Understanding," *TynBul* 40 (1989): 2–23, 223–38.

kingdom of God. Specifically, in relation to the exorcisms, is the kingdom of God already present, arriving, or soon to arrive? Put another way, are the exorcisms thought to prepare for, to herald, or to be some part of the kingdom of God? Answers to these questions revolve around how we understand ἔφθασεν ἐφ᾽ ὑμᾶς ("has come upon you"). Φθάνω has a range of meanings, including "come before," "precede" (1 Thess. 4:15), "just arrived" (Song 2:12), and "reached" (2 Cor. 10:14; 1 Thess. 2:16), as well as "attain" (Rom. 9:31; Phil. 3:16), notably when it is combined with ἐπί ("upon"). This makes φθάνω more specific to mean the actual attainment or presence of something,[65] in this case, the kingdom of God.

That early Christians, such as those represented here in Q, could entertain the idea that Jesus spoke of the kingdom of God being already present is supported by the saying that something greater than Solomon or Jonah is present (Luke 11:31–32).[66] It is reasonable to suppose, then, that the verse that is the focus of our attention is conveying the idea that the kingdom of God has come in the exorcisms. If this is correct, the view that, for Q, the exorcisms of Jesus are *preparatory* to the kingdom of God[67] is unsupported by this verse and to be discarded in the absence of other evidence.

Next we must ask why the exorcisms of Jesus are related to the coming of the kingdom of God and about the nature of that relationship. It cannot be that the kingdom of God has come because, in contrast to the Jews, Jesus was a successful exorcist and the Jews were not or only partially so.[68] For, the previous verse ("If I by Beelzebul cast out demons, by whom do your sons cast them out?" Luke 11:19, my translation), only has force if the exorcisms of Jesus and his contemporaries are both taken to be successful. Indeed, in this verse Q recognizes that the exorcisms of Jesus and the Jews are sufficiently similar to be compared.[69] We are left, then, to ask: In relation to the three key components of Luke 11:20—Jesus, the Spirit, and the kingdom of God—is the kingdom of God coming because Jesus is conducting the exorcisms, or

65. See, e.g., Judg. 20:42 (LXX) and the discussions by Robert F. Berkey, "ΕΓΓΙΖΕΙΝ, ΦΘΑΝΕΙΝ, and Realized Eschatology," *JBL* 82 (1963): 177–87; Gottfried Fitzer, "φθάνω," *TDNT* 9:90–92; George R. Beasley-Murray, *Jesus and the Kingdom of God* (Grand Rapids: Eerdmans; Exeter, UK: Paternoster, 1986), 77–78; Davies and Allison, *Matthew*, 2:340n36; BDAG, "φθάνω," 1053.

66. Cf. Davies and Allison, *Matthew*, 1:389. The saying that Satan has already fallen from heaven (Luke 10:18) supports my case generally, but it was probably not part of Q. See the discussion in Kloppenborg, *Q Parallels*, 76–77.

67. Cf., e.g., Richard H. Hiers, *Jesus and the Future: Unsolved Questions for Understanding and Faith* (Atlanta: John Knox, 1981), 62–71.

68. Against Anthony E. Harvey, *The Constraints of History* (London: Duckworth, 1982), 109. For others who argue that Jesus' opponents were not successful exorcists, see Allison, *Jesus Tradition*, 125–26.

69. Against Caragounis, "Kingdom of God," 230–31, who suggests that Jesus' exorcisms were of a different order because they lacked all *characteristics* of Jewish and Hellenistic exorcisms. Further, see Twelftree, *Exorcist*, 107.

because the exorcisms are being conducted by the Spirit? It is generally agreed that the operative element in this verse is the Spirit (or finger) of God,[70] so that the kingdom of God was understood to be breaking in because exorcisms were being performed in the power of the Spirit of God.

However, a more careful reading of Q shows this to be an incomplete answer for we need to take into account the use of ἐγώ[71] ("I") in the verse. Could it be that Q considered the uniqueness of Jesus' exorcisms to be that it was Jesus who was conducting them? It is true that the use of ἐγώ is not everywhere in the New Testament to be taken as implying an emphasis.[72] However, in the Synoptic Gospels the emphatic ἐγώ is relatively infrequent on the lips of Jesus, being found in warnings, promises, and commands with a sense of Jesus' divine power and authority.[73] In fact, the only other time Q uses ἐγώ is on the lips of the centurion from Capernaum, in drawing attention to his and, by implication, Jesus' personal authority (7:8).[74] Therefore, the use of ἐγώ here in 11:19–20 ought to be taken as significant in Q drawing attention to the person of Jesus.[75]

In turn, as christologically incorrect as it may be, Q is giving the impression that what distinguishes the exorcisms of Jesus from those of his contemporaries is that, at least in part, it is he who is the exorcist. Yet, taking into account what we have said about the importance of "Spirit" in this verse, we have to go on to conclude that Q considered the inbreaking of the kingdom to be linked with Jesus' exorcisms because *Jesus* is casting out demons *in the Spirit*.[76] With this conclusion we have an explanation of the sentence (Luke 11:20) beginning with the adversative δέ ("but"), in which the exorcisms of Jesus are set off over against those of the Jews (cf. 11:19), not because his were successful or more successful, but because it was he, in the Spirit, who was performing these exorcisms.

Another aspect of Q's understanding of exorcism can be gathered from the use of ἐκβάλλω ("drive out") in Luke 11:20, the earliest use I know of the term in relation to exorcism.[77] In Greek literature there are some

---

70. E.g., Dunn, *Jesus and the Spirit*, 44–46.

71. On the status of ἐγώ in Luke 11:20, see NA[27] 196.

72. See Nigel Turner, *A Grammar of New Testament Greek* (vol. 3; Edinburgh: T&T Clark, 1963), 37–38.

73. So Ethelbert Stauffer, "ἐγώ," *TDNT* 2:348.

74. In Matt. 25:27 (cf. Luke 19:23) Jesus uses ἐγώ. However, the source of this story is unclear. Marshall, *Luke*, 702, suggests that this particular story is probably evidence for two recensions of the Q material.

75. Cf. Twelftree, *Exorcist*, 108–9; Davies and Allison, *Matthew*, 2:341. James D. G. Dunn, *Jesus Remembered* (Christianity in the Making 1; Grand Rapids: Eerdmans, 2003), 695, is unconvinced!

76. Twelftree, *Exorcist*, 109.

77. See Twelftree, *Exorcist*, 109. For its later use, see Friedrich Hauck, "Βάλλω . . . ," *TDNT* 1:527.

instances where ἐκβάλλω refers to an enemy being cast out.[78] Indeed, in the Septuagint ἐκβάλλω is most often used when an enemy, frustrating or standing in the way of God fulfilling his purpose for his chosen people, is cast out so that God's purposes can be fulfilled (cf. Exod. 23:30; Deut. 33:27–28).[79] With demons being thought to take up unlawful residence in a person as in a house (Luke 11:24),[80] and Q seeing exorcism as casting out demons or Satan, the enemy of God (11:18), it is not surprising that Q should use ἐκβάλλω to explain what was happening in an exorcism. Therefore, it is reasonable to assume that Q understood that in exorcism Jesus was casting out an enemy of God in order that his purpose might be fulfilled—the coming of the kingdom of God.[81] Insofar as Jesus is seen as the model for early Christian exorcism, God's purpose is also being fulfilled in their exorcisms.

4.8 The Parable of the Strong-Armed Man (Luke 11:21–22)

Given the same order of the Beelzebul controversy material in Matthew and Luke, Q's discussion of exorcism continues after the "Spirit/finger" saying with the parable of the strong man.[82] However, even though it is generally agreed that Luke is following Q,[83] rather than extensively reworking Mark,[84] which would be uncharacteristic of him,[85] the details of the parable are not immediately apparent because Matthew has followed Mark (Mark 3:27 ‖

78. Cf. Aristophanes, *Plut.* 430; Plato, *Gorg.* 468d; Demosthenes, *Epitaph.* 8 (= *Or.* 60.8).

79. See the discussion in Graham H. Twelftree, *Christ Triumphant: Exorcism Then and Now* (London: Hodder & Stoughton, 1985), 104–5.

80. Cf. Hauck, "Βάλλω . . . ," *TDNT* 1:527. See also §5.4 below.

81. See also Twelftree, *Exorcist*, 110.

82. On the parable being part of Q, see Kloppenborg, *Q Parallels*, 92.

83. E.g., Eduard Schweizer, *The Good News according to Luke* (London: SPCK, 1984), 195; Fitzmyer, *Luke (X–XXIV)*, 918. See also Twelftree, *Exorcist*, 111. That Luke is following a different version of Q from Matthew, see Heinz Schürmann, *Das Paschamahlbericht: Lk 22, (7–14.) 15–18*, part 1, *Eine Quellenkritische Untersuchung des Lukanischen Abendmahlsberichtes Lk 22, 7–38* (2nd ed.; NTAbh 19.5; Münster: Aschendorff, 1968), 2.

84. So Erich Klostermann, *Das Lukasevengelium* (2nd ed.; HNT 5; Tübingen: Mohr Siebeck, 1929), 126–27; Simon Légasse, "L'homme fort de Luc 11:21–22," *NovT* 5 (1962): 5–9; Barnabas Lindars, *New Testament Apologetic* (London: SCM, 1961), 84–85; cited by Marshall, *Luke*, 476; also Athanasius Polag, *Fragmenta Q: Textheft zur Logienquelle* (Neukirchen-Vluyn: Neukirchener Verlag, 1979), 52–53.

John Dominic Crossan, *In Fragments: The Aphorisms of Jesus* (San Francisco: Harper & Row, 1983), 189, does not think that Q contained the parable of the strong man—citing Arland Dean Jacobson, "Wisdom Christology in Q" (PhD diss., Claremont Graduate School, 1978), 163—but, following Paul Donald Meyer, "The Community of Q" (PhD diss., University of Iowa, 1967), 71n1, was expanding Mark.

85. Marshall, *Luke*, 477. On the complexity of the problem of Luke's sources, see the discussion by F. G. Downing, "Towards the Rehabilitation of Q," *NTS* 11 (1964–65): 169–81.

Matt. 12:29), leaving us with only what Luke has preserved to enable us to recover Q's version (Luke 11:21–22). Nevertheless, the Lukan contributions to the parable[86] are probably not great.[87] Hence, we can probably say that in Q the parable is about a strong-armed man (ὁ ἰσχυρὸς καθωπλισμένος), along with his possessions, safely in his castle until he is overtaken by a stronger man (ἰσχυρότερος), so that the possessions are taken or abducted[88] from him. The context determines that this parable is about Satan, in some way about exorcism, and particularly about the exorcisms of Jesus. The precise connection between the defeat of Satan, exorcism, and this parable needs elucidation.

It is widely held that the Synoptic writers understood the Temptation story to relate the defeat of Satan or the devil.[89] Indeed, it could be that the aorist subjunctive νικήσῃ ("conquer," Luke 11:22, my translation) is to be taken to refer to a previous definite act—the Temptation story.[90] However, an aorist subjunctive in a final clause does not only describe a single action but can also express an action in which no particular stress is placed on the time of action (cf., e.g., John 17:1, 21). That Q did not think that the devil's defeat was being related in the Temptation story is clear from the story itself, which ended only with simple reference that the devil left Jesus (Luke 4:13). From this we could hardly conclude that such an important matter as the defeat of the devil was being related,[91] especially when there is no vocabulary of defeat, as there is here in the Beelzebul controversy. To the contrary, Satan is assumed to be very much active (cf. 11:15, 19).[92] In light of this, it is probable that, in this parable of the strong-armed man, Q is conveying the idea that, in the exorcisms of Jesus (and as we are about to see, in those of his followers), Satan is being overpowered and his possessions—people—are being taken or abducted from him.

86. The distinctive vocabulary, which Luke has introduced, probably includes: φυλάσσειν ("to guard"): Matthew, 1 occurrence; Mark, 1; Luke, 6; John, 3; Acts, 8; εἰρήνη ("peace"): Matthew, 4; Mark, 1; Luke, 13; John, 6; Acts, 7; ὑπάρχειν ("to possess"): Matthew, 3; Mark, 0; Luke, 15; John, 0; Acts, 25.

87. So also Joachim Jeremias, *Die Sprache des Lukasevangeliums: Redaktion und Tradition im Nicht-Markusstoff des dritten Evangeliums* (Göttingen: Vandenhoeck & Ruprecht, 1980), 201.

88. We should probably read Q as having the simpler idea of "take" or "abduct" (διαρπάζω; Matt. 12:29 ‖ Mark 3:27; cf. LXX: Deut. 28:29; Ps. 88:42 [89:41 MT]), for Luke has probably contributed the more theologically nuanced notion of διαδίδωμι ("divide" or "distribute") to Q—cf. Jeremias, *Die Sprache*, 201—as he probably has at Luke 18:22, where Mark 10:21 has δίδωμι ("give").

89. For this paragraph see also the discussion in Twelftree, *Exorcist*, §11.

90. Cf. Ernest Best, *The Temptation and the Passion: The Markan Soteriology* (SNTSMS 2; Cambridge: Cambridge University Press, 1965), 13, referring to δήσῃ in Mark 3:27.

91. See also Piper, "Jesus and the Conflict," 343.

92. Cf. Joel Marcus, "The Beelzebul Controversy and the Eschatologies of Jesus," in *Authenticating the Activities of Jesus* (ed. Bruce Chilton and Craig A. Evans; Boston and Leiden: Brill, 1999): 259.

4.9 The Spoils of Exorcism (Luke 11:23)

The saying that follows in Q ("Whoever is not with me is against me, and whoever does not gather with me scatters," Luke 11:23) must also be about exorcism for it is sandwiched between the previous saying about the strong-armed man and the next one about the coming and going of evil spirits (11:24–26). The first image in this verse—about being for or against Jesus—calls readers to take sides in a battle.[93] Taking into account the expectation to emulate Jesus (see §4.6 above), this would probably be read as a call to be involved in the same battle as Jesus, which, in the context, is a call to his followers to be involved in exorcism. Thus, in answer to the question of the relation of the coming of the kingdom of God to the exorcisms of the followers of Jesus, we can see again that Q understands them to be as much a part of the eschatological battle as the exorcisms of Jesus in that they also are related to the defeat of Satan.

The second image in Luke 11:23 of gathering and scattering probably also refers to the eschatological scattering and gathering of God's people, for the word "scatter" (σκορπίζω[94]) is used in the Septuagint in relation to the eschatological scattering[95] and gathering[96] of God's people. Notably, C. F. Evans has drawn attention to Isaiah 40:10–11, where there is an abrupt transition from God as the mighty one with his spoil—the rescued exiles—to that of the shepherd gathering Israel.[97] If, as is likely, this is to be seen as the background against which to read this passage, Q also understands the exorcisms of both Jesus and his followers to involve the gathering of the spoils (people) from exorcism (the eschatological battle).

4.10 The "Parable" of the Vacant House (Luke 11:24–26)

This perspective helps us understand the material which follows on the behavior of unclean spirits (Luke 11:24–26). At first sight the material about the wandering spirit appears to be "an extract from a text book on demonology," as C. F. Evans put it.[98] Yet in view of the conclusion Jesus draws to the saying being "the last state of that person is worse than the first" (11:26), it is

93. Nolland, *Luke 9:21–18:34*, 642; and Joel B. Green, *The Gospel of Luke* (Grand Rapids and Cambridge, UK: Eerdmans, 1997), 458; both citing Josh. 5:13.

94. Σκορπίζω occurs in the NT only here (Matt. 12:30 ‖ Luke 11:23) and in John 10:12; 16:32; 2 Cor. 9:9.

95. C. F. Evans, *Saint Luke* (London: SCM; Philadelphia: TPI, 1990), 493, citing Ezek. 5:12; Zech. 11:16; Tob. 3:4; followed by Green, *Luke*, 458.

96. Evans, *Luke*, 493, citing Isa. 11:12; 40:11; 66:18; Ezek. 34:12–13.

97. Evans, *Luke*, 493.

98. Evans, *Luke*, 494. Cf. Ulrich Luz, *Matthew 8–20* (Hermeneia; Minneapolis: Fortress, 2001), 221. See here also for the history of the interpretation of this passage.

equally reasonable to take this to be a parable.[99] Indeed, Matthew takes the description to be a parable, but applies it to "this evil generation" (12:45).[100] However, there is no hint in Q that the description of the activity of the wandering spirit is intended to be like or analogous to any other phenomena.[101] Instead, the description of the spirit is intended to be taken at face value, not even as "parable-like," as Daniel J. Harrington suggests.[102] For also, as we will note when discussing Mark 3:20–35, in terms of the presence or absence of spiritual beings, a person could be described as a house (see §5.4 below).[103]

Nevertheless, it is not immediately clear exactly how the description of the activities of the unclean spirit and its allies is to be understood in relation to exorcism. Since the unclean spirit is portrayed as restless without a host and seeking to return to its "house," it could be that readers are to conclude that part of the process of exorcism needs to involve the then-familiar aspect of commanding or demanding that the demon not return.[104] Or perhaps similarly, as is generally thought, readers are to assume that if a demon is to be kept out, "God must take possession of the vacant dwelling," as T. W. Manson put it.[105] Neither of these options takes into account that Q has this story immediately after the saying about gathering and scattering. (Nor need we entertain the interpretations that take the story away from its relationship with exorcism[106] to connect it in a general way with the evil of the Jews or the Pharisees,[107] or with them refusing his message attested by the exorcisms.[108]) Rather, taking into account the context of the Beelzebul controversy where Jesus asks about the exorcisms of his rivals (Luke 11:19), and also that this story follows the

99. So, e.g., recently, Rudolf Schnackenburg, *The Gospel of Matthew* (Grand Rapids and Cambridge, UK: Eerdmans, 2002), 119. See also, e.g., Adolf Jülicher, *Die Gleichnisreden Jesu* (2 vols.; Tübingen: Mohr Siebeck, 1910), 2:238; Jeremias, *Parables*, 197–98.

100. So also Luz, *Matthew 8–20*, 221.

101. Cf. Luz, *Matthew 8–20*, 220.

102. Daniel J. Harrington, *The Gospel of Matthew* (Collegeville, MN: Glazier, 1991), 191.

103. Luz, *Matthew 8–20*, 220, may be correct in suggesting that the parabolic interpretation of this saying "comes not from the text but from the general human need to apply a Bible text ethically and the modern need to remove Jesus as far as possible from historically conditioned exorcistic practices."

104. Further, see Graham H. Twelftree, "ΕΙ ΔΕ . . . ΕΓΩ . . . ΕΚΒΑΛΛΩ ΤΑ ΔΑΙΜΟΝΙΑ! . . . [Luke 11:19]," in *The Miracles of Jesus* (ed. David Wenham and Craig Blomberg; Gospel Perspectives 6; Sheffield: JSOT Press, 1986), 380–81. Cf. Rudolf Bultmann, *The History of the Synoptic Tradition* (Oxford: Blackwell, 1963), 164, who says that the saying was "not intended to function as a criticism of exorcism, but rather to warn the person who is healed to be wary of demonic powers," citing, e.g., John 5:14 and *Acts of Thomas* 46.

105. T. W. Manson, *The Sayings of Jesus* (London: SCM: 1949), 88. See also, Marshall, *Luke*, 479; Allison, *Jesus Tradition*, 127. Irenaeus took this story to mean that those delivered of evil spirits were not "waiting upon God, but occupied with mere worldly questions" (*Haer.* 1.16.3).

106. E.g., Luz, *Matthew 8–20*, 220–21.

107. See those cited and discussed by Davies and Allison, *Matthew*, 2:359.

108. Marshall, *Luke*, 479, citing Marie-Joseph Lagrange, *Évangile selon Saint Luc* (5th ed.; Paris: Lecoffre, 1941), 333–34; and Schulz, *Q*, 479–80.

saying that those who are not gathering with Jesus are scattering (11:23), this story about the returning evil spirit is probably intended as a call for the readers to make sure that those from whom unclean spirits are cast out are gathered into the followers of Jesus. That is, the readers need to be doing what Jesus was doing (11:23), gathering. If they are not, the results of their (Christian or non-Christian) exorcisms can only be temporary, individuals becoming worse than before the healings. If this reading of Q is correct, this story is not primarily a critique of exorcists outside of the faith[109]—though it would be that as well—but a criticism of Christian exorcists not gathering the healed people into the followers of Jesus.

4.11 Conclusions

Due to there being so many uncertainties regarding Q, in particular about its extent, in the opening of this chapter we acknowledged the provisional nature of any of our conclusions. Notwithstanding, the results that have emerged from our discussion are important, not least because Q may give us an early representation of exorcism among early Christians. The net result of reading the text for clues about the readers themselves is that they can probably be described as poor and beleaguered, conservative, Jewish members of the Jesus movement in northern and western Galilee. Their success in a likely reluctant mission to their fellow Jews, especially in exorcism, has been painful, limited, and rejected. For they probably had to face the criticism that their exorcisms, perhaps at least because of their puzzling simplicity, were empowered by Satan. And with so little thought to distinguish the exorcisms of Jesus from those of his contemporaries—and presumably, therefore, his followers—it is not surprising that those who published Q did not place a high premium on exorcism.

In turn, Q can be read as an encouragement in, and an elucidation of, mission revolving primarily around presenting Jesus as a model. Therefore, through the relatively low showing of exorcism in the ministry of Jesus, and through exorcism never being explicitly portrayed as part of the ministry of his followers, we can speculate that Q is reflecting the low value of exorcism in the Jesus movement. Nevertheless, over against their difficulties with exorcism, through a careful presentation of the traditions, Q conveys a number of points in relation to exorcism that show its practice and assert its importance and significance in the eschatological battle that described its mission.

Early on the readers learn that Jesus is empowered by the Spirit, not by Satan, that he will baptize others with this Spirit, and also that, over against using miraculous power for selfish ends, Jesus and—by implication

---

109. Allison, *Jesus Tradition*, 127.

or association—his followers are to recognize their dependence on God in performing miracles, including exorcisms. Through the harvest metaphor being used both for the mission of the followers of Jesus and for exorcism in particular, as well as tying exorcism to the kingdom of God, and the kingdom of God being the message of the followers of Jesus, Q shows the importance of exorcism and that it is also to be part of the mission of the followers of Jesus as they, with him, engage in the eschatological battle. In the Beelzebul controversy readers are told that the exorcisms of Jesus (and his followers, we can suppose) are not only empowered by the eschatological Spirit of God. The exorcisms of Jesus and his followers are also visible expressions of the coming of the kingdom of God, in which people are rescued as if spoil from a guarded castle so they can be, to use another Q metaphor, harvested or gathered as followers of Jesus. Indeed, in the story of the homeless spirit, readers are informed that exorcism is only part of the eschatological healing process; it needs to include "gathering," or the state of the person involved will be even worse than formerly. The eschatological significance of exorcism is not only conveyed in the mission metaphors of harvest and gathering (cf. §6.2e below). Through a very brief story, exorcism is also portrayed as "casting out" the demon—as if being an enemy of God—so that God's purposes can be fulfilled.

5

Mark

MARK HAS A great deal to say about exorcism.[1] However, the difficulty in setting out Mark's views on the subject in the post-Easter church is that, on a prima facie reading, he tells his readers very little about the post-Easter community[2] and, in particular, nothing about exorcism in that community.[3] Nevertheless, at least for Mark to introduce his book by describing its contents as "gospel" (Mark 1:1)—regardless of whether he is referring to a literary genre or, more probably, the good news it contained about Jesus[4]—shows that he considers he is writing more than "history"; he considers it has

---

1. Mark 1:21–28, 32–34; 3:7–30; 5:1–20; 6:7–13; 7:24–30; 9:14–29, 38–39 relate most directly to exorcism.

2. Mark's post-Easter perspective is clearest at Mark 13:9–13; 14:27–28; 16:7.

3. On the longer ending of Mark, which mentions exorcism, see §11.1 below.

4. The phrase τοῦ εὐαγγελίου Ἰησοῦ Χριστοῦ (Mark 1:1) is more likely to be an objective genitive ("the good news about Jesus Christ") rather than a subjective genitive ("the good news by/of Jesus Christ"), for this corresponds with Mark's redactional use of εὐαγγέλιον (see 8:35; 10:29; 13:10; 14:9) as well as the way the early church used the word (see, e.g., Acts 15:7; Rom. 1:16; 1 Cor. 4:15; 9:14; Gal. 2:5, 14; Eph. 3:6; 6:15, 19; Phil. 1:7, 12, 16, 27; 4:15; Col. 1:5, 23; 2 Thess. 2:14; 2 Tim. 1:10; Philem. 13). Cf. Robert A. Guelich, *Mark 1–8:26* (WBC 34A; Dallas: Word Books, 1989), 9.

positive implications for his readers. Indeed, there are places through his text where he appears to be addressing his readers quite directly,[5] perhaps in Rome[6] around 70 CE.[7]

5.1 A Methodology

Notwithstanding, an important methodological task is to determine a reliable way of discovering what Mark intended to say about exorcism in relation to the post-Easter community.[8] (In this, mindful that New Testament scholarship is increasingly free from the constraints of *Formgeschichte* and that it is no longer necessary or possible to presuppose that the Gospels were written either for or to reflect the views of a particular church or group of churches,[9] I shall assume no more than that, along with the other Gospel writers, Mark is writing for the wider church, expressing his own views on exorcism in the post-Easter community that have been informed by his experiences in a more limited setting; in his case, perhaps in Rome.)

5. The clearest example is Mark 13:14, "Let the reader understand." See also 14:37–38 where, having addressed Peter in the singular ("Could you not [οὐκ ἴσχυσας] keep awake . . . ?"), Jesus then says, in the plural, "Keep awake and pray [γρηγορεῖτε καὶ προσεύχεσθε]. . . ." See Ernest Best, *Disciples and Discipleship: Studies in the Gospel according to Mark* (Edinburgh: T&T Clark, 1986), 130. On 13:37, "What I say to you I say to all," see below.

6. See the discussion by Martin Hengel, *Studies in Mark's Gospel* (London: SCM, 1985), 28–30. Cf. E. Earle Ellis, "The Date and Provenance of Mark's Gospel," in *The Four Gospels, 1992: Festschrift Frans Neirynck* (ed. F. van Segbroeck et al.; 3 vols.; Louvain: Leuven University Press, 1992), 2:809–812, arguing for Caesarea in light of Mark's association with Peter, its Latinisms, Gentile perspective, and Gentile interests.

7. See the brief and balanced discussion by Morna D. Hooker, *The Gospel according to St Mark* (BNTC; London: Black, 1991), 7–8. Although earlier dates have been long supported—see those cited by John S. Kloppenborg, "*Evocatio Deorum* and the Date of Mark," *JBL* 124 (2005): 419–50, esp. 419n1—for a fresh approach to the problem, see James G. Crossley, *The Date of Mark's Gospel: Insight from the Law in Earliest Christianity* (JSNTSup 266; London: T&T Clark, 2004), 208, who suggests a date between the late 30s and the mid-40s.

8. See the discussion by John R. Donahue, "The Quest for the Community of Mark's Gospel," in van Segbroeck et al., *Four Gospels, 1992,* 2:817–38.

9. On the current debate about the audiences of the Gospels sparked by Richard Bauckham, "For Whom Were Gospels Written?" in *The Gospel for All Christians: Rethinking the Gospel Audiences* (ed. Richard Bauckham; Grand Rapids and Cambridge, UK: Eerdmans, 1998), 9–48, see, e.g., Philip F. Esler, "Community and Gospel in Early Christianity: A Response to Richard Bauckham's Gospels for All Christians," *SJT* 51 (1998): 235–48; Ernst van Eck, "A Sitz for the Gospel of Mark? A Critical Reaction to Bauckham's Theory on the Universality of the Gospels," *HvTSt* 56 (2000): 973–1008; David C. Sim, "The Gospels for all Christians? A Response to Richard Bauckham," *JSNT* 84 (2001): 3–27; Wendy E. Sproston North, "John for Readers of Mark? A Response to Richard Bauckham's Proposal," *JSNT* 25 (2003): 449–68, esp. 449–50 and nn. 3–4. On the publication and circulation of literature in the ancient world, see Harry Y. Gamble, *Books and Readers in the Early Church: A History of Early Christian Texts* (New Haven and London: Yale University Press, 1994), chap. 3.

Arguably, the narrational feature through which Mark conveys his understanding of exorcism in the post-Easter community is the theme of disciples and discipleship. However, the complexity of Mark's portrayal of the disciples frequently defies reasonable interpretation.[10] On the one hand, representing a radical approach, T. J. Weeden concluded that Mark was "assiduously involved in a vendetta against the disciples. He is intent on totally discrediting them. He paints them as obtuse, obdurate, recalcitrant men who at first are unperceptive of Jesus' messiahship, then oppose its style and character, and finally totally reject it. As the coup de grâce, Mark closes his Gospel without rehabilitating the disciples."[11] But this view does not take into account the positive aspects of Mark's portrayal of the disciples—as close associates of Jesus,[12] as being given the secret of the kingdom of God (Mark 4:11), as being privy to special teaching (4:34; 9:28–29), and as sharing in Jesus' ministry (6:7–13; 9:14–29).

On the other hand, more traditional approaches emphasize the historical perspective, arguing that Mark sees the historical disciples as providing the means—as well as the theological continuity—for the ministry of Jesus to be extended beyond Easter in the mission of the church.[13] But this approach landlocks the story of Jesus and his immediate followers so that they are put

10. On the variety of approaches to the theme of disciples and discipleship in Mark, see, e.g., Francis J. Maloney, "The Vocation of the Disciples in the Gospel of Mark," *Salesianum* 43 (1981): 487–516; John R. Donahue, "A Neglected Factor in the Theology of Mark," *JBL* 101 (1982): 563–95, esp. 582–87; and particularly C. Clifton Black, *The Disciples according to Mark: Markan Redaction in Current Debate* (JSNTSup 27; Sheffield: JSOT Press, 1989), 46–59.

11. T. J. Weeden, *Mark: Traditions in Conflict* (Philadelphia: Fortress, 1971), 50–51. See the review of Weeden by C. J. A. Hickling, "A Problem of Method in Gospel Research," *RelS* 10 (1974): 339–46; and Ralph P. Martin, *Mark: Evangelist and Theologian* (Exeter, UK: Paternoster, 1972), 150–53. See also T. J. Weeden, "The Heresy That Necessitated Mark's Gospel," *ZNW* 59 (1968): 145–68. For similar perspectives see also, e.g., Joseph B. Tyson, "The Blindness of the Disciples in Mark," *JBL* 80 (1961): 261–68; Werner H. Kelber, *The Kingdom in Mark: A New Place and a New Time* (Philadelphia: Fortress, 1974), 82–84; Werner H. Kelber, "The Hour of the Son of Man and the Temptation of the Disciples (Mark 14:32–42)," in *The Passion in Mark* (ed. Werner H. Kelber; Philadelphia: Fortress, 1976), 41–60; Kim E. Dewey, "Peter's Curse and Cursed Peter (Mark 14:53–54, 66–72)," in Kelber, *Passion in Mark*, 96–114.

12. Mark 1:17, 21; 3:14, 31–35.

13. E.g., Wim Burgers, "De Instelling van de Twaalf in het Evangelie van Marcus," *ETL* 36 (1960): 625–54; Robert P. Meye, "Messianic Secret and Messianic Didache in Mark's Gospel," in *Oikonomia: Heilsgeschichte als Thema der Theologie* (ed. Felix Christ; Hamburg-Bergstedt: Herbert Reich, 1967), 57–68, esp. 60; Robert P. Meye, *Jesus and the Twelve: Discipleship and Revelation in Mark's Gospel* (Grand Rapids: Eerdmans, 1968), esp. 55–56, 71–73, 78, 105, 109, 115, 123–62, 179–81, 219–22; Karl Kertelge, "Die Funktion der 'Zwölf' im Markusevangelium: Eine redaktionsgeschichtliche Auslegung . . . ," *TTZ* 78 (1969): 193–206; Günther Schmahl, "Die Berufung der Zwölf im Markusevangelium," *TTZ* 81 (1972): 203–13; Günther Schmahl, *Die Zwölf im Markusevangelium: Eine redaktionsgeschichtliche Untersuchung* (TThSt 30; Trier: Paulinus, 1974), esp. 143; Klemens Stock, *Boten aus dem Mit-Ihm-Sein: Das Verhältnis zwischen Jesus und den Zwölf nach Markus* (AnBib 70; Rome: Pontifical Biblical Institute, 1975), esp. 191.

out of reach of even Mark's first audience. This view also does not take into account negative aspects of the portrait of the disciples.[14] In other words, all this view does is make a connection between Jesus and the post-Easter community; it does not bring the message of Mark to the world of his readers as effectively as does a median position.

Ernest Best has provided a median position in his detailed and sustained argument for the interpretative key to unlocking the narrative, to hear what Mark wants to say, including about exorcism among post-Easter Christians.[15] Best has drawn attention to two aspects of Mark's redaction that show that the function of the theme of disciples and discipleship in the second Gospel was to teach his readers about discipleship. One feature to take into account is a telling phrase in 13:37.[16] This verse contains not only Jesus' final words in the so-called little apocalypse of chapter 13; it also follows, and is part of, the parable of the doorkeeper and the slaves (Mark 13:34). This parable concludes the whole of the systematic teaching of Jesus before the passion narrative begins (14:1) and is used to apply the teaching of Jesus to his readers.[17] Jesus' final words here include the statement, "And what I say to you"—which Mark's readers would have understood to be the historical disciples (see 13:3)—"I say to all," meaning the readers of the Gospel.[18] In other words, all the teaching to the disciples and on discipleship is intended to be understood as being for the readers of this Gospel.[19]

In the parable of the doorkeeper and the slaves itself (Mark 13:34), there may be further confirmation that what applied to the Twelve—Mark's preferred term for the disciples[20]—also applied to the readers. For, not only is this parable immediately applied to the readers (13:37), but already through

14. Black, *Disciples*, 46.

15. E.g., Ernest Best, "Discipleship in Mark: Mark 8.22–10.52," *SJT* 23 (1970): 323–93; Ernest Best, "The Role of the Disciples in Mark," *NTS* 23 (1976–77): 377–401; Ernest Best, "Mark's Use of the Twelve," *ZNW* 69 (1978): 11–35; Ernest Best, *Following Jesus: Discipleship in the Gospel of Mark* (JSNTSup 4; Sheffield: JSOT Press, 1981); Ernest Best, *Disciples and Discipleship*. See the discussion in Black, *Disciples*, chap. 2.

16. Whether Mark 13:37 is redactional, as generally thought— see, e.g., Rudolf Pesch, *Naherwartungen: Tradition und Redaktion in Mark 13* (KBANT; Düsseldorf: Patmos, 1968), 202—or is from Mark's tradition—see e.g., David Wenham, *The Rediscovery of Jesus' Eschatological Discourse* (Sheffield: JSOT Press, 1984), 57—the significance of this verse is not greatly changed.

17. See C. H. Dodd, *The Parables of the Kingdom* (1935; repr., London and Glasgow: Collins / Fontana, 1961), 122; Charles B. Cousar, "Eschatology and Mark's *Theologia Crucis*: A Critical Analysis of Mark 13," *Int* 24 (1970): 322, 334.

18. See Cousar, "Eschatology," 334. In the use of δοῦλοι in 13:34 Mark may already be applying this parable to his readers. See Pesch, *Naherwartungen*, 198.

19. George R. Beasley-Murray, *Jesus and the Last Days: The Interpretation of the Olivet Discourse* (Peabody, MA: Hendrickson, 1993), 474, noted that, "By a curious coincidence Luke follows the variant parable of the Watching Servants and that of the Burglar with the question of Peter, 'Lord, are you speaking this parable to us or to all?' (Luke 12:41)," making Mark's point explicit.

20. Best, *Disciples and Discipleship*, chap. 8.

the characters of the slaves, Mark's audience would have been drawn into the story because early Christians understood themselves as slaves of Christ.[21] That is, through this parable Mark probably conveys to his readers that the teaching of Jesus applies to them.[22]

Besides Mark 13:37 and its context, the other feature of Mark's narrative that indicates he is using the theme of discipleship to communicate his views about post-Easter Christianity is the way some stories end with instructions to the disciples. Most clear is the example—which we will deal with in more detail in a moment—that, after the fiasco of the disciples' attempt to heal the lad with epileptic-like symptoms, there is teaching on how to conduct an exorcism (Mark 9:28–29).[23] Once one notices these two features—13:37 and some stories ending with instructions to the disciples—it becomes reasonable to maintain that Mark is using the disciples in his narrative as paradigms of discipleship for his readers. Or, as David J. Hawkins put it, "the disciples are made to be figures representative of the church."[24] This means that Mark is using his portrait of the historical disciples to challenge his readers to take up and enter the same discipleship.[25] In turn, it is also reasonable to maintain that through his theme of discipleship Mark will be the most transparent in what he says about exorcism among early Christians. We will find this confirmed narratively as we follow Mark's portrayal of the disciples' attempt to emulate Jesus' ministry (see on 6:7–12, 13 and 9:14–29 below).

Given this conclusion, we will need to give attention to the section 8:22 (or 27)–10:52, which is generally agreed to form the center of Mark's pedagogy on discipleship.[26] Account will also have to be taken of other pericopae in which the disciples feature in relation to exorcism (Mark 3:13–15; 6:7–13; 5:1–20). Some attention will be given to Jesus as an exorcist, on whom Mark models exorcism for his readers. However, before we proceed, we need to determine how Mark wished his motif of exorcism to be understood.

5.2 The Politics of Possession

With the dominance of the scientific approach to understanding sickness and healing among students of the New Testament, demonic possession is

21. See Karl H. Rengstorf, "δοῦλος . . . ," *TDNT* 2:273–77.
22. Cf. Ernst Lohmeyer, *Das Evangelium des Markus* (KEK 2; Göttingen: Vandenhoeck & Ruprecht, 1951), 285, who also sees the plural δοῦλοι indicating that the Markan readers are in mind.
23. See also, e.g., Mark 4:10–34; 7:17–23; 8:34–9:1.
24. David J. Hawkins, "The Incomprehension of the Disciples in the Markan Redaction," *JBL* 91 (1972): 497.
25. Cf. Best, *Following*, "Introduction," 246.
26. Best, "Discipleship in Mark," 323–37.

generally taken to be some form of mental condition or physical illness such as epilepsy.[27] Although this may well be the case, there is no evidence that Mark took this perspective. Alternatively, according to a recurring theme in New Testament scholarship, the demonic is to be interpreted socio-politically, both from Mark's perspective[28] as well as at a historical level.[29] For example, from Mark's perspective in the story of the exorcism in the synagogue at Capernaum, the demon is taken to represent the scribal establishment so that the exorcism itself obliquely symbolizes the casting out of the scribal class.[30] At the historical level, the mental illness—which is to be understood socio-psychologically—is caused, or at least exacerbated, by the social tensions of Roman colonialism, and led to possession functioning as a fix for those who felt politically trapped and unable to cope.[31]

It is one thing to argue that Jesus' acts of power challenged the very social structures of Palestine.[32] Indeed, we see this to be Mark's view of healing in the story of the cleansing of the leper, where Jesus tells the healed man to show himself to the religious authorities (Mark 1:44), and also in the story of the man let down through the roof, in which Jesus is engaged in a debate with the scribes (2:6–10). Further, Mark portrays Jesus' detractors as quick to take up the religious and socio-political implications of his ministry (e.g., 8:10–12; 10:2–12; 12:13–17). However, it is quite another thing to argue "that demon symbolism served not only as a means for the oppressed to express their degradation, but also as a means for the nervous dominant classes to subdue those who protested against their oppressors."[33] In fact, it is not difficult to show that Mark's interest in this theme was not primarily socio-political. Two passages make this clear.

One place that enables us to see that Mark's broad view of Satan or the demonic is other than socio-political is in the Temptation narrative (Mark 1:12–13). By its early position in the Gospel it is narrationally important for informing hearers' opinions about Jesus as well as introducing and characterizing

27. E.g., E. P. Sanders, *The Historical Figure of Jesus* (London: Penguin, 1993), 159; John Dominic Crossan, *Jesus: A Revolutionary Biography* (San Francisco: HarperSanFrancisco, 1994), 84–93. Cf. §1.1 above.

28. E.g., Ched Myers, *Binding the Strong Man: A Political Reading of Mark's Story of Jesus* (Maryknoll, NY: Orbis, 1994), 31.

29. E.g., Paul W. Hollenbach, "Jesus, Demoniacs, and Public Authorities: A Socio-Historical Study," *JAAR* 49 (1981): 567–88; Santiago Guijarro, "The Politics of Exorcism," in *The Social Setting of Jesus and the Gospels* (ed. Wolfgang Stegemann, Bruce J. Malina, and Gerd Theissen; Minneapolis: Fortress, 2002), 165–67, 171–72.

30. Myers, *Binding*, 138, 143; cf. 192–94, 288.

31. Hollenbach, "Demoniacs," 572–84, relying particularly on Erika Bourguignon, *Possession* (San Francisco: Chandler & Sharp, 1976); and Frantz Fanon, *The Wretched of the Earth* (New York: Ballantine, 1963). See also Myers, *Binding*, 31.

32. Myers, *Binding*, 147–48. At the historical level see Guijarro, "Politics," 165–67, 171–72.

33. Hollenbach, "Demoniacs," 580, relying on Thomas S. Szasz, *Ideology and Insanity: Essays on the Psychiatric De-Humanization of Man* (Garden City, NY: Doubleday, 1970).

an anti-hero.[34] By having the Temptation story follow directly after reporting the voice from heaven declaring "You are my Son" (1:11), Mark brings to the hearer's mind Israel's wilderness temptations, in which the nation's faithfulness as a son is being tested (Deut. 8:2–10),[35] rather than Israel's political liberation from the pharaoh's Egypt.[36] Although historically the perceived identity of Jesus as a (or the) Son of God may have had considerable political repercussions, the temporal nature and implications of Jesus' sonship are not uppermost in Mark's mind. Instead, his interest in Jesus' sonship is focused on its otherworldly dimensions.

We see the otherworldly dimensions positively in that, although Jesus' identity is questioned by the chief priest at his Sanhedrin trial (Mark 14:61), Jesus' identity as Son of God is dealt with almost exclusively outside the temporal realm of his story. His sonship is introduced narratively (1:1),[37] established and confirmed by a voice from heaven (1:11; 9:7), reaffirmed by evil spirits (3:11; 5:7), and only finally recognized by a human character (a Roman centurion) at the foot of the cross (15:39). From a negative perspective we can see—in light of Jesus' frequent conflicts with Satan through the debate with the Pharisees, in which their religious error is confronted (8:12; 10:2), and through the disciples in their mistaken messianism (8:33)—that Mark takes the issue of Jesus' identity not into but out of the political arena.

The other passage that gives us insight into Mark's political perspective in relation to the demonic and exorcism is his parable of the strong man (Mark 3:27). Given the context of an exorcism story (3:22–26), Mark most probably intends the parable to be about exorcism and the strong man to represent Satan. So clearly does this parable echo Isaiah 49:24–25[38]—where God says to the doubting that "the captives of the mighty shall be taken, and the prey of the tyrant be rescued" (Isa. 49:25)—that we can expect this Old Testament passage to have informed Mark's hearers' understanding of the parable. Basic to Second Isaiah is God's people being precious to him and the object of his

34. Cf. Bas M. F. van Iersel, *Mark: A Reader-Response Commentary* (JSNTSup 164; Sheffield: Sheffield Academic, 1998), 102–3.

35. Cf., e.g., Robert H. Gundry, *Mark* (Grand Rapids: Eerdmans, 1993), 59; Richard T. France, *The Gospel of Mark* (Grand Rapids and Cambridge, UK: Eerdmans; Carlisle, UK: Paternoster, 2002), 85.

36. So Myers, *Binding*, 130; Herman C. Waetjen, *A Reordering of Power: A Sociopolitical Reading of Mark's Gospel* (Minneapolis: Fortress, 1989), 75.

37. On the textual difficulties relating to the status of "Son of God" (υἱοῦ [τοῦ] θεοῦ) in Mark 1:1, see Vincent Taylor, *The Gospel according to St. Mark* (London: Macmillan, 1952), 152; Bruce M. Metzger, *A Textual Commentary on the Greek New Testament* (2nd ed.; New York: American Bible Society, 1994), 62; and Rudolf Pesch, *Das Markusevangelium* (HTKNT 2.1–2; Freiburg: Herder, 1980), 1.74 n. (a).

38. Cf. France, *Mark*, 173; Eric Sorensen, *Possession and Exorcism in the New Testament and Early Christianity* (WUNT 2.157; Tübingen: Mohr Siebeck, 2002), 140–41.

compassion.[39] In the face of incredulity, God promises to rescue his people from Babylonian captivity (49:24–25); thus the hearers of Mark would probably understand that, in exorcism—theirs as well as those of Jesus—their compassionate God was rescuing people from a mighty enemy. Mark's readers would also have seen that what was a political captivity and promise of rescue is said to be realized in a personal, individual, and internalized fashion in exorcism.[40] In other words, exorcism is taken out of the political arena and interpreted otherwise. We need to note that it cannot be that, through association with the Isaiah passage, exorcism is being politicized, for no corporate or external dimension is given to exorcism to suggest that.

Our conclusion on Mark's broad understanding of Jesus' almost uninterrupted battle with Satan and his disfiguring grip on people (cf. Mark 3:27)[41]— not least in the exorcisms (3:22–27)—is bound to be that Mark does not see it as taking place in the socio-political but in the spiritual or cosmic arena, which is expressed in the personal realm. We can see this lack of interest in the political interpretation of exorcism in a story that is most often taken to lend support to the socio-political explanation of demon possession and exorcism.

The story of the Gerasene demoniac (Mark 5:1–20) appears to have political and military overtones, most obviously in the name "legion" (λεγιών, 5:9, 15) being used of the demon.[42] According to Ched Myers, for example, this Latinism (from *legio*) "had only one meaning in Mark's world: a division of Roman soldiers."[43] Thus, it is argued, when the word was used it always had military connotations. Indeed, Klaus Wengst wonders if any one can "conceive of any ancient hearer or reader who would *not* think of Roman troops in connection with the name 'Legion.'"[44] However, noting the use of the word around the time when Mark was writing considerably modifies this view. Although the word may have had a military origin, it had lost its exclusively military ties to take on a metaphorical meaning that was no longer determined by its origin.

39. Paul D. Hanson, *Isaiah 40–66* (Louisville: John Knox, 1995), 126.

40. Cf. Sorensen, *Possession*, 140.

41. Further see Graham H. Twelftree, "Temptation of Jesus," *DJG* 825–26; James M. Robinson, *The Problem of History in Mark* (SBT 21; London: SCM, 1957), e.g., 33.

42. Cf., e.g., Gerd Theissen, *Miracle Stories of the Early Christian Tradition* (Edinburgh: T&T Clark, 1983), 255–59; Walter Wink, *Unmasking the Powers: The Invisible Forces That Determine Human Existence* (The Powers 2; Philadelphia: Fortress, 1986), 43–47; Richard Dormandy, "The Expulsion of Legion: A Political Reading of Mark 5:1–20," *ExpTim* 111 (2000): 335–37.

43. Myers, *Binding*, 191; cf. 141–43. Cf. J. Duncan M. Derrett, "Contributions to the Study of the Gerasene Demoniac," *JSNT* 3 (1979): 5: "The word 'legion' has only a military association." Also see Dean W. Chapman, *Orphan Gospel: Mark's Perspective on Jesus* (The Biblical Seminar 16; Sheffield: JSOT Press, 1993), 117–22, esp. 121.

44. Klaus Wengst, *Pax Romana and the Peace of Jesus Christ* (Philadelphia: Fortress, 1987), 66 (his emphasis), who also notes that midrash of *Gen. Rab.* 65.1 (fifth or sixth century CE) compares the Roman state to swine.

This can be seen in Pliny the Elder (23/24–79 CE) writing about a legion of crimes (*Nat.* 33.26). Even in Latin, well before the time Mark was writing, the playwright Plautus (ca. 254–184 BCE) was using the word figuratively for a "legion of supporters" (*Cas.* 50).

Also instructive is Matthew's use of the phrase "legions of angels" (Matt. 26:53). In using "legion" just as other writers of the time used "myriads" with angels to indicate a great number,[45] Matthew shows that he did not assume "legion" to be carrying any military connotations. In any case, the number of pigs drowned in Mark 5:13 is said to be 2,000, which is not a number that Mark would have used if he was attempting to call to mind a military legion. For, although the number in a Roman legion varied from 4,200 to 6,000 men, at the time of Augustus as emperor (27 BCE–14 CE) it was around 5,000 soldiers, plus 120 cavalry.[46] Thus, although the word "legion" had military origins and overtones, the deliberate eschewing of a number that would have given exorcism a sociopolitical dimension suggests that Mark is not taking up this perspective.

Considering the setting of the story raises another question against the view that this story is "meant to call to mind the Roman military occupation of Palestine,"[47] as Myers concludes. Mark's setting of the story as "the country of the Gerasenes" (Mark 5:1) is notoriously problematic,[48] though it could be his general term for the region of Decapolis.[49] In any case, the setting is clearly Gentile territory.[50] Mark situates the story on "the other" (πέραν), or east, side of the sea (5:1), and at the end of the story the setting is clearly Decapolis (5:20; cf. 7:31), which is also Gentile territory, not Jewish.[51] From

45. See Hans Dieter Betz, "Legion," *DDD* 507, citing Dan. 7:10; Heb. 12:22; Jude 14; Rev. 5:11; 9:16; *PGM* I. 208–209; IV. 1203–1204; and BDAG, "μυριάς," §2. Cf. *T. Sol.* 11.3.

46. See J. Brian Campbell, "Legio," in *Brill's New Pauly: Encyclopaedia of the Ancient World* (ed. Hubert Cancik and Helmuth Schneider; Leiden and Boston: Brill, 2002–), 7:356–58; BDAG, "λεγιών," 587–88; OCD 839.

47. Myers, *Binding*, 191.

48. See, e.g., Tjitze Baarda, "Gadarenes, Gerasenes, Gergesenes and the 'Diatessaron' Traditions," in *Neotestamentica et Semitica: Studies in Honour of Matthew Black* (ed. E. Earle Ellis and Max Wilcox; Edinburgh: T&T Clark, 1969), 181–97; Metzger, *Commentary*, 72.

49. See the discussion in France, *Mark*, 227. Mark (5:20; 7:31) provides our earliest use of this term, implying that it is a region (cf. Pliny the Elder, *Nat.* 5.16).

50. See Mark 5:20; 7:31; and the discussion by S. Thomas Parker, "The Decapolis Reviewed," *JBL* 94 (1975): 437–41; France, *Mark*, 302 and n. 50.

51. See, e.g., Josephus, *Life* 341–342, 410. Cf. France, *Mark*, 227, 229 and n. 12. Carl H. Kraeling, ed., *Gerasa: City of the Decapolis* (New Haven: American Schools of Oriental Research, 1938), 33–45. It could be that, as Waetjen, *Reordering*, 116, says, "In view of the Parthian threat it would seem that a Roman presence would have to be stationed in Gerasa in order to guard both the frontier and the trade routes from the east and the south." Such in fact appears to have been the case, for Kraeling (*Gerasa*, 40) refers to a Roman garrison stationed in the city. Perhaps the στρατηγός ("chief magistrate") that the Romans under Pompey had placed over the "free" cities of what had once been Coelesyria, as Josephus indicates in *Ant.* 14.74, may have resided in Gerasa. Certainly this was true at least by Mark's time, after the destruction of Jerusalem, because Vespasian had established a garrison there.

such a setting, Mark's readers are unlikely to hear a story about Jewish liberation from Roman occupation.

In light of what we have noted about the use of λεγιών, as well as Mark's general perspective in portraying Jesus' battle with the demonic, it is unlikely that other less significant vocabulary can bear the weight of the theory that this story of the Gerasene demoniac is to be interpreted primarily in military and political terms.[52] Therefore, the idea that this story has such military overtones as to suggest to Mark's readers that it is a symbolic account of Jesus' mission to liberate Palestine from the Romans is unconvincing.[53] In light of Mark's general interest in portraying Jesus in battle with Satan, not the Romans, it is more reasonable to suppose, with Rikki Watts, that Mark understood the ultimate oppressor to be the demonic rather than the Romans.[54]

Further confirmation of this comes in noting that a political perspective is also not easily established in Mark's other exorcism stories. For example, Herman Waetjen has suggested that the exorcism story in the synagogue at Capernaum (Mark 1:21–28) is set in a synagogue "in order to liberate a fellow Jew from its oppression and dispossession."[55] He arrives at this conclusion in two stages. First, without argument, he suggests that the human institutions that consume human acquisitions had been demonized in the Jewish apocalyptic interpretation of the myth of Genesis 6:1–4 by *1 Enoch*.[56] However, this makes short shrift of the long-standing difficulty of identifying the giants and other figures in *1 Enoch* 7.[57] The second step in Waetjen's argument is to say that, in view of the location of the encounter with the demoniac, "it is difficult to avoid the conclusion that the synagogue as a socio-religious institution is insinuated to be one of those giants."[58] For support of this statement, we would be looking to Mark for evidence that he is otherwise critical of the synagogue, evidence we do not find. What we find in Mark is a positive use of the synagogue as a venue for Jesus' ministry (1:39) and criticism not of the synagogue itself but of its misuse (cf. 12:39).[59] Clearly, Waetjen's case does not stand.

52. For a less than convincing discussion of the terms ἀποστείλη ("dispatch"? 5:10), ἀγέλη ("herd" or "troop"? 5:11), ἐπιτρέπειν ("order"? 5:13) and ὥρμησεν ("rushed" into battle? 5:13) in terms of their possible military association, see Derrett, "Contributions," 5–6.

53. Cf. France, *Mark*, 229: "Ingeniously constructed around certain graphic terms in the story, this theory suffers from the apparent inability of virtually all readers of the story until now to have grasped the point Mark allegedly intended to make."

54. Rikki Watts, *Isaiah's New Exodus and Mark* (WUNT 2.88; Tübingen: Mohr Siebeck, 1997), e.g., 163.

55. Waetjen, *Reordering*, 82.

56. Waetjen, *Reordering*, 82.

57. On the difficulty of identifying the meaning of the terms in *1 En.* 7, see George W. E. Nickelsburg, *1 Enoch 1* (Minneapolis: Fortress, 2001), 182–87; and Archie T. Wright, *The Origin of Evil Spirits: The Reception of Genesis 6.1–4 in Early Jewish Literature* (WUNT 2.198; Tübingen: Mohr Siebeck, 2005), chap. 4.

58. Waetjen, *Reordering*, 82.

59. Cf. Wolfgang Schrage, "συναγωγή . . . ," *TDNT* 8:833.

From our discussion of the politics of possession, it is reasonable to conclude that Mark did not intend his readers to interpret the demonic as socio-political domination, or to see exorcism as symbolic of socio-political liberation. Rather, Jesus and (by implication) the readers of this Gospel were battling Satan, not the Romans, and that liberation came not through political freedom but on a personal level through exorcism. We are now in a position to look more closely at what Mark has to say about exorcism among early Christians.

5.3 The Disciples Authorized as Exorcists (Mark 3:13–15)

If, as we argued, Mark's views on exorcism in the post-Easter community will be reflected most clearly in what he says about exorcism in relation to the disciples, we need to give careful attention to those places where Mark deals with exorcism and the disciples.

Immediately after the mission announcement (Mark 1:14–15), Mark has Jesus choose four men to "follow" (ἀκολουθεῖν) him (1:16–20), ἀκολουθεῖν usually being a technical term for discipleship in Mark.[60] The narrative then goes on to depict the newly called disciples often accompanying Jesus, when he teaches (1:21, 29), exorcises (1:21–28), heals (1:29–31), is at dinner in Levi's house (2:15), and is going through a grainfield one Sabbath (2:23–28). There are a few times when Jesus is portrayed as being alone (e.g., 1:35–36), or it is at least implied that he is without the disciples when healing (1:40) or teaching (2:1–12). However, from the point when the Twelve are appointed (3:14) they are almost constantly with him. The clearest notable exceptions of Jesus' absences are when the disciples have difficulty in rowing against the wind (6:45–52), when Jesus is present (but asleep) during a storm (4:35–41), and, important for our study, when the disciples have difficulty in performing an exorcism (9:14–29).

Portraying the followers of Jesus as almost constantly with him plays out the first reason Mark gives for appointing the Twelve—"in order to be with him" (ἵνα ὦσιν μετ' αὐτοῦ, Mark 3:14; see also 5:18).[61] Then, through repeating the word ἵνα ("in order that") in 3:14, Mark gives a second reason—or, more accurately, a pair of reasons—for the Twelve being appointed: "to proclaim the message, and to have authority to cast out demons" (3:14–15). Surprisingly, in light of Jesus' ministry (2:1–12), which the Twelve are portrayed as emulating, there is no mention of the disciples offering forgiveness; Jesus

---

60. "To follow" (ἀκολουθεῖν) is in Mark at 1:18; 2:14, 15; 3:7; 5:24; 6:1; 8:34 (bis); 9:38; 10:21, 28, 32, 52; 11:9; 14:13, 54; 15:41; (16:17). See Martin Hengel, *The Charismatic Leader and His Followers* (Edinburgh: T&T Clark, 1981), 50–57.

61. On Mark's portrayal here in 3:13–35 of characters being either "inside" or "outside" Jesus' circle, see Stephen C. Barton, *Discipleship and Family Ties in Mark and Matthew* (SNTSMS 80; Cambridge: Cambridge University Press, 1994), 74–79.

alone has this authority.[62] Nor is there any mention of healing. In a number of ways this draws attention to the importance of exorcism in the ministry of the followers of Jesus.

First, even though the actual description of the ministry of the Twelve includes curing the sick (Mark 6:13), in both the story of the commissioning (3:14–15) and in the sending out of the Twelve (6:7), other than proclaiming the message, exorcism is the only task assigned to them. Secondly, the authority that arises out of being appointed (3:14–15; cf. 6:7) is frequently associated with exorcism in Mark (1:22, 27; 3:15; 6:7). Importantly for this study, this causes us to consider that the parable of the doorkeeper and the slaves (13:34), where the slaves are also given authority ($\dot{\epsilon}\xi o\upsilon\sigma i\alpha$),[63] may be intended to convey the idea that the ministry of exorcism was the major work to occupy followers of Jesus while waiting for the return of the master of the house. Thirdly, the importance of exorcism in the ministry of the disciples, and hence of the post-Easter community, is seen in the discussion of the authority for ministry in the next story, the Beelzebul controversy (3:21–30) with its theme of exorcism. We also need to examine this story because it establishes not only the credentials for the exorcisms of Jesus and his followers but also describes what Mark thought happened in an exorcism.

5.4 The Beelzebul Controversy: Power-Authority for Exorcism (Mark 3:20–35)[64]

In light of the disciples having just been called to be exorcists (Mark 3:13–19), and the future aspect given to the conclusion of the Beelzebul controversy ("Truly I tell you, people will be forgiven" [$\dot{\alpha}\phi\epsilon\theta\dot{\eta}\sigma\epsilon\tau\alpha\iota$, future indicative passive, 3:28]), we need to note that, for Mark, this pericope functions as a discussion of the power-authority for exorcism not only of Jesus but also of his followers, including Mark's readers.[65] To establish that it is by the Holy Spirit that the exorcisms of Jesus and his followers are taking place, Mark interprets the saying about the unpardonable sin by adding the saying "for they had said, 'He has an unclean spirit'" (3:30).[66] Thus, accusing Jesus (and, probably by association, his followers) of having an unclean spirit was to blaspheme against the Holy Spirit (3:28–30). Therefore, these verses

---

62. See Chapman, *Orphan Gospel*, 76.

63. Cf. Best, *Following*, 152–53.

64. Further see Graham H. Twelftree, *Jesus the Exorcist: A Contribution to the Study of the Historical Jesus* (WUNT 2.54; Tübingen: Mohr Siebeck; Peabody, MA: Hendrickson, 1993), §10.

65. This is not to deny the eschatological reference. Cf. Joachim Gnilka, *Das Evangelium nach Markus (Mk 1–8,26)* (EKK 2.1; Zürich: Benzinger; Neukirchen-Vluyn: Neukirchener Verlag, 1978), 151.

66. With such a great deal at stake, Chapman, *Orphan Gospel*, 200, can hardly be correct in supposing that Mark was not interested in 3:30.

on the unpardonable sin finalize and apply the discussion on the source of power-authority for exorcism, functioning as Matthew 12:28 ‖ Luke 11:20 does in Q, asserting that it is not Satan but the Holy Spirit who is the power-authority for the exorcisms of Jesus and his followers. The seriousness of this point for Mark is driven home by introducing Jesus' words with the saying "Truly [ἀμήν[67]] I tell you . . ." (Mark 3:28), which echoes the authoritative statements of prophets (e.g., Jer. 28:6), drawing attention to and affirming what is said.[68]

Also, in our attempt to elucidate Mark's views on exorcism among post-Easter Christians from this passage, we need to take into account his parable of the strong man (Mark 3:27; cf. 3:23). However, before pursuing the line of thought that this is a parable of exorcism, we must take into account the view that the binding of the strong man (Satan) has already taken place in Mark's narrative. Based on the aorist subjunctive here (δήσῃ, "he bind," 3:27), Ernest Best took it that this binding refers back to the defeat of Satan in the Temptation story (1:12–13).[69] However, an aorist subjunctive in a final clause can express an action with no particular stress on the time of the action (e.g., John 17:1, 21). Also, if Mark intended the binding of Satan to have taken place in the Temptation, we might expect the subsequent plundering mentioned in this verse (Mark 3:27) to be in the present rather than in the future tense (καὶ τότε . . . διαρπάσει, "and then . . . he may plunder," my translation). More importantly, if Mark considered Satan to have been defeated in the Temptation we could expect support for the idea in the Temptation story itself. However, there is nothing in that story to suggest that Mark thought that Satan was defeated at that point.[70] Rather, Mark's objective in the Temptation narrative is probably to show Jesus overcoming Satan in relation to, and in order to

67. Also in Mark 8:12; 9:1, 41; 10:15, 29; 11:23; 12:43; 13:30; 14:9, 18, 25, 30.

68. Gundry, *Mark*, 176. Cf. Heinrich Schlier, "ἀμήν," *TDNT* 1:335–38.

69. Ernest Best, *The Temptation and the Passion: The Markan Soteriology* (SNTSMS 2; Cambridge: Cambridge University Press, 1965), 15. That, in Mark, Satan was defeated in the temptation is widely held: see, e.g., Charles E. Carlston, *The Parables of the Triple Tradition* (Philadelphia: Fortress, 1975), 135 and n. 30; citing Julius Schniewind, *Das Evangelium nach Matthäus* (12th ed.; NTD 2; Göttingen: Vandenhoeck & Ruprecht, 1968), 159; Pierre Bonnard, *L'évangile selon Saint Matthieu* (CNT 1; Neuchâtel: Delachaux & Niestlé, 1963), 182; Werner Foerster, "σατανᾶς," *TDNT* 7:159; Joachim Jeremias, *The Parables of Jesus* (London: SCM, 1972), 122–23. See also, e.g., Morna D. Hooker, *The Message of Mark* (London: Epworth, 1983), 37; Howard C. Kee, *Medicine, Miracle, and Magic in New Testament Times* (SNTSMS 55; Cambridge: Cambridge University Press, 1986), 73; and George R. Beasley-Murray, *Jesus and the Kingdom of God* (Grand Rapids: Eerdmans; Exeter, UK: Paternoster, 1986), 108–11, esp. 110 and 366n4; citing, e.g., Adolf Schlatter, *Die Geschichte des Christus* (Stuttgart: Calwer, 1923), 99; Adolf Schlatter, *Der Evangelist Matthäus* (Stuttgart: Calwer, 1948), 2:406–8; Walter Grundmann, *Das Evangelium nach Markus* (3rd ed.; THKNT 2; Berlin: Evangelische Verlagsanstalt, 1965), 84; Robinson, *History*, 30–31; D. E. Nineham, *The Gospel of St Mark* (PNTC; Harmondsworth, UK: Penguin, 1963), 121.

70. Further, see Twelftree, *Exorcist*, 111–12, 114–17.

begin, his mission.[71] Therefore, we are obliged to leave aside the idea that a premise of what Mark is saying in the parable of the strong man is that Satan was bound or defeated in the Temptation.

We have already noted that Isaiah 49:24–25 would have informed Mark's hearers that he thought exorcism was an internalizing and personalizing of what was (in Isaiah) a promised political rescue. Also, the promise of future rescue in the Isaiah passage, despite its supposed impossibility (cf. Isa. 49:24[72]), would not only be seen by Mark's hearers as an appropriate image for exorcism (which Mark portrays as incurable; Mark 5:3–4). It would also highlight for his hearers that exorcism—including their own—was God's promised eschatological rescue. This eschatological dimension to exorcism is also apparent in the vocabulary of the parable (3:23–27). The parable describes a progression of actions, beginning with adjuring in order to bind (or restrict), before taking action against the demon (cf., e.g., *PGM* IV. 3028–3085), and then plundering—all activities familiar in ancient exorcisms.[73] The strong association of the idea of binding with the binding of Satan in the end times[74] sharpens this eschatological dimension not only for Jesus' exorcisms but also for those of his followers.

We can now return to the strong man parable itself (Mark 3:23–27). As well as its eschatological signals, the parable can be shown to convey Mark's understanding of what happens in an exorcism. In contrast to the parable of the returning spirit (Luke 11:24–26), where a house represents a person (as is still common in the East[75]), here the house represents Satan's domain from which his property (τὰ σκεύη[76])—the person—is taken (διαρπάσαι, "plundered").[77] Thus, the parable relates chiastically to exorcism: in exorcism the undesirable inhabitant (demon) is driven out of the valued place (person); in the parable the valued inhabitant (person) is taken out of the undesirable place (demonic). The parable does not tell us that this is the casting out of Satan. That is already implied in the earlier question in relation to exorcism: "How can Satan cast out Satan?" (Mark 3:23). Thus, from its echoes of Isaiah 49:24–25 and from the context of this question, we see that in this parable Mark views exorcism as a battle in which people illegitimately held by Satan are taken, so that Satan is seen to be overthrown.

71. See Twelftree, *Exorcist*, 117; Twelftree, "Temptation of Jesus," *DJG* 825–26; cf. France, *Mark*, 174.

72. Cf. Claus Westermann, *Isaiah 40–66* (London: SCM, 1969), 222; cf. Werner Grimm and Kurt Dittert, *Deuterojesaja: Deutung, Wirkung, Gegenwart; Ein Kommentar zu Jesaja 40–55* (Calwer Bibelkommentare; Stuttgart: Calwer, 1990), 351–54.

73. Further, see Twelftree, *Exorcist*, 112.

74. See the Jewish literature cited by France, *Mark*, 173.

75. See Paul Joüon, *L'évangile de Notre-Seigneur Jésus-Christ* (2nd ed.; Verbum Salutis 5; Paris: G. Beauchesne, 1930), 83; and also the material cited by Ulrich Luz, *Matthew 8–20* (Hermeneia; Minneapolis: Fortress, 2001), 221n77. Cf. chap. 10, n. 91, below.

76. Σκεῦος in the plural (σκεύη) can be generic: "property." See BDAG, "σκεῦος," 927–28.

77. This corrects Twelftree, *Exorcist*, 111. See also France, *Mark*, 173.

That an exorcism is a cosmic struggle with the demonic is equally clear from the stories of exorcism. James M. Robinson brought to our attention that the characters in the exorcism stories make clear the opponents in the cosmic battle.[78] On the one side are ranged Satan (Mark 3:23) and the unclean spirits.[79] On the other side stands the Holy One (1:24) or Son (3:11; 5:7) of God or of the Most High God (5:7). Further, the sense of battle is conveyed and accentuated in the shouts and violence of each report.[80] As Robinson noted, the only passage where Mark has a conversation between Jesus and the demon(iac)s that approaches normality is in the story of the healing of the Gadarene demoniac (5:9–13). But this comes after the battle and serves to highlight the completeness of Jesus' victory.[81] This victory is also seen in the way Mark portrays the demoniacs as kneeling or falling down before Jesus.[82] That nowhere do the exorcism stories directly identify the Spirit and Satan as involved is not to detract from what is set out in the parable of the strong man; rather, it highlights the clandestine nature of the battle.

The conclusion of the Beelzebul controversy also draws attention to the importance of exorcism in the ministry of the followers of Jesus through Jesus saying, "Whoever does the will of God is my brother and sister and mother" (Mark 3:35). The nature of the will of God is not made explicit; it does not need to be for two reasons. First, the only other place in Mark where the will of God is mentioned (14:36) includes the cross. Hence, with taking up one's cross being central to discipleship (8:34), the phrase "the will of God" becomes a shorthand term for discipleship,[83] in which, as has just been shown (3:14–15), exorcism is the dominant activity. Secondly, the phrase "the will of God" (3:35) is in parallel with the phrase about blaspheming against the Holy Spirit (3:29)[84] so that those doing the will of God—disciples or those "inside"—are involved in, or at least sympathetic to, the exorcisms of Jesus and his followers being empowered by the Holy Spirit.

This teaching that takes place between the appointment (Mark 3:14–16a) and sending out (6:7–13) of the Twelve is not only on the nature of exorcism and the source of power-authority (3:20–30). It is also on the importance of exorcism in discipleship (3:31–35), on the trials of mission (4:1–20), on the

78. Robinson, *History*, 35–38.

79. Mark 1:23, 26, 27; 3:11; 5:2, 8, 13; 6:7; 7:25; 9:25.

80. On the violence of exorcisms, see Campbell Bonner, "The Violence of Departing Demons," *HTR* 37 (1944): 334–36; Twelftree, *Exorcist*, 155–56.

81. Robinson, *History*, 36.

82. Mark 3:11; 5:6; 9:20; cf. 7:25.

83. Cf. Best, *Disciples and Discipleship*, 62.

84. On Mark 3:29 and 35, Donahue, "Neglected Factor," 584, says, "Formally they involve the use of the conditional relative (*hos*) with *an* and a verb in the aorist subjunctive in the protasis."

imperative of mission (4:21–25),[85] on God's sure involvement (4:26–29), as well as on the future breadth of the mission (4:30–32).[86] Mark concludes the disciples' session on teaching: "With many such parables he spoke the word to them, as they were able to hear it; he did not speak to them except in parables, but he explained everything in private to his disciples" (4:33–34). That is, being with Jesus is the only way the teaching of Jesus can be understood.[87]

5.5 Stilling Fears of the Demonic (Mark 4:35–41)

Besides hearing and receiving teaching before they are sent out on their own mission, the disciples are witnesses to the activities of Jesus and to a limited extent involved in them (cf. Mark 5:31). Then comes the story of the stilling of the storm (4:35–41). Keeping in mind that Mark has probably placed this story here[88] between the call and sending out of the Twelve, it has a number of points of interest for us. First, Jesus is described as rebuking (ἐπιτιμάω) the wind (4:39), just as he is described as rebuking the demons.[89] Also, the only other time Jesus uses "be still" (or "be muzzled," πεφίμωσο) in Mark is as a command to a demon (1:25). Thus Mark is probably saying that in the stilling of the storm, Jesus is dealing with and overcoming the demonic.[90] The force of this becomes clear when taken in conjunction with the next point.

Secondly, this pericope is one of the places where Mark uses the theme of the boat to represent the church.[91] Thus, in this story a boat (church?), tossed

---

85. Eduard Schweizer, *Good News according to Mark* (London: SPCK, 1971), 99: "Mark is probably thinking of the time of the world-wide proclamation of the gospel (cf. v. 32), not the time of God's Kingdom after the final judgment."

86. See Dodd, *Parables*, 42–43; Jeremias, *Parables*, 149.

87. Cf. Schweizer, *Mark*, 107.

88. That the story may not have always been in this context, see Ludgar Schenke, *Die Wundererzählungen des Markusevangeliums* (SBB; Stuttgart: KBW, 1974), 3–16; Best, *Following*, 231; to the contrary, see Karl Kertelge, *Die Wunder Jesu im Markusevangeliums* (Munich: Kosel, 1970), 91.

89. Mark 1:25; 3:12; (cf. 8:33); 9:25. Ἐπιτιμάω occurs in Mark at 1:25; 3:12; 4:39; 8:30, 32, 33; 9:25; 10:13, 48.

90. Cf. Robinson, *History*, 40–42; William L. Lane, *The Gospel of Mark* (NICNT; Grand Rapids: Eerdmans, 1974), 174–78; Hugh Anderson, *The Gospel of Mark* (NCB; Grand Rapids: Eerdmans; London: Marshall, Morgan & Scott, 1981), 145; Gnilka, *Markus (Mk 1–8,26)*, 195–96.

91. Πλοιάριον ("small ship" or "boat"), Mark 3:9; πλοῖον ("small fishing vessel"), 1:19, 20; 4:1, 36, 37; 5:2, 18, 21; 6:32, 45, 47, 51, 54; 8:10, 14. See Earle Hilgert, *The Ship and Related Symbols in the New Testament* (Assen: Royal Van Gorcum, 1962); and Best, *Following*, 230–34. With, e.g., Mark 3:7, 20; 4:1, 10 in mind, it may have been expected that others besides the disciples would have been in the boat, but they are not. Note the exclusive context in which the boat is mentioned in 6:30–33. In view of 1:17, 1:19 may be foreshadowing the work of the disciples in the "new boat." Cf. Mark 1:20. Matthew (8:23–27) also interprets this story with the boat representing the church. See Günther Bornkamm, "The Stilling of the Storm," in *Tradition and Interpretation in Matthew* (ed. Günther Bornkamm, Gerhard Barth, and Heinz Joachim Held; London: SCM, 1982), esp. 54–55.

in a (demonic?) storm which had caused great fear in the disciples (church?) because they had no faith, has been saved by Jesus' bringing about a great calm. It is noticeable that when the disciples are out in a boat by themselves (Mark 6:45–52) without Jesus, they face another storm, but "he got into the boat with them and the wind ceased" (6:51). Thus, here in 4:35–41, Mark is probably showing that the mission of the church, when beset by (demonic?) storms of the greatest magnitude, will be kept safe by Jesus being with them and by their faith in him.

5.6 The Disciples as Exorcists (Mark 6:7–12, 13)

Having begun their training at home (Mark 3:19, 31–35), the disciples follow Jesus back to his hometown (πατρίς, 6:1) for the culmination of their preparation for mission. As has been the case in this section (from 3:19) where the disciples witness Jesus teaching and healing, stress is laid on how Jesus' authority, as well as discipleship and mission, are misunderstood[92]—at times even by the disciples themselves.[93] This passage shows the hindrance to faith to be the invisibility of God's power. It concludes with, "And he could do no deed of power there, except that he laid his hands upon a few sick people and healed them. And he was amazed because of their unbelief" (6:5–6, my translation). This passage stresses the importance of faith in healing (cf. 5:36) and in turn, as Eduard Schweizer put it, "may have consoled the Church when it was troubled because of the ineffectiveness of its preaching"[94] and—we add—healing.

Then, against the background of hearing and seeing the ministry of Jesus (Mark 3:13–6:6), the Twelve are sent out (6:7, 12). For Mark, then, Jesus is the model for ministry, including exorcism. Jesus' followers model the methods of Jesus as well as his means of authority, which is God's authority.[95]

Mark says that the disciples go out preaching that people should repent (Mark 6:12). John the Baptist also preaches a baptism of repentance (1:4) in preparation for Jesus' preaching of the kingdom of God (1:14–15). The only other time Mark uses the word "repent" (μετανοέω) is when Jesus preaches the kingdom of God and requires repentance (and belief in the gospel; 1:15). We are probably to assume, then, that Mark understood the disciples to be preaching the kingdom of God, which on the basis of 3:23–27, we should expect, as indeed Mark spells out here in 6:13, involved exorcism. Again, this probably also conveyed to Mark's readers the significance of their exorcistic ministry—it was the casting out of Satan, the destruction of the kingdom of evil.

92. Mark 6:2–3; cf. 3:21–22, 30, 31–35; 5:36.
93. Cf. Mark 4:10, 33, 38, 40; 5:31.
94. Schweizer, *Mark*, 125.
95. Mark 1:22, 27; 2:10; 11:28, 29, 33. Cf. 3:15; 6:7.

We saw, in the appointment of the Twelve (Mark 3:14–15), that it was surprising no mention was made of healing, especially since the Twelve appear to be extending Jesus' ministry, which included more than exorcism. Again, here in the sending out of the Twelve (6:7), exorcism stands alone in their brief (without any mention of preaching). Yet, at the end of the periocope, it is said they "proclaimed that all should repent. They cast out many demons, and anointed with oil many who were sick [ἄρρωστος] and cured them" (6:13). The use of oil in medicine was not uncommon,[96] but we have very little evidence that oil was used in this period to deal with those possessed by demons (*PGM* IV. 3007–3010).[97] The importance of this observation is that, in giving no specific method for exorcism, we are left to suppose that Mark intended his readers to use the methods of Jesus their mentor.

5.7 Jesus as an Exorcist in Mark[98]

Mark portrays Jesus as the model for exorcism among his followers, and has spent a great deal of narrational time expressing the closeness of the disciples to Jesus. We have twice had occasion to suggest that the disciples (as models for the readers) are using the same methods as Jesus, and see that what Mark says about Jesus as an exorcist is important in what he wants to say about exorcism among early Christians.

The importance of exorcism in Jesus' ministry, from Mark's perspective, can be gauged by noting that the first public act of Jesus is an exorcism (Mark 1:21–28). Also, as we noted earlier, of the thirteen healing stories in this Gospel, the largest single category is that of exorcism, of which there are four.[99] Then Mark heightens the impression that exorcism was important in Jesus' ministry, at least in the north, with the little summaries he composes, which focus on exorcism.[100] Jesus, whom readers are to model in their exorcisms, is

96. See Otto Böcher, *Dämonenfurcht und Dämonenabwehr* (Stuttgart: Kohlhammer, 1970), 216–17; France, *Mark*, 250–51.

97. Against Böcher, *Dämonenfurcht*, 216–17, who gives the misleading impression that oil was a common healing medium for demoniacs. For the use of oil at the turn of the second and third centuries CE and later, see Henry Ansgar Kelly, *The Devil at Baptism: Ritual, Theology, and Drama* (Ithaca, NY: Cornell University Press, 1985), e.g., 138–39, 192–94, 230–31. Thus, at a historical level, it is possible that we have evidence here that Jesus only intended his followers to perform exorcisms.

98. See Twelftree, *Exorcist*, chap. 5.

99. Mark 1:21–28; 5:1–20; 7:24–30; 9:14–29.

100. Mark 1:32–34, 39; 3:7–12. That these are Mark's creation, see Gnilka, *Markus (Mk 1–8,26)*, 86; and on the summaries in Mark, see Wilhelm Egger, *Frohbotschaft und Lehre: Die Sammelberichte des Wirkens Jesu im Markusevangelium* (FTS 19; Frankfurt am Main: J. Knecht, 1976). It has to be noted that, although exorcism is important to Mark in the early part of his narrative (note the position of 1:21–28 and the summaries, 1:32–34, 39; 3:7–12), the significance of exorcism is reduced so that, surprisingly, exorcism is not mentioned in the summary statement

empowered by the Spirit (Mark 1:10, 12; cf. 3:28–30) and embattled against Satan (3:20–27). However, Jesus is not only an exorcist, he is also preacher of the kingdom of God (1:14–15) so that teaching and healing form one whole for Mark's view of Jesus' activity (see 1:21–28).

The techniques that Mark portrays Jesus as modeling in his exorcisms are those that would have been familiar to his readers from other exorcists. Jesus "rebukes" (ἐπιτιμάω) demons;[101] he "muzzles" (φιμόω) a demon (cf. Mark 4:39; see above); he orders the demons to "come out" (ἔξελθε)[102] and never to enter a person again (Mark 9:25; see above); he uses the supposed power in a name to gain dominance over a demon (5:9; see above); he transfers demons from one habitat to another (5:12–13); and he exorcises from a distance (7:24–29).

While Jesus is very much an exorcist of his time in his use of contemporary methods (see §2.5 above), for Mark, Jesus' exorcisms are a submission of the demons after being confronted by him and his commands (cf. Mark 3:11). The notion of confrontation sums up these techniques. Just how far Mark understands such techniques as suitable for use in the ministry of the early church will become apparent as we proceed.

5.8 A Lesson in Exorcism (Mark 9:14–29)

As we have already noted,[103] Mark 8:22 or 27 to 10:52 is generally agreed to be the heart of Mark's teaching on discipleship. Since an exorcism is the only miracle story within this section, we are obliged to give it special attention in understanding what Mark wants to say about exorcism among early Christians.[104] The importance of this story for our theme is confirmed in noting that, in contrast to two other exorcism stories only hinting at the presence of the disciples (Mark 1:21, 29; 5:1), and one story not mentioning them (7:24–30), in this story the disciples play a significant role. They are not only specifically mentioned at the beginning of the story (9:14) and play an important role in the body of the narrative (9:18), but they are prominent in being portrayed as unsuccessful in performing an exorcism (9:18, 28–29).[105]

---

of 6:53–56. Exorcism is not mentioned after 9:38–41 (the story of the unknown exorcist), even though Jesus is still portrayed as being in contact with people (e.g., 11:8, 15–19, 27; 12:18, 28, 35–37, 41) and the passion narrative does not commence until 14:1.

101. Mark 1:25; 3:12; (cf. 4:39, on which see below, and 8:33); 9:25; see above.

102. Mark 1:25, 26; 5:8, 13; (7:29, 30); 9:25, 26, (29); see above.

103. Also see Graham H. Twelftree, *Jesus the Miracle Worker: A Historical and Theological Study* (Downers Grove, IL: InterVarsity, 1999), 85–89.

104. Chapman, *Orphan Gospel*, 110, notes that except for the story of the Gadarene demoniac, this is the longest story in the Gospel until the passion narrative.

105. It is inconceivable, therefore, for Chapman, *Orphan Gospel*, 110, to say that this story seems to have no bearing on the theme of this section of Mark.

Being set in the shadow of the story of the Transfiguration (9:2–13), the poverty of the ministry of the disciples is also highlighted. Therefore, we can expect our lengthy discussion of this story to unearth a surprisingly rich lode for understanding Mark's view of exorcism among his hearers.

On rejoining the other nine disciples with Peter, James, and John (who were already with him), Jesus asked about the nature of the argument between the disciples and some scribes (Mark 9:14–16). At first, it does not appear that the subject of the dispute is identified.[106] However, a careful reading of the text shows that Mark thinks the argument is about the authority to cast out demons. That is, as part of Mark's first exorcism story, a discussion is involved that focuses on Jesus' authority being different from the scribes' (1:22). Then, in the Beelzebul controversy, Mark establishes that this unscribe-like authority to cast out demons is the Holy Spirit (3:28–30). Importantly for the story we are discussing, the apostles have been appointed with this same unscribe-like authority (3:15) with a view to being sent out on an exorcism and healing ministry (6:7–13), which turns out to be very successful (6:12–13, 30).

Thus, with the unexpected failure of the disciples to perform an exorcism, it would not be surprising if, in this story, Mark was implying that the dispute with some scribes concerned the disciples' failure in the use of this unique authority. This is possibly confirmed by what Mark goes on to say. He says that when the crowd saw Jesus, they were "immediately overcome with awe" (ἐκθαμβέω) and ran to greet him (Mark 9:15). For Mark, the only writer in the New Testament to use the word, ἐκθαμβέω involves a strong element of distress (9:15; 14:33; 16:5, 6) and is probably better translated here as "perplexed."[107] Thus, Mark is probably conveying the idea that the crowd was perplexed at the disciples' failure in light of the debate they heard with the scribes about the authority the disciples had received from someone who so obviously had authority to heal.[108]

The failure of the disciples as exorcists is described in terms of them not being able or strong enough (οὐκ ἴσχυσαν)[109] to cast out the demon. The word ἰσχύω has a similar meaning to δύναμαι ("to be able"), which Mark uses of Jesus' ability to heal (Mark 9:22–23).[110] However, ἰσχύω carries the idea of self-generated or innate strength.[111] In other words, the father said that the disciples did not possess the innate strength to perform the exorcism. This, as

106. So Thomas L. Budesheim, "Jesus and the Disciples in Conflict with Judaism," ZNW 62 (1971): 206–7, who thinks that the subject was of relative unimportance; it was the *factum* of the debate with the religious leaders that was important.

107. Cf. Georg Bertram, "θάμβος . . . ," TDNT 3:4–7.

108. See also Twelftree, *Miracle*, 86.

109. For the verb ἴσχύω in Mark see 2:17; 5:4; 14:37. The noun (ἰσχυρός) is used at 3:27 and the adjective (ἰσχυρότερός) at 1:7.

110. For δύναμαι in Mark see 1:40, 45; 2:4, 7, 19 (bis); 3:20, 23, 24, 25; 4:32, 33; 5:3; 6:5, 19; 7:15, 18, 24; 8:4; 9:3, 22, 23, 28, 29, 30, 39; 10:26, 38, 39, 40; 14:5, 7; 15:31.

111. See BDAG, "ἰσχύω," 484, §2.

the readers of Mark know, is precisely what the disciples were not given and do not have.[112] According to Mark, while Jesus' ability to heal—dependent on the Spirit (cf. 1:9–11 and 3:28–30)—is innate or self-generated, the ability of the disciples to perform an exorcism is dependent on an ability given to them by Jesus (6:7).[113]

On hearing of the situation, Jesus' response—"O faithless generation" (ὦ γενεὰ ἄπιστος, Mark 9:19)—helps us understand the failure of the exorcism. The readers cannot be surprised that the lack of faith is a key factor in the disciples' lack of success and that of all the miracle stories in Mark, it is this one that treats the subject of faith most thoroughly and requires our close attention.[114] For, in 6:1–6, Jesus' success in conducting miracles is limited because of "their unbelief" (τὴν ἀπιστίαν αὐτῶν), the only other place where ἀπιστία ("unfaith") occurs in Mark.[115] However, it is not immediately clear in this story to whom Jesus is addressing the rebuke about being "faithless."

Even though the rebuke is addressed to "them" (αὐτῶν, plural, Mark 9:19), it is unlikely that the crowd is in mind for it has passed from view in the story (9:14–15), leaving the father and the disciples as the focus of attention. In that the disciples are key characters in this story from beginning to end—and Mark has just portrayed them as failures—he probably intends his readers to understand Jesus to be speaking to the disciples. This is how Matthew and Luke understand Mark for they have each altered their stories to redirect the criticism away from the disciples.[116] Indeed, despite not using the obvious vocabulary of faith, perhaps Jesus' rhetorical questions—"How much longer must I be among you [πρὸς ὑμᾶς]? How much longer must I put up with you [ἀνέξομαι ὑμῶν]?"—are intended by Mark to echo the very purpose of being a follower of Jesus: to be "with him" (μετ' αὐτοῦ, 3:14). Therefore, holding together the vocabulary of faith and the theme of being with Jesus, the error of the disciples is that, perhaps, despite having been with Jesus, they have remained without faith.[117]

Notwithstanding, it is possible that a closer reading may reveal more about the disciples' failure. That is, in view of (1) Mark's depicting discipleship as

112. To divert any criticism, Matt. 17:16 and Luke 9:40 use δύναμαι.

113. However, at this point in the narrative Mark is not interested in the cause of failure—that will come later in the story—but in drawing attention to the grounds of their ability.

114. Cf. Eduard Schweizer, "The Portrayal of the Life of Faith in the Gospel of Mark," *Int* 32 (1978): 389, 396.

115. Also at Mark 16:14, a later ending to Mark.

116. Matt. 17:17 and Luke 9:41 remove αὐτοῖς ("to them") from Mark 9:19 so that Jesus' statement is generalized, and Luke portrays Jesus as addressing the father by ending his rebuke by saying, "Bring your son here" (9:41).

117. In this I can correct the point that the issue is probably not that the disciples are absent from Jesus, for that is the very thing the rebuke affirms: he has been with them (Mark 9:19). Contrast Graham H. Twelftree, *Christ Triumphant: Exorcism Then and Now* (London: Hodder & Stoughton, 1985), 122.

being "with Jesus" (Mark 3:14; 5:18[118]), (2) exorcism arising out of being with Jesus (3:14–15; 6:6–13), (3) the difficulties experienced by the disciples when they are in the boat without Jesus (6:46, 51), and (4) perhaps Mark's depicting total failure as not being with or as leaving Jesus (14:50),[119] we may infer from this story that Mark saw the disciples' failure as also due, to some extent, to the absence of Jesus from the situation.

Yet, despite the clear culpability of the disciples, Jesus' rebuke may also be intended to reflect on the defective faith of the father.[120] For the father asks Jesus to help "if" (εἴ) he is "able" (δύνῃ; from δύναμαι [Mark 9:22]). In this "if" a hint of hesitancy and therefore deficiency may be intended in the expression of the father's faith. After all, at the beginning of the story Mark has portrayed the disciples as unable to heal, so we can expect the father to be pictured as hesitant.[121] Further, it is probably significant that, in the father's request for help, Mark does not use the same word, "to be able" (ἰσχύειν), that was used for the disciples (9:18). Instead, δύναμαι ("to have power") is used with the sense of or potential of choice included.[122] That is, the father is portrayed not as looking to Jesus for his self-generated strength (that is not in question), but hesitantly asks Jesus to choose to do what the father has recognized Jesus has the ability or power to do. Indeed, Jesus said that whether or not he was able to heal the boy did not depend on his ability (δύναμαι)—which all Mark's readers know is not in question— but on trust or faith (9:23). While it may be possible to take the logic of this sentence to refer to the faith of Jesus,[123] it would be unique in Mark. In any case, Mark has the father accept the challenge of the statement.[124] In short, the father's faith is in question. However, it is not his belief that Jesus has the power to heal that is in question, but his belief that Jesus is willing to heal.

The father's immediate response to Jesus is, "I believe; help my unbelief!" (Mark 9:24). In view of the exorcism taking place straight after this statement,

118. Jesus' refusal to grant the healed man's request to "be with him" (Mark 5:19) and, instead, sending him out on mission (5:20) is probably to be understood as Mark saying that being on mission is, for his readers, being with Jesus.

119. See Timothy J. Geddert, *Watchwords: Mark 13 in Markan Eschatology* (JSNTSup 26; Sheffield: JSOT Press, 1989), 101–3.

120. Cf. Christopher D. Marshall, *Faith as a Theme in Mark's Narrative* (Cambridge and New York: Cambridge University Press, 1989), 117–18. That the father is being criticized, see, e.g., Taylor, *Mark*, 398; Gundry, *Mark*, 489.

121. Cf. France, *Mark*, 367.

122. BDAG, "δύναμαι," 262–63; cf. "δύναμις," 263, §1, §2.

123. Cf. Erich Klostermann, *Das Markusevangelium* (HNT 3; Tübingen: Mohr Siebeck, 1950), 91; Nineham, *Mark*, 247. More widely on the debate about "the faith of/in Jesus," see the literature cited by James D. G. Dunn, *Romans 1–8* (2 vols.; WBC 38A; Dallas: Word Books, 1988), 1:161–62; cf. 166–67.

124. Cf. Joachim Jeremias, *New Testament Theology* (London: SCM, 1971), 166. See also, Twelftree, *Miracle*, 87.

Mark cannot mean it to be a confession of (complete?) unbelief.[125] Instead, the statement both establishes faith and shows faith to be understood as a gift. Thus, the father's words are a confession of faith exonerating him from the cause of the failed healing and reinforcing the disciples' culpability.

Mark's description of the healing is also significant in reflecting his view of exorcism in the post-Easter community. He says that Jesus took the boy's hand and "lifted him up" (ἤγειρεν αὐτόν, Mark 9:27). Ἐγείρω is the verb Mark used for Jesus being raised from the dead (16:6), conveying the idea that exorcism is no less significant or miraculous than bringing someone back to life.[126]

The ending of this story mentioning prayer (Mark 9:28–29), which seems at variance with the body of the story, is particularly important in our investigation. The dissonance between the body of the pericope and its ending,[127] along with the distinctive Markan vocabulary[128] and grammar,[129] as well as the Markan theme of a house as a scene of Jesus' teaching[130] indicate a high level of Markan editorial activity and interest in this conclusion. This leads us to suppose that Mark has probably added the ending to the story.[131] What Mark's ending shows is that the story itself did not answer the question as to how to perform this kind of exorcism if Jesus was used as a model by early Christians. Jesus models asking the father of the mute boy for information; the ending answers the question as to what to do when there is no one to ask for such information: they are to pray. This is an unexpected answer, for in light of Jesus chastising the failed disciples for their lack of faith (9:19), we could expect Jesus to say in the conclusion that this kind of demon could be driven out by faith. Indeed, in 6:5–6 the lack of healing by Jesus in his

125. So, e.g., Paul J. Achtemeier, "Miracles and the Historical Jesus: A Study of Mark 9:14–29," *CBQ* 37 (1975): 480.

126. The idea that being healed was akin to being raised from the dead was not new with Mark. Joachim Gnilka, *Das Evangelium nach Markus (Mk 8,27–16,20)* (EKK II.2; Zürich: Benzinger; Neukirchen-Vluyn: Neukirchener Verlag, 1979), 49, notes that the idea is found in Ps. 30:4; cf. 1QH 3.19–20; 5.18–19; 6.24.

127. See Robert H. Stein, "The 'Redaktionsgeschichtlich' Investigation of a Markan Seam (Mc 1 21f.)," *ZNW* 61 (1970): 78–79.

128. Note δύναμαι (twice), εἰς, ἐξέρχομαι, ἐπερωτάω, ἴδιος, μαθητής, οἶκος, and see Lloyd Gaston, *Horae Synopticae Electronicae: Word Statistics of the Synoptic Gospels* (Sources for Biblical Studies 3; Missoula, MT: Society of Biblical Literature, 1973), 18–21, 58–60.

129. Note the genitive absolute (Mark 9:28); see E. J. Pryke, *Redaction Style in the Marcan Gospel* (SNTSMS 33; Cambridge: Cambridge University Press, 1978), 62, and note the ὅτι interrogative (9:28); see C. H. Turner, "Marcan Usage: Notes, Critical and Exegetical on the Second Gospel," in *The Language and Style of the Gospel of Mark* (NovTSup 71; ed. J. K. Elliott; Leiden: Brill, 1993), 63–65; and George D. Kilpatrick, "Recitative λέγων," in Elliot, *Language and Style of the Gospel of Mark*, 177; as well as the absence of λέγων (λέγοντες) after a verb introducing a question (in 9:28, ἐπηρώτων); see Turner, "Marcan Usage," 134.

130. This theme may occur in other redactional passages such as Mark 1:29 (?); 2:1, 15; 3:19–20; 7:17, 24; 10:10. See Pryke, *Style*, 69n3.

131. Cf. Gnilka, *Markus (Mk 8,27–16,20)*, 49; and, e.g., those cited by Pryke, *Style*, 17.

hometown is directly attributed to a lack of faith. Instead, here, Mark says, "This kind can come out only through prayer" (9:29).[132]

This is one of Mark's examples of Jesus giving private instruction when the disciples should not have needed it.[133] By implication, what the disciples should have known is how this kind of demon—a mute and deaf spirit (Mark 9:25)—could be exorcised. Mute spirits were considered particularly difficult to exorcise,[134] not only, presumably, because they could not hear the instructions or incantations, but also because they could not give information about themselves. Therefore, instead of speaking and listening to the demon and employing the usual method of commanding a demon to leave, Jesus says, "This kind can come out only through prayer" (9:29). In that this statement is addressed to the disciples and not the father or the sick boy, the use of prayer is to be taken as a technique (or quality) of the exorcist, not of a needy suppliant.[135]

This leads us to inquire what Mark had in mind in saying that prayer is effective in exorcism. To begin with, we must discount the idea that the prayer is directed toward expecting the parousia, when the Son of Man would show himself the powerful winner over the demons.[136] There is no evidence in the text for that view.[137] Nor is there evidence that Mark understood that one (faith

---

132. To Mark 9:29 many ancient witnesses add "and fasting" (και νηστεια). See NA[27]. It is clear that the words και νηστεια are unlikely to be from Mark's hand. (1) In light of early church interest in fasting, and linking it with prayer—see Luke 2:37; 5:33; Acts 13:(2), 3; 14:23; 27:9; also Justin, 1 Apol. 61—it is easier to explain the addition of the phrase than it being dropped from the text. (2) In view of the Western Text adding that Cornelius was also fasting as well as praying when he had a vision (Acts 10:30; see C. Kingsley Barrett, The Acts of the Apostles [2 vols.; ICC; Edinburgh: T&T Clark, 1994–1998], 1:517), it is notable that important representatives of the Alexandrian and Western types of text do not have the words "and fasting" in Mark 9:29. See Metzger, Commentary, 85. Also (3) with Matthew's interest in associating prayer and fasting (Matt. 6:5–19), he is unlikely to have passed up an opportunity to take up this phrase if it was in the material he had before him (Mark 9:29 ‖ Matt. 17:20); Matt. 17:21 (‖ Mark 9:29) is judged not to be original to the Gospel. See Donald A. Hagner, Matthew 14–28 (WBC 33B; Dallas: Word Books, 1995), 501.

Therefore, this addition is to be left aside in considering Mark's perspective on exorcism. Moreover, 𝔓[45] is dated between the first half and the middle of the third century, placing it outside the period of our study. See, e.g., Frederic G. Kenyon, Chester Beatty Biblical Papyri Codex II/1: The Gospels and Acts, Text (London: Emery Walker, 1933), x; T. C. Skeat, "A Codicological Analysis of the Chester Beatty Papyrus of Gospels and Acts (𝔓[45])," Hermathena 155 (1993): 27–43; reprinted in The Collected Biblical Writings of T. C. Skeat (ed. J. K. Elliott; NovTSup 113; Leiden and Boston: Brill, 2004), 140–57, esp. 141; and Larry W. Hurtado, "𝔓[45] and the Textual History of the Gospel of Mark," in The Earliest Gospels: The Origins and Transmission of the Earliest Christian Gospels—The Contribution of the Chester Beatty Gospel Codex 𝔓[45] (ed. Charles Horton; JSNTSup 258; London and New York: Continuum / T&T Clark, 2004), 133 and n. 4 and works cited.

133. See Mark 4:10–12, 34; 7:17–18; 9:28–29; 10:10; 13:3–4.

134. Cf. PGM IV. 3037–3044; Twelftree, Christ Triumphant, 40.

135. As thought by John Muddiman, "Fast, Fasting," ABD 2:775.

136. Schenke, Wundererzählungen, 340.

137. Cf. Gnilka, Markus (Mk 8,27–16,20), 49n28.

or prayer) was implied by mention of the other. Rather, we probably see what Mark had in mind when we note, that, for him, there is not only a relationship between prayer and faith,[138] but also that prayer is understood to be synonymous with faith, or to be a faith-filled (or based) statement. This is evident in Mark's explanation of Jesus saying, "Have faith in God" (Mark 11:22), uttered in response to Peter pointing out that the fig tree he cursed had withered. Mark's explanation is in the form of two parallel statements. The first statement is about making a faith-filled statement to a mountain (not doubting but believing that what is said will come to pass; 11:23). The second statement is about prayer: "Because of this I say to you, whatever you ask for in prayer, believe that you have received it, and it will be yours" (11:24, my translation). Beginning with "because of this" (διὰ τοῦτο), and being in parallel with the first statement, shows that it depends on and explains the first statement about faith.[139]

In other words, faith-filled statements—to a mountain or a fig tree—are understood to be faith-filled prayers. In turn, for prayer to be effective in exorcism, Mark probably means that, just like Jesus their model, the disciples were to issue commands to the demons, explained here as based on trust in God—"Gott zugewandter Glaube," God-directed faith, as Walter Grundmann put it.[140] Put another way, prayer—directions to the demons—was to be an expression of total trust in, and dependence on, the power and authority used by Jesus and given to the disciples by Jesus.[141] Indeed, this is probably just the matter about which the disciples have been debating with the scribes at the beginning of the story (Mark 9:14).

As anticipated, our extended examination of this exorcism story has realized a valuable and complex lode of information for understanding Mark's views on exorcism among his readers. One further passage requires our attention for it provides some nuancing of what is already clear in Mark.

5.9 The Unknown Exorcist (Mark 9:38–39)

From the context of this story we can see that Mark, perhaps inadvertently, tells us about Christian exorcism. The story is found between material on internal relationships in a Christian community (Mark 9:33–37) and a saying about putting stumbling blocks before one of these "little ones" (9:42)—defined as believers (τούτων τῶν πιστευόντων, "these believing").[142]

138. Cf. Karl-Georg Reploh, *Markus, Lehrer der Gemeinde: Eine redaktionsgeschichtliche Studie zu den Jüngerperikopen des Markus-Evangeliums* (SBM 9; Stuttgart: KBW, 1969), 218–19.

139. Sharyn E. Dowd, *Prayer, Power, and the Problem of Suffering: Mark 11:22–25 in the Context of Markan Theology* (SBLDS 105; Atlanta: Scholars Press, 1988), 63–65.

140. Grundmann cited by Gnilka, *Markus (Mk 8,27–16,20)*, 49.

141. Cf. C. E. B. Cranfield, "St. Mark, 9.14–29," *SJT* 3 (1950): 62–63.

142. Cf. Taylor, *Mark*, 410.

This location strongly suggests that Christians are the subject of this whole section (9:30–50), including this story of the unknown exorcist. Further, that the unknown exorcist was intended to represent other followers of Jesus or people about to become his followers seems probable from Jesus' reply to John: "Do not stop him; for no one who does a deed of power in my name will be able soon afterward to speak evil of me" (9:39). From the perspective of the first readers, this would mean that the person represented by the unknown exorcist was, if not a Christian, on the way to becoming one. Also, that John the disciple says there was an attempt to stop the unknown exorcist "because he was not following *us*" (ὅτι οὐκ ἠκολούθει ἡμῖν, 9:38)[143]—rather than *you* (σοί)—would alert readers to the ongoing relevance of the story beyond that of the situation of the first followers of Jesus. Therefore, Mark's readers would probably have seen the story as reflecting their desire to exclude any Christian who was not a member of their particular community,[144] rather than preventing non-Christians from using the name of Jesus in healing. In other words, Mark gives the impression there were a number of groups of Christians in Rome conducting exorcism indistinguishable from each other.

With this story a new aspect of exorcism appears to emerge in Mark's repertoire: using the name of Jesus. The issue described between the unknown exorcist and the followers of Jesus is allegiance to the particular group of followers of Jesus, not the method of exorcism. There is no criticism of the method, only explanation. Therefore, we can suppose that the method of using the name of Jesus was acceptable to and is being endorsed by Mark. The notion of healing "in the name of" (ἐν τῷ ὀνόματί) someone was not unique to the early Christians.[145] However, as we will see, the phrase became particularly characteristic of their healing techniques.

There may be no technical distinction in meaning between ἐπί ("upon") and ἐν ("in").[146] However, through Mark's repeated and alternate use of the catchphrase "on the name of," and "in the name of," he has not only tied this material together[147] but also probably intends to convey a carefully nuanced understanding of exorcism.[148] Through the voice of John the disciple, Mark describes exorcism as being "in" (ἐν) or by means of the name of Jesus (Mark

143. The textual variations in this verse, on which see France, *Mark*, 375, are not material to our discussion.

144. Cf. Martin, *Mark*, 115; Xabier Pikaza Ibarrondo, "Exorcismo, poder y evangelio: Trasfondo histórico y eclesial de Mc 9,38–40," *EstBíb* 57 (1999): 539–64; France, *Mark*, 378–79.

145. See, e.g., 11Q11 4.4; Josephus, *Ant.* 8.46–47; *PGM* IV. 3019. See the discussion in Twelftree, *Exorcist*, 41–42.

146. See Taylor, *Mark*, 407. The distinction that Gundry, *Mark*, 519–21, wishes to see between ἐπί and ἐν in Mark 9:37 and 38 is groundless when we note that in 9:38 and 39 there is no distinction seen between the words. The very interchange of the words may be Mark's attempt to see the means ("in"/ἐν) and grounds or basis of ("upon"/ἐπί) exorcism to be one and the same.

147. Mark 9:37, 38, 39, 41. So Grundmann, *Markus*, 194.

148. Mark 9:37, 38, 39, 41.

9:38). That is, exorcism is carried out by means of using the name of Jesus as a source of power-authority. Mark gives no examples of how this would work. Perhaps he does not need to; the story of the unknown exorcist probably implies the readers are familiar with such methods. Such methods were clearly well known at the time (see n. 145 above).

In any case, through paralleling this description of exorcism in the next verse (Mark 9:39) as "a deed of power in [ἐπί] my name," Mark adds an important aspect to this notion of exorcism. What is added has been brought forward from the initial use of ἐπί in 9:37: "Whoever welcomes one such child in [ἐπί] my name welcomes me, and . . . [also] the one who sent me" (9:37; cf. 9:41). Here Jesus and the person bearing his name are identified with each other so that what happens to one happens to the other. Thus, an exorcism "in the name of Jesus" would have been an exorcism performed by a follower of Jesus as if it had been done by Jesus himself (cf. 13:6) who, in turn, was identified with and authorized by God (see on 3:20–35 above).

Coming to this point from another perspective, we can see that the rationale for such thinking was that a name went beyond representation to being the essence or hypostasis of a person or god.[149] Hence, to heal "in the name" was to use the name to heal so that the healing was taking place in the sphere of or as if that person or god was performing the healing.[150] Mark does not need to give any examples of this method of exorcism. He has given a sufficient number of examples of Jesus performing exorcisms for this identificatory method to be obvious to his readers. Of course, in light of what we know from this passage, and from other New Testament writers (e.g., Acts 3:6), the simple commands taken up from Jesus implying this identification would probably have been prefaced by words such as "in the name of Jesus. . . ."

5.10 Mark and Exorcism among Early Christians

Against the tide of a recurring theme in Markan studies, rather than interpret the battle with the demonic as symbolic of socio-political struggles, the evidence suggests that the battle was not against the Romans but against Satan, and focused in exorcism. This took the battle—the significance of exorcism—firmly into the personal as well as, especially, into the spiritual or cosmic arena. It is this orientating perspective that helps explain why exorcism plays such a significant role in Mark's narrative for his readers.

149. Cf. Richard Reitzenstein, *Poimandres: Studien zur griechisch-ägyptischen und frühchristlichen Literatur* (Leipzig: Teubner, 1904), 17n6; and see the discussion in Hans Bietenhard, "ὄνομα . . . ," *TDNT* 5:242–81.

150. Cf. H. Cremer, *Biblio-Theological Lexicon of New Testament Greek* (Edinburgh: T&T Clark, 1895), 56.

Given that the interpretive key to unlocking Mark's narrative for his readers—including what he wants to say about exorcism—is his theme of disciples
and discipleship, a number of aspects of Mark's message stand out regarding
exorcism among early Christians. First, perhaps the most astounding result
of our inquiry has been to confirm the importance Mark places on exorcism
in the ministry of his readers. Mark conveys this primarily through portraying exorcism as the major work of Christian ministry while waiting for the
return of their Master—even dominating a preaching ministry of proclaiming the kingdom of God. Exorcism is of such importance because it is God's
promised eschatological rescue of people, no less significant or miraculous
than raising the dead. In other words, in their exorcisms, their compassionate
God is eschatologically active in saving people from a mighty enemy.

Secondly, from Mark's perspective Christian exorcism is empowered by
the Spirit, though that would not always be clear to antagonistic observers.
Indeed, the Beelzebul controversy, with its lengthy discussion of the source of
power-authority for exorcism, suggests that Mark's readers faced the criticism
of being empowered by Satan rather than by the Holy Spirit. Thus we have
seen that it is likely that the ministry of exorcism was associated with fear
or caused turbulence in the church. However, failure in exorcism is caused
not by the absence of authority (which they have been given) but through a
lack of faith or not being "with Jesus."

Thirdly, although in their exorcisms Mark's readers would not always be
expected to use the same techniques as Jesus, they, like Jesus, would confront
the demonic with the divine. Sometimes in their exorcisms, like Jesus, they
would rebuke and muzzle demons as well as order them to come out. As
necessary, they would use the name of the offending demon to gain exorcistic control; they would transfer demons to alternative habitats, and exorcise
at a distance. However, in two places Mark nuances what it also means to
model the method of Jesus. In light of perhaps his readers not being entirely
successful in their efforts as exorcists, he advocates prayer (Mark 9:28–29),
which, from what he says elsewhere on prayer, is a faith-filled statement—
dependent on the Holy Spirit—directed to the demons. Then, in the story of
the unknown exorcist Mark endorses the method of exorcising "in the name
of Jesus" (9:38), which was to perform an exorcism as if it had been done by
Jesus himself. Thus, what appear to be three different methods of exorcism—
imitating Jesus, prayer, and using the name of Jesus—turn out to be aspects
of the same approach: issuing faith-filled statements to the demons as if Jesus
were performing the exorcism.

6

Luke-Acts

ITH THE BOOK of Acts, Luke has given us direct access to his views on exorcism among early Christians.[1] Moreover, Acts also enhances our ability to read his Gospel with a sensitivity to our theme. Then, reciprocally, the Gospel gives further insight into how Acts can be read to shed further light on what he has to say on exorcism among post-Easter Christians.[2] But because of the way the character of Jesus dominates the Gospel and, arguably, remains significant in Acts, Luke invites us to begin with Jesus in understanding what he has to say about exorcism among early Christians.

Before doing that we can note that the majority view is that Luke was writing somewhere between about 70 and 80 CE.[3] Further, as he shows considerable

---

1. See Acts 5:12–16 (summary of apostles' ministry); 8:4–8 (Philip in Samaria); 10:36–43 (summary of Jesus' ministry); 16:16–18 (possessed slave girl); 19:11–20 (the sons of Sceva).

2. Luke 4:33–37 ‖ Mark 1:23–28 (the demoniac in the synagogue); 4:38–39 ‖ Mark 1:29–31 (Simon's mother-in-law); 4:40–44 ‖ Mark 1:32–39 (summary report); 6:17–19 ‖ Mark 3:7–12 (introduction to the Sermon); 7:18–23 ‖ Matt. 11:2–6 (answer to John the Baptist); 8:1–3 ‖ Matt. 9:35 (women followers); 8:26–39 ‖ Mark 5:1–20 (the Gadarene demoniac); 9:1–6, 10 ‖ Mark 6:7–13 (the mission of the Twelve); 9:37–43 ‖ Mark 9:14–29 (the epileptic boy); 9:49–50 ‖ Mark 9:38–41 (the unknown exorcist); 10:1–12, 17–20 ‖ Matt. 9:37–38; 10:7–16 (the mission of the Seventy[-two]); 11:14–26 ‖ Matt. 12:22–30, 43–45 ‖ Mark 3:22–27 (the Beelzebul controversy); 13:10–17 (the woman with a spirit of infirmity); 13:32 (summary report). For a discussion of the relationship between Luke and Acts, see C. Kingsley Barrett, "The Third Gospel as a Preface to Acts? Some Reflections," in *The Four Gospels, 1992: Festschrift Frans Neirynck* (ed. F. van Segbroeck et al.; 3 vols.; Louvain: Leuven University Press, 1992), 2:1451–66.

3. See the outline discussion by Robert Maddox, *The Purpose of Luke-Acts* (Edinburgh: T&T Clark, 1982), 6–9; Joseph A. Fitzmyer, *The Acts of the Apostles* (AB 31; New York and London:

interest in the church at Syrian Antioch, on the Orontes River—certainly in its early stages[4]—this may be the place where Luke's work was composed and published.[5] However, this must remain little more than a guess. In any case, Luke was most likely an experienced traveler, and his writings probably reflect a wider world than a single church. As we consider the possible correlation between social factors and interest in exorcism, we can take into account the social location of Luke, or at least of what he writes. From this we learn that Luke is from the world of cities and villages and is at home among the wealthy, and in administration, travel, writing, cultured speech, and crafts.[6]

6.1 Jesus as Living Model

That Luke encourages his readers to see Jesus as a model for life and ministry has long been agreed.[7] Luke portrays the early Christians as reenacting and paralleling the life of Jesus. Notable are the broad parallels between the deaths of Jesus and Stephen; the appearances of Jesus after his resurrection and Peter after release from prison; the farewell speeches of Jesus and Paul; the journeys to Jerusalem of Jesus and Paul; and the trials of Jesus and Paul.[8] In particular, we can note that, in the farewell discourse at the end of his Gospel, Luke explicitly portrays Jesus as a model for his followers, twice directing them to imitate his actions: in the eucharistic statement Jesus says, "Do this in memory of me" (Luke 22:20), and then Jesus portrays himself as a model for service (22:27).[9] From this it is reasonable to conclude that Luke is clearly among those writers for whom an important rhetorical device was the employment of example to influence the behavior of readers[10] and

Doubleday, 1998), 51–55. Recently Barbara Shellard, *New Light on Luke: Its Purpose, Sources and Literary Context* (JSNTSup 215; London and New York: Sheffield Academic, 2002), 23–34, argues for a date of 100 CE in Rome.

4. Acts 6:5; 11:19–20, 26–27 (Codex Bezae); 13:1–4; 14:26–28; 15:1–3, 13–40; 18:22–23.

5. Cf. John Nolland, *Luke 1–9:20* (WBC 35A; Dallas: Word Books), xxxix; also see the brief discussion and those cited by Frederick W. Norris, "Antioch of Syria," *ABD* 1:266–67.

6. See Vernon K. Robbins, "The Social Location of the Implied Author of Luke-Acts," in *The Social World of Luke-Acts: Models for Interpretation* (ed. Jerome H. Neyrey; Peabody, MA: Hendrickson, 1991), 305–32, esp. 330–32.

7. See, e.g., Charles H. Talbert, *Literary Patterns, Theological Themes, and the Genre of Luke-Acts* (SBLMS 20; Missoula, MT: Scholars Press, 1974), 15–65; and A. J. Mattill, "The Jesus-Paul Parallels and the Purpose of Luke-Acts: H. H. Evans Reconsidered," *NovT* 17 (1975): 15–45.

8. See the discussion by Garry W. Trompf, *The Idea of Historical Recurrence in Western Thought: From Antiquity to the Reformation* (Berkeley: University of California Press, 1979), 122–28.

9. In detail see William S. Kurz, "Luke 22:14–38 and the Greco-Roman and Biblical Farewell Addresses," *JBL* 104 (1985): 251–68.

10. See the discussion by Abraham J. Malherbe, *Moral Exhortation: A Greco-Roman Sourcebook* (Philadelphia: Westminster, 1986), 135–36, citing Heb. 11:4–38; 13:7; *1 Clem.* 9–12; 17–18; 55; Polycarp, *Phil.* 8–9; Isocrates, *To Demonicus* 9–15; Pliny the Younger, *Epistulae* 8.13; Plutarch,

that Luke is inviting his readers to take Jesus as the model for their life and ministry.[11]

Taking another perspective on Luke's view of the continued importance of Jesus for the early Christians, it is arguable that Luke portrays Jesus not only as a model but also as still active in the life of his followers after Easter. For example, Luke probably intends his readers to understand Jesus to be choosing the successor to Judas. For the prayer ("Lord . . . Show us which one of these two you have chosen," Acts 1:24) is most probably addressed to Jesus (cf. 7:59–60; 14:23).[12] Therefore, in opening Acts by saying that his first volume was about what Jesus "began" (ἤρξατο) to do and teach (1:1), Luke does not simply mean that his first volume contained Jesus' activities from the beginning of his ministry.[13] Rather, the second volume was to be about Jesus continuing his ministry through the activities of followers.[14] Therefore, readers of Acts could expect there to be in its characters echoes of the first volume. For example, in light of our interests, we can note that Jesus' ministry is echoed in the ministry of the early church being described as involving "wonders and signs."[15] More particularly, as we will see, both Peter and Paul's involvement in exorcism appears to be modeled on that of Jesus. In short, Luke's readers could expect to see in the stories of exorcism—both of Jesus and also of his followers in Acts— models for their activities.

6.2 Jesus in Luke-Acts

If Luke understands Jesus to be both the pattern for, as well as remaining active in, the ministry of the early church, what he has to say about Jesus as an exorcist can be expected to contribute to what he wants to say about exorcism among early Christians.

Demetr. 1.4–6; Seneca, *Ep.* 6. See also Benjamin Fiore, *The Function of Personal Example in the Socratic and Pastoral Epistles* (AnBib 105; Rome: Pontifical Biblical Institute, 1986), esp. chap. 3.

11. Cf. William S. Kurz, "Narrative Models for Imitation in Luke-Acts," in *Greeks, Romans, and Christians: Essays in Honor of Abraham J. Malherbe* (ed. David L. Balch, Everett Ferguson, and Wayne A. Meeks; Minneapolis: Fortress, 1990), 176.

12. So also Steven F. Plymale, *The Prayer Texts of Luke-Acts* (New York, San Francisco, and Bern: P. Lang, 1991), 77; C. Kingsley Barrett, *The Acts of the Apostles* (2 vols.; ICC; Edinburgh: T&T Clark, 1994–1998), 1:103. Also see mention of Jesus being active in, e.g., Acts 9:5, 10–17, 34; 22:8; 26:15.

13. So, e.g., F. J. Foakes-Jackson and Kirsopp Lake, *The Beginnings of Christianity*, part 1, *The Acts of the Apostles*, vol. 4, *English Translation and Commentary* (1922; repr., Grand Rapids: Baker, 1965), 3; Hans Conzelmann, *Acts of the Apostles* (Hermeneia; Philadelphia: Fortress, 1987), 3.

14. Cf. Barrett, *Acts*, 1:66–67. Also see, e.g., F. F. Bruce, *The Acts of the Apostles* (Grand Rapids: Eerdmans; Leicester, UK: Apollos, 1990), 98; Beverly R. Gaventa, *Acts* (ANTC; Nashville: Abingdon, 2003), 63.

15. Note Acts 2:22. See also 2:43; 4:30; 5:12; 6:8; cf. 8:6.

a. *Jesus: The importance of exorcism*. In Mark we saw that, after giving exorcism the most prominent place in the beginning of the ministry of Jesus, the evangelist reduced its significance until, after the story of the unknown exorcist (Mark 9:38–41), all references to exorcism are dropped (see chap. 5, n. 101). However, Luke both decreases the early significance of exorcism as well as increases its ongoing significance. On the one hand, he begins Jesus' public ministry not with an exorcism story (cf. Mark 1:21–28) but with him teaching in the synagogues (Luke 4:15), only then performing an exorcism (4:31–37). That is, on the other hand, Luke maintains exorcism as of ongoing importance in Jesus' ministry.

First, for example, Luke has cast, or recast, healing stories as exorcisms. The crippled woman in Luke 13:10–17 is portrayed as having "a spirit of sickness" (πνεῦμα ἔχουσα ἀσθενείας, Luke 13:11, my translation), "whom Satan [had] bound" (ἣν ἔδησεν ὁ σατανᾶς, 13:16). Then, to the story of the healing of Peter's mother-in-law (Mark 1:29–34 ‖ Luke 4:38–41), Luke has made two significant additions. He says that Jesus "stood over her" (ἐπιστὰς ἐπάνω αὐτῆς, 4:39) as an exorcist would,[16] and using the language appropriate to an exorcism, "rebuked" (ἐπετίμησεν, 4:39) the fever.[17] Not only does this recast the story as an exorcism, but also, through the word "rebuke," all three initial healing stories in Luke carry an exorcism motif (cf. 4:35, 39, 41).

Secondly, when the disciples of John the Baptist ask Jesus, "Are you the one who is to come, or are we to wait for another?" (Luke 7:20), Luke adds: "In that hour he cured many of diseases and plagues and evil spirits, and to many who were blind he gave sight" (7:21, my translation). This not only makes sense of John's disciples returning able to say what they had seen as well as heard, but Luke has also been able to mention exorcism as an ongoing part of Jesus' ministry (cf. Matt. 11:3–4). Thirdly, in 13:32 Luke introduces a story with a little biographical statement: "Go and tell that fox [Herod], 'Listen, I cast out demons and perform cures today and tomorrow and the third day I finish my work'" (my translation). The saying likewise has the effect of maintaining the high status of exorcism in Luke's portrait of Jesus.

This response to Herod also illustrates Luke's bringing about a balance between exorcism and other aspects of Jesus' ministry. Similarly, looking back to the Markan story of the healing of the demoniac in the synagogue, the theme of Jesus teaching is woven into the first miracle story by having the crowd respond with amazement to both the teaching as well as the

16. Cf. *PGM* IV. 745; also IV. 2735 and Lucian, *Philops*. 31.
17. Further, see Graham H. Twelftree, "ΕΙ ΔΕ . . . ΕΓΩ . . . ΕΚΒΑΛΛΩ ΤΑ ΔΑΙΜΟΝΙΑ! . . . [Luke 11:19]," in *The Miracles of Jesus* (ed. David Wenham and Craig Blomberg; Gospel Perspectives 6; Sheffield: JSOT Press, 1986), 394n17; and Graham H. Twelftree, *Jesus the Miracle Worker: A Historical and Theological Study* (Downers Grove, IL: InterVarsity, 1999), 148.

exorcism (Mark 1:27). Luke, however, has the crowd respond first, and quite separately, to Jesus' teaching (Luke 4:31–32). Then, in the ensuing exorcism story, the mention of teaching is removed, leaving response to him casting out unclean spirits by his word of power-authority (Mark 1:27 ‖ Luke 4:36). The result is that each aspect of Jesus' ministry is dealt with discretely, without subordinating one to the other, contributing to Luke's apparent agenda of balancing word and deed.[18] Also, at the conclusion of the Beelzebul controversy, which focuses on Jesus as an exorcist (Luke 11:14–28), Jesus responds to a woman in the crowd: "Blessed rather are those who *hear the word* of God and obey it" (11:28, emphasis added).[19] Thereby the deed becomes word.

Through these authorial activities, even though Luke could not contribute any new exorcism stories to the latter part of his story, he has been able to heighten the place of exorcism in relating Jesus' ministry. However, we can see that, although Luke wished to emphasize the exorcistic dimension in the Jesus tradition, he did not wish to isolate it or set it against other aspects of Jesus' life. Indeed, Luke goes to considerable lengths to show that exorcism was an integral part of the ministry of Jesus.

Further balancing, even blurring, takes place at another level. Luke can portray Jesus as dealing with the demonic not only through exorcism but also through healing. In the summary of healings at the beginning of the Sermon on the Plain, Luke does not say Jesus rebuked or cast out the unclean spirits, but that those who were troubled with unclean spirits were "healed" or "cured" (ἐθεραπεύοντο, Luke 6:18). This blurring of the distinction between exorcism and other kinds of healing, along with generally enhancing the place of exorcism in the ministry of Jesus, which brings about a balance among the various aspects of Jesus' ministry, is encapsulated in his description of Jesus in Acts 10:38: "he went about doing good [εὐεργετῶν]²⁰ and healing all that were oppressed by the devil."[21] In turn, this not only draws attention to exorcism as an important part of Jesus' ministry, but also, with its generalized reference ("all who were oppressed by the devil"), suggests that the demonic is broader than "possession." That is, for Luke, all sickness has a demonic dimension (is evil), even though it may not be caused

---

18. Cf. Paul J. Achtemeier, "The Lukan Perspective on the Miracles of Jesus: A Preliminary Sketch," in *Perspectives on Luke-Acts* (ed. Charles H. Talbert; Danville, VA: Association of Baptist Professors of Religion; Edinburgh: T&T Clark, 1978), 156–57.

19. Note also Luke 4:40–44; 6:17–26; 7:18–23; 8:1–3.

20. Luke Timothy Johnson, *The Acts of the Apostles* (SP 5; Collegeville, MN: Michael Glazier / Liturgical Press, 1992), 192, notes that Philostratus, *Vit. Apoll.* 8.7, uses "benefactor" for Apollonius.

21. Further see Leo O'Reilly, *Word and Sign in the Acts of the Apostles: A Study in Lucan Theology* (Rome: Editrice Pontifical Università Gregoriana, 1987), 217; and the discussion in Twelftree, *Miracle,* 178–81.

by demons[22] (cf. Luke 13:10–17).[23] In turn, for Luke, in all healing God's adversary is being subdued.[24]

With this reading of Luke's traditions associated with Jesus, we are more sensitive to the significance of exorcism among the early Christians in Acts. To begin with, as in his Gospel, we find the same blurring, as well as balancing, of exorcism and healing that implies all healing involves God's adversary being defeated. For example, Luke describes people coming to Peter from around Jerusalem and "bringing the sick and those tormented by unclean spirits, and they were all cured" (ἐθεραπεύοντο, Acts 5:16). This blurring is also evident in the phrase "signs and wonders." As exorcism was included in Luke's use of the phrase "wonders and signs" of Jesus (2:22), readers would assume that exorcism was included in the "wonders and signs" of his followers.[25] Importantly for us, this also establishes Luke's view of the importance of exorcism among the activities of early Christians.

Luke gives other, more direct, signals of the importance of exorcism for early Christians. His summaries of the early Christians' activities show this most obviously (Acts 5:12–16; esp. 8:4–8). Also, since exorcism and the kingdom of God were so closely tied in the ministry of Jesus, readers could assume that exorcism was involved when Luke says that the early Christians proclaimed the kingdom of God.[26] Then, in a few places, the ongoing and important place of exorcism is explicitly described. First, it is seen to be involved—and mentioned first—in the activities of Philip. Having said that the crowds listened eagerly to Philip, hearing and seeing the signs he did, Luke's explanation is that (γάρ) "unclean spirits, crying with loud shrieks, came out of many who were possessed" (8:7). Secondly, there is an exorcism story associated with Paul in Acts 16:16–18, and thirdly, exorcism is mentioned in a summary of Paul's ministry in 19:11–12. Given its important place in what Luke calls—in shorthand —"proclaiming the kingdom of God," we can turn to explicating the meaning of exorcism through what he says about Jesus.

b. *Jesus: The meaning of exorcism.* For Luke, the exorcisms of Jesus are both the coming of the powerful presence or kingdom of God and the associated defeat of Satan. This is spelled out in Luke 11:20. "If in God's finger I cast

22. There is, e.g., no mention of demons in the healing of the lepers in Luke 5:12–16; 17:11–19.

23. So Twelftree, *Miracle*, 179. Contrast John Christopher Thomas, *The Devil, Disease, and Deliverance: Origins of Illness in New Testament Thought* (JPTSup 13; Sheffield: Sheffield Academic, 1998), 225–26.

24. Graham H. Twelftree, *Christ Triumphant: Exorcism Then and Now* (London: Hodder & Stoughton, 1985), 104.

25. See Acts 2:43; 4:30; 5:12 [cf. 5:16]; 6:8; cf. 8:6–7, 13; and "signs and wonders" in 5:12; 14:3. Again, as in chap. 3, n. 55, we note that no particular or distinct meaning need be assigned to "signs" or "wonders" in these phrases. See Otto Bauernfeind, *Die Apostelgeschichte* (THKNT 5; Leipzig: A. Deichert, 1939), 80.

26. See Acts 8:12 (cf. 8:7); 19:8 (cf. 19:12); 20:25; 28:23, 31.

out demons, then has come upon you the kingdom of God" (my translation). The saying that follows is the parable of the strong man (Luke 11:21–22). As this is most probably a parable of exorcism,[27] and it also associates the coming of the kingdom of God and the defeat of Satan, for Luke, this defeat of Satan was taking place in Jesus' exorcisms.

Luke gives us other signals that the coming of the kingdom of God and the defeat of Satan were central to his understanding of exorcism. First, like Q and Mark before him, Luke uses ἐκβάλλω ("I cast out"),[28] which in the Septuagint is associated with an enemy being cast out so that God's purpose can be fulfilled (see §4.7 above). Also, he uses ἐπιτιμᾶν ("to rebuke"),[29] which had Septuagintal associations with God's reproving word calling down destruction.[30] Therefore, Luke's readers would have understood that in Jesus' exorcisms Satan, God's enemy, was being defeated[31] so that God's purposes could be fulfilled. Secondly, in the story of the woman with a spirit of infirmity, Luke also spells out the view that exorcism is the defeat of Satan. He says that in being released from the spirit of infirmity she was released from Satan's bondage (Luke 13:11–12 and 16).[32] Thirdly, in light of such passages as Exodus 3:20; 7:4–5; 8:19; and 15:6, it may be that in using "finger" Luke wanted to bring out a parallel between the miracles by which God released Israel from bondage and the miracle by which God, in Jesus, also released people from the bondage of Satan.[33] However, Luke does not portray Jesus' exorcisms as the final defeat of Satan.[34] At the end of Jesus' ministry, Satan is still active and is said to enter into Judas (Luke 22:3), as well as demand to have Simon (22:31). Also, in Acts, Satan had filled Ananias' heart (Acts 5:3), and Paul's ministry was the delivery of the Gentiles from the power of Satan (26:18; cf. 10:38).[35]

Not surprisingly, as well as being the coming of the kingdom of God and the defeat of Satan, the exorcisms of Jesus are also said to be the work of God (cf. Luke 8:39 ‖ Mark 5:19)[36] and contribute to God fulfilling his promise to bring salvation to his people.[37] In turn, the exorcisms of his followers are

27. Graham H. Twelftree, *Jesus the Exorcist: A Contribution to the Study of the Historical Jesus* (WUNT 2.54; Tübingen: Mohr Siebeck; Peabody, MA: Hendrickson, 1993), 111–13.

28. See Luke 11:14–15, 18, 19–20 (cf. Matt. 12:27–28); 13:32; cf. 9:40, 49. Also see Mark 1:34, 39; 3:22; 7:26.

29. Cf. Luke 4:35, 39, 41; 8:24; 9:21, 42; 18:39.

30. See Ethelbert Stauffer, "ἐπιτιμάω," *TDNT* 2:624.

31. See Luke 4:35, 39, 41; 9:42.

32. M. Dennis Hamm, "The Freeing of the Bent Woman and the Restoration of Israel: Luke 13.10–17 as Narrative Theology," *JSNT* 31 (1987): 23–44.

33. Cf. Luke 13:16; James D. G. Dunn, *Jesus and the Spirit* (London: SCM, 1975), 46.

34. Cf. Luke 8:31–33, on which see Twelftree, *Miracle*, §5.16.

35. Acts 5:16; 8:7; 16:16–18; 19:11–20.

36. In more detail, see Twelftree, *Christ Triumphant*, 101–2.

37. On "salvation" in Luke-Acts, see, e.g., Ralph P. Martin, "Salvation and Discipleship in Luke's Gospel," *Int* 30 (1976): 366–80; Neal Flanagan, "The What and How of Salvation in Luke-Acts," in *Sin, Salvation, and the Spirit* (ed. Daniel Durken; Collegeville, MN: Liturgical

similarly viewed[38] and, being part of the "wonders and signs," are linked with
salvation (σῴζω, Acts 2:47).[39]

One further aspect of the meaning or significance for Jesus of his exorcisms
can be mentioned since it is illustrated a number of times. In doing the work
of God or, perhaps, as God, Jesus is not only depicted as larger than life, but
pathos is also added to stories, so that he becomes deeply compassionate in
his response to sickness. For example, the Gadarene demoniac is described
as a man from the city but without a home and without clothes (Luke 8:27
‖ Mark 5:3–4). In the report of the healing of the epileptic boy Luke alters
the story so that the boy is an "only" (μονογενής) son, and so that the father
"cries out" (βοάω) and "begs" (δέομαι) Jesus and his disciples to help (Mark
9:17 ‖ Luke 9:38). In Luke, Jesus refers to the boy not as "he" (αὐτός) but as
"your son" (υἱός, Mark 9:19 ‖ Luke 9:41), then he adds that Jesus handed the
healed boy back to the father (Luke 9:42). In this creativity Luke is focusing
primarily on Jesus—that he was powerful, that demons submitted to him, and
that he was all-knowing as well as compassionate. However, insofar as Jesus
is the pattern for life and ministry among early Christians, their ministry was
not only to be associated with the defeat of Satan and the salvific coming of
the powerful presence of God, but also to be one of deep compassion.

c. *Jesus: The methods of exorcism.* Taking a broad understanding of method,
I have already argued elsewhere against the view that Luke ascribes miracles
of Jesus to "power" (δύναμις) and reserves "spirit" (πνεῦμα) for the source of
Jesus' proclamation. Instead, as is true of the preaching, for Luke, miracles
are to be attributed directly to the Spirit or power of the Spirit.[40] I have
also argued elsewhere that John Hull has muddied the waters by saying that
Luke-Acts is a "tradition penetrated by magic."[41] Hull's broad definition of
magic is fed by conceptions from across material from ancient Egypt to the
church in the Middle Ages[42] and includes any sort of belief in angels, demons,
and exorcism.[43] Nevertheless, Hull is more nearly correct to say that, for

---

Press, 1979), 203–13; Joel B. Green, "'The Message of Salvation' in Luke-Acts," *ExAud* 5 (1989):
21–34; Mark Allan Powell, "Salvation in Luke-Acts," *WW* 12 (1992): 5–10.

38. Cf. Luke 4:36 and 9:1. See also Acts 4:30; 19:12.

39. Further see Twelftree, *Miracle*, §6.5.

40. See Twelftree, *Miracle*, §6.2.

41. John M. Hull, *Hellenistic Magic and the Synoptic Tradition* (SBT 2.28; London: SCM,
1974), chap. 6. Further see Twelftree, *Miracle*, §6.4.

42. Max Turner, "The Spirit and the Power of Jesus' Miracles in the Lucan Conception,"
NovT 33 (1991): 136–37 and n. 33.

43. So Howard C. Kee, *Miracle and Magic in New Testament Times* (Cambridge: Cambridge
University Press, 1986), 114. On defining magic, see Twelftree, *Exorcist*, §24; and Graham H.
Twelftree, "Jesus the Exorcist and Ancient Magic," in *A Kind of Magic: Understanding Magic
in the New Testament and Its Religious Environment* (ed. Michael Labahn and Bert Jan Lietaert
Peerbolte; European Studies on Christian Origins; LNTS 306; London and New York: T&T
Clark, 2007), 57–86.

Luke, δύναμις is a mana-like[44] charge working impersonally and responding to the contact of any believer.[45]

For, in Luke 5:17 ("The power of the Lord was with him to heal") and 8:46 ("Someone touched me"), δύναμις works immediately and impersonally, responding to the contact of any believing person without the knowledge or approval of Jesus. This is significant not only in Luke's view of Jesus experiencing fluctuations in the availability of power.[46] It is also probably important in understanding Luke's view of the experience of the early Christians, including in their exorcisms. Luke understands the followers of Jesus to have been given this δύναμις (Luke 9:1).

In Acts, Luke describes δύναμις as appearing to observers to operate in the same way as it did for Jesus. Thus, when Simon Magus believed and was so amazed when he saw the signs and great powers, he offered money for authority to dispense the Spirit through his hands (Acts 8:19). However, Luke corrects this view through Peter saying, "May your silver perish with you!" (8:20). Therefore, we have to fill out Hull's notion of δύναμις for it is more than a mana-like substance working immediately and impersonally. It is the powerful presence of God's Spirit received for healing through faith.[47] When we turn to Acts, we will see more of what Luke has to say about the methods of exorcism among early Christians.

d. *The followers of Jesus as exorcists.* In that the early stories in Acts depict the Twelve as significant (cf. Acts 1:24–25) and playing a leading role in the life of the early Christians, Luke's readers are prompted to recall his portrait of them in his Gospel (cf. Luke 1:1–2). In relation to our interest in exorcism, first to consider in the Gospel is the call and mission of the Twelve (9:1–11). In the period between their call and their commissioning (6:13–7:50), not only is the character of Jesus and his ministry established (see 7:18–50). Also, the wider group (or crowd) of disciples is portrayed as listening to Jesus' teaching (6:17–49; esp. 6:17, 20, 40) and as witnessing him raise the dead (7:11–17; esp. 11). Then from 8:1, Luke narrows the focus of his attention to the Twelve. It is expressly stated that the Twelve were with him as "he went on through cities and villages, preaching and bringing the good news of the kingdom of God" (8:1). Thus, before the Twelve are sent out (9:1–2), they are shown to have heard Jesus preach about the kingdom of God (8:10), declare the true nature of discipleship as hearing and doing the word of God (8:11, 15; cf. 8:39), and have watched him cast out demons (8:26–39), heal a woman's hemorrhage (8:40–48), and raise a dead girl (8:49–56).

---

44. Hull, *Magic*, 105.

45. However, this conception of δύναμις is to be found in the LXX rather than in any universal idea of magical miracles. So also E. P. Sanders and Margaret Davies, *Studying the Synoptic Gospels* (London: SCM; Philadelphia: TPI, 1989), 281.

46. Without evidence, Hull, *Magic*, 107, 115, attributes this view to the historical Jesus.

47. Twelftree, *Miracle*, 172.

When the Twelve are commissioned, they are told to preach what Jesus preached ("the kingdom of God," Luke 9:2; cf. 8:1) and to heal as Jesus did (9:1, 6), and, like Jesus, are given authority over demons (9:1). The scale of this authority and power is seen in light of the stories that have preceded 9:1, especially obvious in light of others being unable to heal (8:43).

That this has direct bearing on Luke's view of exorcism among early Christians is clear when we take into account that he portrays the Twelve as the foundation and leadership of the church. From Luke's saying (6:13) that Jesus "chose" (ἐκλέγομαι)[48] the Twelve from among the disciples and that he called them "apostles" (ἀπόστολοι),[49] readers are probably to understand that the Twelve held a special place of leadership. This is confirmed when we note that they formed the nucleus of the life of the early church (Acts 1:15–2:1; 2:14, 37). Also like Jesus, the Twelve are endowed not only with authority (ἐξουσία)[50] but also with power (δύναμις)[51] to exorcise demons and to heal,[52] and they are sent to preach the kingdom of God.[53]

e. *The Seventy(-two).*[54] The story of the call and mission of the Seventy(-two) is also important for it sheds direct light on Luke's views of exorcism among early Christians (Luke 10:1–12, 17–20). Luke is the only Gospel writer to have two mission stories. Why, having told one story of the sending of disciples, does Luke give us another story, which has many similarities? The answer may be found in exploring the idea that Luke uses a pattern of climactic parallelism as a means of communication.[55] That is, if the parallel story of the call and mission of the Twelve draws attention to Jesus being the model for the mission of his followers, this story draws attention to the scope and nature of the mission.

As Luke has just related a mission (Luke 9:1–6, 10), the "others" here in 10:1 are probably meant as a contrast to the mission of the Twelve—a contrast between those who were particularly associated with the pre-Easter mission of Jesus and those with the post-Easter mission of Jesus. Thus, although the

48. In Luke 6:13; 9:35; 10:42; 14:7; note 9:35, where ἐκλέγω is used of Jesus' being chosen; cf. Acts 1:2, 24; 6:5; 13:17; 15:7, 22, 25, where in each case those chosen are to assume special leadership roles. See Gottlob Schrenk, "ἐκλέγομαι," *TDNT* 4:174.

49. Except for the wider reference in Luke 11:49 and Acts 14:14, Luke uses ἀπόστολος of the Twelve: Luke 6:13; 9:10; 11:49; 17:5; 22:14; 24:10; Acts 1:2, 26; 2:37, 42, 43; 4:33, 35, 36, 37; 5:2, 12, 18, 29, 40; 6:6; 8:1, 14, 18; 9:27; 11:1; 14:4, 14; 15:2, 4, 6, 22, 23; 16:4.

50. As in Mark 6:7. See also Luke 4:32, 36; 5:24.

51. See Luke 4:14, 36; 5:17; 6:19; 8:46.

52. Cf. Luke 4:14, 32, 36; 5:17; 6:19; 7:1–10; 8:46; 20:1–8.

53. Cf. Luke 4:43; 8:1; 16:16; also see 4:18–19.

54. On the status of δύο, see Bruce M. Metzger, "Seventy or Seventy-two Disciples," *NTS* 5 (1959): 299–306; and Bruce M. Metzger, *A Textual Commentary on the Greek New Testament* (2nd ed.; New York: American Bible Society, 1994), 126–27.

55. See Helmut Flender, *St. Luke, Theologian of Redemptive History* (trans. Reginald H. and Ilse Fuller; London: SPCK, 1967), 20–22.

number "seventy" could be modeled on the seventy elders of Israel appointed by Moses (Num. 11:16),[56] with the administrative nature of their role, this probably does not provide a likely background to Luke 10, for leadership is not the major theme of the story. Rather, given that mission is the major theme of the story, the number "seventy" probably represents the nations of the world, thought to be seventy (Gen. 10, table of nations;[57] cf. Exod. 1:5; *1 En.* 89:59–60). Thus Luke is probably prefiguring the universal mission of the church to the wider world.[58] Other points in the story confirm this.

First, in Luke 10:2 the mission is likened to a harvest (θερισμός), which for all the New Testament writers who used the word[59] was a similitude of the eschatological harvest.[60] In this story, then, the eschatological gathering by God of his people from the wider world (Isa. 27:12; cf. Gen. 15:18) is now the task given to the post-Easter followers of Jesus (cf. Luke 10:12; Jude 7).

Secondly, in Luke 10:3 Jesus says, "I am sending you out like lambs into the midst of wolves." The metaphor of wolves and lambs peacefully living together is also associated with the eschaton (Isa. 11:6; 65:25). But the picture of lambs in danger from wolves probably signifies defenseless disciples among the nations of the earth (cf. Acts 20:28–29; *Pss. Sol.* 8:23, 30).[61] We see a further aspect of Luke's parallelism here in that just as Jesus was the Lamb (cf. Acts 8:32, 35; Isa. 53:7), so now the disciples are the lambs sent out.[62] Therefore, Luke tells this story of the sending of the Seventy(-two) as a way of prefiguring the mission of the church, not only as based in and modeled on Jesus and apostolic activity (esp. Luke 9), but also to spell out the nature of the church's mission.

Like the ministry of Jesus, the mission is to comprise healing the sick and saying, "The kingdom of God has come near you."[63] Although exorcism

56. Further, see Karl H. Rengstorf, "ἑπτά," *TDNT* 2:634.

57. In Gen. 10 the MT lists 70 grandsons of Noah; the LXX lists 72. This difference between the MT and LXX helps explain the textual difficulty in Luke 10:1.

58. Rengstorf, "ἑπτά," *TDNT* 2:634; Flender, *Luke*, 23; I. Howard Marshall, *The Gospel of Luke* (Exeter, UK: Paternoster, 1978), 415.

59. Matt. 9:37 ‖ Luke 10:2; John 4:35; Matt. 13:30, 39; Mark 4:29; Rev. 14:15. On the relation of John 4:35 to the Synoptic tradition, see e.g. C. H. Dodd, *Historical Tradition in the Fourth Gospel* (Cambridge: Cambridge University Press, 1963), 392–94.

60. Friedrich Hauck, "θερίζω, θερισμός," *TDNT* 3:133. For background see Isa. 27:12; Joel 3:13; *2 Bar.* 70:2; cf. Isa. 17:5; 18:4–5; Jer. 8:20; 51:33; Hos. 6:11.

61. Cf. *Midr. Tanḥ. Toledot* (generations) 32b: "Hadrian said to R. Jehoshua [ca. 90 CE]: There is something great about the sheep [Israel] that can persist among 70 wolves [the nations]. He replied: Great is the Shepherd who delivers it and watches over it and destroys them [the wolves] before them [Israel]." From Joachim Jeremias, "ἀρήν," *TDNT* 1:340. Note Luke 10:19 in which the readers are assured of protection or care.

62. Thus companionship may have been seen as one of the reasons why the disciples were sent out "two by two." See Luke's pairing at Luke 7:19; Acts 13:2; 15:27, 39, 40; 17:14; 19:22; cf. Eccles. 4:9–12. The witness principle of Deut. 19:15 may also be involved.

63. Luke 10:9, 11; cf. Acts 1:3; 8:12; 19:8; 20:25; 28:23, 31.

is not mentioned in the commission (Luke 10:9; cf. 9:1–2), Luke assumes that it is part of the mission of the church. For the Seventy(-two) are to preach the kingdom of God, which involves exorcism, and the report of their return focuses on exorcism (10:17). However, in contrast to Jesus' restricted mission—note how Luke (9:17–18) omits Mark 6:45–8:26, where Jesus is in Gentile territory[64]—the mission of the church is to be universal (cf. Luke 10:2b, 16;[65] Acts 1:8) and, for our purposes we note, includes exorcism.

f. *The Return of the Seventy(-two)*. In the return of the Seventy(-two) (Luke 10:17–20), Luke conveys three further important aspects of his understanding of exorcism, which have a bearing on his view of exorcism among early Christians. First, Luke tells his readers of the function or significance of the exorcisms: "He said to them, 'I saw Satan fall like lightning from heaven. Behold, I have given you authority to tread upon serpents and scorpions, and over all the power of the enemy; and nothing shall hurt you'" (10:18–19). The understanding of the duration or time of the "falling" (πεσόντα, aorist participle, denoting a point of action) of Satan is governed by the earlier main verb "I saw" (ἐθεώρουν, imperfect tense), which denotes a continuous, protracted action. Thus, we may translate Luke's intention here as "I have been seeing Satan falling like lightning from heaven."

In other words, Luke saw both that Satan's downfall was ongoing and that it was linked to the exorcistic ministry of the early Christians.[66] Just as Jesus had authority to perform exorcisms (Luke 4:36) and to heal (cf. 5:24; 7:8, 10; 20:1–8), and as the apostles received authority over demons (9:1), authority to defeat Satan, so the early Christians had been given that authority to be involved in the same preliminary defeat of Satan. That this downfall of Satan is described "as lightning" (10:18) does not—particularly in the context of what we have just said—necessarily mean that it was "speedy,"[67] as it might to the modern reader. Rather, it probably means bright, spectacular, and obvious.[68] The mention of serpents[69] and scorpions[70] and the enemy (cf. Matt. 13:25; Rom. 16:20; 1 Peter 5:8) highlights the battle aspect of the activity of the early Christians so that it is not surprising that there is the encouragement that no harm will come to them (Luke 10:19).

Secondly, from this story we discover little about the methods of exorcism. However, the returned disciples saying "the demons are subject [ὑποτάσσω;

---

64. Further see John Drury, *Tradition and Design in Luke's Gospel* (London: Darton, Longman & Todd, 1976), 96–102.

65. See Marshall, *Luke*, 416.

66. Cf. W. F. Arndt, *Luke* (St. Louis: Concordia, 1956), 285.

67. Contra Werner Foerster, "ἀστραπή," *TDNT* 1:505; BDAG, "ἀστραπή."

68. Cf. e.g. Dan. 10:6; Matt. 24:27; 28:3; Luke 11:36; 17:24; Rev. 4:5; 8:5; 11:19; 16:18.

69. See 2 Cor. 11:3; Rev. 12:9, 14–15; 20:2.

70. Luke 11:12; Rev. 9:3, 5, 10; cf. Ps. 91:13 (90:13 LXX).

cf. Luke 2:51] to us in your name" (RSV) contains helpful clues. That the demons (or enemies; cf. 10:19) subjected themselves to the Seventy(-two) meant not simply that they obeyed but that they surrendered their rights or wills.[71] The verb ὑποτάσσω often had military associations[72] so that, in the context of the whole saying, the early Christians represented by Luke probably understood that they were confronting the demons with (the authority of) Jesus.[73] This control of the demons was not done on the basis of the disciples' own power-authority. This is in sharp contrast to Jesus' all-but-unique method whereby, although he declared that he exorcised "by the finger of God" (Luke 11:20), in practical terms he appeared to rely on his own power-authority.[74]

That is, despite Jesus being the pattern for the early Christians, Luke is setting out the idea that the disciples were not to use their own power-authority but to confront the demons with (the name of) Jesus in order to gain their submission (see Acts 16:18). Thus, taking Luke as our guide, in its technique of exorcism the early church had reverted to using contemporary "magical" methods of exorcising by some greater source of power-authority (see §§2.1 and 2.2 above) rather than using the innate power-authority of a charismatic.

A third important aspect of Luke's understanding of exorcism among early Christians found in this story of the return of the Seventy(-two) is the statement, "Nevertheless do not rejoice in this, that the spirits are subject to you; but rejoice that your names are written in heaven" (Luke 10:20, my translation). Here Luke could be concerned about an overenthusiastic rejoicing in exorcism. When taken alongside Luke's moderation of Mark's early focus on exorcism, and his bringing about a balance and blurring with other aspects of Jesus' ministry, this may be Luke signaling to his readers that, while exorcism is an integral and important part of the church's ministry, it was to be kept in perspective. The matter of central importance is that their names have been written in heaven (cf. Luke 13:23–24), and that they are part of God's people (cf. Exod. 32:32–33; Ps. 69:28; Dan. 12:1).

In short, what we have tried to show in these paragraphs about the two pre-Easter mission stories is that, in taking Jesus as the model for ministry, Luke was expressing the view that the early Christians had both a warrant—indeed a command—to include exorcism in its ministry of "preaching the kingdom of God" and also a pattern for such a ministry.

71. Gerhard Delling, "ὑποτάσσω," *TDNT* 8:40; cf. 8:41.
72. See 1 Kings 10:15 ‖ 2 Chron. 9:14 (LXX); Esther 3:13a (LXX); Josephus, *C. Ap.* 1.119; 2 Macc. 8:9, 22; 3 Macc. 1:7.
73. This confrontation and subjection of demons to an exorcist (or "magician") was a known method of controlling demons. See, e.g., *PGM* V. 164–166: "Subject all demons to me, that each . . . may be obedient." Cf. IV. 3080: "And every demon and spirit shall be subject to you."
74. See Luke 4:35; 8:29; 9:42; cf. 13:12. Cf. §2.5 above.

6.3 Luke and Exorcism in the Early Church

Having seen what Luke wants to say about exorcism in the early church through stories associated with Jesus, we can turn to what Luke says more directly in his second volume. It is surprising that, compared to Luke's Gospel, exorcism is much less prominent in Acts than we might expect in a book featuring spiritual power.[75] Yet, if Jesus is the pattern for the ministry of exorcism among early Christians, then this is less surprising. What Luke has to say about exorcism in the early church has been prefigured and established in his Gospel as part of the mix of the ministry of the followers of Jesus. Also, in such phrases as "signs and wonders,"[76] Luke's readers would have understood the inclusion of exorcism. Further, given the association of miracles, including exorcism, with "power(s)" ($\delta\acute{u}v\alpha\mu\iota\varsigma/\delta\upsilon\nu\acute{\alpha}\mu\epsilon\iota\varsigma$), some of the occurrences of this word in Acts would have brought exorcism to the minds of the readers.[77] Not withstanding, the relatively small amount of material on exorcism in Acts does not permit us to take exorcism as, in any way, the most important part of the ministry of the early church, at least from Luke's perspective. Not withstanding, as well as taking into account what we have learned from the Gospel, some of Luke's stories in Acts require particular attention in building an idea of what Luke thinks about exorcism among early Christians.

a. *Peter and the Apostles* (Acts 5:12–16). In this summary the focus is not so much on the inner life and worship of the community (as in 2:42–47) or on mutual care and support within it (as in 4:32–37) as on the mission of the apostles. Luke's readers, sensitive to parallels and paradigms in his work, are likely to have seen echoes of the ministry of Jesus in this story. In particular, the final verse is about people gathering from around Jerusalem and bringing their sick and those tormented ($\dot{o}\chi\lambda\acute{e}o\mu\alpha\iota$[78]) by unclean spirits to be healed. This echoes what is found in a number of places in the ministry of Jesus.[79] Thus Luke invites his readers to conclude that the ministry of the early Christians is following the paradigm of Jesus.

The mention of signs and wonders at the beginning of the story (Acts 5:12) not only draws together the threads of the miracles mentioned so far in Acts, but also, at least in part, draws attention to the prayer of 4:30 being

75. See the discussion by Rick Strelan, *Strange Acts: Studies in the Cultural World of the Acts of the Apostles* (BZNW 126; Berlin and New York: de Gruyter, 2004), 101–2.

76. See above and here note Acts 2:43; 4:30; 5:12; 6:8; 14:3; 15:12; as well as 8:6–7, on which see below.

77. See Acts 1:8; 4:33; 6:8; 8:13; on 19:11, see below.

78. To say that those brought to Peter were troubled ($\dot{o}\chi\lambda\acute{e}o\mu\alpha\iota$, Acts 5:16) by the unclean spirits is not, as Strelan, *Strange*, 105, suggests, to portray demon possession more mildly than in the Gospels. For $\dot{o}\chi\lambda\acute{e}o\mu\alpha\iota$ was used, e.g., of the murderous demon in Tob. 6:8 and by Josephus of hardships (Josephus, *C. Ap.* 1.310) and of being attacked by illness (Josephus, *Ant.* 6.217).

79. See Luke 4:40; 5:15; 6:18; 7:21.

answered.[80] In Acts 4:29–30 Luke has the early Christians pray, "And now, Lord, . . . grant [δός] to your servants to speak your word with all boldness, while [ἐν] you stretch out your hand to heal, and signs and wonders are performed through the name of your holy servant Jesus." This is not a request that *they* will be given bold speech *and* that the *Lord* would also perform miracles. Rather, they are asking to be given bold speech *on the basis of*, or because of—note the instrumental ἐν ("in")[81]—God stretching out his hand so that healings and signs and wonders are performed.[82] In other words, Luke sees the bold speech of the early Christians depending on, or based on, the healings and signs and wonders, including exorcisms. This reading is probably immediately confirmed in Luke saying, first, that the place was shaken, as well as those present being filled with the Spirit, before saying they continued speaking (καὶ ἐλάλουν) boldly (Acts 4:31).[83] Also, in the summary here (5:12–16), it is clear the signs and wonders are the cause of believers being "added to the Lord" (5:14) who, in turn (ὥστε, "so that," 5:15), brought the sick and those troubled by unclean spirits to be cured. In short, miracles, including exorcisms, formed the basis of early Christians being able to speak boldly.

The most interesting and difficult aspect of the summary is the idea that people sought healing through Peter's shadow falling on them (Acts 5:15), which, in the light of 5:16, Luke accepts as a Christian method of exorcism.[84] Ancient Egyptian texts are familiar with the idea of the "powerful" shadow and sometimes refer to them as gods.[85] As recently as the eighteenth century, in Germany, it was believed that the shadow of a lime tree could heal the sick.[86] Pieter W. van der Horst has surveyed this and other ancient material[87] and concludes that the shadow was regarded as a person's "soul, soul-substance, spiritual essence, spiritual double, or whatever other term one may use to designate the vital power or life force." Thus, to be in contact with a person's shadow meant to be in contact with that person's life and to be influenced by it.[88] That the impact of a shadow was taken seriously by Cicero, Aulianus, and Pseudo-Aristotle, as well as Pliny the Elder (in relation to property of the

---

80. Cf. Conzelmann, *Acts*, 39.

81. On the instrumental ἐν, see BDF §219; cf. §195.

82. Cf. Barrett, *Acts*, 1:249.

83. Ἐλάλουν; imperfect, "they continued speaking." Cf. Acts 11:20; 19:6.

84. On the considerable number of interpretative difficulties, see Barrett, *Acts*, 1:272–73.

85. Pieter W. van der Horst, "Peter's Shadow: The Religio-Historical Background of Acts 5:15," *NTS* 23 (1976–1977): 206; citing Hans Bonnet, *Reallexikon der Ägyptischen Religionsgeschichte* (Berlin: de Gruyter, 1952), "Schatten," 675–76.

86. J. von Negelein, "Bild, Spiegel und Schatten im Volksglauben," *AR* 5 (1902): 17.

87. E.g., Cicero, *Tusc.* 3.12, 26; Virgil, *Ecl.* 10.75–76; Pliny the Elder, *Nat.* 17.18; 28.69; Dio Chrysostom, *2 Glor.* (*Or.* 67) 4–5; Aelian, *Nat. an.* 6.14; Philostratus of Lemnos, *Her.* 1.3; Porphyry, *Antr. nymph.* 26; Ps.-Aristotle, *Mir. ausc.* 145 (157).

88. Cf. van der Horst, "Shadow," 207.

shadow of trees) suggests that this concept was current in Luke's time and familiar to him when writing this summary.[89] What is significant to conclude here in relation to exorcism among early Christians is that Luke probably understood that people afflicted with unclean spirits were healed as they came in contact with Peter's spiritual essence or life force. In turn, Luke would have seen this power to have been invested in Peter and the apostles by the Holy Spirit (cf. 5:12).[90] We have also seen that exorcisms, along with other miracles, form the basis of the early Christians' ability to speak boldly.

b. *Philip in Samaria* (Acts 8:4–8). Our interest is in Luke's view of the place and practice of exorcism in a story that includes a cleverly constructed flashback to earlier activities of Simon. We can see the nature and role of exorcism not only in noting what is said in relation to it but also in paying attention to aspects of the contrast—indeed contest—Luke sets up between Philip and Simon. Simon is said to have practiced "magic" (μαγεύω, 8:9; cf. μαγεία, 8:11). Luke does not explicitly say what this involved. Nevertheless, that he intended his readers to understand Simon's magic to have involved prophecy may be deduced from his calling Bar-Jesus (Elymas) the magician a false prophet (13:6–8). Simon's magic may also have involved money changing hands (cf. 8:17–24). Further, in view of the competition Luke has set up, the magic probably involved miracles of some kind. Some hint of this might be detected in Luke contrasting Simon's magic with his speaking. That is, the Samaritans "listened eagerly to him because [διά] for a long time he had amazed them with his magic" (8:11). However, Philip's miracle-working is portrayed as superior; after Simon believed and was baptized, he "stayed constantly with Philip and was amazed when he saw the signs and great miracles that took place" (8:13).

Indeed, the crowds are said to listen eagerly to Philip because (γάρ) they heard and saw that "unclean spirits, crying with loud shrieks, came out of many who were possessed; and many others who were paralyzed or lame were cured" (Acts 8:7). Even in the mention of proclaiming the kingdom of God (8:12), readers would assume the miraculous, especially exorcism, to be involved. In that this summary of the results of Philip's ministry closely echoes that of Jesus in the Gospel,[91] readers would also draw conclusions about Philip's ministry that they drew about Jesus, for example, that these exorcisms were part of the subjugation of Satan (Luke 11:20–22; cf. §6.2b above).[92] As a result of what we could call Philip's miracle-laden proclamation, people believed and were baptized (8:12).

89. See the evidence in van der Horst, "Shadow," 207; and in Edwin M. Yamauchi, "Magic in the Biblical World," *TynBul* 34 (1983): 179.

90. Cf. Luke 10:19; 24:49; Acts 1:8; 2:4.

91. See Luke 4:43; 8:1; 9:11; 11:20; 12:1; cf. 10:9.

92. Cf. Susan R. Garrett, *The Demise of the Devil: Magic and the Demonic in Luke's Writings* (Minneapolis: Fortress, 1989), 65.

Alan Richardson called on this passage as part of his evidence that "it is reasonably certain that the ancient practice of baptismal exorcism goes back to apostolic days."[93] However, although the baptisms follow the exorcisms (cf. Acts 8:7, 12), there is no indication that one involved, or was directly associated with, the other.[94] In fact, the baptisms are somewhat detached from the mention of the miraculous signs.[95]

Although it is the miracles that gain both Simon's and the crowds' attention (Acts 8:6–7, 13), on a first reading, Luke appears to give priority to the significance of Philip's message in his activities. That is, Philip is initially described as one of those scattered from Jerusalem proclaiming the word (8:4) and, in Samaria, proclaiming the Christ (8:5). Then, a little later, the Samaritans are not described as believing Philip, a miracle-worker, but one "who was proclaiming the good news about the kingdom of God and the name of Jesus Christ" (8:12). Nevertheless, in Philip modeling the ministry of Jesus, just as Jesus' proclamation of the kingdom of God inextricably involved miracles, especially exorcism, so Philip's miracles, especially exorcism, were a "visible and audible enactment" of the kingdom of God.[96] In other words, for Luke, the exorcism formed a symbiotic relationship with the message, each requiring the other for their completeness and comprehension.

c. *Paul and the slave girl* (Acts 16:16–18). As well as the general principle that Luke sees Jesus as a model for the early Christians, there may be two specific clues in this story suggesting Luke wanted his readers to see this story of Paul as a parallel to that of Jesus in the story of the Gerasene demoniac (Luke 8:26–39): Paul and Jesus are described as "of God Most High" (Luke 8:28 ‖ Acts 16:17, my translation), and the theme of salvation is found in both stories.[97]

In more detail we can note that this short story is helpful in understanding what Luke wants to say about exorcism among early Christians. He is explicit about both the slave girl's condition and the method used in the exorcism, as well as about its function.[98] The girl is said to "have a spirit of python" (ἔχουσαν πνεῦμα πύθωνα, Acts 16:16, my translation) or "divina-

93. Alan Richardson, *An Introduction to the Theology of the New Testament* (New York: Harper & Brothers, 1958), 337–38, also citing Mark 9:14–29; 16:15–17; Acts 8:16; 16:18.

94. Against Richardson's view, Barrett, *Acts*, 1:404, says that Acts 8:7 "will hardly serve as evidence for the origin in apostolic days of the practice of baptismal exorcism!"

95. Cf. Hans-Josef Klauck, *Magic and Paganism in Early Christianity: The World of the Acts of the Apostles* (Edinburgh: T&T Clark, 2000), 14.

96. Garrett, *Demise*, 65.

97. Luke 8:36 (σῴζω) and Acts 16:17 (σωτηρία). Further, see Todd E. Klutz, *The Exorcism Stories in Luke-Acts: A Sociostylistic Reading* (SNTSMS 129; Cambridge: Cambridge University Press, 2004), 217–18.

98. Lisa Maurizio, "Anthropology and Spirit Possession: A Reconsideration of the Pythia's Role at Delphi," *JHS* 115 (1995): 75, notes that, from a cross-cultural perspective, women have often been the agents of spirit possession.

tion." It is difficult to know whether Luke meant that the girl had a spirit named python or a pythonic spirit.[99] In any case, the meaning is clear. Luke describes the spirit as causing the girl to prophesy or give oracles (μαντεύομαι, 16:16)[100] in a way that appears to be ventriloquism.[101] For it was considered that Apollo, the Pythian god, incarnate in a serpent or python, inspired what Plutarch calls Pythones or "belly-talkers" (ἐγγαστρίμυθοι).[102] It is not that the girl was a ventriloquist,[103] for observers would not have considered the girl to be in a trance or spiritual state. Hippocrates compares the noisy breathing of a patient to "the women called belly-talkers,"[104] and as E. R. Dodds notes, ventriloquists do not breathe stertorously.[105]

For Luke, this belly-talking probably had strongly evil connotations, as seen from the Septuagint using ἐγγαστρίμυθος ("belly-talker") of the witch of Endor (1 Sam. 28:7)[106] and from Luke describing her as "soothsaying" or "fortune-telling" (μαντεύομαι). This is the only time the word appears in the New Testament. Its strong negative connotations relating to false prophets in the Septuagint[107] and its use for pagan ecstatic activity in non-Christian literature around the period[108] show that Luke would have viewed the girl as inspired by an evil spirit[109] and in need of exorcism. The error of the girl's prophecy is in its fundamental ambiguity: "These men are slaves of the Most High God, who proclaim to you a way of salvation" (Acts 16:17). Although the Greek Bible has no hesitation in using the divine predicate "the highest," it is found less frequently in the intertestamental literature and, most significantly, Luke only otherwise has the precise term "the Most High God" (τοῦ

99. See Ernst Haenchen, *The Acts of the Apostles: A Commentary* (Oxford: Blackwell, 1971), 495 and n. 4.

100. So also Plutarch, *Def. orac.* 9.414e; see also Plato, *Apologia* 22C; *Ion* 534C; *Menex.* 99C; *Soph.* 252C; Aristophanes, *Vesp.* 1019.

101. See Maurizio, "Anthropology," 69–86; and the discussion by Frederick E. Brenk, "The Exorcism at Philippoi in Acts 16.11–40: Divine Possession or Diabolical Inspiration," *Filología Neotestamentaria* 13 (2000): 11–17.

102. Plutarch, *Def. orac.* 9.414e. Further see Eric R. Dodds, *The Greeks and the Irrational* (London, Berkeley, and Los Angeles: University of California Press, 1951), 71; Werner Foerster, "πύθων," *TDNT* 6:920.

103. So also Brenk, "Exorcism at Philippoi," 8–9.

104. Hippocrates, *Epid.* 5.63 (7.28).

105. Dodds, *Greeks*, 72.

106. Cf. the LXX: Lev. 19:31; 20:6, 27; Deut. 18:11; 1 Chron. 10:13; 2 Chron. 33:6; 35:19; Isa. 8:19; 19:3; 44:25. See also Pseudo-Clement, *Hom.* 9.16.3: "For pythons prophesy, yet they are cast out by us as demons."

107. In the LXX see μαντεῖον ("oracle"): Num. 22:7; Prov. 16:10; Ezek. 21:22–27; μαντεύομαι ("divinize"): Deut. 18:10; 1 Sam. 28:8; 2 Kings 17:17; Jer. 34:9; Ezek. 12:24; 13:6, 23; 21:26, 28, 34; Mic. 3:11; μάντις ("diviner," "seer," or "prophet"): Josh. 13:22; 1 Sam. 6:2; Jer. 36:8; Mic. 3:7; Zech. 10:2.

108. LSJ 1079–80. Further on μαντεύομαι see Klutz, *Exorcism Stories*, 216.

109. Contra Hermann Wolfgang Beyer, *Die Apostelgeschichte* (9th ed.; NTD; Göttingen: Vandenhoeck & Ruprecht, 1959), cited favorably by Haenchen, *Acts*, 495.

θεοῦ τοῦ ὑψίστου)" on the lips of a demoniac (Luke 8:28). This, along with the exceptional absence of the article "the" with "way" (ὁδός),[110] implies that what Paul is said to proclaim is only one among many possibilities for salvation. This ambiguity, coupled with the portrayal of Paul's delay in responding to the girl's false prophecy, shows both that Luke recognizes that he is dealing with the unclear contours between Christianity and its opponents, and why he has Paul react to the girl's statements. In charging the demon to come out of the girl using the name of Jesus—established for the readers as the source of salvation[111]—Paul removes the ambiguity from the girl's reference to the highest God and the way of salvation (16:18).[112] Thus, exorcism is made an unmistakable means of salvation.

Further indication of how abhorrent Luke would have found the girl's situation is the idea that she was earning money from her "soothsaying" or "fortune-telling" (cf. Simon in Acts 8:18–23). Thus, she is exorcised not simply because she is unqualified to proclaim the gospel[113] but because she is inspired or empowered by an evil spirit. Paul is reported as turning and saying to the spirit (πνεῦμα), "I order [παραγγέλλω] you in the name of Jesus Christ to come out of her" (16:18). In Mark we have already come across the idea of exorcism "in the name of Jesus" meaning to perform an exorcism as if it had been done by Jesus himself (§5.9 above); and we have no reason to think that Luke takes it differently.

In relation to the method of exorcism, a key word in the story is παραγγέλλω ("I order"). Luke is particularly fond of the word[114] and in Acts always uses it as a "directive from an authoritative source."[115] Significantly, Luke also uses it of Jesus commanding an unclean spirit to leave the Gadarene demoniac (Luke 8:29; cf. Mark 5:8). Thus, Paul and Jesus—whom Paul is portrayed as modeling—are seen to be issuing a directive to the demons from an authoritative source. This aspect of the word is elucidated when we note that it has strong military associations, where it means "to pass an announcement along (the ranks)."[116] Thus, along with Paul being said to act in the name of Jesus, Luke is again showing exorcism to be confronting the evil spirits or demons

110. In Acts 2:28 the article is absent in a citation of Ps. 16:11 (15:11 LXX).

111. Cf., e.g., Acts 2:14–36; and here in the story in question, 16:30–31.

112. See Klauck, *Magic*, 69; and the review of Klauck by Graham H. Twelftree, in *JTS* 53 (2002): 227.

113. So Hans Hinrich Wendt, *Die Apostelgeschichte* (KEK 3; Göttingen: Vandenhoeck & Ruprecht, 1913), 246; followed by Haenchen, *Acts*, 495n10.

114. In NT = Matt. 10:5; Matt. 15:35 ‖ Mark 8:6; 6:8; Luke 5:14; 8:29, 56; 9:21; Acts 1:4; 4:18; 5:28, 40; 10:42; 15:5; 16:18, 23; 17:30; 23:22, 30; 1 Cor. 7:10; 11:17; 1 Thess. 4:11; 2 Thess. 3:4, 6, 10, 12; 1 Tim. 1:3; 4:11; 5:7; 6:13, 17.

115. Friedrich Hauck, "παραγγέλλω," *TDNT* 5:763. Cf., e.g., Acts 1:4; 10:42; 15:5.

116. Hauck, "παραγγέλλω," *TDNT* 5:761–62n2; citing Eduard Schwyzer, *Griechische Grammatik im Anschluss an Karl Brugmanns "Griechische Grammatik"* (HAT 2.1; 3 vols.; Munich: Beck, 1934–1953), 2:493.

with Jesus. From Luke's perspective, early Christian exorcism was successful because the exorcists brought Jesus into the situation either by using his name or issuing a command as if passed down from him.

While this small story is told in passing to carry forward the larger story of Paul (cf. Acts 16:9–10), and, although we do not know whether the girl was converted, we have seen, embedded in it, reflections of Luke's view of exorcism among early Christians. Exorcisms were to be modeled on those of Jesus and were a combating of evil on the unclear borders on the edge of Christianity. The actual methods of exorcism involved bringing Jesus into the situation, here described in terms of passing on a command from a higher authority. Exorcism was not simply healing a sick person but the bringing of salvation.

d. *Paul's clothing and the sons of Sceva* (Acts 19:11–20). In what is sometimes taken as one paragraph[117] there are actually two stories. The first (19:11–12), which provides a portrait of Paul—parallel to that associated with Peter (5:15–16)—concerns God doing "extraordinary miracles by the hands of Paul" (19:11). It is not that Paul laid hands on the sick and demonized.[118] Rather, the phrase "by the hands" is an expression of agency.[119] For Luke goes on to say, "so that [ὥστε] when the handkerchiefs or aprons that had touched his skin were brought to the sick, their diseases left them, and the evil spirits came out of them" (19:12). In any case, although laying on of hands was part of exorcistic techniques in the New Testament world, Luke seems to avoid this particular method.[120] The idea that objects could be imbibed with, or transmit, spiritual power was well and widely known in the ancient world.[121] In particular, a person's clothing was believed to carry with it the wearer's

117. E.g., Bruce, *Acts*, (1990), 409–10.

118. Foakes-Jackson and Lake, *Acts*, 4:239; Bruce, *Acts* (1990), 410. The most natural reading of Acts 19:11–12 is that Luke makes a distinction between illness and demonization.

119. Cf. Acts 5:12; 11:30; Bruce, *Acts* (1990), 410. Contra Foakes-Jackson and Lake, *Acts*, 4:239, the plural χειρῶν ("hands") is used as an expression of agency without any connection with miracles or the laying on of hands. See Matt. 4:6; Luke 4:11; Acts 7:41; 17:25; 19:26; Heb. 1:10; Rev. 9:20. Contrast Thomas, *Devil*, 280–81, who suggests: "It may include the idea that Paul laid hands on those who were in need, but perhaps should not be limited to this means alone, as v. 12 indicates."

120. Cf. Luke 4:39 and Mark 1:31; Luke 9:42 and Mark 9:27; in Luke 4:41, through using δὲ καί, Luke probably distinguishes healing through the laying on of hands from exorcism (cf. 4:40). See BDF §447 (9).

121. See Twelftree, "Ancient Magic," and §2.1 above. Also, in *PGM* V. 159–171 the exorcist is to write a formula on a piece of new papyrus and extend it across his forehead, with the assurance that "all daimons will be obedient to you," assuming that what is written on the sheet of papyrus is transferred to the mind of the exorcist. Also *PGM* XII. 301–306 is part of a text used to transfer spiritual power into an object to be used in an activity associated with exorcism: "I have called on you . . . that you may give divine and supreme strength to this image [ξόανον] and may make it effective and powerful against all [opponents]." In Luke 8:33 demons are described as being transferred from a person to some pigs.

authority and power.[122] In the New Testament period, Josephus testifies to a similar understanding in that, for example, when relating the story of Elijah choosing Elisha as his successor, he inserts into the narrative that, on receiving Elijah's mantle, "Elisha immediately began to prophesy" (*Ant.* 8.353–354; cf. 1 Kings 19:19–20).

To question whether or not Paul gave his approval to this activity[123] is not to miss the point.[124] It is the point! That is, Luke portrays Paul as playing no active role in the apparent involuntary release and transfer of spiritual power or in the healings and exorcisms.[125] This becomes more obvious when we note that, just as in the story of Jesus (Luke 6:19; 8:44), so also in the stories of Peter (Acts 5:15) and of Philip (Acts 8:4–8), the point conveyed is that the mere powerful presence of the Spirit in Paul (represented here by his clothing) was considered sufficient to heal and send the evil spirits scurrying. How Luke thought these pieces of clothing would have been used, we are not told. Nevertheless, in view of the material just mentioned from Josephus and the Old Testament, as well as clothes taking on the contemporary function of amulets or talismans,[126] Luke probably thought that the clothing would have been placed on the sufferers. Therefore, the reader is led to assume that the success of the exorcisms depended not on any speech or command but simply on the presence of the pieces of clothing impregnated with spiritual power. In turn, the evil sprits are said to "come out"[127] rather than being driven out (cf. 8:7).

Whatever a twenty-first-century reader makes of this method of healing,[128] Luke clearly believed it both possible as well as acceptable; he says that it was God (ὁ θεός) performing[129] the "miracles" (δυνάμεις, Acts 19:11), a word he also

122. E.g., Gen. 35:2; Num. 20:25–26; 1 Sam. 18:4; 1 Kings 19:19–20; 2 Kings 2:8; Ezek. 44:19; Hag. 2:12–14. See Anton Jirku, "Zur magischen Bedeutung der Kleidung in Israel," *ZAW* 37 (1917–1918): 109–25. See also Luke 8:43–48.

123. Discussed by, e.g., Ellen M. Knox, *The Acts of the Apostles* (London: Macmillan, 1908), 306; David J. Williams, *Acts* (Peabody, MA: Hendrickson, 1990), 333: "There is no suggestion that Paul ever encouraged or condoned what they were doing."

124. As thought by Thomas, *Devil*, 281.

125. Cf. Gerhard Schneider, *Die Apostelgeschichte* (HTKNT 5; Freiburg, Basel, and Vienna: Herder, 1982), 2:269n20.

126. Cf. Klauck, *Magic*, 98.

127. Acts 19:12: "Come out," ἐκπορεύεσθαι, present middle or passive deponent.

128. E.g., Johannes Munck, *The Acts of the Apostles* (New York: Doubleday, 1967), 192: "Of course, one may assume that such miracles cannot occur, but it cannot be doubted that they were of decisive importance to primitive Christianity. We shall not be able to understand the latter unless we take the accounts of these healings seriously." I. Howard Marshall, *The Acts of the Apostles* (Leicester, UK: Inter-Varsity, 1980), 310, offers a value judgment: "Perhaps we may suggest that God is capable of condescending to the level of men who still think in such crude ways." See also, e.g., Richard B. Rackham, *The Acts of the Apostles* (WC; London: Methuen, 1951), 353; Haenchen, *Acts*, 562–63.

129. The verb ποιέω ("do/perform") is often used in relation to miracles (e.g., Matt. 7:22; 13:58; Mark 3:8; 6:5, 30; 9:39; Luke 9:10; Acts 6:8; 7:36; 10:39; 14:11) and to God's salvation

associates with the Holy Spirit.[130] Also, Luke sees the healings as remarkable, not only in calling them "deeds of power" (δυνάμεις)[131] but also in saying they are "out of the ordinary" (οὐ τὰς τυχούσας, 19:11, my translation).[132] However, in light of what we have seen as the widely held view that spiritual power could be transferred from one person or object to another, it is probably not the method to which Luke is drawing attention as out of the ordinary.[133] Neither are the distinctive aspects of Paul's healings and exorcisms a puzzle nor, primarily, that he did not accept money.[134] Though, as we will see, a lack of interest in money is probably to be taken as at least part of the background (cf. 8:18–24). Rather, when this little story is read in light of the immediately following story of the failure of the sons of Sceva, what is remarkable about Luke's representation of Paul is the effortless, successful, and numerous[135] healings and exorcisms that have taken place simply because of the powerful presence of God in him.[136]

Further aspects of Luke's attitude to exorcism among early Christians become clear as we look more specifically at the second story in this paragraph, which concerns some Jewish door-to-door exorcists (Acts 19:13–20).[137] In saying these exorcists "then [δέ] . . . tried to use the name of the Lord Jesus over those who had evil spirits, saying, 'I adjure you by the Jesus whom Paul

---

(e.g., Luke 1:51, 68; 18:7; Acts 15:17). See H. Braun, "ποιέω . . . ," *TDNT* 6:464–65, 483; BDAG 839–40.

130. Luke 1:17, 35; 4:14; 24:49; Acts 1:8; 10:38. Note that "power" (δύναμις) is what Luke says the disciples received (Luke 9:1; Acts 1:8), and their work is described as power(s) (Luke 10:13, 19; Acts 4:7, 33; 8:13), just as Jesus received power from God (Luke 1:17, 35; 5:17; Acts 10:38) and his work was described in terms of power(s) (Luke 4:36; 6:19; 19:37; Acts 2:22). See also Friedrich Preisigke, *Die Gotteskraft der frühchristlichen Zeit* (Papyrusinstitut Heidelberg 6; Berlin and Leipzig: de Gruyter, 1922); and Walter Grundmann, "δύναμαι/δύναμις," *TDNT* 2:300–301, 310–13.

131. Luke has used δυνάμεις for the "powers" or miracles of Jesus (Luke 10:13; 19:37) and the heavenly bodies (21:26; cf. 2 Kings 17:16; Dan. 8:10) as well as for the miracles of Philip (Acts 8:13).

132. Cf. BDAG 1019. Also see Otto Bauernfeind, "τυγχάνω . . . ," *TDNT* 8:241–42.

133. Contra Thomas, *Devil*, 281.

134. So Klauck, *Magic*, 98.

135. Note the plurals in Acts 19:11–12: τὰς τυχούσας ("extraordinary things"); δυνάμεις ("miracles" or "deeds of power"); τοὺς ἀσθενοῦντας ("the sick"); σουδάρια ("handkerchiefs" or "face cloths"); σιμικίνθια ("workers' aprons"); αὐτῶν ("their") τὰς νόσους ("sicknesses"); and τά τε πνεύματα τὰ πονηρά ("the evil spirits" [plural]).

136. See Conzelmann, *Acts*, 163, followed by Gerd Lüdemann, *The Acts of the Apostles: What Really Happened in the Earliest Days of the Church* (Amherst, NY: Prometheus Books, 2005), 254n137, is at least partially correct in saying, "The miracle worker is contrasted to those who have no real power."

137. The Western textual tradition (D) has ἐν οἷς (19:14), which is argued by Silva New, "The Michigan Papyrus Fragment 1571," in Foakes-Jackson and Lake, *Acts*, 5:268, to be a Lukan idiom meaning "at this juncture." This gives the impression that there are two groups of exorcists: some itinerant Jews and the sons of Sceva. However, the case made by William A. Strange, "The Sons of Sceva and the Text of Acts 19:14," *JTS* 38 (1987): 97–106, that the Western text is original has not been found convincing. See NA[27] 379.

proclaims'" (19:13), Luke is probably implying that they are modeling Paul.[138] At least this is true in part. For it is likely Luke intends his readers to assume that Paul had been using the name of Jesus. But we have already seen that Paul's exorcisms also involved the involuntary imbibing of clothing with spiritual power. Further, the mention of Paul proclaiming indicates that Luke is assuming that, in the healing and exorcism in which Paul has been involved, there has been proclamation of Jesus.

One of the puzzles of the story is why the exorcisms of these traveling exorcists required condemnation.[139] To begin with, it is notable that the parallel statement by the demon, "Jesus I know, and Paul I know," which bonds Jesus and Paul his follower, is used to set the sons of Sceva over against Paul (Acts 19:15).[140] Also, through repeating the word Ἰουδαῖος ("Jew," 19:13, 14; cf. 19:17), Luke draws attention to the sons of Sceva being Jews.[141] This is not to be taken in any anti-Semitic sense, for all his major characters are Jews, but in the sense of not being Christians.[142] In particular, in light of what he has just narrated about Paul, Luke is probably condemning these peripatetics in that they are not God or Spirit empowered. Luke describes Paul as letting God work directly through him (19:11), but the sons of Sceva are said to rely on a thirdhand source of power-authority: "I adjure you by the Jesus whom Paul proclaims" (19:13).[143] Thus Luke draws attention to the importance of the "spirit" identity of the exorcist.[144] Unlike Jesus and Paul of Luke's narrative, the sons of Sceva are not known in the spirit realm. Therefore, even though, by implication, the spirit would obey Jesus and Paul,[145] their authority is obviated by the intrusion of an unqualified exorcist. Moreover, Luke says the sons of Sceva are attacked (ἴσχυσεν) by the man with the evil spirit.[146] In contrast to

---

138. Cf. Strange, "Sceva," 97; Garrett, *Demise*, 92.

139. See the discussion by Garrett, *Demise*, chap. 5; and the review essay by David Frankfurter, "Luke's μαγεία and Garrett's 'Magic,'" *USQR* 47 (1993): 81–89, esp. 85–86.

140. Luke uses the μὲν . . . δέ (approximately "on the one hand . . . , but") construction.

141. See the discussion by Todd Klutz, "Naked and Wounded: Foregrounding, Relevance and Situation in Acts 19.13–20," in *Discourse Analysis and the New Testament: Approaches and Results* (ed. Stanley E. Porter and Jeffrey T. Reed; JSNTSup 170; Sheffield: Sheffield Academic, 1999), 259–60.

142. Having just described Paul as staying in one place for three months (Acts 19:8) and two years (19:10; cf. 19:22) and then describing the sons of Sceva as peripatetic (19:13), Luke may be giving further cause for their condemnation. See Klutz, "Naked," 269, who notes the pejorative overtones of περιέρχομαι in 1 Tim. 5:13. However, we have to take into account that there is a positive use of the term in Heb. 11:37 (see also, e.g., Plato, *Apologia* 30a).

143. Cf. Robert C. Tannehill, *The Narrative Unity of Luke-Acts: A Literary Interpretation*, vol. 2, *The Acts of the Apostles* (Minneapolis: Fortress, 1990), 237; followed by Thomas, *Devil*, 283n243.

144. Garrett, *Demise*, 93.

145. So Garrett, *Demise*, 93.

146. On the perceived dangers involved in operating in the spiritual realm, see Garrett, *Demise*, 148n66.

Jesus saying that the strong man (ὁ ἰσχυρός, Luke 11:21) is defeated in exorcism, here the evil spirit masters or "strong-arms" (ἴσχυσεν) the sons of Sceva (Acts 19:16); Satan has proved to be divided and has defeated himself.[147]

In this story Luke also condemns Christian exorcisms dependent on texts.[148] First, given the context of an exorcism story, it can be assumed that Luke intended the magic practice confessed by believers to be related to exorcism (Acts 19:18). Secondly, in that the distinguishing feature of this practice is their books, which are publicly burned (19:19), the exorcisms can be assumed to be text-centered. However, Susan Garrett thinks it implausible that Luke is referring to believers in his perfect participle "those who became believers" (τῶν πεπιστευκότων, 19:18).[149] Her prime support is the suggestion that Luke "would hardly have tolerated the notion of even the briefest continuation of magical-satanic practices." However, if we can take this story as an example of Luke dealing with the border clashes between Spirit-empowered and otherwise-empowered statements, lives, and activities in which imperfect Christians (cf. 19:1–8; 18:24–26) or insightful non-Christians (cf. 16:16–18) are involved, it is reasonable to take Luke as having believers in mind as disclosing their practices.

Also, Garrett says that Luke's participial use of πιστεύειν appears to have been "governed by narrative and syntactical context rather than by nuances of meaning inherent in the different tenses."[150] However, there are sufficient cases where the tense of the participle is important in what Luke is saying[151] that the perfect participle here in 19:18 should probably be taken into account in what Luke is communicating. Further, the progress reports in Acts[152]—of which 19:20 ("So the word of the Lord grew mightily and prevailed") is one—are interested in numerical growth.[153] Yet the stories immediately preceding such reports do not have to do with conversions. Therefore, it cannot be assumed that the reference to growth here means that people are becoming believers in the immediately preceding story.[154] In short, we are left taking Luke's

147. Cf. Garrett, *Demise*, 93, 98.

148. Noting the τε and δέ in Acts 19:18–19, Frankfurter, "μαγεία," 86, is right to point out that Luke probably has three different kinds of thaumaturgy in mind in this section: of Paul, of the sons of Sceva, and of the believers.

149. Garrett, *Demise*, 95–96. Cf. Conzelmann, *Acts*, 164: "Luke seems unaware that according to his wording these Christians still continued their 'practices' even after their conversion."

150. Garrett, *Demise*, 96.

151. Luke uses the participle of πιστεύειν at Luke 1:45; 8:12; Acts 2:44; 4:32; 5:14; 9:26; 10:43; 11:17, 21; 13:39; 15:5; 16:34; 18:27; 19:2, 18; 21:20, 25; 22:19 and 24:14. Luke probably invests particular significance into the nuances in the participle's tense at, e.g., Acts 2:44 (present) and 4:32 (aorist), which are both similar parts of cameos of the early Jerusalem church; also cf. 11:17 (aorist) and 13:39 (present), where tense is significant for meaning, as it is in 22:19 (present).

152. Acts 6:7; 9:31; 12:24; 16:5; 19:20; 28:31.

153. Acts 19:20 and 28:31 do not mention numerical growth.

154. As supposed by Jerome Kodell, "The Word of God Grew: The Ecclesial Tendency of Λόγος in Acts 6,7; 12,24; 19,20," *Bib* 55 (1974): 505–19.

perfect participle (τῶν πεπιστευκότων, 19:18) seriously as describing people who were already believers disclosing their text-centered magical practices of which Luke did not approve.

Another aspect brought into relief against Paul's Spirit-empowered exorcisms is probably to be detected in the mention of the great value of the books burned. Over against Spirit-empowered exorcism, considerable amounts of money were involved for those who practice magical exorcisms including, by implication, the sons of Sceva (Acts 19:19).

This story raises the question why the sons of Sceva are condemned while the unknown exorcist in the Gospel is condoned (Luke 9:49–50).[155] In Mark 9:38 John says that he had prevented someone from casting out demons in Jesus' name "because he was not *following us*" (ἠκολούθει[156] ἡμῖν, emphasis added). But Luke alters this to read, "because he does not *follow with us*" (ἀκολουθεῖ[157] μεθ᾽ ἡμῶν, Luke 9:49, emphasis added). What Luke has done in changing the imperfect to the present tense is to transfer the reference of the story from the pre-Easter setting to the post-Easter early Christian situation. This is even more obvious in the following verse where Luke has Jesus say, not "whoever is not against *us* is for *us*" (Mark 9:40, emphasis added), but "whoever is not against *you* is for *you*" (Luke 9:50b, emphasis added).[158] However, the particular post-Easter setting that Luke has in mind is not a debate about the relationship between Christian and non-Christian exorcists, but between exorcists within the Christian community.

For Luke uses the story to develop a point: "An argument arose among them [ἐν αὐτοῖς] as to which one of them was the greatest" (Luke 9:46). In line with this perspective, Luke deletes the bulk of Jesus' reply ("no one who does a deed of power in my name will be able soon afterward to speak evil of me," Mark 9:39); it is no longer applicable to the post-Easter and intrarelational point and application Luke has given the story. In conclusion, here in Luke 9 the story of the unknown exorcist (who is condoned) has to do with different exorcists within the Christian community, and the Acts 19 story of the sons of Sceva (who are condemned) has to do with the problem of non-Christians or those not empowered by God or the Spirit attempting Christian exorcism (see also Luke 11:23[159]).

---

155. See the broader discussions on Luke's distinction between Christian and other miracles, by Dunn, *Jesus and the Spirit*, 167–70; Achtemeier, "Lukan Perspective," 153–67; and Klauck, *Magic*, chap. 6.

156. Imperfect tense, indicating an ongoing activity in the past.

157. Present indicative tense, indicating activity in the present.

158. Cf. BDF §193 (1): "Lk 9:49 μεθ᾽ ἡμῶν not 'follow us,' but 'follow (you) together with us.'"

159. See Marshall, *Luke*, 399, who is unable to resolve this tension between Luke 9:50 and 11:23.

6.4 Luke and Exorcism among Early Christians

Luke has broadened the scope of the demonic. He has blurred the distinction between demon possession and other kinds of sickness so that in effect all sickness (and healing) is given a demonic and cosmic dimension. Luke believes that the church has a warrant for including exorcism as part of its mission. The basis of this warrant comes, first, in the idea that Jesus is the pattern for the ministry of the early church. Just as exorcism was an integral part of Jesus' ministry, so also it was to be an integral—though not the only or the most important—part of the church's ministry. Secondly, particularly in the mission of the Seventy(-two)—which for Luke represents or prefigures the universal mission of the church—Luke gives a warrant for exorcism being an integral part of the ministry of the church. Like other churches represented in the New Testament, the early church with which Luke was familiar did not precisely emulate the methods of Jesus, even though Jesus was seen as the pattern for the life and ministry of the church.

Not only from the other stories in Acts, but also from Luke's narrational decisions, we have learned that the most important aspect of exorcism among early Christians from his perspective is that it is not only to be modeled on Jesus or to use the methods of Jesus, but that it is the continuing activity of Jesus himself—the work of God himself—bringing eschatological salvation or the harvest. However, unlike Mark, this does not make exorcism the most important aspect of Christian ministry; it is part of the balanced approach involving word and deed. Nevertheless, the demonic is broader than possession, and the subjugation of the demonic is wider than mere exorcisms; all healing is defeat of the demonic.

In the two stories we have just discussed—Paul's clothing and the sons of Sceva—we have seen that Luke considered that such power had been made available to the followers of Jesus that their mere presence was sufficient to perform an exorcism. We have also seen that Luke had no compunction about seeing clothing as functioning as an amulet, at least if it was imbibed with the Spirit. As difficult as this notion may be for some twenty-first-century readers, it makes clear that it is the presence of the Spirit rather than anything that is said or done by Christians that defeats the demonic in a powerful and effortless fashion. Concomitantly, Luke condemns text-based exorcism. He also avers any association of payment for bringing this expression of salvation or, indeed, vehicle of salvation. While Luke is happy to accommodate various kinds of Christian exorcists (cf. Luke 9:49–50), he condemns exorcism not empowered by God or the Spirit.

We can also note that the story of Paul's "extraordinary miracles" has been seen as an example of Luke taking up "spectacular thaumaturgy that is more the stock in trade of charlatans and false prophets/apostles" and the "uncritical parading of 'wonders and signs' as an advertisement for the early church."[160] We have found this to be only partly the case. For, placed in the context of the story of the sons of Sceva, Paul's exorcisms are distinguished by their sheer number, their success, and their seeming effortlessness because they are God or Spirit empowered, rather than text based or dependent on a thirdhand power-authority that may involve financial gain.

In short, even though Luke portrays the early Christians adopting the pagan methods of exorcising by a power-authority, in doing so they were confronting the demons with Jesus; they were bringing Jesus into the situation. However, the techniques were not the key to a successful exorcism. Success depended on the exorcist—a person filled and empowered by the Spirit. For Luke the exorcisms of Jesus as well as the church involved the preliminary, though ongoing, defeat of Satan and his kingdom.

---

160. Dunn, *Jesus and the Spirit*, 167, citing Mark 13:22 ‖ Matt. 24:24; John 4:48; 2 Cor. 12:12; 2 Thess. 2:9; cf. Rev. 13:13–14.

7

Matthew

A s with all of the documents we are examining, we are asking what Matthew has to say about exorcism among early Christians.[1] We can expect particularly clear results from this Gospel because of Matthew's more obvious interest in the church.[2] For, as Günther Bornkamm put it, "No other Gospel is so shaped by the thought of the Church as Matthew's, so constructed for use by the Church; for this reason it has exercised, as no other, a normative influence in the later Church."[3] In relation to our subject, John Hull has set the agenda in arguing that Matthew is suspicious of exorcism, tending to purge magical details from the stories.[4] We will see that this is only partly true.

1. I am grateful for conversations with Christopher Gammill, who has helped sharpen my thinking on Matthew.

2. E.g., ἐκκλησία ("church") occurs only three times in the Gospels, all in Matthew (16:18; 18:17 [bis]); cf. Acts, 23 times; Paul, 59; 1 Timothy, 3; Hebrews, 2; James, 1; 3 John, 3; Revelation, 20.

3. Günther Bornkamm, "End Expectation and Church in Matthew," in *Tradition and Interpretation in Matthew* (ed. Günther Bornkamm, Gerhard Barth, and Heinz Joachim Held; London: SCM, 1982), 38.

4. John M. Hull, *Hellenistic Magic and the Synoptic Tradition* (SBT 2.28; London: SCM, 1974), 116–41. See also Morton Smith, *Jesus the Magician* (London: Gollancz, 1978), 145; Susan R. Garrett, *The Demise of the Devil: Magic and the Demonic in Luke's Writings* (Minneapolis: Fortress, 1989), 26.

7.1 Matthew's Church

The church Matthew probably reflects clearest—the place of origin of his Gospel—is generally agreed to be an urban center east of the Mediterranean, perhaps Antioch.[5] In recent years the church situation reflected in Matthew has been interpreted broadly as either a church struggling within the walls of Judaism[6] or a Gentile church outside Judaism considering itself the "true Israel," for whom Judaism was no longer a threat.[7] However, Graham Stanton has cogently championed the view that Matthew "was written in the wake of a recent painful parting from Judaism"[8] following a period of prolonged hostility that involved rejection and persecution. On this reading the vitriolic language, though polemical, is not directed at the scribes and Pharisees. Instead, it is Matthew's expression of anger, frustration, and self-justification in light of Jewish hostility and rejection.[9] The import of this for us is that we should be reading Matthew not as an attack on the synagogue, but as addressing issues faced by the Christian community.[10] As we will see, one of these issues relates to exorcism.

Concerning the date of Matthew, there is ongoing pressure on the critical orthodoxy, which holds to a post-70 CE date.[11] However, because the parable of the marriage feast contains the words "The king . . . sent his troops, destroyed those murderers, and burned their city" (Matt. 22:7),[12] and because Matthew

5. See the discussion by David C. Sim, *The Gospel of Matthew and Christian Judaism: The History and Social Setting of the Matthean Community* (SNTW; Edinburgh: T&T Clark, 1998), 40–62.

6. See, e.g., Bornkamm, "End Expectation," 39; though see his later essay, Günther Bornkamm, "The Authority to 'Bind' and 'Loose' in the Church in Matthew's Gospel: The Problem of Sources in Matthew's Gospel," in *Jesus and Man's Hope* (ed. Donald G. Miller; 2 vols.; Pittsburgh: Pittsburgh Theological Seminary, 1970), 1:41; William D. Davies, *The Setting of the Sermon on the Mount* (Cambridge: Cambridge University Press, 1966), 290, 332.

7. See, e.g., Rolf Walker, *Die Heilsgeschichte im ersten Evangelium* (FRLANT 91; Göttingen: Vandenhoeck & Ruprecht, 1967), 145 and n. 107; Sjef van Tilborg, *The Jewish Leaders in Matthew* (Leiden: Brill, 1972), 171.

8. Graham N. Stanton, *A Gospel for a New People: Studies in Matthew* (Edinburgh: T&T Clark, 1993), 114, and works cited on 124–26; cf. 156.

9. Stanton, *New People*, 156–57.

10. Cf. Robert H. Smith, "Matthew's Message for Insiders: Charisma and Commandment in a First-Century Community," *Int* 46 (1992): 229–39.

11. What William D. Davies and Dale C. Allison Jr., *The Gospel according to Saint Matthew* (ICC; 3 vols.; Edinburgh: T&T Clark, 1988–1997), 1:128, call "a weighty minority" include Bo Reicke, "Synoptic Prophecies on the Destruction of Jerusalem," in *Studies in the New Testament and Early Christian Literature* (ed. David E. Aune; NovTSup 33; Leiden: Brill, 1972), 121–34; E. E. Ellis, "Dating the New Testament," *NTS* 26 (1980): 487–502; John A. T. Robinson, *Redating the New Testament* (London: SCM, 1976), 104; Gerhard Maier, *Matthäus-Evangelium* (2 vols.; Stuttgart: Hänssler, 1988–1989), 9–10; C. F. D. Moule, *The Birth of the New Testament* (3rd ed.; London: Black, 1981), 173–74; and Robert H. Gundry, *Matthew: A Commentary on His Literary and Theological Art* (Grand Rapids: Eerdmans, 1982), 599–609.

12. To the contrary see, e.g., Reicke, "Synoptic Prophecies," 123.

reflects the recent parting of the ways between Judaism and the followers of Jesus, general opinion continues to favor seeing the Gospel written after the destruction of Jerusalem, in the last twenty years of the first century.[13]

Matthew signals to his readers the relevance of the story of the earthly Jesus and his first followers by setting the narrative against a wide backdrop that includes the time of the readers. For example, in 19:28 Jesus refers to a time beyond the setting of the Gospel when his followers will judge Israel (cf. Matt. 25:46). Also, in the early promise that Jesus will be "with us" (1:23) being fulfilled not only in Jesus never leaving the stage (even in the last scene of the book[14]) but also especially in his promise to be with his followers "to the end of the age" (28:17–20),[15] readers can see the forward reach and relevance of this Gospel for them.

7.2 The Matthean Narrative

Since one of the most impressive aspects of Matthew's writing is his attention to the details of numbers and arrangement, as well as the overall architecture of his work,[16] we can expect that giving attention to the structure of this Gospel will yield significant information about what he has to say, including on exorcism among early Christians. Giving such attention yields a very different message from that found in Mark or Luke. Gone is Luke's blurring and balance between word and deed. And in contrast to Mark, who has exorcism as Jesus' first public act (Mark 1:21–28), setting it as a programmatic function, Matthew has Jesus as the teacher of the Sermon on the Mount dominating the early part of his Gospel. Indeed, Matthew does not mention exorcism until 4:23–25,[17] the summary of the ministry he is about to relate, and then only among other healings: "They brought to him all the sick, those who were afflicted with various diseases and pains, demoniacs, epileptics, and paralytics, and he cured them" (Matt. 4:24). Nevertheless, significantly, the first part of this summary—which closely parallels the paired summary in 9:35 closing this section (chaps. 5–9)—draws attention to the word-and-deed structure of the section[18] and, hence, the implied nature of

13. See the brief discussion by Davies and Allison, *Matthew*, 1:131; and Sim, *Matthew and Christian Judaism*, 33–40.

14. Noted by Terence L. Donaldson, *Jesus on the Mountain: A Study in Matthean Theology* (JSNTSup 8; Sheffield: JSOT Press, 1985), 184. See also his discussion 186–87.

15. Cf. Graham H. Twelftree, *Jesus the Miracle Worker: A Historical and Theological Study* (Downers Grove, IL: InterVarsity, 1999), 105–6.

16. Cf. Davies, *Sermon*, 14.

17. Cf. Mark 1:21–28, 32, 34, 39; 3:7–12. See Davies and Allison, *Matthew*, 1:412; Ulrich Luz, *Matthew 1–7* (Edinburgh: T&T Clark, 1989), 204.

18. Cf. Eduard Schweizer, *The Good News according to Matthew* (London: SPCK, 1976), 233. See also Julius Schniewind, *Das Evangelium nach Matthäus* (8th ed.; NTD 2; Göttingen: Vandenhoeck & Ruprecht, 1956), 36; followed by Luz, *Matthew 1–7*, 203.

the ministry of Jesus: "Jesus went throughout Galilee, teaching in their synagogues and proclaiming the good news of the kingdom and curing every disease and every sickness among the people" (4:23). However, exorcism is not mentioned in this verse. Further, not only does a miracle story not appear in Matthew until that of the leper being cleansed in 8:1–4, but a full exorcism story—that of the Gadarene demoniacs—does not come until 8:28–34. This major (re)arrangement of material establishes Jesus not as a healer or exorcist who preaches but as a teacher who heals—and also performs exorcisms. In this we see that Matthew not only emphasizes Jesus the teacher-preacher over above Jesus the miracle-worker, but he also plays down the role of exorcism among Jesus' miracles.[19] This emphasis on teaching is maintained even to the end in the summary instructions at the close of the Gospel: the disciples are to baptize and to teach; there is no mention of miracle-working or exorcism (28:16–20).

Nevertheless, despite the apparent downplaying of miracles and exorcism, the instruction to teach does not preclude but includes other aspects of Jesus' ministry.[20] That is, the disciples are told to teach new disciples "to keep [τηρεῖν] everything that I have commanded you [ἐνετειλάμην ὑμῖν]" (Matt. 28:20, my translation). The direction "to keep" (τηρεῖν) involves guarding, preserving, or watching over something (or someone)[21] rather than simply knowing or obeying laws. Thus, in Matthew 23:3 Jesus says to the crowds and his disciples regarding the scribes and Pharisees, "Do whatever they teach you and follow it [τηρεῖτε]; but do not do as they do, for they do not practice what they teach." This implies that "keeping" or "following" involves lifestyle as well as command. Also, "to command" (ἐντέλλεσθαι) is not only to issue or set out a law (cf. Heb. 9:20), but also includes the idea of leaving general instructions.[22] Thus, in the closing verse of his Gospel, Matthew is not suggesting that the followers of Jesus teach his laws. Rather, the disciples are to teach new followers to keep or guard "everything I have instructed you" (Matt. 28:20, my translation). Most obviously, this is what is found in this Gospel, including the material on exorcism. Davies and Allison are right, then, to suppose that the mention of Jesus instructing or commanding in Matthew 28:20 "unifies word and deed and so recalls the entire book: everything is in view. The earthly ministry as a whole is an imperative."[23]

Therefore, even if not as important as other aspects of ministry, part of this imperative would be for early Christians to perform exorcisms. Looking at the body of his Gospel, we see the place of exorcism confirmed when we

19. Cf. Graham H. Twelftree, *Christ Triumphant: Exorcism Then and Now* (London: Hodder & Stoughton, 1985), 123.

20. This is a correction of Twelftree, *Miracle*, 104.

21. For τηρέω in Matthew, see 19:17; 23:3; 27:36, 54; 28:4, 20. See Harald Riesenfeld, "τηρέω," *TDNT* 8:140–46; BDAG, "τηρέω."

22. See BDAG, "ἐντέλλω." Cf. Matt. 4:6; 17:9.

23. Davies and Allison, *Matthew*, 3:686.

note that the chapters on miracles (Matt. 8:1–9:38) and the one on the mission of the disciples (10:1–42) are bound together by the two statements, "and when Jesus had finished" (my translation), which come just before the miracle stories (7:28) and immediately after the instructions to the commissioned disciples (11:1). Thus, even though exorcism is relatively unimportant in Matthew, and the preaching and teaching are his main interests over and above healing or exorcism in particular, exorcism is still established as an aspect of an integrated ministry model for the readers. More detail on what Matthew has to say about exorcism among early Christians comes as we look at specific texts in this Gospel.

7.3 Peripatetic Christian Exorcists (Matthew 7:15–23)

The first time Matthew mentions exorcism, implying a post-Easter situation, he does so negatively.

> Beware of false prophets, who come to you in sheep's clothing but inwardly are ravenous wolves. You will know them by their fruits. Are grapes gathered from thorns, or figs from thistles? In the same way, every good tree bears good fruit, but the bad tree bears bad fruit. A good tree cannot bear bad fruit, nor can a bad tree bear good fruit. Every tree that does not bear good fruit is cut down and thrown into the fire. Thus you will know them by their fruits. (Matt. 7:15–20)

> Not everyone who says to me, "Lord, Lord," will enter the kingdom of heaven, but only the one who does the will of my Father in heaven. On that day many will say to me, "Lord, Lord, did we not prophesy in your name, and cast out demons in your name, and do many deeds of power in your name?" Then I will declare to them, "I never knew you; go away from me, you evildoers." (Matt. 7:21–23)

The level of Matthean activity in this passage[24] suggests that Matthew is dealing with a real rather than imaginary issue among his readers.[25] With our interests in mind, it is noticeable that, in assembling material from M and Q (cf. Luke 6:43–45; 13:25–27), Matthew is able to connect exorcism with antinomianism and false prophecy (Matt. 7:21–23). The identity of the false prophets has been a puzzle.[26] In that the two sections (7:15–20 and 21–23) have been connected by Matthew (through the specific vocabulary

24. See the brief discussion by Luz, *Matthew 1–7*, 440–41.
25. Cf. Luz, *Matthew 1–7*, 441.
26. See the discussion by David Hill, "False Prophets and Charismatics: Structure and Interpretation in Mt. 7:15–23," *Bib* 57 (1976): 327–48; and the summary discussion by Davies and Allison, *Matthew*, 1:701; Luz, *Matthew 1–7*, 441–42; and Dieter Trunk, *Der messianische Heiler: Eine redaktions- und religionsgeschichtliche Studie zu den Exorzismen im Matthäusevangelium* (HBS 3; Freiburg, Basel, and Vienna: Herder, 1994), 224–27.

relating to these individuals being known,[27] and the general theme of sound-ness or integrity of those in question), he is most probably dealing with one group, not two.[28] That they represent Christians[29] is probable because it would heighten narrational tension and also seems plain from their use of "Lord," which Matthew otherwise reserves for use by the disciples,[30] or at least the expressing of faith before Jesus.[31] That they are Christians is also supported by their activities of prophecy, exorcism, and "mighty works [δυνάμεις][32] in your name" (7:22–23; cf. 24:11, 24).[33]

However, in that these false prophets—about whom he warns his readers—are said "to come" to the readers (ἔρχονται πρὸς ὑμᾶς, Matt. 7:15), we may assume that these Christian prophets are peripatetic[34] and likely to be ac-tive within the Christian community. From other things Matthew has told his readers, we cannot conclude that, in principle, Matthew is opposed to wandering charismatics. For, in 10:1–15, 41 and 23:34, he assumes that there will be (from time to time? see 7:15; 23:34[35]) wandering charismatics in the Christian community. Indeed, in this passage Matthew does not condemn such people outright but warns of particular aspects of prophets who are false (7:15). Further, in Matthew not being critical of the methods of these Christian exorcists, we can suppose that he takes exorcism in "the name of Jesus" (7:22) as the accepted method. Therefore, in line with what we have seen among other early Christian exorcists, this method involved performing an exorcism by the authority of Jesus or as if Jesus was present or performing it (cf. 10:41–42; 18:5; 21:9).[36]

27. Note: ἐπιγινώσκω (Matt. 7:16, 20) and γινώσκω (7:23).

28. As thought by Hill, "False Prophets," 327–48.

29. So also David E. Aune, *Prophecy in Early Christianity and the Ancient Mediterranean World* (Grand Rapids: Eerdmans, 1983), 223; Joachim Gnilka, *Das Matthäusevangelium*, part 1, *Kommentar zu Kap. 1,1–13,58* (HTKNT 1.1; Freiburg, Basel, and Vienna: Herder, 1986), 274, drawing attention to *Did.* 11; and Trunk, *Heiler*, 226.

30. Matt. 8:21, 25; 14:28, 30; 16:22; 17:4; 18:21; 26:22.

31. Matt. 8:2, 6, 8; 9:28; 15:22, 25, 27; 17:15; 20:30, 31, 33. See Luz, *Matthew 1–7*, 444.

32. Δυνάμεις is otherwise only used by Jesus in Matthew (13:58).

33. Cf. Pierre Bonnard, *L'évangile selon Saint Matthieu* (2nd ed.; CNT 1; Neuchâtel: Dela-chaux & Niestlé, 1970), 104.

34. More widely on the subject, see the stimulating work by Martin Hengel, *The Charismatic Leader and His Followers* (Edinburgh: T&T Clark, 1981); also Schweizer, *Matthew*, 178–80.

35. Cf. Max Weber, "The Sociology of Charismatic Authority," in *From Max Weber: Essays in Sociology* (ed. and trans. H. Gerth and C. W. Mills; London: Routledge & Kegan Paul, 1948), 248: "Those who are the bearers of the charisma—the master and his disciples—must, if they are to do justice to their mission, stand outside the ties of this world, outside the everyday vocations and also outside the everyday family duties" (quoted in Hengel, *Leader*, 34). Cf. *Did.* 11.4–5.

36. Davies and Allison, *Matthew*, 1:716, note that Matthew probably does not use the phrase "in the name of Jesus" consistently; thus in 24:5 "the speaker is trying to make himself out to be Jesus or a messianic figure."

Matthew is also not opposed to their ecstatic experience or utterances, if this is the way to understand the statement "Not everyone who says to me, 'Lord, Lord'" (Matt. 7:21; cf. 1 Cor. 12:3).[37] Rather, Matthew's warning is against wandering charismatics who come proposing to offer care but savage or plunder (ἅρπαξ[38]) the community. He says they will be known by their fruits. Since, in its transferred sense, "fruit" (καρπός) carries the meaning of behavior (Matt. 3:8; 12:33),[39] and he describes them as "workers of lawlessness" (ἐργαζόμενοι τὴν ἀνομίαν, 7:23, my translation), Matthew is warning his readers against these itinerants on the basis of their damaging lifestyle.[40] He proceeds to explain (7:21–23) that the required lifestyle goes beyond ecstatic utterances, prophecy, exorcising, or mighty deeds and extends to doing "the will of my Father" (7:21).

As this warning comes in the closing lines of the Sermon on the Mount, where Matthew has just set out his interpretation of the law for his community, readers are most likely to consider that the will of the Father—the law—has been set out there.[41] But from what Matthew says later about how peripatetic exorcists should behave (Matt. 10:8), this savagery done to the Christian community by itinerant exorcists probably involved taking money for services.[42] Thus, while Matthew admits wandering exorcists to operate in and in relation to his community,[43] their legitimacy depends on their submit-

---

37. Cf. David Hill, *The Gospel of Matthew* (NCB; 1972; repr., Grand Rapids: Eerdmans; London: Marshall, Morgan & Scott, 1990), 152; Davies and Allison, *Matthew*, 1:716n38; less certain is Luz, *Matthew 1–7*, 446–47. Against Schweizer, *Matthew*, 158, in the statement being associated with prophecy, exorcism, and performing miracles, it is unlikely that Matthew is "thinking of a liturgical acclamation."

38. Matt. 7:15. Cf. Ezek. 22:27; Zeph. 3:3.

39. For this meaning in antiquity, see LSJ; BDAG; and Friedrich Hauck, "καρπός . . . ," *TDNT* 3:614–15. Here the debate between Origen and Celsus comes to mind in that the integrity of a miracle-worker was evidenced by his behavior. Further, see Graham H. Twelftree, *Jesus the Exorcist: A Contribution to the Study of the Historical Jesus* (WUNT 2.54; Tübingen: Mohr Siebeck; Peabody, MA: Hendrickson, 1993), chap. 5. Cf. *Did.* 11.8: "But not everyone who speaks in the spirit is a prophet, but only if he has the ways of the Lord. So the false prophet and the prophet will be known by their ways."

40. In the LXX ἐργαζόμενοι τὴν ἀνομίαν ("workers of lawlessness") generally refers to "evil persons of influence able to harm the vulnerable." So Ernest James Bursey, "Exorcism in Matthew" (PhD diss., Yale University, 1992), 144.

41. Cf. Donald A. Hagner, *Matthew 1–13* (WBC 33A; Dallas: Word Books, 1993), 187, who draws attention to Matt. 6:10; 12:50; 21:31; 26:42.

42. In light of Matt. 10:6, this does not trivialize the danger that threatens the community, as thought by Luz, *Matthew 1–7*, 443. Cf. *Did.* 11.6. Corroborative evidence that Matthew (7:15) is warning against financial plundering comes from Acts 20:29 (the only other use of λύκοι, "wolves," in this way in the NT), where, on the one hand, Paul warns the Ephesian elders of fierce wolves (λύκοι βαρεῖς), and, on the other hand, says that he "coveted no one's silver or gold or clothing" (20:33; cf. 1 Thess. 2:5, 9).

43. Cf. Luz, *Matthew 1–7*, 445.

ting to the regulations of the Matthean community,[44] notably in relation to behavior, for truth and ethics are inseparable.[45]

7.4 A Commission for Exorcism (Matthew 9:37–10:42)

Next to consider is Matthew's missionary discourse in 9:37–10:42. Early in the discourse it is said that Jesus "gave them authority over unclean spirits, to cast them out" (Matt. 10:1). A key question in trying to discover what Matthew has in mind about exorcism among early Christians is whether he intends these instructions to be for the companions of Jesus, or whether they are intended to apply to his readers. The question is not easily answered. On the one hand, the narrative setting of the mission discourse is a particular occasion in Jesus' own mission in Galilee.[46] From this readers could assume that the instructions are for the companions of Jesus rather than for them. However, on the other hand, later in the story (10:18), a much wider mission is presumed than the Galilean ministry of Jesus. The twelve apostles are warned that they will be "dragged before governors and kings . . . as a testimony to them and the Gentiles." Further, in 10:22–23 a longer mission is presumed than the Galilean ministry of Jesus; he talks of enduring "to the end" and the coming of the Son of Man. Moreover, the latter part of the mission charge (10:24–42) is adrift from the specific chronological and geographical settings that were given or assumed in 9:35–10:15. In particular, the referents are frequently designated in general terms (e.g., ὅστις, "everyone," as in 10:32 and 33).[47]

There have been various attempts to resolve this disjunct between setting and content, which makes Matthew's purpose unclear.[48] For example, it could be that Matthew is showing that the opponents Jesus had to face are the same as those faced by his disciples. Thus, the references to the governors, kings, and Gentiles (Matt. 10:18) have been taken to refer, respectively, to Pilate (e.g., 27:11), the Herods (e.g., 14:1), and the Gentiles (20:19), which Jesus also had to face.[49] But this does not take into account the sayings that

44. Cf. Luz, *Matthew 1–7*, 445–46; Gerhard Barth, "Matthew's Understanding of the Law," in Bornkamm, Barth, and Held, *Tradition and Interpretation*, 75: "The false prophets are thus clearly designated antinomians."

45. Cf. Daniel Marguerat, *Le jugement dans l'évangile de Matthieu* (MdB; Genève: Labor et Fides, 1981), 192: "*la vérité chrétienne est éthique*" (his emphasis); also cited by Luz, *Matthew 1–7*, 446n48.

46. See Matt. 4:18, 23; 8:18, 23, 28; 9:1, 35; 11:1.

47. For more detail, see Dorothy Jean Weaver, *Matthew's Missionary Discourse: A Literary Critical Analysis* (JSNTSup 38; Sheffield: JSOT Press, 1990), 16.

48. Here I am dependent on Weaver, *Discourse*, 17–29.

49. Joachim Lange, *Das Erscheinen des Auferstandenen im Evangelium nach Matthäus: Eine traditions- und redaktionsgeschichtliche Untersuchung zu Mt 28, 16–20* (FB 11; Würzburg: Echter, 1973), 258.

go beyond the geographic and chronological frames of the setting of the narrative. Alternatively, the whole mission charge,[50] or just the latter part of it (10:24–42),[51] has been taken to be addressed to the church rather than the twelve apostles. However, this ignores the time and setting Matthew has given the story and that he has not changed the setting of the discourse for the material in 10:24–42.

A way forward in determining the intended audience of the discourse is in noting that it has been long recognized that at the end of the discourse, unlike Mark (6:12–13, 30) and Luke (9:6, 10; 10:17), Matthew does not have the disciples proceed on their mission.[52] Instead, Matthew says that "when Jesus had finished instructing his twelve disciples," it was Jesus who "went on from there to teach and proclaim his message in their cities" (Matt. 11:1). Given that Matthew is writing a unified and coherent narrative, it follows that the mission of the disciples is not fulfilled within the framework of this particular narrative.[53] Indeed, it is not even fulfilled in the narrative of the entire Gospel. This impression is not altered by the implication that the disciples had been involved in some form of mission. In 15:23 it is implied that the Canaanite woman had asked the disciples to help—we can assume, exorcise—her daughter. In turn, this implies that the followers of Jesus, like their Master, were expected to be exorcists. However, their resistance shows them both fulfilling the injunction of 10:5–6 ("Go nowhere among the Gentiles") as well as confirming that the mission to the Gentiles was outside the time of the narrative.[54] Also, a mission of the disciples is implied in relation to the epileptic boy (17:14–21). But not only is the mission a failure; the father has also taken the initiative in asking for a cure. In this, Matthew again confirms that the time for the mission of Jesus' followers is not yet, not only because more training is required, but also because the time of the mission is to be in the narrative world of the readers.

Notably, then, at the conclusion of the Gospel, the mission charge is not to "Go" (ὑπάγετε, present imperative, as in Matt. 28:10), with the assumption that it will be immediately fulfilled. Rather, the disciples are given instructions for "having gone" or "in going" (πορευθέντες, aorist participle), with the assumption that they are still to fulfill the command (28:19).[55] Thus,

50. So, e.g., Francis W. Beare, "The Mission of the Disciples and the Charge: Matthew 10 and Parallels," *JBL* 89 (1970): 3.

51. So, e.g., Bornkamm, "End Expectation," 18.

52. E.g., Beare, "Mission," 3; Gundry, *Matthew*, 203; Hagner, *Matthew 1–13*, 296.

53. This means we need to set aside the assumption of Ernst Bammel, "πτωχός," *TDNT* 6:903–4, and Hill, *Matthew*, 196, that the reader is to presume the disciples were sent out.

54. Cf. Amy-Jill Levine, *The Social and Ethnic Dimension of Matthean Social History: "Go nowhere among the Gentiles . . ." (Matt 10:5b)* (SBEC 14; Lewiston, NY: Mellen, 1988), 131–64, 191–92.

55. In saying that the text "doesn't say that *they didn't go!*" Karen Barta, "Mission in Matthew: The Second Discourse as Narratives," SBLSP 27 (1988): 530, has not taken sufficient account of these subtleties.

to conclude this important point, it remains reasonable to assume that, for Matthew, the fulfillment of the commission of 10:1–42 takes place outside the narrative of his Gospel, in the time of his readers.

Two things follow from this. First, the narrative of Jesus' own ministry that precedes (cf. Matt. 5:1–9:34), as well as what follows the commission, is the means of interpreting and explicating the mission discourse.[56] In other words, the ministry of his followers, including the suffering and persecution as well as the teaching, healing, and exorcising, is to mirror the ministry of Jesus.[57] In turn, secondly, along with its commentary in Jesus' ministry, the commission for mission confirms and supplies context for what is only implied indirectly in the Great Commission. That is, the Great Commission, which is to be fulfilled in the narrative world of the readers, is to parallel the mission of Jesus. In other words, to answer the question about the intended audience for the commissioning instructions: Matthew intends the instructions of the commission for mission, including those relating to exorcism, to apply to his readers.

What Matthew wants to say about exorcism in this mission by early Christians is set out in a number of ways and places in the commission:

a. The giving of authority for exorcism takes pride of place over healing in the commission (Matt. 10:1); teaching or preaching is not mentioned until later (10:7). At first this seems to be at variance with Matthew's low view of exorcism (see n. 4 above). However, as if to counterbalance the importance of exorcism in his tradition (cf. Mark 6:7; Luke 9:1), he includes the instruction regarding other healing activity. Thus exorcism is only one of a number of tasks set for these wandering preachers (10:8), and they have a much wider brief than the disciples in Mark (6:12–13) and Luke (9:1–2, 6; 10:9).[58]

b. Exorcism, along with healing, is to be part of evangelistic activities, rather than reserved for the community of followers of Jesus. This is clear from the space Matthew gives the peripatetic aspects of the mission (Matt. 10:5–23).

c. The restriction of the mission to "the house of Israel" (Matt. 10:6)—to the exclusion of Gentiles and Samaritans—has the effect of underscoring that their ministry is to parallel that of Jesus' ministry,[59] which the narrative is about to take up (11:1b). This restriction also has the effect of highlighting the exception of the story of the Canaanite woman, showing that Gentiles receive mercy also on the basis of their faith (15:21–28).

d. From the statement "The kingdom of heaven has come near" (Matt. 10:7), readers are led to understand that Matthew accords the traveling

56. Cf. Weaver, Discourse, 126.

57. Cf. John P. Meier, The Vision of Matthew (New York: Paulist Press, 1979), 73.

58. Cf. Heinz Joachim Held, "Matthew as Interpreter of the Miracle Stories," in Bornkamm, Barth, and Held, Tradition and Interpretation, 250.

59. Weaver, Discourse, 84.

healers a share in Jesus' eschatological work (note 9:37). Their exorcisms are part of the destruction of Satan's kingdom and the realization of the powerful presence of God. This view is perhaps also evident at 17:17 (see below): in the context of exorcism in the early church, the example of operative faith, "moving mountains," is an echo of eschatological expectation in Isaiah 40:4.

e. The mission charge also includes the instruction, "You received without payment; give without payment" (Matt. 10:8). This saying, as well as it being accepted practice that medical treatment required payment,[60] suggests that Matthew is countering what the early Christians are likely to do, perhaps like the false prophets who come to them (see above). Likewise, it distances what they are doing from general medical practice. That accepting money is a particular issue for Matthew is confirmed when we note that the peripatetic Christian missionaries conducting exorcism are said to be able to receive food instead of money.[61] Like those of their Master, the exorcisms of the early Christians were not the work of medical healers but an expression of the grace of the coming of the kingdom of God.[62]

f. Matthew implies that the wandering exorcists connected with his church faced great difficulties and were neither very successful nor well received. Indeed, Douglas Hare has noted the large proportion of material concerned with hostility and rejection.[63] There is mention of not being welcomed or listened to (Matt. 10:14). Instead, Jesus' followers are handed over to sanhedrins (= local "councils") and flogged (10:17), dragged before political leaders (10:17), hated (10:22) and maligned, perhaps in being accused of being of the house of Beelzebul[64] (10:25). Not surprisingly, there is a clear potential for unfaithfulness to Jesus (10:32–33). However, they are assured

---

60. See Xenophon, *Mem.* 1.2.4–8; Aristotle, *Politica* 3.16; cf. Arthur R. Hands, *Charities and Social Aid in Greece and Rome* (Ithaca, NY: Cornell University Press, 1968), 131–41, and 202–5 (documents). BDAG, "ἰατρός," cites P.Stras. 73.18–19 for a physician's fee of 20 drachmas, though see Fridolf Kudlien, "'Krankensicherung' in der griechisch-römischen Antike," in *Sozialmassnahmen und Fürsorge: Zur Eigenart antiker Sozialpolitik* (ed. Hans Kloft; GBSup 3; Graz: Berger, 1988), 90–92; and Frederick W. Danker, *Benefactor: Epigraphic Study of a Graeco-Roman and New Testament Semantic Field* (St. Louis: Clayton, 1982), nos. 1–4, for physicians accepting no payment.

61. Matthew has changed the proverbial statement from "The laborer deserves his wages" (μισθός, Luke 10:7 RSV; cf. Ps.-Phoc. 19; also 1 Cor. 9:14) to "The laborer deserves his food" (τροφή, Matt. 10:10 RSV).

The *Didache* singles out the seeking of reward as the mark of a false prophet: "Whoever says in the Spirit, 'Give me money,' or something else, you shall not listen to him, but if he tells you to give for others who are in want, let no one judge him" (*Did.* 11.12). See also Acts 8:18–24.

62. Cf. Bursey, "Exorcism," 167.

63. Douglas R. A. Hare, *The Theme of Jewish Persecution of Christians in the Gospel according to St Matthew* (SNTSMS 6; Cambridge: Cambridge University Press, 1967), 98.

64. On the origin, meaning, and use of this word as a euphemism for Satan, see Graham H. Twelftree, "Beelzebul," *NIDB*, 1:417–18.

of the consolation of the soon-returning Son of Man[65] and of the care of the Father (10:26–31).

7.5 The Essence of Exorcism: The Beelzebul Controversy (Matthew 12:22–30)

If, as we have noted, the narrative of Jesus' ministry that follows the commission is to function, at least in part, as its commentary on the commission, then some further passages, including the Beelzebul controversy, require our attention to fill out what Matthew says about exorcism among early Christians. Particularly through taking into account the attention Matthew gives to the structure of his book, we have seen that exorcism is given a relatively low priority in the ministry of Jesus. Nevertheless, we have also seen that this form of healing still remained important to Matthew. This is especially obvious in this passage, which gathers up much that Matthew says elsewhere on Jesus and exorcism and that has significant implications for the exorcisms of his readers.[66] This passage introduces a section on a dispute about Jesus' power-authority for exorcism (12:22–45). It begins with a brief exorcism story: "Then they brought to him a demoniac who was blind and mute; and he cured him, so that the one who had been mute could speak and see. All the crowds were amazed and said, 'Can this be the Son of David?'" (Matt. 12:22–23).

Introducing the idea that the demoniac was blind (cf. Matt. 9:32 ‖ Luke 11:14) shows that, for Matthew, the fond hope of the new age was being realized in the exorcism.[67] That the crowd responds by suggesting that Jesus is the Son of David also shows that Matthew is using the exorcism story to contribute to his Christology. Indeed, it is his christological considerations that give rise to Matthew's habit of abbreviating his miracle stories—including those of exorcism.[68] For example, in the story of the healing of the Gadarene demoniacs, Matthew has severely abbreviated the dialogue, which was considered part of the healing technique (Matt. 8:28–34; cf. Mark 5:1–20). All that remains is Jesus' simple authoritative command, "Go," the only time Matthew actually mentions Jesus' words to demons.[69] From Matthew's perspective the Son of God does not need to use involved techniques. From this the readers of Matthew could deduce that precise technique was also not important in their success.

65. Cf. Meier, *Vision*, 73–74.

66. Matt. 9:32–34 ‖ Mark 3:22–27 ‖ Luke 11:14–15, 17–23. In more detail see Twelftree, *Christ Triumphant*, 123–25.

67. Further, see Twelftree, *Christ Triumphant*, 124.

68. See the discussion of Held, "Miracle Stories," 165–200, in Twelftree, *Miracle*, chap. 4.

69. Cf. Hull, *Magic*, 130.

Following the brief exorcism and the crowd's response (Matt. 12:22–23), there is the accusation by the Pharisees that Jesus was operating as an exorcist "by Beelzebul, the ruler of the demons" (12:24).[70] Jesus' reply, in effect, is that this blasphemous accusation (see 12:31–32) cannot be correct for, as exorcisms are directed against Satan, to be empowered by Satan would mean that the exorcisms would be ineffectual. Matthew illustrates this point with the parable of the strong man (12:29), where the strong man obviously represents Satan being cast out by the exorcisms.[71] In this, Matthew follows his received tradition, linking the exorcisms of Jesus with the first of what was understood to be a two-stage defeat of Satan.[72]

Negatively then, for Matthew, the exorcisms of Jesus are the first stage in the defeat of Satan. Positively, Jesus' exorcistic ministry is then clearly set out in a saying that Eduard Schweizer has called "one of the most amazing in the Gospels."[73] "But if in the Spirit of God I cast out demons, then has come upon you the kingdom of God" (Matt. 12:28, my translation). This spells out that Jesus' exorcisms are empowered by the Spirit. This saying also sets out the implications of the long-awaited eschatological Spirit being upon Jesus (12:18): the kingdom of God has already come in his Spirit-empowered exorcisms.[74] Given that Matthew thinks that Jesus' ministry is to be modeled by early Christian exorcists, and that they are to say, "The kingdom of heaven has come near" (10:7), readers are to conclude not only that their exorcisms are to be empowered by the eschatological Spirit, but also that the kingdom of heaven is coming in their exorcisms.

7.6 The Returning Spirit (Matthew 12:43–44)

Matthew began this section about Jesus' power-authority with an exorcism story (Matt. 12:22); he finishes the section with the saying about an unclean spirit wandering without a home after coming out of a person. Finding the old host empty or at leisure (σχολάζοντα), the spirit returns with seven other spirits, making the state of the person worse than before (12:43–44). Although, for Luke, this was a comment on exorcism (11:24–26), for Matthew the saying

70. Matt. cf. 9:34; 12:24 ‖ Mark 3:22 ‖ Luke 11:15.

71. One view, e.g., Ernest Best, *The Temptation and the Passion: The Markan Soteriology* (SNTSMS 2; Cambridge: Cambridge University Press, 1965), 13, is that Satan was defeated at the Temptation. But, not least because of this pericope, this view is untenable. See Twelftree, *Exorcist*, chap. 3.

72. On the idea of a two-stage defeat of Satan see Graham H. Twelftree, "ΕΙ ΔΕ ... ΕΓΩ ... ΕΚΒΑΛΛΩ ΤΑ ΔΑΙΜΟΝΙΑ! ... [Luke 11:19]," in *The Miracles of Jesus* (ed. David Wenham and Craig Blomberg; Gospel Perspectives 6; Sheffield: JSOT Press, 1986), 391–92. Cf. 2 Pet. 2:4; Jude 6; Rev. 20:1–3.

73. Schweizer, *Matthew*, 286–87.

74. Cf. James D. G. Dunn, *Jesus and the Spirit* (London: SCM, 1975), 47.

is made in relation to the scribes and Pharisees (12:38–39) and applied to "this evil generation" (12:45), which was rejecting Jesus. In other words, keeping in mind the judgment theme introduced just before this saying (12:41–42), Israel's rejection of Jesus will leave it in a worse situation at the judgment than it was without or before knowing him.[75]

Although Matthew probably chose σχολάζοντα[76] as an appropriate description of those rejecting Jesus, for rhetorical force it would also probably have been a fitting description of the vulnerable state of the person without the spirit and therefore susceptible to further attack. Some precaution had to be taken to prevent its return—with reinforcements. Central to the meaning of σχολάζω was the idea of being lazy, at leisure, or unoccupied.[77] Therefore, Matthew is probably reflecting the view that a successful exorcism involved the person not only being free of the unclean spirit but also going on to be the opposite to σχολάζοντα—that is, most probably, adopting the lifestyle of a disciple.

7.7 Training in Exorcism (Matt. 17:14–21 ‖ Mark 9:14–29 ‖ Luke 9:37–43)

The pericope in which Matthew appears to give specific teaching on exorcism is in the story of the healing of the so-called epileptic boy (Matt. 17:14–21 ‖ Mark 9:14–29 ‖ Luke 9:37–43). We have already noted that this story is not so much about the disciples being on mission as about receiving training for the mission that is to be fulfilled in the horizon of the readers.

In light of the reported failure of the disciples to heal the boy, at the end of the story Matthew says, "Then the disciples came to Jesus privately and said, 'Why could we not cast it out?' He said to them, 'Because of your little faith. For truly I tell you, if you have faith the size of a mustard seed, you will say to this mountain, "Move from here to there," and it will move; and nothing will be impossible for you'" (Matt. 17:19–21).[78] The significance of this teaching

75. Cf. Ulrich Luz, *Matthew 8–20* (Hermeneia; Minneapolis: Fortress, 2001), 221; also Gundry, *Matthew*, 246; Davies and Allison, *Matthew*, 2:360; Donald Senior, *Matthew* (ANTC; Nashville: Abingdon, 1998), 144.

76. That σχολάζοντα (12:44) was not in Matthew's source, see Bruce M. Metzger, *A Textual Commentary on the Greek New Testament* (2nd ed.; New York: American Bible Society, 1994), 134.

77. See, e.g., in LXX: Exod. 5:8, 17; Ps. 45:11 (46:10 ET); also see Philo, *Mos.* 2.211; *Decal.* 98; *Spec.* 2.60, 101; 3.1; *Flacc.* 33; *Legat.* 128; cf. σχολή in LXX: Prov. 28:19; MM, "σχολάζω"; and LSJ, "σχολάζω." See also the insightful comments by Douglas R. A. Hare, *Matthew* (IBC; Louisville: John Knox, 1993), 144.

78. Matt. 17:21, found mostly in the Byzantine group of texts (cf. Mark 9:29), is missing in the best witnesses (e.g., ℵ* B Θ). "Since there is no satisfactory reason why the passage, if originally present in Matthew, should have been omitted, and since copyists frequently inserted

for the disciples is apparent when we note that, unlike Mark, who often has the disciples involved in some way in the healings, this is the only healing story in which Matthew has the disciples play an indispensable part.[79] If we compare Matthew's abbreviated story with his tradition (Mark 9:14–29), the commentary on Jesus' healing technique is truncated so that what stands out is the disciples' inability to heal (Matt. 17:16). In particular, the saying "O faithless and perverse generation . . ." remains directed to the disciples (cf. Mark 9:19), and the phrase "they were not able" (οὐκ ἠδυνήθησαν/-θημεν) concerning them occurs twice (Matt. 17:16, 19) so that, with the addition of the saying on faith (17:20b), their failure and, therefore, Jesus' response to dominate loom large the purpose of the story.[80]

In Matthew's source the faith of the father appears as an important aspect of the success of the exorcism (Mark 9:23–24). However, Matthew (Matt. 17:17–18) removes the reference to the father's faith[81] so that the failure of the exorcism is attributed entirely to the disciples. Before the disciples have asked the reason for their failure, the readers know that it is related to their being faithless (17:17). This is filled out at the end of the pericope with Jesus saying that they could not cast out the demon "because of your little faith" (διὰ τὴν ὀλιγοπιστίαν ὑμῶν, 17:20). In Matthew it is always Jesus who uses the term "little faith" (ὀλιγόπιστος),[82] and it is always directed to his followers. The word is used to help convey the idea that, although they have faith sufficient to keep them in the community, they do not trust God to provide their unexpected needs in difficult circumstances.[83] The magnitude of Jesus' criticism, and therefore the small amount of faith required to perform an exorcism, is seen in light of the saying that "faith the size of a mustard seed" is sufficient to do even the impossible (17:20). From the example given of telling a mountain to move, the expression of faith that is required for a successful exorcism is, as it was for Mark, a faith-filled command to the demon.

7.8 Matthew and Exorcism among Early Christians

From this chapter a number of points emerge as important for our study of exorcism among early Christians:

---

material derived from another Gospel, it appears that most manuscripts have been assimilated to the parallel in Mk 9.29" (Metzger, *Commentary*, 35).

79. Cf. Held, "Miracle Stories," 181.

80. Held, "Miracle Stories," 189.

81. In other places, however, Matthew sees the importance of the faith of those seeking healing: 8:10; 9:2, 22, 29; 15:28.

82. Some manuscripts (e.g., C, D, L, W) have ἀπιστίαν ("no faith"). See the discussion in Donald A. Hagner, *Matthew 14–28* (WBC 33B; Dallas: Word Books, 1995), 296.

83. See Matt. 6:30; 8:26; 14:31; 16:8; 17:20. For rabbinic parallels, see Davies and Allison, *Matthew*, 1:656; and Luz, *Matthew 1–7*, 406.

a. Arguably the most interesting result from our look across Matthew's Gospel is that we learn that, in the last couple decades of the first century, perhaps in urban Antioch, there were visiting peripatetic ecstatic Christians whose ministry included conducting exorcisms, along with prophesying and performing miracles. However, at least from Matthew's perspective, they were "savaging" the community with their perceived libertine lifestyle, not least through probably taking money for their services.

b. Most likely because of this experience, when compared with the other two Synoptic writers, the most notable aspect of Matthew's view of exorcism among early Christians is its low priority. Yet we cannot with Hull (see n. 4 above) say that Matthew is suspicious of the subject. Nevertheless, while still important in Christian mission, exorcism does not have the preeminent position it held for Mark, nor is it even kept in balance with preaching, as it is by Luke. Instead, for Matthew, it is the spoken word that is given pride of place in the ministry of the early Christians. Notwithstanding, even in the final lines of the text, the teaching that was enjoined would have been understood by the readers to involve the whole of what preceded in the Gospel, which included exorcism as part of ministry for early Christians.

c. In contrast to Paul (see §3.5 above), the peripatetic exorcists appear to have been active within Matthew's already-Christian community. However, by including exorcism in the commission for mission, it is clear that Matthew also saw exorcism as part of the evangelistic activity of the early Christians; exorcism was not only an activity for the benefit of the community of believers.

d. In portraying early Christian exorcism as modeled on that of Jesus, as well as from the explicit direction for those going on mission to say, "The kingdom of heaven has come near" (Matt. 10:7), the exorcisms of the early Christians were vested with the same significance as those of Jesus. Exorcisms were part of the first stage of the destruction of Satan as well as the complementary eschatological coming of the powerful presence of God.

e. We have been able to deduce that Matthew did not place much significance in any particular methods used by early Christian exorcists. They were to be simple. In that the methods of the wandering charismatics were both conventional and acceptable to Matthew, we can assume that exorcists of whom Matthew would approve used "the name of Jesus." Further, we saw that, as for Mark, the use of faith-filled statements empowered by the Spirit that were directed to the demons was a method to be used in exorcism.

f. The story of the so-called wandering or returning spirit reflects a view of exorcism among early Christians known to Matthew that understood a successful exorcism to be more than the removal of an unclean spirit from a person. Unless the precaution was taken of adopting the lifestyle of a disciple, the person was susceptible to further demonic attack that would leave the person in a worse state than before.

g. Sadly, we have seen that Matthew implies that those conducting exorcism have neither been very successful nor, just like their Master before them, been well received. They therefore were in need of the encouragement Matthew offered.

h. More generally, though of considerable significance for our overall study, given that we have Mark, one of Matthew's primary sources, we can see that the exigencies of his situation were thought to enable him to handle his tradition in a way that changed how exorcism was understood, both from that of Jesus as well as from the way other Christian communities were viewing exorcism. In relation to what we will see took place in the Johannine tradition, Matthew made but small changes. However, first, we must take note of 1 Peter, Hebrews, and the letter of James.

8

---

1 Peter, Hebrews, and James

Treating the New Testament material in as near chronological order as possible brings us to 1 Peter, Hebrews, and James. As they do not require extensive treatment, as a matter of convenience we can take them together, though this implies no particular relationship between them. The letter of 1 Peter has an intriguing statement about Christ proclaiming to the spirits. The book of Hebrews offers a promising, even if brief, reference for our consideration of the place of exorcism among early Christians. James may reveal an even more interesting insight into exorcism.

8.1 1 Peter

For various aspects on locating the readers of 1 Peter, we are greatly indebted to John H. Elliott. Through an examination of the way the readers are described as, for example, "aliens" (πάροικοι, 1 Pet. 2:11), Elliott has given good reason to think that they are poor rural people, which the epistle's author locates in five areas of Anatolia (Asia Minor; 1:1).[1] The majority view is that

1. John H. Elliott, *A Home for the Homeless* (Minneapolis: Fortress, 1990), 67–72.

this letter is most likely to have come from Rome somewhere in the years 70 to 90 CE,[2] from the hand of an unknown disciple of Peter.[3]

In 3:18–19 and 22 the author says, "He was put to death in the flesh, but made alive in the spirit, in which also [ἐν ᾧ καί] he went and made a proclamation to the spirits in prison [ἐν φυλακῇ]," and Christ Jesus "is at the right hand of God, with angels, authorities, and powers made subject to him." Since "spirits" (πνεύματα) is used in the Gospels especially for the spiritual beings confronted by Jesus (e.g., Matt. 8:16), and 1 Enoch 6 (about the origin of demons) is generally agreed to be influential here, 1 Peter probably has in mind Christ's dealing with evil spirits. One of the puzzles of this passage is how "in which also" (ἐν ᾧ καί) functions. It could be taken to mean that "in the state of being made alive," Christ dealt with the spirits.[4] It is more likely that, in light of both his death and resurrection, Jesus preached to the spirits and is now in a position in which they are subject to him. In any case, the complexities involved in a more complete understanding of this passage do not need to distract us from noting that it is not the ministry of Jesus, including exorcism, that is connected with his dealing with the demonic. Rather, it is in Christ's being alive in the spirit—or perhaps both his death and resurrection—that is associated with his being over them.

8.2 Hebrews 2:3–4

Hebrews was probably written before the mid-90s, when 1 Clement mined it for ideas,[5] though perhaps not earlier than the 60s for the writer is dependent on the first generation of followers of Jesus (Heb. 2:3), yet his readers have been Christians for some time (5:12).[6] Although there have been many suggestions as to the location of the readers,[7] Rome is the choice of the majority of scholars, not least because of its attestation there by 1 Clement.[8]

2. Raymond E. Brown, An Introduction to the New Testament (ABRL; New York: Doubleday, 1997), 721–22.

3. See the discussions by Marion L. Soards, "1 Peter, 2 Peter, and Jude as Evidence for a Petrine School," ANRW II.25.5 (1988): 3828–49; Leonhard Goppelt, A Commentary on 1 Peter (Grand Rapids: Eerdmans, 1993), 7–15.

4. William J. Dalton, Christ's Proclamation to the Spirits: A Study of 1 Peter 3.18–4.6 (AnBib 23; Rome: Pontifical Biblical Institute, 1965), 140.

5. See Donald A. Hagner, The Use of the Old and New Testaments in Clement of Rome (NovTSup 34; Leiden: Brill, 1973), 179–95; Gareth L. Cockerill, "Heb 1:1–14, 1 Clem. 36:1–6 and the High Priest Title," JBL 97 (1978): 437–40.

6. See the discussion of dating in Harold W. Attridge, Hebrews (Hermeneia; Philadelphia: Fortress, 1989), 7–9.

7. Attridge, Hebrews, 9–10, lists Palestine, Jerusalem, Samaria, Antioch, Corinth, Cyprus, Ephesus, Bithynia, Pontus, and Colossae.

8. See Eusebius, Hist. eccl. 6.14.2; and the brief discussion in William L. Lane, Hebrews 1–8 (WBC 47A; Dallas: Word Books, 1991), lviii–lx.

The relatively wealthy socio-economic location of the readers, at least in the past, is likely to be suggested in the comment that they have experienced a plundering of their possessions (10:32–34).[9]

Apart from his suffering and death, and its theological significance, the writer to the Hebrews pays scant attention to the ministry of Jesus.[10] However, the author says the message of salvation "was declared at first through the Lord, and it was attested to us by those who heard him, while God added his testimony [συνεπιμαρτυροῦντος] by signs and wonders [σημείοις τε καὶ τέρασιν] and various miracles [ποικίλαις δυνάμεσιν], and by gifts [μερισμοῖς] of the Holy Spirit, distributed according to his will" (Heb. 2:3–4). It is clearly the conviction of the writer that the message of salvation came not only initially through the Lord but also to him or his generation through the spoken word and also—taking into account συνεπιμαρτυροῦντος (simultaneous testimony) being a present participle—in and with the miracles. Further, mentioning the "distributions" (μερισμοῖς) of the Holy Spirit suggests that the community's experience of miracles was ongoing (cf. 6:5).[11] Just what any of these miracles were is not said. Perhaps, in light of the all-encompassing nature of the terms used ("signs and wonders and various miracles"), it is at least likely that exorcisms would have been included. Further, that the same three words (signs, wonders, and powers) are used by Paul of his ministry (Rom. 15:18–19; 2 Cor. 12:12), as well as—though in reverse order—in Acts 2:22 of Jesus' ministry, suggests that the early Christians were using the collection of terms to cover the whole range of miracles. If, as is probable, exorcisms are to be numbered among the miracles, they were likely to be seen not only as part of the expression of the coming of salvation, but also as part of the ongoing life of the early church.

8.3 James 2:19

That the letter of James reflects a Jewish-Christianity for whom the biblical Torah is important is clear.[12] However, the letter has proved signally

9. See the discussion in William L. Lane, *Hebrews 9–13* (WBC 47B; Dallas: Word Books, 1991), 300–301; and David A. deSilva, "The Epistle to the Hebrews in Social-Scientific Perspective," *ResQ* 36 (1994): 1–21.

10. On the life of the historical Jesus, Hebrews offers only three statements: Heb. 5:7; 7:14; and 13:12; on which see Erich Grässer, "Der historische Jesus im Hebräerbrief," *ZNW* 56 (1965): 63–91. Also on the historical Jesus in Hebrews, see, e.g., Graham Hughes, *Hebrews and Hermeneutics* (SNTSMS 36; Cambridge: Cambridge University Press, 1979), 75–100; Bertram L. Melbourne, "An Examination of the Historical-Jesus Motif in the Epistle to the Hebrews," *AUSS* 26 (1988): 281–97.

11. Cf. Lane, *Hebrews 1–8*, 40.

12. James 1:25; 2:8–12; 4:11–12. On the law in James, see Robert W. Wall, *Community of the Wise: The Letter of James* (The New Testament in Context; Valley Forge, PA: TPI, 1997), 83–98;

resistant to disclosing a more specific social setting,[13] so the identity of the author and the provenance of the book remain focal points of considerable debate.[14] Nevertheless, it is likely that the readers are poor since they are portrayed as vulnerable to the rich.[15] If, rather than a pseudepigrapher,[16] a specific author is sought, the suggestion of James the "Just,"[17] the James of Mark 6:3, a "brother"[18] of Jesus is, as Raymond Brown put it, "the only truly plausible" one.[19] This could place the origins of the book in the middle of the first century, perhaps with later editing.[20] However, if, as Brown suggests, James 3:1 implies there was an office of teacher and in 5:14–15 the elders or presbyters have a quasi-liturgical role, then the letter is likely to have been written in the late first century.[21]

Notwithstanding, the parallels with Q and the Community Rule of Qumran (1QS) and the association of Christology and imminent eschatology,[22] as well as the mention of Gehenna (γεέννη, James 3:6)—which suggests knowledge of Palestine[23]—argue for James arising in early Palestinian Christianity. Moreover,

Patrick J. Hartin, *A Spirituality of Perfection: Faith in Action in the Letter of James* (Collegeville, MN: Michael Glazier / Liturgical Press, 1999), 78–85. The attempt to broaden the understanding of νόμος ("law") in James to include the Stoic notion of natural, as done by Matt A. Jackson-McCabe, *Logos and Law in the Letter of James: The Law of Nature, the Law of Moses, and the Law of Freedom* (NovTSup 100; Leiden: Brill, 2001), has not been well received; see the reviews by Joel Marcus in *CBQ* 64 (2002): 577–79, and by Matthias Konradt in *JBL* 122 (2003): 187–89.

13. On the difficulty of establishing the social world of James, see Luke Timothy Johnson, "The Social World of James: Literary Analysis and Historical Reconstruction," in *The Social World of the First Christians: Essays in Honor of Wayne A. Meeks* (ed. L. Michael White and O. Larry Yarbrough; Minneapolis: Fortress, 1995), 178–97; repr. in Luke Timothy Johnson, *Brother of Jesus, Friend of God: Studies in the Letter of James* (Grand Rapids and Cambridge, UK: Eerdmans, 2004), 101–22.

14. See, e.g., Todd C. Penner, *The Epistle of James and Eschatology: Re-Reading an Ancient Christian Letter* (JSNTSup 121; Sheffield: Sheffield Academic, 1996), chap. 2.

15. See James 2:1–7; 4:13–17; 5:1–6. Also see Pedrito U. Maynard-Reid, *Poverty and Wealth in James* (Maryknoll, NY: Orbis, 1987), e.g., 8–10, 97–98; Robert B. Crotty, "Identifying the Poor in the Letter of James," *Colloq* 27 (1995): 11–21.

16. This is the view of the vast majority of scholars. See those cited by John Painter, *Just James: The Brother of Jesus in History and Tradition* (Minneapolis: Fortress, 1999), 240–41.

17. See Robert Crotty, "James the Just in the History of Early Christianity," *ABR* 44 (1996): 42–52.

18. See Richard Bauckham, *Jude and the Relatives of Jesus in Early Christianity* (Edinburgh: T&T Clark, 1990), 19–32; and summarily, Richard Bauckham, "The Relatives of Jesus," *Them* 21 (1996):18–21.

19. Brown, *Introduction*, 725. So also James B. Adamson, *James: The Man and His Message* (Grand Rapids: Eerdmans, 1989), 9–11. For a discussion of the criticism of this view, see Painter, *Just James*, 236–48.

20. See Peter H. Davids, *The Epistle of James* (NIGTC; Exeter, UK: Paternoster, 1982), 22–23.

21. Brown, *Introduction*, 742.

22. See Penner, *James and Eschatology*, 234–54, 266–68.

23. Johnson, "Social World," 178–97; repr. in Johnson, *Brother of Jesus*, 106n16.

now that it has been shown that the polished Greek of James could readily come from a Palestinian writer,[24] such a provenance is, arguably, a reasonable conclusion.[25] In any case, it would probably be agreed at least that James represents the ongoing influence of the traditions of the Jerusalem church.[26]

Of particular interest to us is James 2:19: "You believe that God is one; you do well. Even the demons believe—and shudder." In this section (2:14–26) the nature and scope of faith are being defined. In this particular verse the point is that belief is to involve not merely intellectual assent to a proposition,[27] but also requires a response, which in the case of demons was for them to "shudder" (φρίσσειν). To shudder was to respond in disabling fear to something,[28] including to God.[29]

A number of factors suggest that this statement probably reflects exorcistic practice known to James. To begin with, he has a general interest in evil or the demonic that is concomitant with exorcistic practice; there are enticing evil desires (James 1:13–14);[30] there is devilish (δαιμονιώδης) as well as divine wisdom (3:15); and the devil is to be resisted (4:7). More particularly, the notion of demons shuddering is well documented in apotropaic or exorcistic texts. For example, one text for exorcism from the magical papyri has the direction: "Write this phylactery upon a little sheet of tin: 'IAĒO ABRAŌTH IŌCH PHTHA MESENPSIN IAŌ PHEŌCH IAĒŌ CHARSOK,' and hang it on the patient. It is of every demon a thing to be trembled at [φρικτόν], which he fears" (*PGM* IV. 3014–3019).[31] Another aspect of James 2:19, which suggests it may reflect exorcistic practice, is the phrase "God is one" (εἷς ἐσιν ὁ θεός;[32] cf. Deut. 6:4),

24. See Jan N. Sevenster, *Do You Know Greek? How Much Greek Could the First Jewish Christians Have Known?* (NovTSup 19; Leiden: Brill, 1968), 3–21, 191. See the summary discussion in Penner, *James and Eschatology*, 35–47.

25. Cf. Richard Bauckham, *James: Wisdom of James, Disciple of Jesus the Sage* (New Testament Readings; London and New York: Routledge, 1999), 11–25. On the metaphorical interpretation of "the twelve tribes of the Diaspora" (James 1:1), see Wall, *Community*, 11–18.

26. Cf. Helmut Koester, *Introduction to the New Testament* (2 vols.; New York: de Gruyter, 1982), 2:157.

27. See Sophie Laws, *A Commentary on the Epistle of James* (BNTC; London: Black, 1980), 126, over against Hugh W. Montefiore, *The Epistle to the Hebrews* (BNTC; London: Black, 1964), 187.

28. Cf. LSJ, "φρίσσω."

29. E.g., *Prayer of Manasseh* 4; Josephus, *J.W.* 5.438.

30. Davids, *James*, 84, notes "a strong tendency in Jewish tradition to personify the evil impulse and make it interchangeable with Satan" citing *b. Sukkah* 52b and *b. B. Bat.* 16a.

31. See also the material assembled by Samson Eitrem and Leiv Amundsen, eds., *P.Oslo* 2:98; and Martin Dibelius and H. Greeven, *James* (Hermeneia; Philadelphia: Fortress, 1976), 160. Cf. *PGM* XII. 239–240.

32. The phrase εἷς ἐσιν ὁ θεός ("God is one"), one of a number of attested readings in James 2:19, is the best supported (e.g., 𝔓74 ℵ A vg syrᵖ copˢᵃ, ᵇᵒ) and is in conformity with the prevailing formula of Jewish orthodoxy rather than being assimilated to Christian theology. See Joseph B. Mayor, *James* (London: Macmillan, 1913), 100; Dibelius and Greeven, *James*, 158n50; Davids, *James*, 125; Ralph P. Martin, *James* (WBC 48; Waco: Word Books, 1988), 77; Bruce M. Metzger,

for such creedal statements found their way into the vocabulary of exorcists, to be used to identify their sources of power-authority.[33] For example, Justin says that in Jewish exorcisms, "the God of Abraham, and the God of Isaac, and the God of Jacob" was used (*Dial.* 85.3) as a source of power-authority.[34] However, although exorcisms that were dependent on using the name of "God" were probably widely known,[35] for rhetorical impact, the exorcisms that James is reflecting were most probably those conducted by Christians. We can suppose, therefore, that even if they used the name of Jesus, as might be expected,[36] perhaps out of habit or tradition, this text shows that the exorcisms known to James also included using the name of "God" and would be of the kind just cited from *PGM* IV. 3014–3020 and particularly from Justin (*Dial.* 85.3).

8.4 "In the Name of the Lord"

There is corroborating evidence for the use of the name of God in exorcisms James is reflecting in the above passage (James 2:19) through noting James 5:14:[37] "Are any among you sick [ἀσθενεῖ]?[38] They should call for the elders

---

A Textual Commentary on the Greek New Testament (2nd ed.; New York: American Bible Society, 1994), 610. Cf. Erik Peterson, *ΕΙΣ ΘΕΟΣ: Epigraphische, formgeschichtliche und religionsgeschichtliche Untersuchungen* (FRLANT 24; Göttingen: Vandenhoeck & Ruprecht, 1926), 295–99.

33. The Jewish milieu of James probably precludes taking into account that, "when used of a pagan god, εἷς expresses the great power or preëminence of the deity rather than a definitely monotheistic belief." Campbell Bonner, *Studies in Magical Amulets: Chiefly Graeco-Egyptian* (Ann Arbor: University of Michigan Press; London: Oxford University Press, 1950), 174–75, citing the example used in P.Oxy. 1382 after the narrative of a miracle by Sarapis.

34. Cf. *PGM* IV. 1231–1239; Origen, *Cels.* 1.24–25; 4.33–34. See the discussion by John G. Gager, "A New Translation of Ancient Greek and Demotic Papyri, Sometimes Called Magical," *JR* 67 (1987): 84.

35. Cf., e.g., 4Q511 frg. 35; 8Q5 frg. 1; 11Q11 3.1–12; on which see Joseph M. Baumgarten, "On the Nature of the Seductress, in 4Q184," *RevQ* 15 (1991): 136; Esther Eshel, "Genres of Magical Texts in the Dead Sea Scrolls," in Lange, 401–2, 404. For the free use of the tetragrammaton up to the beginning of the second century BCE and at Qumran, see Armin Lange, "The Essene Position on Magic and Divination," in *Legal Texts and Legal Issues: Proceedings of the Second Meeting of the International Organization for Qumran Studies Cambridge 1995* (STDJ 23; ed. M. Bernstein, F. García Martínez, and J. Kampen; Leiden: Brill, 1997), 380–81 and nn. 8 and 14. See also *PGM* XII. 270–350 and the discussion in Graham H. Twelftree, "Jesus the Exorcist and Ancient Magic," in *A Kind of Magic: Understanding Magic in the New Testament and Its Religious Environment* (ed. Michael Labahn and Bert Jan Lietaert Peerbolte; European Studies on Christian Origins; LNTS 306; London and New York: T&T Clark, 2007), 57–86.

36. See Acts 3:6; 4:10, 30; 16:18; cf. 19:13.

37. On which also see Martin C. Albl, "'Are Any among You Sick?' The Health Care System in the Letter of James," *JBL* 121 (2002): 123–43. Dibelius and Greeven, *James*, 252, mistakenly call this a procedure for exorcism. They cite Mark 6:13, but Mark distinguishes between exorcism and anointing the sick with oil.

38. In that the person is assumed to be unable to go to the elders, the translation "sick" (ἀσθενεῖ) is to be preferred over "weak"; cf. BDAG, "ἀσθένεια."

[πρεσβυτέρους] of the church and have them pray over [ἐπί] them, anointing them with oil in the name of the Lord [τοῦ κυρίου]."[39] In this way it is expected that the sick will be "healed" or "saved" (σῴζω). To begin with, it is quite likely that κύριος ("Lord") was intended to refer to God rather than Jesus. For, on the one hand, most of the occurrences of κύριος in James refer to God,[40] with only two specifically designated as referring to Jesus (James 1:1; 2:1). Then, at 5:7–8 it cannot be ruled out that "the coming of the Lord" refers not to the messianic coming of Jesus but to the coming of God at Judgment (cf. 1 En. 92–105),[41] not least because the next verse mentions the Judge—probably God (cf. James 4:12)[42]—standing at the door (5:9). On the other hand, given that, for Jews, healing could be by prayer to the Lord[43] and oil was used therapeutically (Isa. 1:6; b. Šabb. 53b; PGM IV. 3007–3020[44]), it is quite likely that this direction has maintained or taken up from their Jewish heritage, so that it was God[45] rather than Jesus who was understood to be doing the healing.

Nevertheless, given that early Christians commonly made a distinction between demon possession and other sicknesses, as well as how they were to be healed (e.g., see §5.6 above on Mark 6:13), we cannot suppose that this is an instruction for an exorcism.[46] Yet it can still be taken to reflect exorcistic practices familiar to James. Given the blurring of the distinction between exorcism and healing that we see in Luke and that, here, the healing prayer was to take place "over" (ἐπί) the sufferer—an approach well known in exorcism at the time[47]—and that oil is involved (see PGM IV. 3007–3010), we can

39. Dibelius and Greeven, James, 253n67, rightly note that "the very infrequent expansion 'the Lord Jesus (Christ)' (τοῦ κυρίου Ἰησοῦ [Χριστοῦ]) is worthless."

40. James 1:7; 3:9; 4:10, 15; 5:4, 10, 11.

41. See the discussion by Dibelius and Greeven, James, 242–43 and n. 6. On James and the Epistle of Enoch (1 En. 92–105), see Patrick J. Hartin, "'Who Is Wise and Understanding among You?' (James 3:13): An Analysis of Wisdom, Eschatology, and Apocalypticism in the Epistle of James," SBLSP 35 (1996): 495–98.

42. Cf. Laws, James, 213. To the contrary, less persuasively, Davids, James, 185; and Franz Mussner, Der Jakobusbrief (HTKNT 13.1; Freiburg: Herder, 1975), 205.

43. Cf. the third-century BCE Jewish author Ben Sirach: "My child, when you are ill, do not delay, but pray to the Lord [κυρίῳ], and he will heal you" (Sir. 38:9).

44. Cf. §5.6 above. On the strong Jewish character of this and other magical papyri (e.g., PGM IV. 1231–1239), see Morton Smith, "The Jewish Elements in the Magical Papyri," SBLSP 25 (1986): 455–62, noting (on 456) the difficulty of distinguishing characteristically Jewish elements. See also Twelftree, "Ancient Magic."

45. On God (Yahweh) as healer, see Albrecht Oepke, "ἰάομαι . . . ," TDNT 3:201–2. On the use of divine names by rabbis to control angelic forces and power, see Rebecca Lesses, "The Adjuration of the Prince of the Presence: Performative Utterances in Jewish Ritual," in Ancient Magic and Ritual Power (ed. Marvin W. Meyer and Paul Mirecki; RGRW 129; New York and Leiden: Brill, 1995), 185–206.

46. Dibelius and Greeven, James, 252: "The whole procedure is an exorcism." To the contrary, John Wilkinson, "Healing in the Epistle of James," SJT 24 (1971): 326–45, esp. 332, 341.

47. See 11Q5 (11QPsᵃ), which states that David was responsible for composing songs for making music "over the stricken" (על הפגועים, 27.9–10); cf. Luke 4:39; Lucian, Philops. 31;

conclude that the injunction is also reflecting an approach to exorcism that would have been familiar to James.[48] Notably, this verse shows the continuing Jewish-Christian tradition of healing (and exorcising) in the name of the Lord, rather than the more specific "Jesus." Further, since this verse (James 5:14) quite likely reflects what he knows about exorcism as well as healing, his church probably confined conducting exorcism to the "elders" (πρεσβύτεροι) or leaders.[49] We found a similar approach evident in the Qumran texts (§2.1 above). Although healing in the name of the Lord was conducted among the Christians, we cannot tell whether James considered exorcism to be for those in or outside the church. From 1 Peter we see the resurrected Christ as the one exercising authority over the spirits. From Hebrews we learn that miracles, likely including exorcism, were understood to be part of the message of salvation.

PGM IV. 745, 2735. In the exorcistic text of PGM IV. 1227–1264 there is the direction to speak "over" (ἐπί) the person's head. See also Twelftree, "Ancient Magic."

48. We have already seen (§6.2 above) that this attitude and posture was an expression of dominance in what was understood to be a battle. Contrast Luke Timothy Johnson, "The Letter of James," NIB 12:222, who suggests ἐπί is a "sign of the community's commitment and support in times of crisis."

49. Contrast the probable situation in the Pauline church (1 Cor. 12:9–10, 28–30). See Dibelius and Greeven, James, 252. That James 5:16 goes on to say, "Therefore [οὖν] confess your sins to one another [ἀλλήλοις], and pray for one another [ἀλλήλων], so that you may be healed [ἰαθῆτε]" does not necessarily widen the group praying to include the whole community, as implied by Davids, James, 195–96. For this injunction of 5:16 connects most appropriately to the immediately preceding verse about sin and forgiveness (5:15b): "And anyone who has committed sins will be forgiven."

9

Johannine Christianity

C OMING TO THE Fourth Gospel, we are faced with a puzzle: silence on the
matter of Jesus and his followers being exorcists while in the Synoptic
traditions the subject is prominent. One of the purposes of this chapter is to
offer a solution to this problem as well as to explain its implication for our
understanding of exorcism among early Christians.[1]

As with most ancient documents, dating the Fourth Gospel cannot be
very precise. The best guess at present is that this Gospel began to circulate
in its final form somewhere between 90 and 110 CE.[2] It is equally difficult
to locate the book geographically: Galilee or Antioch is a possibility, though
Ephesus is more likely.[3] Socially, the Johannine Christianity reflected in the
Fourth Gospel is of those who are free citizens and, although not part of the
established society, have considerable financial and social security.[4]

---

1. What follows corrects and develops Graham H. Twelftree, "Exorcism in the Fourth Gospel and the Synoptics," in *Jesus in Johannine Tradition* (ed. Robert T. Fortna and Tom Thatcher;
Louisville: Westminster John Knox, 2001), 135–43.

2. Recently, see Andrew T. Lincoln, *The Gospel according to Saint John* (BNTC; Peabody, MA:
Hendrickson; London and New York: Continuum, 2005), 18. See also Raymond E. Brown, *The
Gospel according to John* (2 vols.; AB 29–29A; London: Chapman, 1971), 1:lxxx–lxxxvi; D. Moody
Smith, *John* (Nashville: Abingdon, 1999), 41–43.

3. See Irenaeus, *Haer.* 2.22.5; 3.3.4; Eusebius, *Hist. eccl.* 3.23.3–4. See the discussion by
Craig S. Keener, *The Gospel of John: A Commentary* (2 vols.; Peabody, MA: Hendrickson, 2003),
1:142–49; and Sjef van Tilborg, *Reading John in Ephesus* (NovTSup 83; Leiden: Brill, 1996),
esp. 1–4.

4. Van Tilborg, *Reading John*, esp. 82–83.

The puzzle of the Johannine silence on exorcism has another side to it; although the Fourth Gospel has no interest in Jesus being an exorcist,[5] the writer expresses interest in the category of demon possession in that Jesus is portrayed as having a demon.[6] In understanding what the Fourth Gospel means by the accusation that Jesus had a demon, we will be able to see how Johannine theology dealt with the demonic. More broadly, we will attempt to draw some tentative conclusions about the implications of both the problem as well as the explanation we offer for our understanding of the diversity of the early church, as well as the varying attitudes toward the Jesus tradition.

Surveying the Synoptic traditions and noting evidence from outside the New Testament, there could hardly be any doubt that Jesus was a very powerful, successful, and widely known exorcist.[7] Indeed, on a prima facie reading, the Fourth Gospel could be expected to contain exorcism stories. In view of the messianic function of the exorcism stories in the Synoptic tradition (e.g., Matt. 12:28 ‖ Luke 11:20) and the Fourth Gospel's stated agenda that readers "may come to believe that Jesus is the Messiah" (John 20:31), exorcism stories might be seen to serve such an agenda well. Also, if the signs of the Fourth Gospel anticipate the great sign of the cross (e.g., 2:4; 6:11), would not exorcism stories aptly prefigure the casting down of Satan in the cross (12:31)? But the Fourth Gospel has not followed this path. Why? As we will see, our answer to this question needs to take into account that there are other kinds of miracle stories missing from the Fourth Gospel.

9.1 Inadequate Solutions

a. The simplest answer to the Johannine silence regarding exorcism is that the Fourth Evangelist did not know of Jesus as an exorcist. For at least two reasons this is highly unlikely. First, as we have seen, Jesus had a wide and strong reputation as a powerful and popular exorcist. In line with this, if we accept the emerging view that the Gospels were not written for particular audiences but for Christian readers at large, it is difficult to maintain that the Christians involved in the development of the Johannine tradition were

5. The only trace of the language familiar from the Synoptic evangelists is the report of the healing of an official's son, where it is said that "the fever left [ἀφῆκεν] him" (John 4:52). However, we cannot press this evidence for ἀφίημι had a wide range of use that extended beyond demons and healing. See BDAG.

6. John 7:20; 8:48–49, 52; 10:20–21. See also Graham H. Twelftree, "Spiritual Powers," in *New Dictionary of Biblical Theology* (ed. T. D. Alexander and Brian S. Rosner; Leicester, UK, and Downers Grove, IL: InterVarsity, 2000), 801.

7. Graham H. Twelftree, *Jesus the Exorcist: A Contribution to the Study of the Historical Jesus* (WUNT 2.54; Tübingen: Mohr Siebeck; Peabody, MA: Hendrickson, 1993), 136–42 and those cited.

unaware of Jesus being known as an exorcist.[8] Secondly, there are possible hints that the Fourth Evangelist was aware of exorcistic traditions reflected in the Synoptic traditions. The story of many disciples turning back from following Jesus (John 6:66–71) uses the phrase "the Holy One of God" for Jesus (6:69), a title in this precise form unknown in the period apart from its use in Mark 1:24 ‖ Luke 4.34 on the lips of a demoniac. Supportive of Johannine and Synoptic connections in this pericope is the occurrence of the well-used Synoptic title "the Twelve,"[9] which occurs elsewhere only in the Fourth Gospel appendix at 20:24.[10]

To these points we could add that, with Mary Magdalene playing such a key role in the Johannine passion narrative (John 19:25; 20:1, 18), it is possible that the Fourth Evangelist was aware of the tradition that she was known as the one "from whom seven demons had gone out" (Luke 8:2). Also, the phrase "they saw the signs that he was doing for the sick" (John 6:2) is reminiscent of the brief reports of healings found in the Synoptic traditions (e.g., Mark 1:32) and perhaps, therefore, a hint that the Fourth Evangelist was aware of healings similar to those reported in the Synoptic tradition. Further, we can note that the Synoptic charge of Jesus being accused of madness and being empowered by Beelzebul or Satan (Mark 3:22–27; Matt. 12:22–30 ‖ Luke 11:14–23) has a counterpart in the crowd in the Fourth Gospel charging Jesus with being mad and having a demon (John 7:20; 8:48–52; 10:20–21).

Slight as they are, these points are probably internal evidence that the Fourth Evangelist was aware of the exorcistic traditions now available to us in the Synoptic Gospels. Therefore it is unreasonable to maintain that the Fourth Evangelist was unaware of the strong and widespread tradition that Jesus was a popular and powerful exorcist. It is only reasonable to conclude that the Fourth Evangelist has deliberately excluded reference to exorcism from his Gospel.[11]

b. Could it be that in eliminating reference to Jesus being an exorcist, the Fourth Gospel avoided facing the charge reflected in Mark 3:22 that Jesus performed his exorcisms by the power of Satan? Probably not. As we have just noted, the Fourth Gospel does not avoid the similarly damaging charge of Jesus having a demon (John 7:20; 8:48–52; 10:20–21).

8. Richard Bauckham, ed., *The Gospels for All Christians: Rethinking the Gospel Audience* (Edinburgh: T&T Clark; Grand Rapids: Eerdmans, 1998).

9. John 6:67, 70, 71 and Matt. 10:5; 26:14, 20, 47; Mark 3:16; 4:10; 6:7; 9:35; 10:32; 11:11, 17, 20, 43; Luke 8:1; 9:1, 12; 18:31; 22:3, 47.

10. Cf. Edwin K. Broadhead, "Echoes of an Exorcism in the Fourth Gospel?" *ZNW* 86 (1995): 111–19. On the possibility of the residue of an exorcism in John 11, see Barnabas Lindars, "Rebuking the Spirit: A New Analysis of the Lazarus Story of John 11," *NTS* 38 (1992): 84–104.

11. We can keep in mind that the Fourth Gospel gives no hint that exorcism is to be included as part of the general category of healing.

c. It could be that the absence of exorcism stories in the Fourth Gospel is linked with its origins in Judea. That is, none of the Synoptic exorcism stories has its origin in Judea, the supposed home of the Beloved Disciple upon which the Fourth Gospel may depend.[12] But this is an unlikely explanation. To begin with, four of the seven signs or miracles in the Fourth Gospel have a Galilean setting,[13] the very setting of at least two Synoptic exorcism stories (Mark 1:21–28; 5:1–20). Secondly, we can note again that it is probably unreasonable to suppose that the author of John's Gospel knew nothing of at least the Synoptic story line, if not the traditions that have come to us in the first three Gospels.[14]

d. Another solution to the problem of the absence of exorcisms in the Fourth Gospel is to postulate that the Fourth Evangelist was using a signs source of seven miracle stories, none of which was an exorcism story. However, even if the Fourth Gospel had been dependent upon such a source, the question remains why the source contained no allusion to exorcism. Further, we still need to ask why the Fourth Evangelist did not supplement a supposed signs source with either a story or a reference or at least a clear allusion to Jesus' ministry of exorcism, perhaps from among the many other reports of miracles or signs of Jesus that he repeatedly mentions.[15]

e. An older explanation relied upon the speculative view that the Fourth Evangelist belonged to the Sadducean party, which rejected belief in angels and demons (specifically attested only by Acts 23:8). On this view, there are no exorcism stories in the Fourth Gospel because the author found them uncongenial. But this will not do. The positive association of ascending and descending angels of God with the Son of Man (John 1:51), the key role of angels in witnessing to the resurrection (20:12), and the ease with which the Fourth Evangelist reports Jesus being accused of demon possession (7:20; 8:48–52; 10:20–21) fly in the face of this assertion.

f. It cannot be that the Fourth Evangelist was embarrassed about portraying Jesus using the healing techniques of his contemporaries. Nor can we take the option of supposing that in ignoring exorcism the Fourth Gospel is avoiding a possible charge of magic because of Jesus' healing techniques.[16] For the Fourth Gospel relates Jesus healing from a distance (John 4:46–54), a method familiar in the ancient world (Flavius Philostratus, *Vit. Apoll.* 3.38; *b. Ber.* 34b). Also, Jesus uses spittle (John 9:1–7), a common feature of cures.[17]

12. Reported in Eric Plumer, "The Absence of Exorcisms in the Fourth Gospel," *Bib* 78 (1997): 350–51.

13. John 2:1–12; 4:46–54; 6:1–14, 16–21.

14. Cf. D. Moody Smith, *John among the Gospels* (Columbia, SC: University of South Carolina Press, 2001), chap. 8, esp. 234–41.

15. Cf. John 2:23; 3:2; 4:45; 6:2, 26; 7:31; 10:32; 11:47; 12:37; 20:30.

16. So Plumer, "Absence of Exorcisms," 356–58.

17. Twelftree, *Exorcist*, 158.

Nevertheless, supposing the Fourth Gospel is to be associated with Ephesus, a notorious center of magic,[18] it could be that in avoiding exorcisms the Fourth Evangelist was distancing Jesus from any possible association with these kinds of known healers.[19] Even though there can be little confidence in the specific association between this Gospel and Ephesus,[20] later we will pick up a more nuanced perspective on this point (see §9.5 below).

g. Not only is exorcism not mentioned in the Fourth Gospel, in contrast to its high frequency of occurrence in the Synoptic traditions, but the phrase "kingdom of God" is also lost, virtually without trace. In the Synoptic traditions of Q, Matthew, and Luke, exorcism and the kingdom of God are inextricably linked so that exorcism is portrayed as the actualization or coming into operation of the kingdom of God (Matt. 12:28 ‖ Luke 11:20). However, it cannot be that exorcism is lost to the Johannine traditions because of an aversion to the notion of the kingdom of God for the phrase does occur in John 3:3 and 5. More likely, leaving aside exorcism has led to the indissolubly linked idea of the kingdom of God being excluded, replacing it with a focus on Jesus' kingship, which is mentioned fifteen times, nearly double that of any other Gospel.

Having set aside these inadequate explanations for the absence of exorcism in the Fourth Gospel, we must look elsewhere. We shall see, on the one hand, that a number of aspects of the Fourth Evangelist's intentions and theology—particularly his view of the ministry of Jesus and his understanding of the miracles and the demonic—have probably converged to contribute to the deliberate suppression of Jesus' association with exorcism. Instead, on the other hand, in light of his notion of the nature and scope of the demonic, exorcism is replaced by a radical two-part alternative for the overthrow of the demonic. We begin with an examination of the intentions of the Fourth Evangelist.

9.2 The Johannine Purpose and Audience

Echoing views held at the beginning of the twentieth century, that the Fourth Gospel presupposes the general Synoptic tradition,[21] Richard Bauckham has argued that the Fourth Gospel was published to supplement Mark's

18. See Clinton E. Arnold, *Power and Magic: The Concept of Power in Ephesians* (Eugene, OR: Wipf & Stock, 1989), chap. 2.

19. Cf. Philostratus who says that Apollonius, the wandering Neopythagorean philosopher-healer and exorcist, was warmly welcomed at Ephesus (*Vit. Apoll.* 4.1). On the historical reliability of Philostratus, see Graham Anderson, *Philostratus: Biography and Belles Lettres in the Third Century A.D.* (London and Dover, NH: Croom Helm, 1986), 175–97.

20. See the brief comments by Lincoln, *John*, 88–89.

21. See James Moffatt, *An Introduction to the Literature of the New Testament* (New York: C. Scribner's Sons, 1914), 533.

Gospel.[22] Even if we were to reject this specific thesis,[23] as does Moody Smith because of the sophistication he argues it would require of the readers of John,[24] there is a growing consensus that we are still able to take up the general view that the Fourth Gospel was aware of traditions reflected in the Synoptics[25] and intended to correct and surpass them.[26]

Given this supplementary nature of the Fourth Evangelist's purpose, we may be helped to understand the Fourth Evangelist's selection of miracle stories. Not only are there no exorcisms; there also are no stories of people with withered limbs healed, cleansing of lepers, fevers cured, hemorrhages stopped, deaf made to hear, dropsy cured, stilling of a storm, or the withering of a fig tree.

It cannot be that the Fourth Evangelist wished to avoid repeating the kinds of stories his readers may have already known. The Fourth Evangelist parallels Mark's stories of Jesus feeding a multitude and walking on the sea, and also has stories of the blind receiving their sight and the dead being raised.[27] The Fourth Gospel also shares with Matthew and Luke the stories of the disciples catching many fish and of the official's servant or son being healed. The only entirely unique story in the Fourth Gospel is that of the changing of water into wine.

Nor can it be that the Fourth Evangelist wanted to downplay Jesus being a healer, even though most of the kinds of miracle stories not found in the Fourth Gospel are of healings. For three (four if raising Lazarus is included) of the seven miracle stories in the body of the Fourth Gospel deal with healing. Rather, part of the explanation for the absence of the mention of exorcism in the Fourth Gospel is probably related to the Fourth Evangelist attempting to supplement Synoptic tradition. Indeed, this may be at least part of the reason other kinds of miracle stories are missing from the Fourth Gospel. A closer examination of both the miracles in the Fourth Gospel and the exorcisms in the Synoptic traditions confirms this and shows the way

22. Bauckham, ed., *Gospels*, 147–71.

23. On the criticisms of Bauckham, see chap 5, n. 9 (above).

24. Smith, *John among the Gospels*, 240n65.

25. See, e.g., Frans Neirynck, "John and the Synoptics: 1975–1990," in *John and the Synoptics* (ed. Adelbert Denaux; BETL 101; Louvain: Leuven University Press, 1992), 3–62; Paul N. Anderson, "John and Mark: The Bi-Optic Gospels," in *Jesus in Johannine Tradition* (ed. Robert T. Fortna and Tom Thatcher; Louisville: Westminster John Knox, 2001), 180–85; and Lincoln, *John*, 26–39.

26. Martin Hengel, *The Johannine Question* (London: SCM; Philadelphia: TPI, 1989), 91, 193–94n8, acknowledging Hans Windisch, *Johannes und die Synoptiker: Wollte der vierte Evangelist die älteren Evangelien ergänzen oder ersetzen?* (UNT 12; Leipzig: Hinrichs, 1926); and Martin Hengel, *The Four Gospels and the One Gospel of Jesus Christ: An Investigation of the Collection and Origin of the Canonical Gospels* (Harrisburg, PA: TPI, 2000), 105–6.

27. A point also made long ago by David Friedrich Strauss, *The Life of Jesus Critically Examined* (trans. George Eliot from 4th German ed., 1840; Philadelphia: Fortress, 1972), 437.

in which the Fourth Gospel wishes to supplement the traditions already known to its readers.

9.3 Johannine Miracles Are Astounding and Unambiguously by a Divine Being

When compared with the other Gospels, the most obvious features of the miracle stories in the Fourth Gospel are that there are fewer of them and that they take up less direct space than in the other Gospels. Nevertheless, the miracle stories dominate the narrative of the Fourth Gospel through being spectacular and relatively uncommon. We will also see that, in light of supposed parallels, as well as through the Fourth Evangelist's narrative creativity, the Johannine miracles are intended to be understood as unambiguously divine both in origin and as a revelation of the divine.

The turning of water into wine is related as a miracle of immense proportions; six jars of twenty or thirty gallons of water each are turned into wine (John 2:1–11). The story would probably have reminded readers of those connected with Dionysus, a god associated with wine,[28] so that readers probably concluded—at least—that the one performing the miracle was divine and superior to Dionysus. In any case, the Fourth Evangelist says that miracle revealed the glory or divine presence of God (2:11; Exod. 16:7).

The healing of the official's son (John 4:46–54) is not only a healing of a sick boy at a distance of more than seventeen miles, but it is also an astounding miracle of bringing back to life a person "at the point of death" (4:47). The divine origins of this story would have been perceived not only through possible parallels[29] but also through the repeated variations of the declaration "Your son will live" (4:50, 51, 53). In the Fourth Gospel "life" (ζωή) is always what God gives (e.g., 4:10; 6:58) or what Jesus has on being raised from the dead (14:19). Therefore, this is a miracle performed by one who has the life of God and who was raised from the dead.

The astounding thing about the story of the paralytic at Bethesda (John 5:1–18) is that the person is said to have been paralyzed for thirty-eight years and yet immediately made well by Jesus speaking to him (5:8–9). Again, this story is shown to reveal the divine and to have divine origins not only through possible parallels[30] but, this time, through Jesus being said to perform the healing on the Sabbath (5:9, 16). For Jesus justifies his working on the Sabbath

---

28. Cf. Julius J. G. Vürtheim, "The Miracle of the Wine at Dionysos' Advent: On the Lenaea Festival," CQ 14 (1920): 92–96.

29. Cf. Wendy Cotter, *Miracles in Greco-Roman Antiquity: A Sourcebook* (London and New York: Routledge, 1999), 18–19.

30. See Hendrik van der Loos, *The Miracles of Jesus* (NovTSup 9; Leiden: Brill, 1965), 435–36; Cotter, *Miracles*, 20–22.

on the grounds that—as Jewish tradition had it at the time—God his Father worked on the Sabbath (5:16–17; cf. Philo, *Alleg. Interp.* 1.5–6). In this the Jews say he was "making himself equal to God" (John 5:18), a clear signal to the readers of the divine revelation in and the divine origin of the healing.

The astonishing magnitude of the miracle of the feeding of a crowd (John 6:1–14) is portrayed principally through saying five thousand men (ἄνδρες, 6:10) were fed, as well as in saying that even six months' wages would not buy enough bread for each person to receive a little (6:7). The magnitude of the miracle is reinforced through the closest known parallel to this story, which is insignificant by comparison: Elisha feeding a mere one hundred people with twenty loaves of barley as well as some grain (2 Kings 4:42–44; cf. Elijah in 1 Kings 17:8–16). This Old Testament story of a prophet would probably have caused the first readers to conclude that the Jesus story had divine origins and was revealing the divine because the miraculous feeding took place "according to the word of the Lord" (2 Kings 4:44; cf. 1 Kings 17:16). Indeed, at the conclusion of the Johannine story the people say, "This is indeed the prophet who is to come into the world" (John 6:14).

The report of Jesus walking on the sea is self-evidently stupendous (John 6:16–21). Also, it was widely held that gods and heroes could walk on seas and across rivers.[31] However, since none of these stories is as clear and as graphic as the one in the Fourth Gospel, it can be supposed that Jesus' miracle would have been seen as undoubtedly astounding. In that Jesus says, in the absolute, "I am!" (Ἐγώ εἰμι, John 6:20), the readers of the Fourth Gospel are likely to have recalled God saying to Moses, "I am who I am" (Exod. 3:14). Therefore, the Fourth Gospel is using this story to indicate Jesus' unique and extremely close relationship with God, giving the miracle an unambiguously divine origin and a capacity to reveal the divine nature of Jesus.

Similarly, the giving of sight to a blind person (John 9:1–7) is an astounding act, increased by describing the man as having been born blind (9:1). With stories of the healing of the blind being largely from legendary traditions[32] and rare from historical figures,[33] the report associated with Jesus would probably have been considered spectacular. As inaccurate as it may be, the Johannine position on this story is: "Never since the world began has it been heard that anyone opened the eyes of a person born blind" (9:32). Parallels in the literature may have ranked Jesus among the gods. In any case, that healing the blind in the Old Testament was an activity of God (Ps. 146:8) and that eschatological hopes were being fulfilled[34] gave this miracle a thoroughly divine dimension.

31. E.g., Homer, *Il.* 13.27–30; Dio Chrysostom, *3 Regn.* 30–31; cf., e.g., Job 9:8.
32. See Cotter, *Miracles*, 17–18.
33. Tacitus, *Hist.* 4.81; Philostratus, *Vit. Apoll.* 3.39.
34. Isa. 29:18; 35:5; 42:7, 16, 18.

As incredible as is raising the dead, there are a number of parallels to the story of Lazarus (John 11:1–57), mostly from the Greek legends of gods and heroes, but also from the Old Testament and religious figures of the New Testament period.[35] Such stories probably helped readers of the Fourth Gospel to conclude at least that the story of the raising of Lazarus was the outstanding work of a god, or at least a holy man (cf. 11:4, 40). Also, Lazarus is said to have been in a tomb four days (11:17). It was held that a person's soul hovered in the vicinity of the body for three days after death, after which time a resuscitation was considered to be impossible.[36] Indeed, 11:39 implies that the body is already rotting.

The story of the large catch of fish (John 21:4–14) was probably appended to an earlier edition of the Fourth Gospel and intended to be understood allegorically, at least in parts. When this story is placed alongside other miracles in the Fourth Gospel, it is not particularly spectacular, in itself highlighting the magnitude of the seven miracles in the body of the Gospel. We have no known parallel to this story, which would help us see if the first readers of the Fourth Gospel may have been alerted to its magnitude or intended divine origins or character. However, it is the Fourth Evangelist's use of κύριος ("Lord") that provides clear signals of the supposed divine origin and revelatory capacity of the miracle. While κύριος is used fifty-two times in the Fourth Gospel, it is not until some of the uses in chapter 20 (vv. 2, 13, 18, 20, 25, 28), and here in the story of the large catch of fish, that it is clear that a character in the narrative refers to Jesus as "Lord" in the transcendent sense (21:7, 12).

For our purposes we need to note two things about the Johannine miracle stories. First, apart from the appended story of the large catch of fish, the miracles in the Fourth Gospel are portrayed, foremost, as *consistently* of an order of magnitude that contrasts with the relatively commonplace nature of the exorcism stories in the Synoptics. It is not that the Synoptic traditions do not have stupendous miracles; the feeding of a multitude, giving sight to the blind, the raising of Jairus's daughter and the widow's son are certainly stories that would have been seen as spectacular. However, it is the consistently astounding and extraordinary or uncommon nature of the Johannine miracles that would have stood out to the readers. Moreover, taken at their face value, that John intends the miracles to be considered stupendous—even to the point of being unique—can be seen from Jesus' exaggerated statement that he has done "the works that no one else did" (John 15:24).

Secondly—in themselves and sometimes in light of possible parallels—the Johannine miracles are also reported as unambiguously divine both in ori-

---

35. See Loos, *Miracles*, 559–66; Cotter, *Miracles*, chap. 1.

36. See C. Kingsley Barrett, *The Gospel according to St John* (2nd ed.; London: SPCK, 1978), 401, who cites *Eccl. Rab.* 12.6; *Lev. Rab.* 18.1 and notes that, despite the doubt by Marie-Joseph Lagrange, *Évangile selon Saint Jean* (7th ed.; Paris: Gabalda, 1948), 307, about the belief existing in the time of Jesus, the idea is probably assumed here.

gin and as a revelation of the divine. The perspective on the miracles in the Fourth Gospel is summed up by the character Nicodemus: "No one can do these signs that you [Jesus] do apart from God being with him" (John 3:2). This view is also captured through the Fourth Evangelist's notion that the glory of God is seen in Jesus' miracles.[37] That is, in that the glory of God in Jesus refers to his manifesting God's presence and power,[38] there could be no doubt that Jesus was the Messiah (20:30–31). These two perspectives are in sharp contrast to how exorcisms were viewed at the time.

9.4 Exorcisms Are Common and Unspectacular

In preserving numerous incantations and recipes for exorcists, the Greek magical papyri offer the best evidence for the widespread and common occurrence of exorcism by healers whose identity mattered little in the success of their art.[39] The historical data we have leaves no evidence of any exorcist being as powerful and prolific as Jesus. Nevertheless, the New Testament and the literature of the period witness to a number of historical figures who were exorcists, such as the sons of Sceva, Rabbi Simeon bar Yoḥai, and Apollonius of Tyana.[40] Even the Synoptic traditions portray exorcism as commonplace in Jesus' own ministry.[41]

Further, most of the Synoptic stories of exorcism are far from astounding, either in the description of the sufferer or the manner of the healing. In Mark 1:21–28, until confronted with Jesus, either the symptoms of the possessed person were not known to the crowd, or perhaps even to the man, or at least he was not disruptive. Similarly, in 9:14–29, the so-called epileptic boy is described as suffering only intermittently (cf. Mark 9:21). In Mark 7:24–30 there is the report of an exorcism from a distance; however, we are not told of any great distance involved, nor of the ailment being particularly severe (7:26).

Therefore, apart from the report of the exorcism of the Gerasene demoniac (Mark 5:1–20), the Synoptic exorcisms are reported as unspectacular events. This would have stood in stark contrast to what we have seen of the miracles of the Fourth Gospel. We can suppose, then, that the inclusion of exorcism

37. John 11:40; cf. 1:14; 2:11; 11:4; 17:24.

38. See the discussion by C. H. Dodd, *The Interpretation of the Fourth Gospel* (Cambridge: Cambridge University Press, 1953), 206–8. More recently, see Dirk G. van der Merwe, "The Glory-Motif in John 17:1–5: An Exercise in Biblical Semantics," *Verbum et Ecclesia* 23 (2002): 226–49.

39. Graham H. Twelftree, "Jesus the Exorcist and Ancient Magic," in *A Kind of Magic: Understanding Magic in the New Testament and Its Religious Environment* (ed. Michael Labahn and Bert Jan Lietaert Peerbolte; European Studies on Christian Origins; LNTS 306; London and New York: T&T Clark, 2007), 57–86; Twelftree, *Exorcist*, 38–39.

40. Twelftree, *Exorcist*, 22–47.

41. Cf. Matt. 12:22–23 ‖ Luke 11:14; Mark 1:32–34, 39; 3:11–12.

among his other stories would have detracted from the Fourth Evangelist's consistent perspective that Jesus' miracles were astounding and grand in scale.[42] Thus, not only would such a relatively common healing as an exorcism fail as a programmatic act for the ministry of Jesus, as in Mark 1:21–28 (cf. John 2:1–11), but it could never carry the significance (as divine acts) the Fourth Evangelist sought to invest in his miracle stories.

9.5 Exorcisms Are Ambiguous in Significance and Origin

The ambiguity of exorcisms—which left Jesus open to severe criticism as to their origin—is clear from the Synoptic Beelzebul controversy. On witnessing an exorcism, Jesus' critics are reported as saying: "It is only by Beelzebul, the ruler of the demons, that this fellow casts out the demons" (Matt. 12:24 ‖ Luke 11:15). From what we know about exorcisms, Jesus' success could have been understood to have depended on what he said or what he did, or upon a source of power-authority outside himself. In eschewing exorcisms, the Fourth Evangelist avoided the ambiguity of the origin of Jesus' source of power-authority for his miracles.[43] It is not that the Fourth Evangelist was distancing Jesus from other healers; in his other healings he was much like others. Any distancing that took place was a by-product of his maintaining the unambiguously divine origin and revelatory character of the miracles of Jesus.

This leads directly to a related view of exorcism that would probably have helped cause the Fourth Evangelist to leave aside mention of exorcism. That is, some exorcists were thought to be effective because they were dependent not so much on any particular technique but on an outside power-authority for effectiveness.[44] Even though Jesus is reported as relying on his own power-authority in using the emphatic, "I [ἐγώ] command you," there is evidence in the Synoptic traditions that this is precisely how the exorcisms of Jesus were understood in that Luke has Jesus saying, "It is by the Spirit [Luke has 'finger'] of God that I cast out demons" (Matt. 12:28 ‖ Luke 11:20). On the other hand, even if Jesus is given the tasks and is authorized by the Father (John 5:36), the Fourth Gospel portrays Jesus as relying on no source of power-authority outside himself in performing miracles.

Here we are taking up a more nuanced version of the view that the Fourth Evangelist avoided exorcism in order to distance Jesus from other healers,

42. Cf. Frederick E. Brenk, "In the Light of the Moon: Demonology in the Early Imperial Period," *ANRW* II.16.3 (1986): 2113: "Jesus as the divine *logos* in the world would be put in a demeaning position if he were portrayed as a mere wonder-worker exerting his power over individual demons within possessed persons."

43. Cf. Smith, *John*, 110, citing Mark 3:22–23.

44. See Mark 9:38–39 ‖ Luke 9:49–50; Acts 19:13–19; *PGM* IV. 3019–3020; cf. 1227. See §2.2 above.

not because of their technique (see §9.1f above), but because they could be dependent on unspecified or unknown sources of power-authority. In establishing the uniqueness of Jesus and his miracles, the Fourth Evangelist focuses on the close relationship or even identity between the Father and the Son, as advertised in the prologue (John 1:1–18) and repeated one way or another through the ensuing narrative (e.g., 1:51; 5:18). Thus, in the miracle stories themselves, the Fourth Gospel is able to go beyond Q's notion that it was by the finger or Spirit of God that Jesus worked to establish the idea that Jesus was a self-sufficient divine miracle-worker.

Noting the Fourth Evangelist's selection of miracle stories that were "larger than life," and to a lesser extent the unambiguously divine origin and nature of the miracles, probably also helps explain why the Fourth Evangelist has left aside miracle stories about the deaf, those with dropsy, people with withered limbs, the lepers, people with fevers and hemorrhages, even stories of a storm being calmed and a fig tree withering: they were comparatively minor and—in the case of exorcism—ambiguous in their origin.

9.6 Johannine Miracles Are Signs

One of the distinctive features of the Johannine miracles is that they are called signs (σημεῖα). In the Synoptic Gospels this word is never used for the miracles of Jesus. With the probability that all but two of the uses of σημεῖον are redactional (John 2:18; 6:30), the concept of miracle as sign is to be taken as highly significant, confirming what we have already discovered about the contrast between the miracles in the Fourth Gospel and those (including the exorcisms) in the Synoptic traditions.

The Fourth Gospel's use of "sign" is best understood in light of the Septuagint, where the word is almost always used of God showing himself to be the Almighty and Israel to be his chosen people through the miraculous events associated with Moses leading the Israelites out of Egypt (e.g., Deut. 26:8; Jer. 32:20–21). Also, a sign could be either a natural or supernatural event demonstrating the authenticity of the word of a prophet of God as well as the prophet himself (e.g., Exod. 3:12; 4:1–9; 1 Sam. 10:1–9). Further, as an Old Testament sign could represent (Ezek. 4:1–3) or announce things to come (e.g., Isa. 7:10–16), we are not surprised that, for the Fourth Evangelist, the miracles of Jesus are also a foretaste of a future time when God will do even greater things (John 14:10–12).

Thus, while the miracles in the Fourth Gospel may be unambiguously of a divine origin, and innately reveal the divine, they also signify more than the immediately obvious. This is seen from the misunderstandings imbedded in the stories. To what the miracles point is easily determined. First, in light of the Septuagint, the Fourth Evangelist is probably declaring that in these acts of Jesus, God himself is at work as the author and is revealing his character. Thus, in turn, the signs reveal the glory of Jesus or point to the true identity or glory of Jesus and his filial relationship or even identity with the Father. Even the appended story of the large catch of fish (John 21:4–14) is consistent with this Johannine theology of miracles, at least in that it is used to reveal (φανερόω) Jesus to the disciples (21:1, 14; cf. 2:11; 9:3), encouraging them to trust in him.

Secondly, the signs point to the death and resurrection of Jesus, where the glory of Jesus is also seen clearly. Two examples can establish this: (a) The healing of the official's son (John 4:46–54) is not simply a healing of a sick boy. In repeating the phrase "your son will live" (4:50, 51, 53), there is probably to be seen an echo of the resurrection of Jesus (cf. 14:19). (b) If we take an overview of the story of the giving of sight to a blind man (9:1–7) it reflects the life of Jesus. For both men, a washing is followed by an illumination. Both Jesus and the man born blind are subjects of disputes over their identity and cause a division in their families. When the healed man is interrogated he uses the same self-identification as Jesus ("I am"), and both men elicit hostile responses. And as if prefiguring the trial of Jesus, the man is not believed when he testifies before the authorities.

Turning to the Synoptic stories, we see that they can have a symbolic function, as in the case of Mark understanding the cursing of the fig tree to be a prophetic action regarding the rejection of Israel (Mark 11:12–14, 20–24). Also, Luke has the story of the miraculous catch of fish, a prophetic action symbolizing the catching of people (Luke 5:1–11). In Matthew, the miraculous appearance of a coin in the mouth of a fish is probably to be understood as a symbolic action (Matt. 17:24–27).

However, the exorcisms in the Synoptic traditions function differently. For Jesus, the exorcisms carried out what they signified—the coming into existence of the kingdom of God (cf. Matt. 12:28 ‖ Luke 11:20). If the exorcisms pointed to anything, it was to the new state of affairs attending the appearance of Jesus. Then, for the Synoptic evangelists, although exorcisms were not primarily signs, they did, secondarily, point to the identity of Jesus (e.g., Mark 1:27–28). In the Fourth Gospel, however, as signs, the miracles were primarily pointing to God himself being at work in Jesus, whose true identity was being revealed.

9.7 Jesus' Whole Ministry Is a Battle with Satan

There is no doubt that in the Synoptic exorcisms Jesus is involved in a battle. But in that battle Jesus is confronted, verbally abused, cursed, disobeyed, and appears to have difficulties in being successful. Such a perspective is so completely at variance with the decisively powerful, self-determining Jesus of the Fourth Gospel that this alone may have been enough for the Fourth Evangelist to omit such stories.

Be that as it may, on the other hand, while the Synoptic Gospels affirm the notion, apart from the isolated exorcism stories, there is little indication that Jesus' whole ministry is to be understood as a battle with Satan (e.g., Mark 3:22–27). Even the demons with which Jesus contends in the Synoptics are not strongly or often tied to Satan, and the latter part of Jesus' ministry—including the passion narrative—reflects little of the battle. However, in portraying Jesus' antagonists as children of Satan (John 8:44), and Jesus bringing light to a world darkened by Satan, the whole Johannine ministry of Jesus remains a battlefield with Satan. Further, that Jesus, not his suppliants, is portrayed as possessed heightens the readers' attention to the sense of battle as well as the unambiguous revelatory power of the miracles. That Jesus' whole ministry is to be seen as a battle is strengthened by the Fourth Evangelist's interpretation of the death of Jesus.[45]

In concert with the thinking of the time, Jesus, as well as the early Christians reflected in the Synoptic traditions, expected Satan's defeat to take place in two stages (e.g., Isa. 24:22; *1 En.* 10:4–6). However, for the Synoptic writers the first stage took place in the exorcisms of Jesus (e.g., Matt. 12:26 ‖ Mark 3:26 ‖ Luke 11:18) and also in those of his followers (e.g., Luke 10:18). The second stage of the defeat of Satan was thought to take place at the end of history (cf. Matt. 13:24–30, 36–43).

To put the matter sharply, although the Synoptic traditions focus the battle with Satan in the ministry of Jesus (particularly in exorcism), and that battle is severely attenuated in the passion narrative, the reverse is the case for the Fourth Gospel. The battle with Satan, though pervading the proleptic ministry of Jesus, reaches its climax and realization in the cross event, the grand cosmic exorcism.[46] Looking to the cross (cf. John 12:23–25, 33), Jesus says, "Now is the judgment of this world; now the ruler of this world will be driven out" (12:31). In a single act involving the heavenly realm,[47] Satan is to be dealt with directly, without recourse to his malevolent minions on earth. In this way the Fourth Evangelist is able to affirm that the lie of Satan's control of this world is far more pervasive than the possession of individual people, and that the defeat of Satan requires more than isolated activity by Jesus. Nevertheless, like the Synoptic traditions, the Fourth Evangelist sees Satan as continuing to be active beyond the Jesus event (17:15).

45. John 12:31; 14:30; 16:11; cf. 13:27.
46. John 6:70; 12:31; 13:2; 14:30; 16:11. Cf. *1 En.* 1–36 (The Book of Watchers).
47. Keener, *John*, 2:880, notes similar language used by the Stoic philosopher Cornutus (first century CE) for the expulsion of Cronus by Zeus at the fall of the Titans. See Pieter W. van der Horst, "Cornutus and the New Testament: A Contribution to the Corpus Hellenisticum," *NovT* 23 (1981): 171, referring to Cornutus, *Nat. d.* 7.7.20.

With his consistent view of the death of Jesus, it can be postulated that the Fourth Evangelist would want nothing to detract from the centrality of the cross event as the locus of the defeat of Satan. Also, from what we have seen of the stupendous and unambiguously divine nature of the miracles in the Fourth Gospel, it is unlikely that commonplace and ambiguous exorcisms could aptly prefigure the casting down of Satan to take place in the cross, let alone encapsulate it. Also, in that Jesus' kingdom was not of this world (John 18:36) and that his battle was not terrestrial but focused in the cross, pre-Easter exorcisms would not have been able to carry the notion of the magnitude of that battle.

9.8 Synoptic Exorcisms and Johannine Signs

Although the Synoptic Gospels cause readers to consider the exorcistic traditions as central to Jesus' eschatology, the Fourth Evangelist was under no obligation to portray the Messiah as an exorcist. Before the time of Jesus, there was no connection between exorcism and eschatology.[48] We have seen a number of reasons why the Fourth Evangelist did not use exorcism in his Gospel. Even if crudely, these can be represented in a table.

Sign-Miracles of the Fourth Gospel	Exorcisms of the Synoptic Traditions
Spectacular	Commonplace
Rare	Prevalent
Divine in origin	Of ambiguous origins
Reveal God at work in the miracles	Of ambiguous origins
Jesus a self-sufficient miracle-worker	Jesus empowered by the Spirit
Signs of the cross event	Actualization of the kingdom of God
Jesus' whole ministry is a battle with Satan	Exorcisms are the focus of the battle with Satan
Battle and defeat of Satan focused in the cross event	Battle and defeat of Satan focused in exorcisms

Insofar as we have explained why other Synoptic miracle stories like exorcisms—the commonplace, prevalent, and those of ambiguous origins actualizing the kingdom of God—are not found in the Fourth Gospel, we have, at least in part, also explained the absence of exorcisms. More importantly, insofar as the Fourth Evangelist saw his Gospel as supplementing that of the Synoptic tradition(s), we can see that he wanted to use a consistently different kind of miracle to convey the uniqueness of Jesus in his divine nature

---

48. Twelftree, *Exorcist*, 182–89.

and his relationship to the Father: God himself is encountered and seen at work in activities that can only portray him as God himself at work among his people.

In short, from the perspective of the Fourth Gospel, an exorcism could not, without further and considerable explanation, be expected to reflect on the identity or origin of Jesus, nor on the divine dimension of a miracle. Nor could any number of exorcisms convey the grand cosmic scale and otherworldly setting of the battle the Fourth Evangelist wished to convey was taking place and was won in the cross event, yet adumbrated throughout the life and ministry of Jesus. For that, the Fourth Evangelist was able to take over from his (signs?) source stories, which were unambiguously divine both in origin and revelatory capacity. To allay any possible remaining misunderstandings, he called them "signs."

9.9 Dealing with Demons

Despite the complete avoidance of the idea of Jesus or his followers being exorcists, the Fourth Evangelist not only maintains the category of demon possession but does so through having—at least at first sight—Jesus, and Jesus alone, charged with having a demon.[49] That this charge is significant is seen in it being repeated a number of times in the Gospel,[50] for repetition, widely used in literature, was not only important in the Old Testament,[51] but of all the New Testament writers, it was a literary device most frequently used by the Fourth Evangelist to draw attention to various themes.[52] In that irony—thriving on the contrast between what a character or the surface text says and what the readers are privileged to understand—functions alongside the repetition of the charge of demon possession, the significance of the multiple charges is further highlighted.[53] Not surprisingly, therefore, an examination of these charges in their Johannine context shows that they have clear theological content.[54] We will see that they also carry with them the Fourth Evangelist's

49. On the equivalence of "having a demon" and being "demon possessed," see Twelftree, *Exorcist*, 198–99.

50. John 7:20; 8:48, 49, 52; 10:20, 21.

51. See James Muilenburg, "A Study in Hebrew Rhetoric: Repetition and Style," in *Congress Volume: Copenhagen 1953* (VTSup 1; Leiden: Brill, 1953): 97–111.

52. See Paul D. Duke, *Irony in the Fourth Gospel* (Atlanta: John Knox, 1985), 91, citing John 3:10; 6:42; 7:20, 28, 35–36; 8:22, 58; 11:16; 13:38; 16:17–18, 29–30. On repetition in the Fourth Gospel, see Urban C. von Wahlde, "A Redactional Technique in the Fourth Gospel," *CBQ* 38 (1976): 520–33; David Alan Black, "On the Style and Significance of John 17," *CTR* 3 (1988): 141–59, esp. 150–52.

53. For a report of recent discussions of irony in the Fourth Gospel, see R. Alan Culpepper, "Reading Johannine Irony," in *Exploring the Gospel of John: In Honor of D. Moody Smith* (ed. R. Alan Culpepper and C. Clifton Black; Louisville: Westminster John Knox, 1996), chap. 10.

54. Against Barrett, *St John*, 319, who says, "There is no theological treatment of the charge [δαιμόνιον ἔχεις] in John."

distinct understanding of the demonic and demonic possession, as well as its remedy. In two places the mention of demon possession is brief (John 7:20; 10:20–21). They are dependent for their full understanding and significance on a third longer passage (8:48–52), as well as on an earlier passage that we will need to take into account for it has established some axioms for the readers (4:2–42).

John 7:20. Leading up to this point in the narrative, the Jews (οἱ Ἰουδαῖοι), who are authorities rather than the common people,[55] represent the world viewed from a religious perspective.[56] They are also Jesus' opponents, particularly in chapters 7 and 8 (as well as in 19), who have decided to kill Jesus (John 5:18; 7:1) and are now looking for him (7:11); but the crowd (ὄχλος), who will later be shown as ignorant of the truth (12:29), knows nothing of this.[57] Therefore, in response to Jesus asking, "Why are you looking for an opportunity to kill me?" the crowd expresses its disbelief: "You have a demon! Who is trying to kill you?"

This charge is often taken to be one of madness (cf. John 10:20).[58] However, in this particular context, the crowd's saying that Jesus has a demon is a way of saying that he is not believable or not telling the truth (cf. 10:20–21). Through a characteristic of this Gospel, where incorrect statements and unanswered questions imply unknowing truth,[59] and through their narrational advantage (cf. 7:1 and 20), the readers are invited to conclude that Jesus does not have a demon, that he is telling the truth, and that his life is being

55. On the difficulty of identifying "the Jews" in John, see Urban C. von Wahlde, "The Johannine 'Jews': A Critical Survey," *NTS* 28 (1982): 33–60. See also the bibliographical note, 54n1. He states: "If we speak of the meaning [of οἱ Ἰουδαῖοι] intended by the original author, we are most probably correct to say that he saw them as the religious authorities exclusively. If we speak about the present state of the text, we may point to 6:41, 52 as one text which seemingly was considered by the redactor to be representative of the attitudes and opinions of the common people" (45).

56. Cf., e.g., John 1:19; 2:13, 18, 20; 3:1, 25; 4:9; 5:1, 10, 16, 18; 6:4, 41; 7:2, 15; and C. Dekker, "Grundschrift und Redaktion im Johannesevangelium," *NTS* 13 (1966): esp. 66–71.

57. Cf. R. Alan Culpepper, *Anatomy of the Fourth Gospel* (Philadelphia: Fortress, 1983), 132. If the Fourth Evangelist does not wish the reader to presuppose the innocence of the crowd here (John 7:20), the protesting voices may be "of the murderer smiling reassuringly while fondling the knife behind his back." So Duke, *Irony*, 74. On the confusing presentation of the roles of the crowd, the Jews, and the Pharisees and the chief priest in John 7–8, see John Painter, *The Quest for the Messiah: The History, Literature, and Theology of the Johannine Community* (2nd ed.; Nashville: Abingdon, 1993), 288–90.

58. E.g., Barrett, *St John*, 319; Barnabas Lindars, *The Gospel of John* (London: Oliphants / Marshall, Morgan & Scott, 1972), 290; Rudolf Schnackenburg, *The Gospel according to St. John* (3 vols.; New York: Crossroad, 1982), 2:133; George R. Beasley-Murray, *John* (WBC 36; Waco: Word Books, 1987), 109.

59. Cf. Culpepper, *Anatomy*, 176, citing John 1:46; 4:12; 6:42, 52; 7:20, 26, 35, 42, 48; 8:22, 53; 9:40; 18:38. Gail R. O'Day, *Revelation in the Fourth Gospel: Narrative Mode and Theological Claim* (Philadelphia: Fortress, 1986), 130n38, contests 4:12 in that Jesus offers an indirect answer (cf. 4:11–14).

sought.[60] Therefore, although the precise charge is of no particular importance to the argument here,[61] through being alerted to its error (and perhaps to the ignorant and lying characteristics of his opponents), and at least picking up its superficial meaning of not telling the truth, the readers are given an interpretive perspective for understanding the full import of the accusation of having a demon when it is repeated and expanded later in the passages to which we now turn.

John 8:48–52. Principally through the use of irony, it is in this longer passage that the Fourth Evangelist brings into play the major interpretive keys to convey the understanding of the nature and function of the charge of demon possession brought against Jesus. As in the other two passages (John 7:20; 10:20–21), Jesus is set over against the Jews, here in a narrative that has a forensic structure.[62] The Jews are described as not loving Jesus (8:42), not accepting his word (8:43), but having the devil as their father, who "does not stand in the truth" because he is a liar (8:44).[63] This portrait gives detail to what has already been said of the Jews earlier in the Gospel as not trusted by Jesus (2:23–25), as having one of their leaders unable to accept Jesus' teaching (3:1–12), and so antagonistic to him that he left Judea (4:1–3). Narratively, therefore, readers can be expected to have taken up this perspective as a portrait of the Jews who are about to bring an accusation against Jesus: "Are we not right in saying that you are a Samaritan and have a demon?" (8:48). In other words, in view of the sustained negative portrayal of the Jews, as well as knowing from 7:20 that the charge against Jesus is false, readers can be expected to be alert to the irony here, which is rendered pellucid in the framing of the accusation itself.

The two-part accusation ("you are a Samaritan and have a demon") amounts to one and the same thing for Jesus gives a simple catch-all response: "I do not have a demon" (John 8:49). Yet we are able to note the irony of Jesus not denying being a Samaritan. In view of Jesus' simple reply, we can anticipate, therefore, understanding what the Fourth Evangelist means by demon possession, not only from the irony involved in the description of the Jews in this context (8:42–44), but also by understanding what the accusation to be a Samaritan meant. John Bowman has shown that the accusation of being a Samaritan, though not intended literally, was meant as

60. Also, insofar as the crowd is to be implicated as part of his opposition, they are shown to be liars.

61. Rudolf Bultmann, *The Gospel of John* (Oxford: Blackwell, 1971), 277.

62. Jerome H. Neyrey, "Jesus the Judge: Forensic Process in John 8,21–59," *Bib* 68 (1987): 509–42. See also the discussion by Andrew T. Lincoln, *Truth on Trial: The Lawsuit Motif in the Fourth Gospel* (Peabody, MA: Hendrickson, 2000), 82–96, esp. 96.

63. Cf. Felix Porsch, "'Ihr hat den Teufel zum Vater' (Joh 8,44): Antijudaismus im Johannesevangelium," *BK* 44 (1989): 50–57. Miroslaw Stanislaw Wróbel, *Who Are the Father and His Children in JN 8:44 and Its Context?* (CahRB 63; Paris: Gabalda, 2005), came to my attention too late to be taken into account.

a charge of acting the Samaritan, or being responsible for false prophecy (cf. 8:52),[64] ironically, by putting forth unbelievable opinions centering around faith and belief instead of ritual acts.[65] Such an accusation of deception echoed in the charge of demon possession (cf. 7:20; 10:20–21). This association of the demonic or Satan with false information or prophecy, embedded here in John 8, was well established in a Jewish context (e.g., *Mart. Isa.* 1:8–9).[66] Thus, of a piece with the charge in John 7:20 of not telling the truth, this two-part accusation amounts to the charge of being a liar. We have some support for this interpretation in a second-century comment about the Samaritans. In *Against Heresies*, Irenaeus calls the Simon of Acts 8:9–24 a Samaritan and the person from whom all heresies originated (*Haer.* 1.23.1–2). Further, he attributes Simon with being the author of the "Simonians," a "most impious doctrine, from whom the falsely called knowledge took its origin" (*Haer.* 1.23.4). Even though Irenaeus is writing around three generations later, his concern for the past and for handing on traditions, as well as having grown up in the same area in which the Johannine traditions developed (see §11.6 below), suggests he is probably casting reliable light on the use of the term "Samaritan" in the Johannine material as a cipher for purveyors of lies.

However, the irony involved in the Jews' charge that Jesus was a Samaritan (or demon possessed) has already been signaled by their unbelievable question: "Are we not right in saying . . . ?" (οὐ καλῶς λέγομεν . . .? John 8:48). For with the Jews being cast as having a liar as their father (8:44), readers have already been informed that the Jews could be anything but right. In light of this context, the irony unfolds and becomes poignant when we also take into account the contrary ways the Jews and the Samaritans have been described.

For by way of contrast to the portrait of the Jews,[67] it was in his journey through Samaria (from Judea where, as a prophet, he was without honor; John 4:44), as a result of the effective testimony (4:39, διὰ τὸν λόγον[68]) not

64. Cf. 2 Kings 17:29, where "the people of Samaria" are connected with the making of shrines for gods.

65. John Bowman, "Samaritan Studies," *BJRL* 40 (1957–1958): 306–8. Further, see Twelftree, *Exorcist*, 200. On the Jewish belief that Samaritan prophets were demon possessed, see Walter Bauer, *Das Johannesevangelium: Erklärt von Walter Bauer* (3rd ed.; HNT 6; Tübingen: Mohr Siebeck, 1933), 130–31.

66. See Jannes Reiling, "The Use of ΨΕΥΔΟΠΡΟΦΗΤΗΣ in the Septuagint, Philo and Josephus," *NovT* 13 (1971): 147–56.

67. In this context, the contrasting Johannine portraits of Nicodemus the Pharisee and the Samaritan woman are to be noted. See, e.g., Winsome Munro, "The Pharisee and the Samaritan in John: Polar or Parallel?" *CBQ* 57 (1995): 710–28.

68. Although λόγος is used of Jesus' words (John 4:41) and λαλιά of what the woman said (4:42), there is no intended denigration of her testimony, as suggested by Bultmann, *John*, 201. For

of a Jew but of a Samaritan woman,[69] that Jesus was acclaimed by Samaritans as "truly the Savior of the world" (4:42, cf. 39). The irony here—signaled by the Gospel's only use of σωτηρία ("salvation," 4:22) and σωτήρ ("savior," 4:42)—is that the salvation the Samaritans recognized would come from the Jews (4:22) was rejected by the Jews and accepted by the Samaritans (4:44).[70] Further irony is found in the acclaim of the Samaritans in that they recognize Jesus not as *a*, or *their*, national savior, as might the Jews, but in the climax of the story as "Savior of the world" (4:42).[71] The Samaritans also ask Jesus to stay (μένω, "remain")[72] with them (4:40). In that μένω is such a frequent and significant term for this Gospel,[73] denoting intimacy and permanency in a relationship,[74] the Samaritans are not simply offering casual accommodation but inviting their newfound Savior to live or dwell with them in intimacy.[75] The intimacy and permanency denoted here is heightened in this being a (water) well scene, which in literary instances can be a betrothal scene.[76]

With such a high view of the Samaritans,[77] it is no wonder the rebuttal of the two-part accusation ("you are a Samaritan and have a demon") is not a

λόγος was used initially for what she said in leading many Samaritans to believe (4:39). See O'Day, *Fourth Gospel*, 88.

69. She recognized Jesus as a prophet (John 4:19; cf. 4:29, 39) and proclaimed Jesus as the Christ (4:29). Jeffrey A. Trumbower, *Born from Above: The Anthropology of the Gospel of John* (HUT 29; Tübingen: Mohr Siebeck, 1992), 79, calls her one of the Fourth Gospel's "paradigms of correct belief."

70. O'Day, *Fourth Gospel*, 89.

71. Cf. P. Joseph Cahill, "Narrative Art in John IV," *RelSBul* 2 (1982): 43–44.

72. Cf. Friedrich Hauck, "μένω . . . ," *TDNT* 4:576.

73. In the NT μένω occurs 118 times; in John 40 times: 1:32, 33, 38, 39 (bis); 2:12; 3:36; 4:40 (bis); 5:38; 6:27, 56; 7:9; 8:31, 35 (bis); 9:41; 10:40; 11:6, 54; 12:24, 34, 46; 14:10, 17, 25; 15:4 (tris), 5, 6, 7 (bis), 9, 10 (bis), 16; 19:31; 21:22, 23; in Matthew, thrice (10:11; 11:23; 26:38); in Mark, twice (6:10; 14:34); and in Luke 7 times (1:56; 8:27; 9:4; 10:7; 19:5; 24:29, bis).

74. See Georgius Pecorara, "De verbo 'manere' apud Ioannem," *DivThom* 40 (1937): 159–71, esp. 162–64; followed by Brown, *John*, 1:510–12, esp. 511; and also see Rudolf Schnackenburg, *The Johannine Epistles* (Tunbridge Wells, UK: Burns & Oates, 1992), 99–104.

75. Jesus staying for the specified period of "two days" (John 4:40) is a puzzle. See, e.g., Francis J. Moloney, *The Gospel of John* (Collegeville, MN: Liturgical Press, 1998), 149. It could simply denote a brief period of time. Alternatively, since at the end of the period the "two days" are mentioned again (4:43), this time in connection with Jesus being a prophet traveling to Galilee, the Fourth Gospel may wish the "two days" to signal a reinforcement of the view (4:39) that Jesus is an authentic prophet. For in *Did.* 11:5 a peripatetic prophet may stay only two days; a stay of three is a mark of being a false prophet.

76. Cf., e.g., Cahill, "Narrative Art," 45–47, citing Walter Arend, *Die typischen Scenen bei Homer* (Problemata: Forschungen zur klassischen Philologie 7; Berlin: Weidmann, 1933).

77. Bowman, "Samaritan Studies," 298–327, esp. 299, 310–11, took up the proposal of Hugo Odeberg, *The Fourth Gospel: Interpreted in Its Relation to Contemporary Religious Currents in Palestine and the Hellenistic-Oriental World* (Uppsala and Stockholm: Almquist & Wiksell, 1929), 171–90, that Samaritan concepts had influenced the formulation of parts of the Fourth Gospel. See Wayne A. Meeks, *The Prophet-King: Moses Traditions and the Johannine Christology* (NovTSup 14; Leiden: Brill, 1967), esp. 318–19; followed by Edwin D. Freed, "Did John Write His Gospel

denial of being a Samaritan. In other words, for the readers, the charge brought against Jesus turns out to be both an echo of the positive assessment of the Samaritans and a shorthand description of their own plight—being liars and having the devil as their father. That is, *for the readers it is the Jews*, not Jesus, *who are to be seen as demon possessed.*

John 10:20–21: "Many of them were saying, 'He has a demon and is out of his mind. Why listen to him?' Others were saying, 'These are not the words of one who has a demon. Can a demon open the eyes of the blind?'" Here the charge of being demon possessed is immediately followed and linked with the accusation of being mad (μαίνεται, "he is mad") and unbelievable.[78] In all the other occurrences in the New Testament of μαίνομαι ("to be mad"), the word characterizes a disbelieved message.[79] For example, in Acts 12:15 Rhoda is said to be mad (μαίνομαι) or disbelieved when she relates the news that Peter is standing at the door.[80] Thus, as in John 7:20, the charge of demon possession is associated with promulgating lies and, in light of the passage we have just discussed, would have become a signal to the readers of the very opposite conclusion to be drawn—it is Jesus' opponents who have a demon and are not to be heard.

From examining the Johannine category of demon possession we can see that, through dramatic and verbal irony, the charge that Jesus is demon possessed turns out to be the proper, though veiled, description not of Jesus but of his opponents, showing that the evangelist is charging all of them with being demon possessed: being of the devil, being children of the father of lies.[81] In turn, this enables the reader to see how demon possession—to be in error—was to be combated. That is, being full of truth (ἀλήθεια) is a description of Jesus (John 1:14; cf. 14:6), and truth from the Father (15:26) came into the world through him (1:17). Also, the discussion centering around the charge of demon possession in 8:48–52, which frequently touches on the issue of truth and falsehood (8:40, 44, 45, 46), has its origin in a statement of Jesus, "You will know the truth, and the truth will make you free" (8:32).[82]

Partly to Win Samaritan Converts?" *NovT* 12 (1970): 241–56, arguing that the Fourth Gospel had as one of its purposes the winning of the Samaritans. The view of John MacDonald, *The Theology of the Samaritans* (London: SCM, 1964), that Samaritan sources borrowed from Christianity, especially the Fourth Gospel, found no support. See Meeks, *Prophet-King*, esp. 256–57.

78. See Twelftree, *Exorcist*, 199; Brown, *John*, 1:387; Lindars, *John*, 365; Barrett, *St John*, 378.

79. See Acts 12:15; 26:24, 25; 1 Cor. 14:23.

80. Further, see Twelftree, *Exorcist*, 199–200.

81. This understanding of the impact of evil spirits on individuals matches the view found in the Dead Sea Scrolls. See the tractate on the two spirits in 1QS 3.13–26, where the evil spirits "affect the ethical behaviour of an individual in an effort to separate him or her from God and his law." Archie T. Wright, *The Origin of Evil Spirits: The Reception of Genesis 6.1–4 in Early Jewish Literature* (WUNT 2.198; Tübingen: Mohr Siebeck, 2005), 179.

82. Bernard C. Lategan, "The Truth That Sets Man Free: John 8:31–36," *Neot* 2 (1968): 70–80.

Hence, we can see that, from the Johannine perspective, *demon possession is combated through knowing the truth: Jesus.*[83]

With this all-pervasive notion of demon possession and its required anti-dote, we cannot be surprised that the Fourth Gospel does not have stories of exorcism. To use exorcism would belie the deep and all-encompassing hold that Satan is portrayed as having not on a few but on the many. Demon possession is, then, not fought with the hand of a healer but with accepting Jesus (John 1:12) and his truth and honoring God as one's Father (cf. 8:49). It is salvation—knowing and remaining in Jesus and the truth he brings—that is the antidote to error and the demonic, not a healing encounter reserved for a few.[84]

9.10 Revelation and the Johannine letters

The Apocalypse shows considerable interest in Satan or the devil, who is mentioned more often than in any other book in the canon. He is also called an angel (Rev. 9:11)—as are his followers (12:7, 9)—who, by inspiring civil authorities (2:9, 13), emperor worship (2:13), immorality, idolatry (2:22–24), and some of the Jews (3:9), not only attacks the church (12:13–17) but, in the exercise of fearsome power, attempts to thwart God's redemptive plan in Jesus (12:1–3). Thus, in John 8:44, as in Revelation 2:9 and 3:9, Satan's hold is not over a few individuals who may need exorcism but over all who, not accepting the truth in Jesus, stand deceived (cf. Rev. 9:20; 12:9) over against the Christians. Indeed, the performance of signs or miracles is associated with the work of a beast or false prophet (13:13–14), demonic spirits (16:14), and with deception (19:20). Also, familiar from the Fourth Gospel is Satan's defeat not being at the level of individuals. Perhaps alluding to the victory of the cross, Satan is thrown down to the earth (12:7–12; cf. John 12:31). As his army is consumed by fire so also is Satan finally bound and thrown into the lake of fire (cf. 2 Kings 1:10) to be tormented forever (Rev. 20:1–3, 7–10) so that readers can receive encouragement knowing that the various attacks on them inspired by evil spiritual power will eventually be defeated. Thus, the battle against Satan is cosmic (12:12; cf. 20:2, 7–8) yet expressed on earth through the faithfulness of the martyrs (12:11).

83. For a similar view of truth combating the deceit of evil spirits, see 1QS 3.13–26. Note John 20:31 on the importance of "authentic belief that leads to life" in the Fourth Gospel; Lincoln, *John*, 88.

84. The test for this acceptance of the truth or salvation taking place may well be embedded in John 10:21. In some of the Jews asking, "Can a demon open the eyes of the blind?" the assumption is that one who can open the eyes of the blind will not be demon possessed. Perhaps we can extrapolate from this that, from the perspective of the Fourth Evangelist, a test for Christians accepting Jesus and his truth and honoring God as Father was Jesus' ability to perform miracles.

Similarly, in the Johannine letters where evil or false spirits are a concern (cf. 1 John 3:24; 4:1–6), the activity of the spirit of the antichrist has to do with correct belief in relation to Jesus rather than sickness (4:2–3). Again, conquering this spirit takes place not through exorcism but through knowing God (2:14) and loving him rather than the world, as well as having the word of God living in them (2:14–16).

9.11 Conclusion

In this chapter we have seen that in the Fourth Gospel the whole of the ministry of Jesus takes on the character of a battle with Satan. However, that battle is radically reinterpreted. As the battle is set up in the Fourth Gospel, Jesus does not confront Satan in the form of demons in a few demented or deranged people. Instead, he confronts the unbelief of all those who, inspired by the father of lies (John 8:44), refuse to see the truth revealed in his teaching and his glory revealed in his miracles. On receiving him, they know the truth and are freed from the father of lies (cf. 8:31–32, 44). In view of such a reinterpretation of the way Satan is to be fought and defeated, it is unlikely the Fourth Gospel, or any of the Johannine literature, could be seen by readers familiar with Mark as any encouragement in exorcism. Indeed, the Johannine perspective on the ministry of Jesus with its attendant worldview may also help us understand the perspective of other Christian literature in relation to the absence of exorcism among those Christians. That we will explore in the next part of our study.

9.12 The Next Step . . .

So far in this study we have examined those New Testament writings that could most contribute to answering our questions about the place and practice of exorcism among early Christians. Since we have already set out conclusions to each of the chapters in this part, we will not repeat them here. Rather, we will turn to the second-century data as we begin constructing a lens of literature that will enable us to look back with greater precision and clarity on the New Testament documents we have been examining.

Part 3

The Second Century

I N LIGHT OF an ongoing debate, the principal question driving this study of the New Testament is, what was the place of exorcism among early Christians, not least in relation to the growth of the church? Secondly, if exorcism had a place, we are interested in discovering its importance and how it was practiced. From what we have seen so far, the New Testament documents witness to a broad spectrum of views on exorcism among the early Christians. Even among the Synoptic Gospel writers, there is a diversity of opinions, though to varying degrees they shared the view that exorcism was an important factor in early Christianity. Matthew showed the least interest in exorcism among early Christians while Mark most probably held the view that exorcism was the most significant aspect of post-Easter Christian ministry. Though our evidence is somewhat circumstantial, for James exorcism was also probably a part of early Christianity, but its practice was very different from that found in the Synoptic Gospels. However, on the other hand, Johannine theology saw no place for exorcism, not because there was no category of demonic or demonic possession but because the demonic was overcome by truth rather than by the power-encounter of an exorcism. We speculated that Paul probably represented a middle position: exorcism was simply one form of healing in which Christians could expect to be involved in their evangelism.

It is these findings that open up the further question of the perceived function of the memory of Jesus as an exorcist in determining the role and practice of exorcism among early Christians. We will return to this issue in our conclusions in part 4. In any case, from our examination of the New Testament, it seems that, despite the apparent strong tradition of Jesus as an exorcist, not only did interest in exorcism vary, but there may have been Christians and churches who were not interested in it and did not practice exorcism because they expected the demonic to be defeated by other means.

In order to test this tentative conclusion and also to help account for this variety of interest and approaches, as well as not torture the New Testament texts to say more than their authors intended, especially on a subject that is unevenly represented among them, I earlier suggested that we would attempt to look back from beyond the canon as through a lens of later literature. Also, I have already set 200 CE as the terminus ad quem for this material (§1.3 above). Even though so much has been lost to us, there is still an enormous amount of material available so that it will be better managed if we consider it over two chapters. In these chapters we will take into account only that literature which came to be recognized as "orthodox" and thought to be faithful to the trajectories of the canon of the great or catholic church. For this reason we will leave aside all but the mainstream literature of the so-called Apostolic Fathers and the Greek apologists. Nevertheless, in view of what we saw earlier of the important place of what we could call "magical exorcisms" in the background to Christian exorcism (§2.1 above), it is appropriate that a comment be included on them as we seek to understand exorcism among early Christians (see §11.11 below). Thus, from the great wealth of literature available to us, we will examine only those which either mention exorcism or, equally important, could be expected to mention exorcism. To this list is to be added the longer ending of Mark for, although not originally part of the Second Gospel, it was written in our period of interest and taken up into mainstream Christianity in the canon. Also, as I will argue, this longer ending is important for, geographically and chronologically, it marks a renaissance of interest in exorcism, helping to explain the varied interest we see in exorcism among early Christians.

Further, during the period of our interest, Christianity had sufficient impact on society to receive considerable critical attention in the literature of outsiders. In the third chapter in this part of our study (chap. 12), we will take advantage of this material, looking to these outsiders for insight into the place of exorcism among the early Christians they knew. To begin we will look briefly at some passing comments made by the earliest-known critics of Christianity: Tacitus and Suetonius, for example. Then we will briefly examine the three great second-century critics of Christianity: Celsus, Lucian of Samosata, and Galen. This will enable us to give a slightly sharper focus to our lens of the early Christian literature discussed in the first two chapters of this part (chaps. 10–11) before using that lens to look back more clearly on the New Testament documents.

10

Fathers, Apologists,
and the Early Second Century

Tʜᴇ ᴘᴜʀᴘᴏsᴇ ᴏꜰ this and the next chapter is to examine mainstream early Christian writers up to the end of the second century, to discover and explain what interest they may have had in exorcism, as well as how it may have been practiced. Although this will have value in itself, for us this material will provide the lens with which we may be able to detect aspects of exorcism in the New Testament not otherwise immediately obvious to us. For example, if in the New Testament the impressive miracles were losing their demonstrative power, or they were no longer necessary to give rise to faith, so that there was a move away from the appeal to miracle, these documents may help us to see that. This material may also show us how the Jesus tradition was viewed and handled in the period, at least in relation to exorcism. Further, if the New Testament writers' interests in exorcism were influenced by theological, social, cultural, or geographical factors, these documents may also help us to see that. Therefore, as well as dating and provenance, as the evidence permits, we will also take note of these factors as possibly important in accounting for the varying interest in our subject. Taking them in as nearly a chronological order as we can determine, in this chapter we will deal with Clement of Rome, the *Shepherd of Hermas*, the *Didache*, Quadratus, Aristides of Athens, the *Preaching of Peter*, the *Letter of Barnabas*, and Ignatius of Antioch. In the next chapter we will examine the longer ending of Mark, the *Letter to Diognetus*, Justin Martyr, Tatian, Athenagoras of Athens, Irenaeus of

Lyons, Theophilus of Antioch, Montanism, Clement of Alexandria, and the *Apostolic Tradition*. We will conclude that chapter with some comments on Christian magical exorcisms and their relevance to our purposes.

10.1 Clement of Rome

This letter from Clement[1] of Rome in the mid-90s[2] was called forth by the rejection of the leaders in the church at Corinth (*1 Clem.*, preface). Nevertheless, we can assume that it still reflects the "concerns and convictions of a Roman Christian congregation."[3] The frequent and positive or neutral allusion to slavery and the identifying of God as Master[4] suggest that Clement belonged to a Christian community, not to what Tacitus called the "shabby poor" (*Hist.* 1.4), but to freed people and slaves of the great families of Rome.[5]

Addressing the Corinthians, Clement condemned the self-willed rebellion and discord, calling for submission, peace, and harmony to replace the jealousy, envy, and pride.[6] With such an agenda it is not surprising that *1 Clement* does not mention exorcism. However, from what the writer says, there is good reason to think that he has no interest in the subject. That is, first, in describing the mission of Paul, he is said to teach (διδάσκω, *1 Clem.* 5.7); there is no mention of miracles or exorcism in relation to the spread of the gospel. Secondly, in 49.6 Clement says that the love of the Lord, which drew us to him, was his blood; there is no mention of love that might be expressed in the healings or exorcisms. Thirdly, in support of his view that

1. For a discussion of the identity of this probably otherwise unknown writer (cf. *Herm.* 8.3), see Bart D. Ehrman, *The Apostolic Fathers* (2 vols.; LCL; Cambridge, MA, and London: Harvard University Press, 2003), 1:21–23.

2. See David G. Horrell, *The Social Ethos of the Corinthian Correspondence: Interests and Ideology from 1 Corinthians to 1 Clement* (Studies in the New Testament and Its World; Edinburgh: T&T Clark, 1996), 239–41, including 239n7 listing, e.g., J. B. Lightfoot, K. Lake, O. Knoch, L. W. Barnard, P. Mikat, A. Jaubert, J. Fuellenbach, M. W. Holmes, J. S. Jeffers, and A. Lindemann. Cf. the succinct discussion in Ehrman, *Fathers*, 1:23–25. For a less convincing case for an earlier date, see Thomas J. Herron, "The Most Probable Date of the First Epistle of Clement to the Corinthians," *StPatr* 21 (1989): 106–21; and the comments by Ehrman, *Fathers*, 1:25.

3. James S. Jeffers, *Conflict at Rome: Social Order and Hierarchy in Early Christianity* (Minneapolis: Fortress, 1991), 90.

4. *1 Clement* uses δεσπότης more than any other New Testament or early church writer. So Jeffers, *Conflict*, 102.

5. Jeffers, *Conflict*, 100–104.

6. E.g., *1 Clem.* 1.1; 44.3–6; 47.6; 63.4. See the discussion by Horrell, *Social Ethos*, 250–58. Christian Eggenberger, *Die Quellen der politischen Ethik des 1. Klemensbriefes* (Zürich: Zwingli, 1951), 189–93, has found little support for his view that the stated occasion of *1 Clement* is a fiction. See Karlmann Beyschlag, *Clemens Romanus und der Frühkatholismus: Untersuchungen zu 1 Clemens 1–7* (BHT 35; Tübingen: Mohr Siebeck, 1966), 17–19.

ministry ought to be conducted as Jesus commanded (40.1), Clement says that, after the resurrection, Christ sent the apostles "forth in the assurance of the Holy Spirit, proclaiming the good news [εὐαγγελιζόμενοι] that the kingdom of God was about to come [μέλλειν ἔρχεσθαι]" (42.3).

There is no mention of the apostles healing or performing exorcisms; they are, like Paul described earlier (1 Clem. 5.5–7), preachers[7] without appeal to miracle. Indeed, given this interest in the kingdom of God, if exorcism was part of the mission, we might expect that the kingdom would be described as having come (ἤγγικεν, Matt. 10:7; Mark 1:15) or to have come upon the hearers (ἔφθασεν ἐφ᾽ ὑμᾶς, Matt. 12:28 ‖ Luke 11:20). However, other than their preaching, Clement's only interest in this mission is in the apostles' testing converts with a view to appointing bishops and deacons (1 Clem. 42.5).

Later, in the course of assuring his readers of his prayers, Clement slips into addressing God directly: "Save those of us who are in affliction, show mercy to those who are humble, raise those who have fallen, show yourself to those who are in need, heal those who are sick [τοὺς ἀσθενεῖς ἴασαι], set straight those among your people who are going astray. Feed the hungry, ransom our prisoners, raise up the weak, encourage the despondent" (1 Clem. 59.4). Here we have evidence of healing being part of the life of the church. Yet, at a point where mention of exorcism could have been expected, it is not found. Of course, exorcism could have been understood to be part of healing the sick. More likely, however, exorcism is not mentioned because his view of salvation obviates its need. Using Abraham as the model, salvation is not seen in terms of being rescued from a spiritual enemy but in terms of becoming and being obedient "to the words of God" (τοῖς ῥήμασιν τοῦ θεοῦ, 10.1).

In view of the lack of interest in exorcism, the question is raised about the writer's knowledge of the Synoptic tradition. From the way 1 Clement alludes to the Synoptic tradition a number of times[8] and possibly quotes it twice,[9] there is the probability that he knew traditions that are now found in Matthew or Mark.[10] Allusions to the Fourth Gospel—all lacking verbal

7. On the use of εὐαγγελίζομαι, see Gerhard Friedrich, "εὐαγγελίζομαι . . . ," TDNT 2:718; Lampe 261; BDAG 402. In particular see 1 Clem. 42.1–3; Barn. 8.3; 14.9; Polycarp, Phil. 6.3. On the contrast between Clement's interests and those of Paul, forty years earlier, see Bruce Chilton and Jacob Neusner, Types of Authority in Formative Christianity and Judaism (London and New York: Routledge, 1999), 105.

8. See 1 Clem. 7.4; 16.17; 23.4; 24.5; 30.3; 48.4 (cf. OT citations or allusions also found in the Synoptics: 4.10; 7.7; 15.2; 16.15–16; 18.10; 36.5; 50.4; 52.3); and the discussion by Donald A. Hagner, The Use of the Old and New Testaments in Clement of Rome (NovTSup 34; Leiden: Brill, 1973), 164–71.

9. See 1 Clem. 13.2 (cf. Matt. 5:7; 6:14–15; 7:1–2, 12; Mark 4:24; 11:25; Luke 6:31, 35–38) and 1 Clem. 46.8 (cf. Matt. 18:6; 26:24; Mark 9:42; 14:21; Luke 17:2; 22:22), on which see Hagner, Use of the Old, 135–64.

10. So Hagner, Use of the Old, 164, 171, 178; see also Arthur J. Bellinzoni, "The Gospel of Matthew in the Second Century," SecCent 9 (1992): 201–4.

agreement[11]—probably mean that Clement did not know that book.[12] Instead, ideas and expressions which became part of the Johannine literature influenced his theology.[13] Therefore, although he knew traditions that became part of the canon, we can suppose that Clement did not think that these inherited traditions, including their emphasis on exorcism, were determinative for Christianity. Notably, the connection between mission and exorcism found in the Synoptic Gospel traditions has been entirely ignored by Clement. Instead, he reflects a Christianity that sees mission as preaching and teaching. There is the encouragement to heal the sick, but this is not in the context of mission.

10.2 *Shepherd of Hermas*

This document was widely known and often highly regarded in the early church.[14] It sets out a series of visions to Hermas in order to deal with the issues of, for example, the availability of forgiveness for postbaptismal sin, as well as the lifestyle of the rich Christians and their relationship with poorer members of the church. Even though there has been considerable discussion about this document having multiple authors, it reasonably claims to be written—though probably in stages[15]—by a certain Hermas, a former slave who was brought up in Rome, freed, and then became a Christian.[16] It is generally agreed that the *Shepherd of Hermas* originated in Rome (*Herm.* 1.1–2; 22.2)[17] somewhere around the turn of the first and second centuries CE.[18] Though not poor himself (1.8), those who would have identified with the message

11. See, e.g., *1 Clem.* 42.1 (John 17:18; 20:21); *1 Clem.* 43.6 (John 17:3; cf. 12:28); *1 Clem.* 49.1 (John 14:15, 21, 23; 15:10); *1 Clem.* 49.6 (John 6:51); *1 Clem.* 54.2 and 57.2 (John 10:2–16, 26–28; 21:16–17); *1 Clem.* 59.3–4 (John 17:3); *1 Clem.* 60.2 (John 17:17); on which see Hagner, *Use of the Old*, 263–68.

12. Hagner concludes that "the evidence indicates only the possibility of . . . dependence upon the Gospel of John" (*Use of the Old*, 268).

13. Cf. Robert M. Grant, *An Introduction* (vol. 1 of *The Apostolic Fathers: A New Translation and Commentary*; ed. Robert M. Grant; New York: Nelson, 1964), 43.

14. See the discussion in Carolyn Osiek, *Shepherd of Hermas: A Commentary* (Hermeneia; Minneapolis: Fortress, 1999), 4–7.

15. Norbert Brox, *Der Hirt des Hermas* (Kommentar zu den Apostolischen Vätern 7; Göttingen: Vandenhoeck & Ruprecht, 1991), 26–28.

16. William J. Wilson, "The Career of the Prophet Hermas," *HTR* 20 (1927): 21–62.

17. The view of Erik Peterson, "Kritische Analyse der fünften Vision des Hermes," in *Frühkirche, Judentum und Gnosis: Studien und Untersuchungen* (Freiburg: Herder, 1959), 271–84, that the *Shepherd of Hermas* is to be located in a Palestinian ascetic milieu, has not been taken up by scholars.

18. See the discussions in J. Christian Wilson, *Toward a Reassessment of the Shepherd of Hermas: Its Date and Its Pneumatology* (Lewiston, NY: Edwin Mellen, 1993), 9–61; Osiek, *Shepherd*, 18–20; and Charles E. Hill, *The Johannine Corpus in the Early Church* (Oxford: Oxford University Press, 2004), 474–80.

of Hermas came from the lower levels of urban society and, while being free people, faced the struggle with poverty.[19]

In the *Shepherd* the activities of evil spirits, demons, or the devil are frequently mentioned. For example, they are involved in factions, doubt, and doing evil, not least in people being angry and proud.[20] In 33.1–3 there is discussion of evil spirits and the Holy Spirit competing for living space in a person (cf. *Herm.* 34.7). Hermas says that when the Holy Spirit is forced out, "the person becomes void of the upright spirit and at last, being filled with evil spirits, vacillates in everything he does, being dragged back and forth by the evil spirits, entirely blinded from any good understanding" (34.7). Later, it is said that the end result of the work of the devil (τοῦ δαιμονίου) is death (100.5).

Regardless of how evil spirits are understood to control people, exorcism is never considered as the response. Rather, it is repentance and belief in the Lord, as well as clothing oneself with patience and standing against irascibility and bitterness—what could be called a self-applied moral or intellectual exorcism—that brings power over the devil and purification from the devil (*Herm.* 100.5; cf. 34.1–8).[21] For, in contrast to the Lord, the devil is not seen as powerful nor to be feared (37.2; 39.10); it is God who is powerful and, being feared, brings power over the devil (37.2; cf. 33.1). Ongoing freedom from the works of the devil is maintained through the fear of the Lord (37.3–4) and a decision to refrain from evil as well as to be patient and understanding (33.1, 6). Since the method of being free from the devil involves personal intellectual decisions and fear of the Lord, even in addressing non-Christians, we can assume that Hermas would not entertain the need for exorcism. Instead, we could expect he would enjoin the behavioral and cognitively based exercises of repentance and faith, for in 30.1–2 conversion is equated with understanding and with "great understanding" (σύνεσίς ἐστιν μεγάλη; cf. 100.5).

In light of this self-applied moral approach to subduing the demonic, two issues arise. First, the question is raised as to whether or not the *Shepherd* knew and was reacting against the Synoptic traditions. However, for a book with no quotations[22] and, at best, only allusions to the Synoptic Gospels,[23] it is unlikely to be seeking to correct that tradition, even though he seems to know it in some form. On the other hand, secondly, it is tempting to consider

19. See Jeffers, *Conflict*, 116–20.

20. *Herm.* 33.3; 39.10–11; 99.3. References are to the continuous numbering system introduced by Molly Whittaker, *Die Apostolischen Väter*, vol. 1, *Der Hirt des Hermas* (GCS; 1956; 2nd ed., Berlin: Akademie-Verlag, 1967), and used in *TLG*. See the discussion in Jeffers, *Conflict*, viii.

21. Cf. Osiek, *Shepherd*, 248.

22. Osiek, *Shepherd*, 26.

23. See the discussion by Robert Joly, *Le pasteur: Hermas* (2nd ed., 1968; SC 53; repr., Paris: Cerf, 1997), 414–15.

a direct connection between the Fourth Gospel and the *Shepherd of Hermas*.[24] For, keeping the commandments to find life and live to God (*Herm*. 30.4; cf. John 8:51; 15:10), knowing and remaining in the truth for spiritual security (*Herm*. 14.2; cf. John 8:31–32), and especially self-generated decisions of repentance and right behavior (*Herm*. 33.1–7; 100.5; John 8:48–52) are all examples of ideas shared by both writings.[25] Also, in the ninth parable (esp. 89–93) there is a concentration of allusions to John 1:2–3; 10:7; and 14:6. But there are no exact quotations. Therefore, more likely going beyond possible borrowing by Hermas, there is probably a sharing in a common pool of ideas.[26] In particular, what has probably been decisive in shaping this aspect of the thought of the *Shepherd* is likely to be access to the same dualistic ideas. In the case of Hermas, this is drawn from the widely known tradition variously identified as the "two spirits" (also familiar to those at Qumran; cf. 1QS 3.13–4.26), "two ways," or "two inclinations."[27]

What is important for the purposes of our study is to note that the *Shepherd* is evidence of there existing early in Christianity a way of dealing with the demonic without resorting to exorcism, as in the Synoptic traditions. On the other hand, the *Shepherd* is also evidence of an approach that, while similar to that found in the Fourth Gospel though not directly dependent on it, indicates that self-applied moral or intellectual exorcism was more widespread than evidenced from the Johannine literature.

10.3 *Didache*

Even though the *Didache* was important during the first Christian centuries for its "apostolic" rules,[28] for most of its history before its rediscovery in 1883, its existence had only been known through its mention by Eusebius (*Hist*.

---

24. How any connection between the two documents is understood is partly dependent on the date of the *Shepherd*. See the discussion by Hill, *Johannine Corpus*, 374–80. For an early dating, in the last two decades of the first century, see Wilson, *Toward a Reassessment of the Shepherd of Hermas*, chap. 2.

25. In more detail see Hill, *Johannine Corpus*, 376–80.

26. Although he admits the evidence "may not be too impressive," Hill concludes: "It appears . . . the author did know the Fourth Gospel, at least by the time he wrote Similitude 9" (*Johannine Corpus*, 378, 380).

27. On the material covered by this collection of antithetical terms or images in early Christianity and beyond, see Oscar J. F. Seitz, "Two Spirits in Man: An Essay in Biblical Exegesis," *NTS* 6 (1959–1960): 82–95; Leslie W. Barnard, "The Dead Sea Scrolls, Barnabas, the *Didache* and the Later History of the 'Two Ways,'" in his *Studies in the Apostolic Fathers and Their Background* (New York: Schocken, 1966), 87–107; and Sebastian Brock, "The Two Ways and the Palestinian Targum," in *A Tribute to Geza Vermes: Essays on Jewish and Christian Literature and History* (ed. Philip R. Davies and Richard T. White; JSOTSup 100; Sheffield: JSOT Press, 1990), 139–52.

28. Huub van de Sandt and David Flusser, *The Didache: Its Jewish Sources and Its Place in Early Judaism and Christianity* (Assen: Royal Van Gorcum; Minneapolis: Fortress, 2002), 2–3.

eccl. 3.25) and by Athanasius in his *Festal Letter 39*.[29] There is no agreement on the date of writing or, more accurately, the editing of older traditions. Important in setting a date is the Didachist's argued dependence on Synoptic tradition, notably Matthew. However, the jury is still out on this matter.[30] If the Didachist is independent of the Synoptic Gospels, there would be no convincing obstacle to dating the *Didache* in the middle of the first century.[31] Nevertheless, the turn of the first and second centuries is the view of an increasing number of scholars.[32]

The provenance of the book is also an enigma.[33] The early circulation in Egypt[34] and the correspondence between the doxology of the Lord's Prayer (*Did.* 8.2) and the Coptic translation of Matthew 6:13 could point to Egypt as the place of composition.[35] However, the mention of cereal crops growing on hills (*Did.* 9.4) and the lack of running water (7.2) favor Syria or Palestine,[36] the most frequently argued suggestion for its origin.[37] It is probable that the place of composition can be further narrowed. In light of the relative wealth

29. The last mention of the *Didache* from personal knowledge was by Patriarch Nicephorus of Constantinople (ca. 758–828). See van de Sandt and Flusser, *The Didache*, 1, 4–5, for the complexities of the use of the *Didache* in early Christianity.

30. On the one hand John S. Kloppenborg, "Didache 16:6–8 and Special Matthaean Tradition," *ZNW* 70 (1979): 54–67, convincingly argued that "Matthew combined Marcan tradition with another free-floating apocalyptic tradition which had been incorporated into the Didache quite independently of Matthew" (67). On the other hand, in relation to *Did.* 16 Christopher M. Tuckett, "Synoptic Tradition in the Didache," in *The New Testament in Early Christianity* (BETL 86; ed. Jean-Marie Sevrin; Louvain: Leuven University Press, 1989), 197–230, and reprinted in *The Didache in Modern Research* (ed. Jonathan A. Draper; AGJU 37; Leiden: Brill, 1996), 92–128, concluded: "The pattern of parallels between the Didache and Matthew is thus most easily explained if the Didache here presupposes Matthew's finished Gospel" (104; cf. 128). See the debate set out by Tuckett, "Didache," in *Modern Research*, 92–93; and Bellinzoni, "Matthew," 204–6.

31. E.g., Aaron Milavec, "Distinguishing True and False Prophets: The Protective Wisdom of the *Didache*," *JECS* 2 (1994): 118; and the discussion by Michelle Slee, *The Church in Antioch in the First Century CE* (JSNTSup 244; London: Sheffield Academic, 2003), 57–76.

32. See Kurt Niederwimmer, *The Didache* (Hermeneia; Minneapolis: Fortress, 1998), 53n71; van de Sandt and Flusser, *The Didache*, 48, and those cited in n. 128.

33. Cf. John M. Court, "The Didache and St. Matthew's Gospel," *SJT* 34 (1981): 109.

34. See Andrew Louth and Maxwell Staniforth, *Early Christian Writings: The Apostolic Fathers* (London: Penguin, 1987), 189, noting that Clement of Alexandria witnesses to it as Scripture (*Strom.* 1.20.100).

35. See Niederwimmer, *The Didache*, 53n75; van de Sandt and Flusser, *The Didache*, 51.

36. In Egypt soil suitable for crops is limited to the Nile valley. See Richard S. Ascough, "An Analysis of the Baptismal Ritual of the *Didache*," *StLit* 24 (1994): 205–6n23; and Robert A. Kraft, *Barnabas and the Didache* (vol. 3 of *The Apostolic Fathers*; ed. Robert M. Grant; New York: Nelson, 1965), 74–75.

37. See Niederwimmer, *The Didache*, 53n77. Against Niederwimmer, the mention of apostles in *Did.* 11 does not argue for a Syrian or Palestinian setting since the writer could be referring to persons other than the followers of Jesus. In any case, movement of the apostles cannot be assumed to be restricted to Syria or Palestine.

of the community (13), as well as the number of visitors (11) and Christians coming in to join the community (12), along with the Jewish elements (1–6), and a concern for the needs of Gentiles (6.2–3; 7; 9.5), Antioch is a reasonable suggestion for its origin.[38]

As a composite document the *Didache* deals with ethical (*Did*. 1–6), liturgical (7–10), organizational (11–15), as well as eschatological (16) matters. Although there are instructions that make most sense if there are Gentiles present who had been converted from paganism (e.g., the instruction to abstain from food sacrificed to idols; 6.3),[39] the document has such a strong Jewish flavor[40] that it was most likely written for a church dominated by Jewish Christians.[41] The Didachist may have initially brought his material together in an attempt to help the readers distinguish true Christianity from an attractive aberration that mimicked Judaism. For in 8.1 his readers are to distinguish themselves from the "hypocrites" (ὑποκριταί), a word he uses elsewhere probably to indicate not pious Jews[42] but lapsed or wayward Christians (2.6; 4.12) who fast on Mondays and Thursdays (8.1), the same days set aside by the Jews for fasting.[43] After dealing with ethical and liturgical matters, the Didachist goes on, perhaps in subsequently enlarged editions, to deal with the problem of internal relationships and leadership (14–15) and then peripatetic propagandists (16),[44] which will be of particular interest to us.

As is apparent with other writings included among the Apostolic Fathers, this document shows little or no ongoing interest in the miracles of Jesus, let alone his followers being exorcists. An interest in the miracles of Jesus might be expected to have surfaced in the words spoken over the broken bread in *Didache* 9.3: "We give you thanks, our Father, for the life and knowledge that you made known to us through Jesus your child." However, thanks is given for "the life and knowledge" (τῆς ζωῆς καὶ γνώσεως) made known through Jesus (9.3). There is no mention of, for example, his miracles or power to perform miracles.

---

38. Slee, *Antioch*, 55–57.

39. To this could perhaps be added *Did*. 9.4 and 10.5, which van de Sandt and Flusser, *The Didache*, 33, suggest that the transfer of the concept of the gathering of Israel on the day of salvation (Deut. 30:3–5a; Isa. 11:12b–c; Ezek. 37:21) to the Christian church "is a conspicuous characteristic of gentile Christian refashioning."

40. Van de Sandt and Flusser, *The Didache*, 32, note that "the ritual of baptism, the Lord's Prayer, and the eucharistic celebration are deeply affected by the pattern of Jewish daily worship."

41. The address "to the nations" or "gentiles" (τοῖς ἔθνεσιν) is of little help in determining the purpose and audience of the *Didache* because it is probably secondary. See Niederwimmer, *The Didache*, 56.

42. Against Niederwimmer, *The Didache*, 131–32.

43. J. Behm, "νῆστις," *TDNT* 4:930–31.

44. On the history of the composition of the *Didache*, see van de Sandt and Flusser, *The Didache*, 28–35.

Also notable is the lack of mention of any kinds of miracles associated with the itinerant apostles and prophets, about whom the readers are being instructed and warned (*Did.* 11–13).[45] From the Jesus traditions now in the canon, we could expect these traveling Christians to have included miracles in their repertoire.[46] However, the only possible "miraculous" activity mentioned of the prophets is being "in Spirit" (ἐν πνεύματι), which is limited to speaking (11.7).

Since the Didachist does not associate miracles with the traveling apostles and prophets, it would be difficult to maintain that miracles, including exorcism, were a legitimate part of the life and community of those reflected in the *Didache*. Furthermore, in that the visiting apostles and prophets are to be accepted only if they adhere to "all that has been said above" (ταῦτα πάντα τὰ προειρημένα, *Did.* 11.1), and part of what has been set out is that they are to practice "not magic nor sorcery" (οὐ μαγεύσεις, οὐ φαρμακεύσεις, 2.2;[47] cf. 3.4; 5.1), which is how the magicians who duplicated the miracles of Moses and Aaron in Exodus are described,[48] it can safely be concluded that these prohibitions are understood to be real and that miracle-working was acknowledged but associated with false Christians. In their miracle-working they may have been described as soothsayers, enchanters, or astrologers (3.4).

The only time there is a clear mention of miracles in the *Didache* is in the chapter on eschatology.[49] In 16.4 the writer says that, in the last days, "the world-deceiver will be manifest as a son of God. He will perform signs and wonders [καὶ ποιήσει σημεῖα καὶ τέρατα]." To begin with, it is notable that the currency of the phrase "signs and wonders" included use as a term for misleading deeds.[50] Then, in a way familiar from 2 Thessalonians 2:9[51] and echoing a tradition shared by Matthew 24:24[52] (about false messiahs and

45. On the debate as to whether or not the teaching mentioned in *Did.* 11.1–2 is intended to refer to a class separate from the apostles and prophets or to one of their functions, see van de Sandt and Flusser, *The Didache*, 342–43, who conclude the latter.

46. Cf. Matt. 7:21–23; 10:5–8; 24:24 in light of Matthew being the Gospel closest to the *Didache*. See Richard Glover, "The Didache's Quotations and the Synoptic Gospels," *NTS* 5 (1958): 25–29.

47. Jean-Paul Audet, *La Didachè: Instructions des apôtres* (Paris: Gabalda, 1958), 287, notes that from the context it is not possible to distinguish the meanings of the terms μαγεία and φαρμακεία. On the paralleling of these two terms, see Pieter W. van der Horst, *The Sentences of Pseudo-Phocylides, with Introduction and Commentary* (SVTP 4; Leiden: Brill, 1978), 212–13.

48. In the LXX see Exod. 7:11, 22; 8:3, 14. Cf. Wilfred L. Knox, "Περικαθαίρων (Didache III, 4)," *JTS* 40 (1939): 146–49.

49. Though not critical for our purposes, the difference in style suggests that this chapter may once have been a separate tradition. See the discussion by Torsten Löfstedt, "A Message for the Last Days: Didache 16:1–8 and the New Testament Traditions," *EstBib* 60 (2002): 375–78; and Niederwimmer, *The Didache*, 207–13.

50. See Graham H. Twelftree, "Signs, Wonders, Miracles," *DPL* 875.

51. Cf. Glover, "Quotations," 24.

52. See the synopsis in Niederwimmer, *The Didache*, 211.

false prophets producing signs and wonders), as well as using the word "son" for the figure,[53] this probably means that readers are intended to see this as a parody on the ministry of Jesus, especially his miracles.

In light of this warning, and that, as just suggested, the wandering preachers to be turned away may have been miracle-workers, Jesus is implied to be the only one who performed miracles.[54] Rather than performing ambiguous signs and wonders that could be confused with those of a Messianic pretender, the *Didache* says that the signs preceding the coming of the Lord are "signs of truth" of a more cosmic and spectacular kind—the opening of heaven, the trumpet's voice, and the raising of the dead (*Did.* 16.6, 8). In other words, after Jesus, the *Didache* associates miracles with the false messiah and false Christianity.

The explanation of this aversion to the miraculous is not difficult to find. Not only is it apparent that false Christianity was thought to involve miracles, which mislead the faithful (*Did.* 3.4; cf. Deut. 18:10–13), but also, as it has been cogently argued, the Didachist was dependent on a Q-like sayings source with no detectable biographical interest in Jesus.[55] Further, as Ian Henderson has argued, not only is "teacher" the nearest term to describing the implied author, but also the considerable use of διδασκ- ("teach-") words—especially as they are coordinated with prophet and apostle—suggest that the writer is uniting his readers around a Christianity less uncontrollably numinous than that associated with prophets and apostles.[56] In other words, the Didachist is promoting a Christianity free of miracles, which (we note) would rule out exorcism. Thus, while we saw that Matthew lowered the importance of exorcism in the face of adverse experience, the Didachist, also probably in Antioch, has relegated exorcism to false Christianity.

Before leaving the Didachist, we need to note the mention of baptism in *Didache* 7 (cf. *Did.* 9.5),[57] the earliest account of baptism outside the New Testament canon. This is of interest to us in light of the modern discussion about the relationship between baptism and exorcism in the early church.[58] Chapter 7 begins: "But with respect to baptism, baptize as follows. Having said all these things in advance [ταῦτα πάντα προειπόντες], baptize . . ." (7.1). Regardless whether or not this means the "two ways" of chapters 1–6 were to

---

53. In *Did.* 7.1, 3 υἱός ("son") is used of Jesus.

54. Cf. the translation by Louth and Staniforth, *Apostolic Fathers*, 197–98: "Then the Deceiver of the World will show himself, pretending to be a Son of God and doing signs and wonders."

55. See particularly Glover, "Quotations," 25–29; Kloppenborg, "Didache 16:6–8," 54–67; Jonathan A. Draper, "The Jesus Tradition in the Didache," in *The Miracles of Jesus* (ed. David Wenham and Craig Blomberg; Gospel Perspectives 6; Sheffield: JSOT Press, 1986), 283.

56. Ian H. Henderson, "*Didache* and Orality in Synoptic Comparison," *JBL* 111 (1992): 286–87.

57. See the discussion by Ascough, "Baptismal Ritual," 201–13.

58. See the discussion by Willy Rordorf, "Baptism according to the *Didache*," in *The Didache in Modern Research* (ed. Jonathan A. Draper; AGJU 37; Leiden and New York: Brill, 1996), 212–22.

be recited immediately before the baptismal rite or taught to the candidates previously,[59] there is nothing in 7.1 or the preceding material that could be construed to relate baptism and exorcism. There is not even any mention of the renunciation of Satan (cf. *Trad. ap.* 21.9).[60] There is, however, a few lines later, a direction that "both the one baptizing and the one being baptized should fast before the baptism, along with some others if they can. But command the one being baptized to fast one or two days in advance" (*Did.* 7.4). It is true that, a few decades later, in the middle of the second century, there is a clear connection made between baptism, unclean spirits, and exorcism.[61] Theodotus of Alexandria,[62] the Valentinian Gnostic, says that "since unclean spirits often go down into the water with some . . . [t]herefore let there be fastings, supplications, prayers, raising of hands, kneelings" (*Exc.* 84–85). However, in the *Didache* the connection between exorcism and baptism is not made, and we cannot argue from the later evidence that it was present earlier in the *Didache*.

10.4 Quadratus

Our interest in Quadratus lies in what this earliest Christian apologist has to say about the miracles of Jesus, and perhaps what he does not say about Christian miracles of his own time. Unfortunately, we know no more about Quadratus than what we can deduce from Eusebius.[63] In his *Chronicle*, Eusebius says that Quadratus was a disciple of the apostles and that his apology was delivered to Hadrian in the ninth year of his reign.[64] That would be in the middle of the third decade of the century, when Hadrian was touring Asia Minor (Dio Cassius 69.9–12).[65] In his *History* Eusebius says: "When Trajan

59. See the discussion by van de Sandt and Flusser, *The Didache*, 280.

60. Cf. Rordorf, "Baptism," 221.

61. Elizabeth A. Leeper, "From Alexandria to Rome: The Valentinian Connection to the Incorporation of Exorcism as a Prebaptismal Rite," *VC* 44 (1990): 7: "The Theodotian rite contains the earliest known evidence explicitly stating the need to rid a person of all evil spirits before baptism."

62. Our knowledge of Theodotus is limited to what we know of him from fragments of his work preserved in Clement of Alexandria's *Excerpta ex Theodoto*. See Robert Pierce Casey, *The Excerpta ex Theodoto of Clement of Alexandria* (London: Christophers, 1934); and François M. M. Sagnard, *Clément d'Alexandrie: Extraits de Théodote* (SC 23; Paris: Cerf, 1970).

63. On the three different people named Quadratus by Eusebius, see Johannes Quasten, *Patrology* (4 vols.; Utrecht-Antwerp: Spectrum, 1950–1986), 1:191; Robert M. Grant, "Quadratus, The First Christian Apologist," in *A Tribute to Arthur Vööbus: Studies in Early Christian Literature and Its Environment, Primarily in the Syrian East* (ed. R. H. Fischer; Chicago: Lutheran School of Theology, 1977), 178–79. Contrast the article "Quadratus," ODCC³ 1354, which sees no compelling reason to take the three names as referring to the same person.

64. Eusebius, *Chronicon;* Grant, "Quadratus," 182n31.

65. See Quasten, *Patrology*, 1:191; Ehrman, *Fathers*, 1:89. This relatively late date is not inconsistent with what Quadratus says for he does not say that the healed and raised people

had reigned for nineteen and a half years, Aelius Hadrian succeeded to the sovereignty. To him Quadratus addressed a treatise composing a defense for our religion because some wicked men were trying to trouble the Christians" (*Hist. eccl.* 4.3.1). From a copy he has of the work in question, Eusebius says both the intellect and orthodoxy of Quadratus can be seen.

It is to illustrate the early date of Quadratus that Eusebius cites him: "But the works of our Savior were always present, for they were true, those who were cured, those who rose from the dead, who not merely appeared as cured and risen, but were constantly present, not only while the Savior was living, but even for some time after he had gone, so that some of them survived even till our time" (*Hist. eccl.* 4.3.2).[66] Quadratus appears to be contrasting Jesus—"but our Savior" (δέ σωτῆρος ἡμῶν)—with some other savior figure, or figures, on the strength of his enduring miracles.[67] Exorcism is not mentioned, though the catch-all term "those . . . cured" (οἱ θεραπευθέντες) could be said to cover such healings. In any case, although it can only be an argument from silence—especially obvious when we have only a small quotation from a third party—we can note that in arguing against the miracles of his opponents, Quadratus makes no mention of Christian miracles taking place in his own time. It is to be wondered then if such miracles were taking place, at least on any significant scale, and if they were thought to be authentic, that Quadratus would have mentioned them. We can only speculate that miracles, including exorcism, were not important in the church of the third decade of the second century known to Quadratus in Asia Minor.

10.5 Aristides

Having introduced Quadratus, Eusebius goes on to say that "Aristides again, a loyal and devoted Christian, has like Quadratus left us a *Defense of the Faith*

---

are alive at the actual time of writing. Cf. Geoffrey W. H. Lampe, "Miracles and Early Christian Apologetic," in *Miracles: Cambridge Studies in Their Philosophy and History* (ed. C. F. D. Moule; London: Mowbray, 1965), 209; Maurice F. Wiles, "Miracles in the Early Church," in Moule, ed., *Miracles*, 221. Also, since Eusebius does not say that he actually knows any of the survivors from the time of Jesus—see also Robert M. Grant, *Miracle and Natural Law in Graeco-Roman and Early Christian Thought* (Amsterdam: North-Holland, 1952), 188—Quadratus does not have to be located in the Levant.

66. Andriessen's proposal that this fragment of Quadratus fits well into the lacuna between *Diogn.* 7.6 and 7 has not met with approval: Paul Andriessen, "L'Apologie de Quadratus conservée sous le titre d'Épître à Diognète," *RTAM* 13 (1946): 5–39, 125–49, 237–60; 14 (1947): 121–56; and Paul Andriessen, "The Authorship of the *Epistula ad Diognetum*," *VC* 1 (1947): 129–32. See, e.g., Eugene Fairweather, "The So-Called Letter to Diognetus," in *Early Christian Fathers* (ed. Cyril C. Richardson; LCC 1; 1953; repr., New York: Collier / Macmillan, 1970), 206–7; and Grant, "Quadratus," 178.

67. On the various possible figures that Quadratus may have in mind—Hadrian, Aesclepius, the Gnostics—see Grant, "Quadratus," 180–82.

addressed to Hadrian. Many people still preserve copies of his work also" (*Hist. eccl.* 4.3.3). Aristides was a philosopher in Athens,[68] perhaps handing over his apology when Hadrian visited the city in 125 CE.[69] However, unlike that from the hand of Quadratus, the text of Aristides' apology is now known to us in a number of forms.[70] Early in the text in his description of the four kinds of people—pagans, Greeks, Jews, and Christians—he introduces the Christian religion as beginning from Jesus the Messiah. Included in his brief description of Jesus there is mention, for example, of his Hebrew birth, his having twelve disciples, that he was "pierced by the Jews," and that after three days he rose and ascended into heaven. The description finishes by saying, "Thereupon these twelve disciples went forth throughout the known parts of the world, and kept showing his greatness with all modesty and uprightness. And hence also those of the present day who believed that preaching are called Christians" (Aristides, *Apol.* 2). In neither the description of Jesus nor in the mission of his disciples is there any mention of miracles, let alone exorcism; preaching is what is central to evangelism.

In a longer paragraph describing the Christians, Aristides gives attention primarily to their lifestyle, including marital fidelity, honoring parents, and not harming others, as well as not worshipping strange gods. In illustrating the Christians' love for others, Aristides gives an example of Christian evangelism: "If one or other of them have bondmen and bondwomen or children, through love towards them they persuade them to become Christians" (*Apol.* 15). Most notable, again, there is no mention of the miraculous being part of evangelism. Nor is there to be seen any need to defend the conducting of miracles in the face of possible skepticism. Given that the main features of Christianity are being described, it is reasonable to conclude that miracles, including exorcism, were not part of the Christianity (including its evangelism) that Aristides knew and was defending.

10.6 *Preaching of Peter*

This document is known to us primarily from quotations in Clement of Alexandria's *Stromateis* (or *Miscellanies*).[71] Given that the second-century

68. Eusebius, *Chron.* 2.166; cf. Jerome, *Vir. ill.* 20. On the ancient witnesses to Aristides, see Bernard Pouderon et al., *Aristide: Apologie* (SC 470; Paris: Cerf, 2003), 25–31.

69. See *Hadr.* 13, in David Magie, *Scriptores historiae Augustae* (vol. 1; LCL; 1921; repr., London: Heinemann; Cambridge, MA: Harvard University Press, 1979) 39–43. On the dating of Aristides, see Pouderon et al., *Aristide*, 32–37.

70. On the discovery and rediscovery of the text, see the brief description in Quasten, *Patrology*, 1:192.

71. See Clement of Alexandria, *Strom.* 1.29.182; 2.15.68; 6.5.39–41, 43; 6.6.48; 6.7.58; 6.15.128. For a discussion of possible citations in other writings, see Wilhelm Schneemelcher,

Gnostic Heracleon (flourished ca. 145–180 CE) used it,[72] the composition of the *Preaching of Peter* can be placed in the first half of the second century.[73] Though not demonstrable, it is generally agreed to have come from Egypt.[74] There is so much we do not know about the *Preaching of Peter*: its length, its structure, the order of most of the extant fragments, and the overall purpose remain a mystery to us. However, the title may suggest that it was supposed to be a compendium of at least Peter's preaching, if not a reflection of apostolic preaching generally, with Peter's name being representative of the apostles.[75] The fragments that are available to us (see n. 71) deal with the topics of Christian monotheism, pagan polytheism, Jewish worship, the old covenant being for the Greeks and the Jews, the new for the Christians, and the Scriptures being written about Christ Jesus and determining the Christian message. From this it seems that the writer was particularly interested in the relationship between Christians and others, especially the Jews.

There is just one fragment where there is a hint of a perspective on miracles and exorcism that is of interest to us. In *Stromata* 6.6.48 Clement says that in the *Preaching of Peter* the resurrected Lord says concerning his disciples: "I sent them . . . into the world to *proclaim* to men in all the world the joyous message that they may know that there is (only) one God, and to reveal what future happenings there would be through faith in me, to the end that those who *hear* and believe may be saved; and that those who believe not may testify that they have *heard* it and not be able to excuse themselves saying, 'We have not *heard*.'" The preponderance of vocabulary relating to speaking and hearing (emphasis added), as well as Jesus being called "Law and Word" (*Strom.* 1.29.182) and being described as a covenant maker (*Strom.* 6.5.39) rather than a miracle-worker are strong indications that both Jesus and his followers are understood to be preachers only. There is no hint of accompanying or authenticating exorcisms or other miracles being performed. Although we have so little information about the contents of the *Preaching of Peter*, at the very point where the performing of exorcism could be expected to be mentioned in a description of the disciples, it is not. Also, in view of Clement's interest in the demonic (see §11.9 below), it is unlikely that he would have filtered out references to exorcism. From this it is reasonable to conclude that exorcism was not seen to be at all important to the early second-century Christians in Egypt responsible for this docu-

---

NTApoc[2] 2:36–37. The text is also known from, e.g., Eusebius, *Hist. eccl.* 3.3.2; Origen, *Comm. Jo.* 13.17.

72. So Origen, *Comm. Jo.* 13.17; cited by Schneemelcher, *NTApoc*[2] 2:41n14.

73. Henning Paulsen, "Das Kerygma Petri und die urchristliche Apologetik," *ZKG* 88 (1977): 13, suggests 100–120 CE; Wilhelm Schneemelcher, "Kerygma Petri," *NTApoc*[2], 2.34, suggests 100–140 CE.

74. See Schneemelcher, *NTApoc*[2], 2:34.

75. See Schneemelcher, *NTApoc*[2], 2.35.

ment, probably because Jesus was seen as a covenant maker and the mission of the church as preaching.

10.7 *Letter of Barnabas*

Perhaps on the strength of the portrait of Barnabas in the canonical book of Acts,[76] what may have been an anonymous work (cf. Eusebius, *Hist. eccl.* 3.25.4) could later have been ascribed to Barnabas because of its Jewish content.[77] However, we cannot tell whether or not the author himself was Jewish.[78] The puissance of the Jewish content, not least the use of the "two ways," which is likely to be of Jewish origin,[79] does not allow us to deem the author Jewish for he nowhere distinguishes himself from the uncircumcised Gentile readers.[80] In any case, the letter was probably written by a teacher[81] to Gentile Christians (*Barn.* 3.6; 16.7) who were tempted to convert to Judaism,[82] in a setting where Jews and Christians, who had separated from each other,[83] were competing for the same Gentiles associated with the synagogues.[84] In the context of this struggle for their loyalty,[85] Barnabas says that he has received God-given knowledge or pneumatic insight into the readers.[86] A reading of *Barnabas* makes it fairly clear that neither miracles in general nor exorcisms in particular were part of the church known to the writer in Alexandria[87] around the year 130 CE, for in 16.3–4 there is probably a reference to the

76. See, e.g., Acts 13:1, 43, 46; 15:2, 35.

77. Hans Windisch, *Der Barnabasbrief* (HNT, Ergänzungs-Band: Die apostolischen Väter 3; Tübingen: Mohr Siebeck, 1920), 413.

78. Whether or not the author was a Jew is a matter of considerable debate. See the summary discussion by James Carleton Paget, *The Epistle of Barnabas: Outlook and Background* (WUNT 2.64; Tübingen: Mohr Siebeck, 1994), 7–9; and the review of Paget by Leslie W. Barnard, "The Epistle of Barnabas: Outlook and Background," *JTS* 46 (1995): 696–98.

79. See Leslie W. Barnard, "The Epistle of Barnabas in Its Jewish Setting," in *Studies in Church History and Patristics* (Analecta Vlatadon 26; Thessaloniki: Patriarchikon Hidryma Paterikon Meleton, 1978), 52–106, esp. 90–91; and Niederwimmer, *The Didache*, 36–37.

80. Kraft, *Barnabas and the Didache*, 39, citing 1.8; 3.6; 4.6; 13.7; 14.5–8; 16.7–9.

81. See the discussion in Reidar Hvalvik, *The Struggle for Scripture and Covenant: The Purpose of the Epistle of Barnabas and Jewish-Christian Competition in the Second Century* (WUNT 2.82; Tübingen: Mohr Siebeck, 1996), 47–49.

82. See S. Lowy, "The Confutation of Judaism in the Epistle of Barnabas," *JJS* 11 (1960): 1–33; Hvalvik, *Struggle*, 164; Ehrman, *Fathers*, 2:8–9.

83. William Horbury, "Jewish-Christian Relations in Barnabas and Justin Martyr," in *Jews and Christians: The Parting of the Ways A.D. 70 to 135* (ed. James D. G. Dunn; WUNT 2.66; Tübingen: Mohr Siebeck, 1992), 315, notes the "us" and "them" language in *Barn.* 2.7; 3.6; 8.7; 10.12; 13.1; 14.1, 4–5.

84. Hvalvik, *Struggle*, 319–20.

85. See the discussion in Paget, *Barnabas*, 46–49.

86. See the discussion of λαμβάνω (esp. at *Barn.* 1.5) in Hvalvik, *Struggle*, 49–51.

87. See Paget, *Barnabas*, 30–42.

hope, alive in the period leading up to the second Jewish revolt (132–135 CE), that the Jerusalem temple would soon be reconstructed.[88]

The subject of miracles first arises at the end of a section warning of approaching judgment, where the writer says that the readers are to bear in mind that, "even after such great signs and wonders [σημεῖα καὶ τέρατα] had been wrought in Israel, they were none the less rejected." From this Barnabas concludes that the readers were to "be very careful not to be found among those of whom it is written that many are called, but few are chosen" (4.14).[89] It could be that the readers were placing store in their experience of miracles. Indeed, the readers' personal experience of miracles would increase the force of his argument. Slight evidence of this could soon follow. Barnabas goes on to deal with the incarnation and describes Jesus as teaching the people of Israel and doing "wonders and signs" (τέρατα καὶ σημεῖα, 5:8). However, in saying that Jesus chose apostles, he only says that they "were to preach his gospel"; there is no mention of them doing wonders and signs (5.9).

Therefore, it is possible that, in both pointing out the dangers of relying on wonders and signs and not mentioning the apostles conducting them, Barnabas wishes to restrict the value of miracles to the exodus and Jesus' ministry. That Barnabas wishes to downplay miracles may also be evident in chapter 14. There the citation of Isaiah 42:6–7 and 61:1–2 (LXX; each mentions opening the eyes of the blind) is applied not to any miracle-working by Jesus or his followers but to the general notion of salvation (*Barn.* 14.4–9). Further, in light of the suggestion that miracles, especially exorcisms, were important in the growth of the church (see §1.1 above), it is notable that at a point where this could have been raised, Barnabas has nothing to say on them. He clearly did not think miracles were significant in relation to mission. Indeed, if what we have suggested is near what he had in mind, for Barnabas, miracles were a hindrance to mission, which is seen in terms of preaching (5.9; 8.3) that elicits a faith response (9.3).

Notwithstanding, the ideas of demons and their removal come into view in a discussion about the old and new temples (*Barn.* 16). Echoing Old Testament ideas of demons as idols or foreign deities,[90] rather than notions familiar from the exorcism stories in the Synoptic Gospels, Barnabas says, "Before we believed in God, the dwelling place of our heart . . . was full of

88. See, e.g., Hvalvik, *Struggle*; and the summary discussion by Ehrman, *Fathers*, 2:6–7. For an earlier date see, e.g., Peter Richardson and Martin B. Shukster, "Barnabas, Nerva, and the Yavnean Rabbis," *JTS* 34 (1983): 31–55; Horbury, "Jewish-Christian Relations," 319–21; and Paget, *Barnabas*, 9–30.

89. Translation from Louth and Staniforth, *Apostolic Fathers*.

90. See Graham H. Twelftree, "Devil, Demons," in *New Dictionary of Theology* (ed. Sinclair B. Ferguson and David F. Wright; Leicester, UK, and Downers Grove, IL: InterVarsity, 1988), 197, citing Deut. 32:17; Pss. 91:6 (LXX); 96:5; 106:37; Isa. 13:21; 34:14; 65:3, 11. Cf. Acts 17:18.

idolatry and was a house of demons" (οἶκος δαιμονίων, 16.7).[91] He goes on to say that the new temple is built in which God truly resides "within us . . . because we have received the forgiveness of sins and have hoped in the name" (16.8). That this experience of being made new (16.8) and of God's living in the person rids the person of demons and maintains a healthy condition is clear from the ensuing explanation.

Barnabas says that the new temple is built or comes about through "his word of faith, his call to us through his promise, the wisdom of his upright demands, the commandments of the teaching, he himself prophesying in us and dwelling in us, who had served death, opening up to us the door of the temple, which is the mouth [i.e., 'word'[92]], and giving repentance to us" (*Barn.* 16.9). Thus, even though a person could be described as a house of demons, the cure was not any rite of exorcism or even baptism,[93] which was administered by immersion (11.11). Rather, the cure was located in the whole conversion complex (or coming to faith), including and epitomized by God dwelling in the person. Thus it is not a single experience (conversion) but an ongoing experience of God living in a person that brings and maintains health in relation to the demonic. What is striking for us is that the method of dealing with demons is reminiscent of the Fourth Gospel (see chap. 9 above).

There has been a long debate over the relationship between *Barnabas* and the Fourth Gospel.[94] That there is some connection beyond coincidence is arguable in light of what they share: some typologies (e.g., the bronze serpent and the figure of Abraham), the incarnational theology, the preexistence of Christ (whose death is related to the forgiveness of sins), and the anti-Judaism, for example.[95] Also, in view of our interests, it is notable that the Jews are said to be instructed by "an evil angel" (ἄγγελος πονηρός, *Barn.* 9.4; cf. John 8:44). However, any direct relationship between *Barnabas* and the Fourth Gospel is unlikely: *Barnabas* has no *logos* theology and, in particular, salvation could not be said to be from the Jews for Judaism has been a religion dead

91. For a house as representation of a person inhabited by a demon, see §5.4 above. More generally on the image, see Francis X. Gokey, *The Terminology for the Devil and Evil Spirits in the Apostolic Fathers* (Patristic Studies 93; Washington, DC: Catholic University of America Press, 1961), 108–9n5. Commensurate with this understanding of the human being's relationship with the spiritual realm, Barnabas goes on to discuss the "two ways" (of teaching and of wielding power): "For over the one are appointed light-bearing angels of God, but over the other the angels of Satan" (*Barn.* 18.1).

92. On στόμα see Kraft, *Barnabas and the Didache*, 132, citing *Odes Sol.* 12:3; 42:6; Ignatius, *Rom.* 8.2.

93. Without evidence, suggested by Gokey, *Terminology*, 100.

94. See the discussion by Paget, *Barnabas*, 225–30.

95. In more detail see Paget, *Barnabas*, 226–28, and notes. This is not to deny the strong Jewish character of either document. See Paget, *Barnabas*, esp. 9, and the collection of papers by Reimund Bieringer, D. Pollefeyt, and F. Vandecasteele-Vanneuville, eds., *Anti-Judaism and the Fourth Gospel: Papers of the Leuven Colloquium, 2000* (Jewish and Christian Heritage Series 1; Assen: Royal Van Gorcum, 2001).

since the golden calf fiasco. Therefore, it is not that *Barnabas* is dependent on the Fourth Gospel.[96] Rather, in *Barnabas* and the Johannine literature, we are probably dealing with ideas expressing the same zeitgeist.[97] Once again, we have an example (cf. *Shepherd*) of an expression of Christianity in which demons and their possession of human beings is assumed but without recourse to exorcism to provide a cure. Instead, it is, if we may paraphrase, the presence of God that removes the demonic. Finally, in our interest in the relationship between baptism and exorcism, we can note that although Barnabas discusses baptism, it is in relation to the cross, not exorcism (11.1–11).

10.8 Ignatius of Antioch

Nothing is known of this early—perhaps second—Christian bishop of Antioch (Ignatius, *Rom.* 2.2; cf. Eusebius, *Hist. eccl.* 3.22) save what can be gleaned from seven letters he wrote to a number of churches as he was accompanied by ten soldiers on his way to martyrdom in Rome (Ignatius, *Rom.* 5.1).[98] Reading between the lines of the letters, J. B. Lightfoot reasonably conjectured that Ignatius was mature in life when he was converted from paganism.[99] If, as has reasonably been argued, Eusebius is to be relied upon for the martyrdom of Ignatius taking place in 107 CE, during the days of Trajan (98–117 CE),[100] it is likely that Ignatius was writing early in the second century.[101]

96. As has been argued by François-Marie Braun, "La 'Lettre de Barnabé' et l'Évangile de Saint Jean (simples réflectiones)," *NTS* 4 (1957–58): 119–24; and François-Marie Braun, *Jean le Théologien et son évangile dans l'église ancienne* (Paris: Gabalda, 1959), 81–86. See the discussion by Paget, *Barnabas*, 225–30; and Hill, *Johannine Corpus*, 19–20.

97. So H. Holtzmann, "Barnabas und Johannes," *ZWT* (1871): 336–51; cited by Paget, *Barnabas*, 230.

98. For a list of the earliest patristic references to Ignatius, see Cyril C. Richardson, *The Christianity of Ignatius of Antioch* (New York: Columbia University Press, 1935), 89n1. On the three traditional listed recensions of the letters, see William R. Schoedel, *Ignatius of Antioch: A Commentary on the Letters of Ignatius of Antioch* (Hermeneia; Philadelphia: Fortress, 1985), 3–4. Although confidence in the authenticity of the letters of Ignatius has fluctuated, the consensus remains in favor of the authenticity of the letters. See Caroline P. Hamond Bammel, "Ignatian Problems," *JTS* 33 (1982): 62–97; and Mark J. Edwards, "Ignatius and the Second Century: An Answer to R. Hübner," *ZAC* 2 (1998): 214–26.

99. See Joseph B. Lightfoot, *The Apostolic Fathers*, part 2, *Ignatius and Polycarp* (2nd ed.; 2 parts in 5 vols.; London: Macmillan, 1889–1890; repr., Grand Rapids: Baker, 1981), 1:28.

100. Eusebius, *Hist. eccl.* 3.21–22, 35. For a discussion of this evidence for dating Ignatius, see Christine Trevett, *A Study of Ignatius of Antioch in Syria and Asia* (SBEC 29; Lewiston, NY; Queenston, ON; and Lampeter, UK: Edwin Mellen, 1992), 3–9.

101. See William R. Schoedel, "Ignatius and the Reception of the Gospel of Matthew in Antioch," in *Social History of the Matthean Community* (ed. David L. Balch; Minneapolis: Fortress, 1991), 130–31; and William R. Schoedel, "Polycarp of Smyrna and Ignatius of Antioch," *ANRW* II.27.1 (1993): 347–58.

Apart from his imminent death, for which he longs (e.g., *Rom.* 1–2, 8), in general, Ignatius is concerned about false teachers in the church (e.g., *Eph.* 6.2; *Trall.* 6.1)[102] and, above all, about the unity of the church (*Magn.* 1.2; *Phld.* 5.2; 8.1).[103] Nevertheless, compared to others of this period, Ignatius shows considerable interest in the life of Jesus.[104] Yet, apart from his eating and drinking (e.g., *Trall.* 9.1), having apostles and being a teacher (*Magn.* 7.1; 9:1–2), Ignatius has little to say on the public life and ministry of Jesus.[105] It is possible, nevertheless, that there is a hint of his knowing that Jesus was a healer. In his letter to Polycarp he urges the bishop: "Bear [βάσταζε] with all people, just as the Lord bears with you" (*Pol.* 1.2). Since Ignatius here reflects Isaiah 53:4, as found in Matthew 8:17, where it is used to describe the healing ministry of Jesus—including exorcism—Ignatius is probably aware of this aspect of Jesus' ministry. However, Ignatius interprets the passage not in terms of a healing ministry of the church but of a bishop enduring his role.[106]

Ignatius has provided us with sufficient information for us to ask why he did not take up from his traditions and develop the idea of Jesus and his followers being healers or exorcists. To begin with, perhaps a small part of the explanation can be taken as his considerable dependence on Matthew[107] (or at least his sources[108]), who, before him, had subsumed Jesus the miracle-

102. See, e.g., Einer Molland, "The Heretics Combatted by Ignatius of Antioch," *JEH* 5 (1954): 1–6; Jerry L. Sumney, "Those Who 'Ignorantly Deny Him': The Opponents of Ignatius of Antioch," *JECS* 1 (1993): 345–65; and Michael D. Goulder, "Ignatius' 'Docetics,'" *VC* 53 (1999): 16–30.

103. See the discussion by Schoedel, *Ignatius*, 21–22. According to Christine Trevett, "Prophecy and Anti-Episcopal Activity: A Third Error Combatted by Ignatius?" *JEH* 34 (1983): 1–18; and Christine Trevett, "Apocalypse, Ignatius, Montanism: Seeking the Seeds," *VC* 43 (1989): 313–38, Ignatius was combating a third error, prophetic activity that was the seedbed for Montanism; this theory has been discussed and criticized by Schoedel, "Polycarp of Smyrna and Ignatius of Antioch," 342.

104. Ignatius mentions or alludes to a number of aspects of Jesus' life: the virgin birth (*Eph.* 19.1; *Smyrn.* 1.1) from Mary (*Eph.* 7.2; *Trall.* 9.1); the star of the nativity (*Eph.* 19.2) and perhaps the magi (*Eph.* 19.3); that Jesus was of the line of David (e.g., *Eph.* 20.2; *Trall.* 9.1); that he was baptized by John (*Smyrn.* 1.1; cf. *Eph.* 18.2); perhaps the temptation by Satan (*Rom.* 6.1); that Jesus ate and drank (*Trall.* 9.1); that he was anointed (*Eph.* 17.1); probably the last supper (*Rom.* 7.3); possibly the trial (*Eph.* 15.2); that Jesus was persecuted at the time of Pontius Pilate (*Trall.* 9.1) and the tetrarch Herod (*Smyrn.* 1.2); that he "was truly crucified and died" (*Trall.* 9.1; *Smyrn.* 1.2); and that "he was also truly raised from the dead" (*Trall.* 9.2) in the flesh so that he ate and drank and his followers could see and touch him (*Smyrn.* 3.1–3). In more detail see Schoedel, "Reception," 154–75. See also the earlier essay by Graydon F. Snyder, "The Historical Jesus in the Letters of Ignatius of Antioch," *BR* 8 (1963): 3–12.

105. See Schoedel, "Reception," 164–65.

106. Schoedel, "Reception," 167.

107. See Christine Trevett, "Approaching Matthew from the Second Century: The Under-Used Ignatian Correspondence," *JSNT* 20 (1984): 59–67, esp. 65.

108. See the discussion by Trevett, *Ignatius*, 22–23; see also the discussion by Schoedel, "Reception," 129–77, esp. 175–77; John P. Meier, "Matthew and Ignatius: A Response to William R. Schoedel," in Balch, ed., *Social History of the Matthean Community*, 178–86; and Bellinzoni, "Matthew," 206–7.

worker under that of Jesus the teacher.[109] Secondly, in reading the Fourth Gospel,[110] Ignatius would have been familiar with an approach to the defeat of the demonic that did not require exorcism.

Thirdly, in view of his own immediate and anticipated circumstances, it is not surprising that Ignatius could describe the gospel in terms of the death and, particularly, the resurrection of Jesus. In one place he defines the gospel as "the coming of the Savior, our Lord Jesus Christ, his suffering, and resurrection" (*Phld.* 9.2; cf. 8.2; *Smyrn.* 7.2). Further, for Ignatius, this is a gospel that is spoken or preached (e.g., *Eph.* 6.2).[111] Apart from the way one lives (e.g., *Eph.* 14), Ignatius makes no mention of demonstrating or enacting the gospel in miracles or exorcism.

Fourthly, for Ignatius, at least some of the defeat of Satan and the powers of evil took place in the incarnation. He says that "the virginity of Mary and her giving birth escaped the notice of the ruler of this age; so too did the death of the Lord" (*Eph.* 19.1).[112] As a result, he says, "all magic was vanquished and every bondage [δεσμός] of evil came to nought" (19.3). Readers would probably have understood the bonds to refer not only to fate, magic spells, and dissension,[113] but also to evil powers.[114] However, in the face of a broader description of Jesus that includes not only his birth but also his eating, drinking, persecution, and death, Ignatius portrays "those in heaven and on earth and under the earth" as looking on (*Trall.* 9.1), perhaps intending to portray them as powerless. In any case, there is no mention of teaching or miracles, including exorcism.

Fifthly, Ignatius associates the activity of Satan with false doctrine and disunity. Thus, he encourages his readers to meet together more frequently to give thanks and glory to God (*Eph.* 13.1–2) so that "the powers of Satan are overthrown."[115] He also goes on to say that Satan's "destructiveness is nullified by the unanimity of your faith" (13.1). Similarly, in *Ephesians* 17,

109. Schoedel, "Reception," e.g., 164.

110. That Ignatius did not use the Fourth Gospel, see Henning Paulsen, *Studien zur Theologie des Ignatius von Antiochien* (Forschungen zur Kirchen- und Dogmengeschichte 29; Göttingen: Vandenhoeck & Ruprecht, 1978), 36–37. However, persuasively to the contrary, see Hill, *Johannine Corpus*, 421–43. On Ignatius, *Rom.* 7.2–3 (John 4:10, 14; 6:33; etc.); *Magn.* 7.1 (John 5:19; 8:28); *Magn.* 8.2 (John 1:1; 8:28–29); *Phld.* 7.1 (John 3:6, 8; 8:14); *Phld.* 9.1–2 (John 8:30–59; 10:7, 9; 14:6; 17:20–23), see the discussion by Hill, *Johannine Corpus*, 431–41.

111. See the discussion by Charles T. Brown, *The Gospel and Ignatius of Antioch* (New York: P. Lang, 2000), 118–21; cf. 209.

112. Cf. Virginia Corwin, *St. Ignatius and Christianity in Antioch* (New Haven: Yale University Press, 1960), 156, 177.

113. See Schoedel, *Ignatius*, 93.

114. Schoedel, *Ignatius*, 93n37, citing Luke 13:16; Hippolytus, *Comm. Dan.* 4:33; *Odes Sol.* 21:2; 25:1; 42:16; *Trim. Prot.* (NHC XIII,*1*) 41.4–5; 44.14–17.

115. The vocabulary of thanksgiving and glory (εἰς εὐχαριστίαν θεοῦ καὶ εἰς δόξαν) suggests that Ignatius is thinking of the Eucharist. See Gerhardus J. M. Bartelink, *Lexicologisch-semantische studie over de taal van de Apostolische Vaders* (Nijmegen: Centrale Drukkerij N.V.; Utrecht: Beyers, 1952), 113–14; Justin, *1 Apol.* 65.3; *Did.* 9.1, cited by Schoedel, *Ignatius*, 74.

instead of taking up doctrines of "the prince of this world," the readers are encouraged to accept the knowledge of God in the person of Jesus Christ. Thus, Satan is overthrown not by exorcism or any powerful confrontation, but by expressions of attention to God (or God in Jesus) and to unity. Once again, we see an approach that is not far from that we have encountered in the Fourth Gospel.

In this chapter we have dealt with Clement of Rome, the *Shepherd of Hermas*, the *Didache*, Quadratus, Aristides, the *Preaching of Peter*, the *Letter of Barnabas*, and Ignatius of Antioch. In light of the view that exorcism was very important in the early church it is remarkable that, so far, we have not come across any interest in exorcism. However, as we turn to the material dealt with in the next chapter, a change takes place, at least among some Christians.

11

Mark's Longer Ending
and the Later Second Century

I N CONTRAST TO what we saw in the last chapter, beginning with the longer ending of Mark, some of the literature of the latter half of the second century—the *Letter to Diognetus*, Justin Martyr, Tatian, Athenagoras of Athens, Irenaeus of Lyons, Theophilus of Antioch, Montanism, Clement of Alexandria, and the *Apostolic Tradition*—shows a marked change of interest in exorcism. We will conclude this chapter with some comments on Christian magical exorcisms and their relevance to our purposes.

11.1 The Longer Ending of Mark (Mark 16:9–20)

Two references to exorcism in only twelve verses of the so-called longer ending of Mark show that the writer may have had considerable interest in the subject. In Mark 16:9 Mary Magdalene is identified as the one "from whom he had cast out seven demons" (cf. Luke 8:2), and near the end of the passage Mark 16:17 says: "By using my name they will cast out demons." A discussion of these references and their literary contexts can be expected to give us further insight into exorcism among some early Christians represented by this material.

Even though it is probably an exaggeration to say that the ending of Mark is "the greatest of all literary mysteries,"[1] no explanation of the enigma has been forthcoming that has commanded general appeal.[2] Whether or not Mark intended to conclude his Gospel at 16:8,[3] there are good reasons to think that the longer ending is not from the hand of the one who wrote the body of the book.[4] For, besides these twelve verses being absent in the two earliest parchment codices, Codex Sinaiticus (ℵ) and Codex Vaticanus (B), as well as many other manuscripts,[5] the passage contains significant differences in vocabulary and style from the rest of Mark,[6] and the pericope is not well connected to what precedes it in that the women are the subject of 16:8 but Jesus is the subject of 16:9. Further, this longer ending interrupts the sequence of thought established up to 16:8 in failing to relate the promised appearance of the risen Lord in Galilee (16:7) in the list of appearances that are probably taken from the other three Gospels.[7] Thus, what stylistic affinities there are

1. Dennis E. Nineham, *The Gospel of St Mark* (PNTC; Harmondsworth, UK: Penguin, 1963), 439.

2. See the discussion by, e.g., Garry W. Trompf, "The Markusschluss in Recent Research," *ABR* 21 (1973): 15–26; and Steven Lynn Cox, *A History and Critique of Scholarship concerning the Markan Endings* (Lewiston, NY: Mellen, 1993).

3. See the argument and evidence collected by Robert H. Gundry, *Mark* (Grand Rapids: Eerdmans, 1993), 1009–21, that at 16:8 Mark was not ending his Gospel but starting a new paragraph on a subsequent meeting between Jesus and the women; this is what Richard T. France, *The Gospel of Mark* (Grand Rapids and Cambridge, UK: Eerdmans; Carlisle, UK: Paternoster, 2002), 684, calls "the least unsatisfactory of the proposed understandings of Mark's enigmatic final verses."

4. The comment on the treatment of "The Conclusion of Mark" by Ned B. Stonehouse, *The Witness of Matthew and Mark to Christ* (Philadelphia: The Presbyterian Guardian, 1944), 86–118, by F. F. Bruce, "The End of the Second Gospel," *EvQ* 17 (1945): 169, that "the result is a demonstration as conclusive as any proof of this kind can be that these twelve verse are not an integral part of the Gospel to which they have so long been attached," still stands. Nevertheless, to the contrary see, e.g., Eta Linnemann, "Der (wiedergefundene) Markusschluss," *ZTK* 66 (1969): 255–87. See the critique of Linnemann by Kurt Aland, "Die wiedergefundene Markusschluss? Eine methodologische Bermerkung zur textkritischen Arbeit," *ZTK* 67 (1970): 3–13; and J. K. Elliott, "The Text and Language of the Endings to Mark's Gospel," *TZ* 27 (1971): 255–62; repr. in J. K. Elliott, *The Language and Style of the Gospel of Mark* (Leiden: Brill, 1993), esp. 204–5.

5. See Bruce M. Metzger, *The Text of the New Testament* (4th ed.; Oxford: Oxford University Press, 2005), 322–23; Elliott, "Text and Language," 203–4.

6. E.g., sixteen words do not occur in the body of Mark: πορεύομαι (Mark 16:10, 12, 15), πενθέω (16:10), θεάομαι (16:11, 14), ἀπιστέω (16:11, 16), ἕτερος (16:12), μορφή (16:12); ὕστερον (16:14), ἕνδεκα (16:14), παρακολουθέω (16:17), ὄφις (16:18), θανάσιμον (16:18), βλάπτω (16:18), ἀναλαμβάνω (16:19), συνεργέω (16:20), βεβαιόω (16:20), and ἐπακολουθέω (16:20). See Paul L. Danove, *The End of Mark's Story: A Methodological Study* (Leiden: Brill, 1993), 122–23, 125–26, for further differences in vocabulary and grammar between Mark 1:1–16:8 and 16:9–20. See also William R. Farmer, *The Last Twelve Verses of Mark* (SNTSMS 25; Cambridge: Cambridge University Press, 1974), 83–103, esp. 85, who also notes the points of contact with the body of Mark's Gospel.

7. See Farmer, *Last Twelve*, 103. Cf. Craig A. Evans, *Mark 8:27–16:20* (WBC 34B; Nashville: Nelson, 2001), 546–47.

between the longer ending and the body of Mark[8] suggest that it was written as a secondary ending for this Gospel rather than by the evangelist.

In fixing the terminus a quo for this material, we are dependent on two factors. First, since the longer ending has clear echoes of John's Gospel,[9] the earliest it can be dated is the beginning of the second century. Similarly, the possible dependence of the longer ending of Mark on the *Epistula Apostolorum*,[10] which, according to Martin Hengel, "is to be put at the latest in the middle of the second century, and very probably earlier,"[11] also means that the longer ending is likely to have been in existence early in the second century. To these points we can add that the earliest entire citation of the longer ending, by Tatian, is in his *Diatessaron*,[12] which may be dated just before his departure from Rome, likely in 172 CE.[13] Also, Irenaeus cites Mark 16:19 as part of Mark's Gospel in his *Against Heresies* (3.10.5),[14] which was written in Lyons and sent, as each part was written, to Eleutherus during his Roman episcopate (ca. 175–189).[15] Irenaeus was most probably relying on sources independent of Tatian, for not only does he never mention the *Diatessaron*,[16] but he is unlikely to have cited this material after him without explanation if it was known to have been used by Tatian, of whom he was critical (*Haer.* 1.28.1; 3.23.8). It is reasonable, therefore, to

---

8. Farmer, *Last Twelve*, 85, suggests that the phrasing of Mark 16:9 "*evidences that kind of stylistic affinity with the rest of Mark that would be expected were it to have been composed by the same writer responsible for Mk. 1:1–16:8*" (his italics).

9. Cf. Mark 16:9 and John 20:1; Mark 16:10 and John 20:18; Mark 16:16 and John 3:18. Ἐκείνη, for "that woman" (feminine nominative singular substantive), is found elsewhere in the Gospels only in John 11:29; 20:15, 16; see Farmer, *Last Twelve*, 85, who adds, "Interestingly enough the closest parallel to ἐκείνη πορευθεῖσα is found in John 20:15, ἐκείνη δοκοῦσα, where we are struck by the fact that the woman concerned is precisely the same person."

10. See Manfred Hornschuh, *Studien zur Epistula Apostolorum* (PTS 5; Berlin: de Gruyter, 1965), 14, cited by Martin Hengel, *Studies in Mark's Gospel* (London: SCM, 1985), 168. Dependence on the longer ending is denied by James A. Kelhoffer, *Miracle and Mission: The Authentication of Missionaries and Their Message in the Longer Ending of Mark* (WUNT 2.112; Tübingen: Mohr Siebeck, 2000), 171n49, though see 186n91; such dependence is seen as "still quite possible" by Charles E. Hill, *The Johannine Corpus in the Early Church* (Oxford: Oxford University Press, 2004), 405.

11. Hengel, *Studies*, 168. See the discussion in Johannes Quasten, *Patrology* (4 vols.; Utrecht-Antwerp: Spectrum, 1950–1986), 1:150–51.

12. See Tatian, *Diat.* 53.25, 35, 37, 39, 61; 55.3, 5, 8–10, 12, 13, 16.

13. Molly Whittaker, *Tatian: Oratio ad Graecos and Fragments* (Oxford: Clarendon, 1982), "Introduction," ix.

14. Irenaeus, *Haer.* 3.10.5: "Towards the conclusion of his Gospel, Mark says: 'So then, after the Lord Jesus had spoken to them, he was received up into heaven, and sitteth on the right hand of God.'"

15. Robert M. Grant, *Irenaeus of Lyons* (London and New York: Routledge, 1997), 6.

16. Bruce M. Metzger, *The Early Versions of the New Testament: Their Origin, Transmission, and Limitations* (Oxford: Clarendon, 1977), 32. However, Irenaeus (*Haer.* 1.28.1) knows Tatian's *Discourse to the Greeks*.

suppose that Irenaeus knew about the longer ending of Mark, at least from his time in Rome in 177 CE (Eusebius, *Hist. eccl.* 5.4.1–2). Allowing time for this material to be accepted as part of Mark, it can be supposed that it was established in Rome probably a generation earlier, in the middle of the second century.[17] Then, further, the reference to drinking poison (Mark 16:18) tends to place the composition in the first half of the second century. For Papias, who probably wrote his *Exposition of the Logia of the Lord* around 110 CE,[18] is cited by Eusebius as saying that Justus Barsabas drank poison without suffering harm (*Hist. eccl.* 3.39.9).[19] From this evidence we can reasonably conclude that the longer ending of Mark was in existence around the third decade of the second century and well established by the middle of that century.[20]

For the provenance of the longer ending, the evidence, such as we have, points to Rome. Even if Tatian's *Diatessaron* was written in Syriac,[21] there was a considerable Syriac Christian community in Rome,[22] where in the second and third centuries the *Diatessaron* was well known.[23] Also, Tatian's teacher, Justin Martyr (Eusebius, *Hist. eccl.* 4.29.3), who probably alludes to the ending,[24] was also in Rome.[25] Then, despite the dissonance we have noted between the longer ending and the Gospel as a whole, the longer ending was probably intended as a conclusion to Mark, which is also traditionally said to originate in Rome (see chap. 5, n. 6). Further, the writer appears to be familiar with all four Gospel traditions, as well as Acts.[26] Since Rome is one of the

17. See Cox, *Markan Endings*, 15–17.

18. See William R. Schoedel, *Polycarp, Martyrdom of Polycarp, Fragments of Papias* (vol. 5 of *The Apostolic Fathers*; ed. Robert M. Grant; Camden, NJ: Nelson, 1967), 91–92; and Ulrich H. J. Körtner, *Papias von Hierapolis* (Göttingen: Vandenhoeck & Ruprecht, 1983), 225–26.

19. For other later references to Christians drinking poison, see Henry B. Swete, *The Gospel according to St. Mark* (London: Macmillan, 1908), 406.

20. Cf. Kelhoffer, *Miracle and Mission*, 175, who says: "With confidence one may thus date the LE [Longer Ending] to ca. 120–150 C.E." and (475) "possibly to the earlier part of this range."

21. On the original language of the *Diatessaron*, see n. 89 below.

22. Louis Duchesne, *Le liber pontificalis: Texte, introduction et commentaire* (2 vols.; Paris: E. Thorin, 1886–1892), 1:134, says that Anicet, a Syrian, was bishop of Rome from 145 to 165 CE; cited by William L. Petersen, "Tatian's Diatessaron," in *Ancient Christian Gospels: Their History and Development* (ed. Helmut Koester; London: SCM; Philadelphia: TPI, 1990), 429n1.

23. Petersen, "Tatian's Diatessaron," 429.

24. In Justin Martyr, *1 Apol.* 1.45, written in the late 150s CE (*1 Apol.* 1.46) in Rome—see Adolf von Harnack, *Die Chronologie der altchristlichen Litteratur bis Eusebius* (2 vols.; Leipzig: Hinrichs, 1897), 1: 274–84—there is a possible allusion to Mark 16:20: "His apostles going forth preached everywhere."

25. See Justin Martyr, *1 Apol.* 1.

26. Rudolf Pesch, *Das Markusevangelium* (HTKNT 2.1–2; Freiburg: Herder, 1980), 2.544–47; Hengel, *Studies*, 168–69; Evans, *Mark 8:27–16:20*, 546–47. On the *Diatessaron* also depending the living tradition of the words of Jesus, see, e.g., Eric F. Osborn, *Irenaeus of Lyons* (Cambridge: Cambridge University Press, 2001), 181; Kelhoffer, *Miracle and Mission*, e.g., 121–22, 138–39, 147–50.

likely places for all these traditions to be known, it is more than reasonable to maintain that the longer ending was also composed there.

Turning to the content of these verses, it is notable that the motif holding these verses together is that of belief and unbelief.[27] The initial interest of the passage is in the Eleven; not believing the message of those who saw Jesus after he had risen, they are upbraided by the risen Lord (Mark 16:14) so that they can believe and go out to proclaim the good news (16:15). Yet the focus of the passage is on those who believe the ones who proclaim this message. Not only will they be saved (16:16), but also "signs will accompany"—literally, "will follow" (παρακολουθήσει)—"those who believe" (16:17). That is, the signs or miracles are seen as proofs or evidence of belief. In other words, for the writer of this material, belief is shown through the miracles that take place in association with the person. It is against this theology of miracles that the references to exorcism are to be understood.

Important for our study, Mary Magdalene is identified as the one "from whom he had cast out seven demons" (παρ' ἧς εκβεβλήκει ἑπτὰ δαιμόνια, Mark 16:9). In using ἐκβάλλω ("cast out"), the writer of the longer ending maintains the Markan as well as wider early Christian idea of exorcism as God fulfilling his purpose for his people in casting out an enemy.[28] That our writer took up the idea that Mary had seven demons cast out from her draws attention to the power of Jesus to deal with a person who was so demonized that there could be no worse state imagined.[29] In turn, this powerful ability of Jesus provides the backdrop for the exorcism of the early Christians in the second reference, in 16:17.

In the second reference that is of interest to us, exorcism heads the list of the signs: "Signs will accompany those who believe: by using my name [ἐν τῷ ὀνόματί μου] they will cast out demons [δαιμόνια ἐκβαλοῦσιν]" (Mark 16:17; cf. 9:37–41). This connection between belief and the ability to perform miracles is not Synoptic but Johannine: "The one who believes in me will also do the works that I do" (John 14:12). In the Johannine tradition this ability to perform works (ἔργα) or miracles[30] is based on the shared unity of

---

27. "Believe" (πιστεύω, Mark 16:16, 17), "not believe" (ἀπιστέω, 16:11, 16), "not believe" (οὐδέ . . . πιστεύω, 16:13; οὐ . . . πιστεύω, 16:14) and "unbelief" (ἀπιστία, 16:14). Against Linnemann, "Markusschluss," 255–87, that verses 9–14 and 15–20 are to be treated separately, linguistically Mark 16:9–20 is also held together by the verb πορεύομαι, which is not Markan. Πορεύομαι occurs at Mark 16:10, 12, 15; 29 times in Matthew; and 51 times in Luke. Only at Mark 9:30 does the compound verb παραπορεύομαι occur with a secondary reading of the simple verb. See Elliott, "Text and Language," esp. 206–7.

28. Graham H. Twelftree, *Jesus the Exorcist: A Contribution to the Study of the Historical Jesus* (WUNT 2.54; Tübingen: Mohr Siebeck; Peabody, MA: Hendrickson, 1993), 110.

29. Cf. Karl H. Rengstorf, "ἑπτά . . . ," *TDNT* 2:630–31; Otto Böcher, *Das Neue Testament und die dämonischen Mächte* (SBS 58; Stuttgart: KBW, 1972), 9–10.

30. That "works" (ἔργα) in John 14:12 are intended to include miracles; see Graham H. Twelftree, *Jesus the Miracle Worker: A Historical and Theological Study* (Downers Grove, IL:

Jesus with his followers and the presence of the Spirit continuing the work of Jesus (15:18–16:11). However, the signs or miracles listed in the longer ending—exorcism (e.g., Mark 1:21–28), speaking in tongues (e.g., Acts 2:4; 1 Cor. 12:28), picking up poisonous snakes (cf. Luke 10:19), and laying hands on the sick (e.g., Mark 5:23; 1 Cor. 12:9–10, 28–30)—are not Johannine but Synoptic or Pauline. This synthesis of a pneumatological perspective with these particular miracles is reminiscent of Paul.

The method of exorcism, involving the use of the formula "in my name" (ἐν τῷ ὀνόματί μου), shows that the writer has the same view of this kind of healing as expressed in Mark 9:38. That is, an exorcism would have been understood to be performed as if it had been done by Jesus himself (see §5.9 above). The final verse of this passage confirms this by saying that the Lord "worked with" (συνεργέω) them and "confirmed" (βεβαιόω) the message by the signs that "accompanied" (ἐπακολουθέω) it (Mark 16:20). That is, the miracles—performed "in the name of" the Lord—are attributed to the Lord (cf. Heb. 2:4). Not only does this associate the Lord (Jesus) with the exorcisms of the early Christians, but also, as we have just noted, the healing of Mary from seven demons by Jesus being the backdrop to this material—confirmed by the vocabulary link in ἐκβάλλω and δαιμόνια—suggests their success and power.

The final verse of the passage develops the function of miracles a stage further in stating that the miracles not only gave evidence of the belief of the one proclaiming but also—in accompanying (ἐπακολουθέω) or following the message—"confirmed" (βεβαιόω) the message (Mark 16:20). For a sign or miracle to "follow" (ἐπακολουθέω) a message meant that it followed so closely after that it could be said to be the result of the message,[31] perhaps even inherent in the message.[32] The verb ἐπακολουθέω also contains the notion of following in the sense of authenticating the message.[33] Hence, there is the appropriate use of "sign" here for the miracles which inherently follow the message as well as confirm it.

If our discussion of the longer ending of Mark reasonably reflects the evidence, we have in this material a glimpse of the important place of exorcism among Christians in Rome in the first half of the second century. They have maintained the view (cf. Mark 9:37–41) that their practice of exorcism was as if Jesus were performing them in person—perhaps understood to be

---

InterVarsity, 1999), 233–34; following, e.g., Rudolf Schnackenburg, *The Gospel according to St. John* (3 vols.; New York: Crossroad, 1982), 2:71.

31. See Gerhard Kittel, "ἐπακολουθέω," *TDNT* 1:215, citing, e.g., Mark 16:20; 1 Tim. 5:10; Josh. 6:8 LXX; Polybius, *Historiae* 30.9.10; against Erwin Preuschen, *Vollständiges Griechisch-Deutsches Handwörterbuch zu den Schriften des Neuen Testaments* (ed. Walter Bauer; 2nd ed.; Giessen: Töpelmann, 1928), 438.

32. Cf. MM, "ἐπακολουθέω," citing P.Petr. 2.40(*b*)[6] and P.Oxy 7.1024[33] as evidence that this verb came to mean "am personally present."

33. See BDAG, "ἐπακολουθέω."

through his Spirit. We can extrapolate that this pneumatological Christianity included exorcism among its "works" or "gifts." More broadly, the fact that they were able to perform exorcisms not only provided evidence for their ("orthodox"?) faith, but also showed the veracity of their message, which was being sanctioned by God through the accompanying miracles.

11.2 *Letter to Diognetus*

As none of the early Christian writings refer to it, at worst *Diognetus* could be a forgery by the first-known editor of the work in the late sixteenth century. However, few scholars are impressed with this view.[34] Instead, because it uses the *Preaching of Peter* (from the first half of the second century),[35] is known only from quotations in Clement of Alexandria, and Clement himself and the *Letter of Barnabas* have affinities with it, *Diognetus* was probably written in Alexandria at least by the end of the second century,[36] and most probably in the middle of the second century,[37] by a highly educated Greek-speaking Christian.[38]

What the first editor incorrectly called a letter is actually a treatise going beyond apology to protreptic and recruitment (*Diogn.* 10.1). What is of interest to us is that in the positive description of Christianity and in the effort of recruitment (chaps. 7–12) there is no mention of miracles, those of Jesus or his followers. Instead, God's action in sending Jesus (whose name is not mentioned) is cryptically described as sending his "own holy and incomprehensible word" (7.2). Also, even though he says that we should regard the Savior as, among other things, healer (ἰατρόν, 9.6), his description of Jesus is one who "bore with us," "took our sins" (9.2), and persuades and calls (7.4; 10.6). There is no mention of miracles or exorcism.

In the last two chapters—of uncertain relationship to the others[39]—the writer describes himself as a pupil of the apostles (*Diogn.* 11.1). They also

---

34. Andrew Louth and Maxwell Staniforth, *Early Christian Writings: The Apostolic Fathers* (London: Penguin, 1987), 139.

35. See chap. 10, n. 73, above.

36. Theofried Baumeister, "Zur Datierung der Schrift an Diognet," *VC* 42 (1988): 105–11.

37. See Leslie W. Barnard, "The Enigma of the Epistle to Diognetus," in *Studies in the Apostolic Fathers and Their Background* (New York: Schocken, 1966), 165–73, esp. 173; and W. H. C. Frend, *The Rise of Christianity* (Philadelphia: Fortress, 1984), 261n24. For later dates see Robert M. Grant, *Greek Apologists of the Second Century* (Philadelphia: Westminster, 1988), 178 (ca. 177 CE); and Henri Irénée Marrou, *A Diognète* (2nd ed. revised and augmented; SC 33 bis; Paris: Cerf, 1997), 241–68 (ca. 190–200); both are discussed by Hill, *Johannine Corpus*, 361–62.

38. See Bart D. Ehrman, *The Apostolic Fathers* (2 vols.; LCL; Cambridge, MA, and London: Harvard University Press, 2003), 2:124–27. For a list of the names that have been canvassed, see Barnard, "Diognetus," 171–72.

39. Barnard, "Diognetus," 171, sees "no insuperable objections to regarding Chs. i–x and xi–xii of *Ad Diognetum* as coming from the same writer."

are not portrayed as having anything to do with healing but as being given understanding (12.9) and handing on truth, the Word, or revelations (11.2). Not surprisingly, the writer describes himself as a teacher (διδάσκαλος, 11.1) at pains to communicate truths revealed to him. These truths have to be spoken and understood by his readers (11.7–8). He goes on to say that the way of life he is commending lies in knowledge (12.1–9). The simplest and most probable explanation of this lack of interest in miracles or exorcism as part of the ministry of Jesus or the church comes from noting that the Synoptic traditions have had little impact on *Diognetus*.[40] On the other hand, as Eugene Fairweather put it, "the Johannine outlook dominates the work."[41] It is not that *Diognetus* had a copy of any of the canonical Johannine literature in front of him—no sure quotation can be found. Rather, the writer of *Diognetus* is so imbibed with the Johannine perspective that exorcism is not part of his purview.

11.3 Justin Martyr

Although Quadratus and Aristides are the earliest apologists, with Justin we leave the period of the so-called Apostolic Fathers and turn to the period in which the apologists flourished. Much of what we know about the life of Justin is to be gleaned from his own work, especially the early chapters of *1 Apology* (cf. *Dial.* 1–8; 28.2), though there is the question of how much can be taken as autobiographical.[42] Of Roman descent and born of pagan parents in Samarian Flavia Neapolis (now Nablus) either in the last years of the first or early years of the second century,[43] Justin maintained an interest

40. Seen in noting the only slight echoes, at best, of the Synoptic traditions: Matt. 3:17 ‖ *Diogn.* 8.11; 11.5; Matt. 6:31 ‖ *Diogn.* 9.6; Matt. 17:5 ‖ *Diogn.* 8.11; Matt. 19:17 ‖ *Diogn.* 8.8; Matt. 20:28 ‖ *Diogn.* 9.2; Mark 3:4 ‖ *Diogn.* 4.3; Mark 9:7 ‖ *Diogn.* 8.11; Mark 10:18 ‖ *Diogn.* 8.8; Mark 10:45 ‖ *Diogn.* 9.2; Luke 6:27 ‖ *Diogn.* 6.6; Luke 18:19 ‖ *Diogn.* 8.8.

41. Eugene R. Fairweather, "In Defense of the Faith: The So-Called Letter to Diognetus," in *Early Christian Fathers* (ed. Cyril C. Richardson; LCC 1; 1953; repr., New York: Macmillan / Collier, 1970), 207 (cf. n. 3); cited with approval by Hill, *Johannine Corpus*, 363, who gives further evidence, 363–66.

42. In various ways Erwin R. Goodenough, *The Theology of Justin Martyr* (Amsterdam: Philo, 1968), 58–59—relying on Rudolf Helm, *Lucian und Menipp* (Leipzig and Berlin: Teubner, 1906), 40–42—as well as, e.g., Carl Andresen, "Justin und der mittlere Platonismus," *ZNW* 44 (1952–1953), 157–95, and Niels Hyldahl, *Philosophie und Christentum: Eine Interpretation der Einleitung zum Dialog Justins* (Copenhagen: Prostant apud Munksgaard, 1966), 45–50, have doubted the historical veracity of Justin's autobiographical material. To the contrary see Leslie W. Barnard, *The First and Second Apologies: St. Justin Martyr* (ACW 56; New York and Mahwah, NJ: Paulist Press, 1997), 3–5, 11–12; Leslie W. Barnard, "Justin Martyr in Recent Study," *SJT* 22 (1966): 152–56; and Leslie W. Barnard, *Justin Martyr: His Life and Thought* (London: Cambridge University Press, 1967), chap. 1.

43. Barnard, *Life and Thought*, 3; Eric F. Osborn, *Justin Martyr* (BHT 47; Tübingen: Mohr Siebeck, 1973), 6. Cf. Eusebius, *Hist. eccl.* 4.11, 16.

in Samaritan affairs.[44] Even after he was converted from Platonism at the age of about thirty,[45] he continued to regard himself as a Gentile.[46] He was well educated, considered himself a philosopher, and exercised intellectual rigor in his writing.[47] Justin spent time in Corinth, where his dialogue with Trypho the Jew took place in about 137 (*Dial.* 1.3[48]) and was written down later, perhaps in the late 150s.[49] His *1 Apology* may have been written around the same time, and *2 Apology* shortly afterward.[50] Justin was twice in Rome,[51] including for the last days of his life (Eusebius, *Hist. eccl.* 4.11, 16).[52] Eusebius says his writings were "the products of a cultured mind deeply versed in theology" (4.18.1). It is still generally agreed that he became the greatest and most prolific apologist of the second century, defending the Christians against the state, the Jews, the heretics, and the intellectuals.[53] Justin said he wrote "on behalf of those from every race who are unjustly hated and ill-treated." His interest in doing so was, as he said, in "being one of them myself" (*1 Apol.* 1.1).

In combating the various threats to Christians, the heart of Justin's interests was to pass on the basic message of the early church concerning God's love and care for people as expressed supremely in the incarnation.[54] Nevertheless, he gives considerable attention to demons or evil spirits.[55]

44. Justin, *1 Apol.* 1; 26; 53; 56; *Dial.* 120.6.

45. Edward R. Hardy, "The First Apology of Justin, the Martyr: Introduction," in Richardson, ed., *Early Christian Fathers*, 230.

46. *2 Apol.* 12; *Dial.* 2–7; 41.3. On Justin's retention of Platonic ideas after his conversion, see Barnard, *First and Second Apologies*, 16.

47. See Osborn, *Justin Martyr*, 6–7; and more recently, Craig D. Allert, *Revelation, Truth, Canon, and Interpretation: Studies in Justin Martyr's "Dialogue with Trypho"* (VCSup 64; Leiden: Brill, 2002), 28–29.

48. Eusebius, *Hist. eccl.* 4.18.6, says the *Dialogue* reproduces the argument that took place in Ephesus. On the historicity of the *Dialogue*, see J. C. M. van Winden, *An Early Christian Philosopher: Justin Martyr's Dialogue with Trypho, Chapters One to Nine: Introduction, Text and Commentary* (Philosophia patrum 1; Leiden: Brill, 1971), 127.

49. On the problem of establishing the main contours of the life of Justin and the dating of his work, see, e.g., Hardy, "First Apology," 228–31; Cullen I. K. Story, *The Nature of Truth in "The Gospel of Truth" and in the Writings of Justin Martyr* (NovTSup 25; Leiden: Brill, 1970), xiii–xv; Osborn, *Justin Martyr*, 6–10.

50. Barnard, *First and Second Apologies*, 11.

51. Jon Nilson, "To Whom Is Justin's *Dialogue with Trypho* Addressed?" *TS* (1977): 538, "seeks to locate the *Dialogue* in a specific context of Jewish-Christian relations in mid-second-century Rome."

52. *The Acts of Justin and Companions* 1; see Herbert Musurillo, *The Acts of the Christian Martyrs: Introduction, Texts and Translations* (Oxford: Clarendon, 1972), 43. At least in that Eusebius knew the two *Apologies* and the *Dialogue* but not the *Acts of Justin*, the question of the historical value of the *Acts of Justin* is raised.

53. See Osborn, *Justin Martyr*, 13–14; Eric F. Osborn, "Justin Martyr and the Logos Spermatikos," *StMiss* 42 (1993): 143–44.

54. Hardy, "First Apology," 231–32.

55. See Osborn, *Justin Martyr*, chap. 4; Barnard, *First and Second Apologies*, 108–9; Goodenough, *Justin Martyr*, 201–5.

He describes them as "strange" (ἀλλοτρίων), by which he means "evil" or "deceitful" spirits (τῶν πονηρῶν καὶ πλάνων πνευμάτων, *Dial.* 30.2). For an explanation of the origin of demons, he looks to Genesis 6:1–4. The Old Testament says "the sons of God" were attracted to women and, by them, produced "the heroes" (הַגִּבֹּרִים, 6:4 MT) or "the giants" (οἱ γίγαντες, 6:4 LXX). Justin substitutes angels (ἄγγελοι) for sons[56] and says demons (δαίμονες) were produced (*2 Apol.* 5.3).[57] In this he was perhaps influenced by *1 Enoch*'s version of this story (cf. *1 En.* 6:1–8)[58] being immediately followed by the mention of Azazel (cf. Lev. 16:10, עֲזָאזֵל; 17:7), who is taken by *1 Enoch* to be a demon.[59] Probably still relying on *1 Enoch* (see *1 En.* 8.1–4), Justin says the demons have "enslaved" (ἐδούλωσαν) people to themselves by magical writings, as well as fears and vengeances (or "punishments," τιμωριῶν[60]), and partly by teaching people to offer sacrifices and incense and to enter into pacts or treaties (σπονδῶν[61]) with them. The result was murder, war, adultery, intemperate deeds, and wickedness (*2 Apol.* 5.4). The demons, headed by Satan (*Dial.* 131.2; *1 Apol.* 28.1), are also responsible for stirring up persecution,[62] for heretics such as Simon, Menander, and Marcion (*1 Apol.* 26), as well as for "godless, blasphemous, and unholy doctrines" in the church (*Dial.* 82.3). Justin also thinks that demons possess people (*1 Apol.* 18.4; *2 Apol.* 6). At this point in his demonology, Justin is as close to the thinking of the Synoptic Gospels as anywhere in his ideas.[63] However, he goes beyond them in thinking the demons so significant in what they have done, and counting as so essential their destruction as well as ongoing protection from them (*1 Apol.* 14.1; *Dial.* 30.3), that he says the purpose of the incarnation "is for the sake of believing men, and for the destruction of the demons" (*2 Apol.* 6.5).

56. Following R. Simeon ben Yoḥai, ca. 140, rabbis rejected this exegesis (*Gen. Rab.* 26.5.2). See Oskar Skarsaune, *The Proof from Prophecy: A Study in Justin Martyr's Proof-Text Tradition: Text-Type, Provenance, Theological Profile* (NovTSup 56; Leiden: Brill, 1987), 368.

57. Justin, the first to suggest that the union of angels and women produced demons, is followed by Athenagoras, *Leg.* 25.1; and Tertullian, *Apologeticus* 22. So says Goodenough, *Justin Martyr*, 199, who also notes that Justin's explanation of Gen. 6 was expressly rejected by Christian theologians, citing Philastrius, *Liber de haeresibus* 107; and Augustine, *Civ.* 15.23.

58. Goodenough, *Justin Martyr*, 200, notes that the Ebionites had the same explanation as Justin (Pseudo-Clement, *Hom.* 6.18) and suggests that both are relying on an earlier Jewish tradition. See also the major study by Archie T. Wright, *The Origin of Evil Spirits: The Reception of Genesis 6.1–4 in Early Jewish Literature* (WUNT 2.198; Tübingen: Mohr Siebeck, 2005).

59. See *1 En.* 8:1; 9:6; 10:4–8; 13:1; 54:5–6; 55:4; 69:2.

60. See Lampe 1394.

61. Justin uses σπονδῶν (*2 Apol.* 5.4), which is often translated "libations," e.g., by Barnard, *First and Second Apologies*, 77. However, in view of the context here, it ought to be translated "treaties" or "pacts." See Lampe 1250.

62. Justin, *1 Apol.* 5.3; 10.6; 12.5; 44.12; 63.10; *2 Apol.* 1.2; 7.2–3; 8.2; 10.5–8; *Dial.* 18.3; 131.2.

63. Goodenough, *Justin Martyr*, 205.

As this quotation from the *Second Apology* illustrates, exorcism is not a separate topic of interest for Justin. Instead, he discusses it in conjunction with other subjects,[64] generally in seeking to establish a high view of Jesus. For example, in *2 Apology* 6.6 the only evidence he offers for both the significance of the name "Jesus" and the purpose of the incarnation is the many demoniacs throughout the world, including in Rome, who have been exorcised (cf. *Dial.* 85.2). From this we can see that Justin probably considered exorcism to be not only the most important but also the most common form of Christian healing.

Also, Justin mentions demons after he has described baptism, saying that the demons hear this washing (*1 Apol.* 61.1). However, we cannot conclude from this that Justin is saying that exorcism took place as part of baptism.[65] Indeed, when Justin goes on to give evidence of the defeat of the demons, he points not to baptism but to exorcism: "Numberless demoniacs throughout the whole world, and in your city," have been exorcised "in the name of Jesus Christ" (*2 Apol.* 6.6). Consistent with this, Justin refers to the activity of exorcism distinct from baptism.[66]

In relation to method, Justin sets the practice of Christian exorcism over against those who are using "incantations and drugs" (ἐπᾳστῶν καὶ φαρμακευτῶν, *2 Apol.* 6.6). In *Dialogue* 85.3 he says the Jews and Greeks were using "craft" (τῇ τέχνῃ), perhaps best described as a methodological approach that involved "incense and spells" or incantations (θυμιάμασι καὶ καταδέσμοις). In other words, for Justin, Christian exorcism was distinct in not depending on the use of practical aids. Instead, positively, he says that many Christians were exorcising "in the name of Jesus Christ, who was crucified under Pontius Pilate" (*2 Apol.* 6.6; cf. *Dial.* 30.3).

Nevertheless, prima facie this method seems little, if any, different from the incantational methods of other exorcists in which the power-authority was understood to reside in particular words.[67] However, two factors militate against drawing this conclusion. One is that, in line with both Christian[68] and non-Christian exorcisms,[69] a careful descriptive statement about the power-authority could be appended to the name being used so that there was a precise identification of the power-authority sought. That Justin understands

64. James Edwin Davidson, "Spiritual Gifts in the Roman Church: 1 Clement, Hermas and Justin Martyr" (PhD diss., Graduate College of the University of Iowa, 1981), 149.

65. Cf. Barnard, *First and Second Apologies*, 175n378, refers to *1 Apol.* 61.13: "It is not clear, from Justin's account, whether exorcism was connected with the baptismal rite." The only clear connection between baptism and exorcism is in the same statement about Jesus being used in relation to both. Cf. *1 Apol.* 61.13 (καὶ ἐπ᾽ ὀνόματος δὲ Ἰησοῦ Χριστοῦ, τοῦ σταυρωθέντος ἐπὶ Ποντίου Πιλάτου); and *2 Apol.* 6.6 (κατὰ τοῦ ὀνόματος Ἰησοῦ Χριστοῦ, τοῦ σταυρωθέντος ἐπὶ Ποντίου Πιλάτου).

66. Justin, *Dial.* 30; 76.6; 85; *2 Apol.* 6.6.

67. See the discussion in Twelftree, *Exorcist*, 38–43.

68. See, e.g., Acts 19:13; Irenaeus, *Haer.* 2.32.4.

69. See, e.g., *PGM* IV. 3034–3036; *L.A.B.* 60.

the statement about Jesus to be identificatory rather than charged with innate power can be seen in that he uses a similar but more brief set of words to identify believers as "those believing on the one crucified by Pontius Pilate, Jesus our Lord" (*Dial.* 76.6). Moreover, this point is made abundantly clear in that he can state that exorcisms defeat or overthrow demons simply "through [διά] the name of Jesus" (*2 Apol.* 8.4; cf. *Dial.* 121.3). This was the view of the use of the words used in exorcism that we saw in Acts (see §6.3c above).

The other factor militating against seeing Justin's method of exorcism as incantational is that a close reading of this statement in *Dialogue* 76.6 nuances what Justin probably has in mind in describing Jesus as "crucified under Pontius Pilate." Speaking in the first person of his involvement, Justin says, "Now we—those believing on the one crucified by Pontius Pilate, Jesus our Lord—exorcising, have all demons and evil spirits subject to us" (*Dial.* 76.6). Here exorcism does not depend on any particular method or formula. Instead, the exorcisms are dependent on the exorcist believing in Jesus our Lord. Yet, in passing we can note, Justin is not saying that exorcism is a proof of right belief; he is saying that right belief enables exorcism to be successful. In this he has an understanding of exorcism that we came across in the longer ending of Mark (§11.1 above). Put another way, although a Christian exorcism may appear like other exorcisms in the use of recurring words and phrases, it is different in that these phrases are not considered the source of power or success. Rather, success depends on the association between the exorcist and a particular power-authority, Jesus. And in this association the believer can be assured to have received the power and authority to cast out demons, for in discussing exorcism in *Dialogue* 73.6 he quotes Luke 10:19, "I have given you . . . all power over the enemy," and draws the same conclusion as Luke: authority has been given to them by Jesus.[70]

From this it is clear that Justin considered exorcism the most important weapon of evangelism Christians possessed against the various threats to the church in a demon-infested world. Not surprisingly, then, exorcism was the most common form of healing in which Christians were involved. However, Christian exorcism was at least superficially much like other exorcisms. This is clear from the defense he has to offer of their distinctive features, which he says is the success itself and the simplicity of the cures. In particular, it was not that any special words or materials used in the healings were considered to be the locus of power-authority. Instead, it was the name of Jesus or the power given by him to his believers that was the means of the widespread success of Christian exorcism.

In this we see Justin was involved in a practice of exorcism little if any different from that portrayed as practiced by Jesus as well as his followers before and immediately after Easter. However, Justin goes beyond the very

70. Davidson, "Spiritual Gifts," 154.

early followers of Jesus in that, from his perspective, the magnitude of the success of the simple exorcisms performed in the name of Jesus were part of the proof of both the truth and superiority of the Christian faith, as well as of the faith of the particular believers involved.

It is reading too much into the evidence and misrepresenting Justin to say that the church of his time had a rite of exorcism that involved the recital of an embryonic creed.[71] Rather, what was said at an exorcism was the embryonic creed;[72] however, the words spoken functioned not as a statement of belief or as having innate power, but as a means of identifying the source of power-authority for the healing.

As important as exorcism was for Justin in combating the demons, he did not consider it the only means of escape from them. In *1 Apology* 56 Simon and Menander are inspired by wicked demons and said to continue to deceive people. This deception is through myths and stories invented as well as taken up from other religions (*1 Apol.* 23.3). Justin warns his readers, offering the antidote not of exorcism but of learning the truth, thereby escaping error (56).

In both the central use of exorcism and its being an important apology for Christianity, we can see Justin's dependence on Synoptic traditions, especially Matthew[73] or, more likely, tradition that was heavily dependent on Matthew.[74] His preference for the Synoptic Gospels[75] is seen in that, even though his knowledge of the Fourth Gospel is demonstrable, he lacks any formal quotation of it.[76] Given the status of Justin in the mid-second century as "one of the most recognized orthodox and antiheretical teachers of his day in Rome or elsewhere,"[77] we need to be especially mindful of his attitudes toward exorcism and the Fourth Gospel when we come to draw conclusions from our study.

11.4 Tatian

We became briefly acquainted with Tatian when we noted that he provides us with the earliest and entire citation of the longer ending of Mark (see §11.1

---

71. See Barnard, *First and Second Apologies*, 191n34.

72. Cf. John N. D. Kelly, *Early Christian Creeds* (London: Longman, 1972), 70–76.

73. See Édouard Massaux, *Influence de l'évangile de saint Matthieu sur la littérature chrétienne avant saint Irénée* (BETL 75; Louvain: Leuven University Press, 1986), 466–505, 510–55. See also the discussion by Arthur J. Bellinzoni, "The Gospel of Matthew in the Second Century," *SecCent* 9 (1992): 197–258.

74. Arthur J. Bellinzoni, *The Sayings of Jesus in the Writings of Justin Martyr* (NovTSup 17; Leiden: Brill, 1967), 30, 36, 43, 88, offers a critique of Massaux and of A. Baldus. On Justin using a harmony of the Synoptic Gospels, see Bellinzoni, *Sayings*, 140–42.

75. See Henry Chadwick, *Early Christian Thought and the Classical Tradition* (Oxford: Clarendon, 1966), 124–25n5; Bellinzoni, *Sayings*, 140; Skarsaune, *Proof*, 106.

76. Hill, *Johannine Corpus*, 312–37, esp. 337.

77. Hill, *Johannine Corpus*, 312.

above). Here our interest is in what Tatian can tell us about exorcism, either concerning his own views or those of other Christians.

In the last lines of his *Address to the Greeks*, he tells us that he was born in Assyria but had a Greek education before being converted to Christianity (*Orat.* 42.1). Earlier he says this was after a great deal of travel (35.1) and after having come upon and read Christian writings, perhaps in Rome (29.1–2), around 155 CE. There he was a disciple of Justin,[78] of whom he speaks well (18.2; 19.1). After the death of Justin between 163 and 167,[79] tradition has it that Tatian left the orthodox church and, in the East, founded the Encratite church.[80] We know nothing of his death. Only two of his works survive: his *Address to the Greeks*[81] and the *Diatessaron*. The latter—on which his fame rests and in which our primary interest lies—survives in a single Greek fragment as well as in secondary and tertiary witnesses.[82] Of his other works we have only passing hints in his own works[83] and comments in the writings of others.[84]

Since the *Diatessaron* has influenced all Latin versions and their descendants,[85] it is likely that Tatian wrote it in Rome just before his departure from the city in 172 CE.[86] The *Diatessaron* is a continuous narrative compiled from traditions now known to us in the four canonical Gospels.[87] Therefore, a comparison of Tatian with the canonical Gospel traditions can be expected to yield interesting results on his view of exorcism.[88]

---

78. Cf. Eusebius, *Hist. eccl.* 4.29.3.

79. Robert M. Grant, "The Heresy of Tatian," *JTS* 5 (1954): 62; Whittaker, *Tatian*, ix–xvii.

80. Irenaeus, *Haer.* 1.28.1; 3.23.8; Eusebius, *Hist. eccl.* 4.29.1–2. See also Grant, "Tatian," 62–68.

81. Written after the year 176, when he had already left the church. See Robert M. Grant, "Date of Tatian's Oratio," *HTR* 46 (1953): 99–101; Whittaker, *Tatian*, ix–x.

82. Metzger, *Early Versions*, 10–25.

83. In *Orat.* 15, Tatian refers to his work *On Animals*.

84. Clement of Alexandria cites and refutes *Perfection according to the Savior* (*Strom.* 3.12.81.1–3) and cites Tatian's *Problems* (*Eclogae propheticae* 38.1; cf. Origen, *Cels.* 6.51. See Whittaker, *Tatian*, x.

85. Otis C. Edwards Jr., "Diatessaron or Diatessara?" *StPatr* 16, part 2 (1985): 91.

86. See Whittaker, *Tatian*, ix.

87. On the sources of the *Diatessaron*, see William L. Petersen, *Tatian's Diatessaron: Its Creation, Dissemination, Significance, and History in Scholarship* (VCSup 25; Leiden and New York: Brill, 1994), 427–28. Gilles Quispel's case that Tatian used a fifth, Jewish Christian, Gospel that reflects the same tradition as the *Gospel of Thomas* has generally been deemed not to have been carried. See, e.g., Gilles Quispel, "The Gospel of Thomas and the New Testament," *VC* 11 (1957): 189–207; and the discussion by William L. Petersen, "Textual Evidence of Tatian's Dependence upon Justin's ΑΠΟΜΝΗΜΟΝΕΥΜΑΤΑ," *NTS* 36 (1990): 512–34.

88. One of the great conundrums of Tatian research is the question of the language in which the *Diatessaron* was written: Greek or Syriac? Against the prevailing view that the *Diatessaron* was written in Greek, see William L. Petersen, "New Evidence for the Question of the Original Language of the Diatessaron," in *Studien zum Text und zur Ethik des Neuen Testaments* (ed. Wolfgang Schrage; Berlin: de Gruyter, 1986), 325–43. The dilemma is solved and the evidence explained if

Tatian begins his harmony with extracts from the first few lines of John's Gospel (*Diat.* 1:1–5)[89] and then, broadly, takes up material from the birth narratives, first from Luke and then from Matthew, before using the baptism and temptation narratives, as well as telling of Jesus calling the disciples. The impression left on the reader in the early part of the book is of a truly divine Spirit-empowered figure striding the earth. This image is enhanced by Tatian choosing the story of Jesus turning water into wine as Jesus' first public act (*Diat.* 5.22–33 ‖ John 2:1–11). This establishes Jesus as a powerful miracle-worker for the story precedes that of Jesus teaching in the synagogue at Nazareth (*Diat.* 5.34–41).

It is in 6.40 that Tatian introduces the idea that Jesus performed exorcisms. He does this through using Luke's version of the story of the healing of the demoniac in the Capernaum synagogue (Luke 4:33–37). This version probably appealed to Tatian because some of the details suit him: the man not being harmed, and Luke's simplifying the response of the crowd to "What is this word that orders unclean spirits . . . ?" (*Diat.* 6.44 ‖ Luke 4:36). Tatian follows this story with that of the healing of Simon's mother-in-law, which again using Luke, is also told as an exorcism. For the woman is said to be oppressed with a great fever, and Jesus is said to stand over her and rebuke the fever.[90] Then Tatian uses Matthew 8:16 to say that "in the evening they brought many that had demons: and he cast out their devils with the word" (*Diat.* 6.50). Although Tatian includes all the exorcism stories from the canonical Gospels—usually following Luke, as well as numerous other references to Jesus casting out demons, the result of taking up the opening chapters of Matthew and Luke, as well as John, is that the *Diatessaron* removes exorcism from its prime position in Mark so that the theme appears relatively late in the *Diatessaron* and makes it clear Tatian did not consider exorcism to have a particularly special place in the ministry of Jesus.

The one exorcism story Tatian takes up almost entirely from Mark is that of Jesus healing the so-called epileptic boy (Mark 9:14–29), which Tatian calls a case of lunacy (*Diat.* 24.31).[91] It is of particular interest to us because the end of the story includes teaching on how a follower of Jesus can heal

we suppose that Tatian composed the work in Greek (hence the title) but, as could be expected in a bilingual area, soon thereafter translated it into Syriac, perhaps for those in Rome who needed such a document or for those among whom he found himself when he moved to the East, where it became established and particularly popular among Christians. See Petersen, *Tatian's Diatessaron*, 328–29; and the older summary discussion by Metzger, *Early Versions*, 31–32.

89. On the problem of establishing the opening sentence of the *Diatessaron*, see Metzger, *Early Versions*, 27–28.

90. *Diat.* 6.48–49 ‖ Luke 4:38–39. On Luke telling this story as an exorcism, see §6.2a above.

91. For his story of the Gadarene demoniac, Tatian uses primarily Luke 8:26–39, with a little material from Mark 5:1–20 (cf. *Diat.* 11.38–12.1). In the story Tatian probably left Matthew aside because Mark and Luke had all the material he needed.

and conduct exorcism. Choosing to follow Mark is probably due to the story offering more detail than provided by either Matthew 17:14–21 or Luke 9:37–43a.[92] In any case, in following Mark's Gospel, which includes the conversation between Jesus and the father, Tatian is also able to pick up a theme that interests him: faith.[93] This becomes obvious from the way Tatian ends the story by switching to Matthew as his source:

> And when Jesus entered into the house, his disciples came, and asked him privately, and said unto him, Why were we not able to heal him? Jesus said unto them, Because of your unbelief. Verily I say unto you, If ye have faith as a grain of mustard seed, ye shall say to this mountain, Remove hence; and it shall remove; and nothing shall overcome you. But it is impossible to cast out this kind by anything except by fasting and prayer. (*Diat.* 24.45–47)[94]

In using this Matthean ending (Matt. 17:20–21) and changing the question to "Why were we not able to *heal* him?" rather than "cast it out," as in Matthew, Tatian is able to give his readers an answer to the general question of failure in healing, as well as provide a specific answer to failure in dealing with this particular kind of demon. To the general question as to why a healing would fail, Tatian has Jesus say that it is because of unbelief. Not only has Tatian probably picked up this theme from the body of Mark's story (Mark 9:19–24), but he also is able to follow the theme through in using this ending which Matthew provides as well as, in particular, changing Matthew's "little faith" (Matt. 17:20) to "unbelief."

Tatian is able to answer the specific question as to why this particular kind of exorcism would fail in ending the story—beginning with an adversative— "But it is impossible to cast out this kind by anything except by fasting and prayer." As we saw in discussing this story in a Markan context (§5.8 above), this kind of demon would have been considered difficult to exorcise because, being mute, the exorcist could not enter into any diagnostic or combative dialogue. Therefore, a different strategy was required: fasting and prayer. As the sentence is cast as a reply to the disciples' question, the prayer and fasting most naturally read as instruction to the healers rather than the sick person.

92. Probably for the same reason, for the story of the healing of the Syrophoencian (Canaanite) woman's daughter, Tatian uses the Matthean version (*Diat.* 20.46–58 ‖ Matt. 15:21–28). See the following note.

93. E.g., for the story of the healing of the Syrophoenician (Canaanite) woman, Tatian chooses the Matthean version (Matt. 15:21–29), which concludes with an emphasis on faith (cf. *Diat.* 20.46–58). In the story of the healing of the centurion's servant, Tatian (*Diat.* 11.4–16) uses both Matthew 8:5–13 and Luke 7:1–10, but he chooses to follow Matthew's ending at the point where faith is mentioned (*Diat.* 11.15 ‖ Matt. 8:13).

94. Since this last sentence was probably not in Matthew—see Bruce M. Metzger, *A Textual Commentary on the Greek New Testament* (2nd ed.; New York: American Bible Society, 1994), 35; and Donald A. Hagner, *Matthew 14–28* (WBC 33B; Dallas: Word Books, 1995), 501—Tatian can probably be assumed to be using a text that has been assimilated to Mark.

Since Tatian included this story, as well as the stories of the followers of Jesus being sent out on mission to teach, heal, and to exorcise successfully,[95] it is reasonable to assume that Tatian considered exorcism—modeled on Jesus' ministry—to be part of the ministry of the followers of Jesus, including those of his own time. We have just seen corroborative evidence for this conclusion in Tatian's particular interest in the ending of the story about healing the so-called epileptic boy.

Notwithstanding, Tatian's prime interest in publishing his *Diatessaron* is not so much to make the story of Jesus applicable to his own time as to provide a full and continuous narrative from the various traditions that were before him. In relation to our theme, we gather this from a hint in the way he has related the story of the unknown exorcist. As we would expect, he has chosen the longer version, Mark 9:38–41 (cf. Luke 9:49–50). However, through changing John the disciple's statement from "He was not following us" to "He was not following you with us," Tatian has tied the story back into the life of Jesus. For the contemporary application, Tatian turns to a line in the Lukan version of the story: "Every one who is not in opposition to you is with you" (*Diat.* 25.16 ‖ Luke 9:50).

From his general attention to exorcism and from what we have seen in this particular story, we can conclude that Tatian had considerable interest in exorcism and that he probably understood exorcism among his contemporary Christians to be possible as well as, perhaps, important. Indeed, in his *Address to the Greeks*, he says that demons can "shake the body's system with a fit of their own madness." But, he goes on to say that being "smitten by a word of God's power, they go away in fear, and the sick man is healed" (*Orat.* 16.3). Since we have seen Jesus is said to exorcise by "the word" (see above, on *Diat.* 6.44, 50), it is reasonable to suppose Tatian saw exorcism among Christians as being modeled on that of Jesus. Further, we can see that this ministry would have been understood to take place not only on the basis of the authority Jesus gave his followers but also because of their faith. We note also that, from Tatian's handling of the Gospel traditions, there was understood to be considerable freedom with regard to the use of the tradition even at this relatively late date.

11.5 Athenagoras

Next to nothing is known about this second-century apologist.[96] He probably flourished in Athens, for the early tenth-century Arethas Codex (Parisinus Graecus 451) calls him "the philosopher of Athens." Also, his *Embassy for the*

---

95. *Diat.* 13.36–37; 14.43; 15.33, 36.

96. Of the patristic writers, only Methodius of Olympus mentions him (*Res.* 3.7; cf. Athenagoras, *Leg.* 24.2).

Christians (*Legatio pro Christianis*)[97] was likely presented to the emperor Marcus Aurelius and his son (emperor-to-be) Commodus (*Leg.* 1) in the early autumn of 176 CE, when they were in Athens.[98] Athenagoras sets out to answer three charges brought against the Christians: atheism (*Leg.* 4–30), Thyestian banquets (31), and Oedipean incest (32–36). In relation to our interest in exorcism, it is notable that Athenagoras did not see the need to answer any questions related to the working of miracles or magic that might have arisen if Christians were thought to be involved in exorcism. Given that Athenagoras was aware of at least the philosophical beliefs of Marcus,[99] and that the emperor had a disdain for "wizards and wonder-workers with their tales of spells, exorcism [δαιμόνων ἀποπομπῆς], and the like" (*Med.* 1.6),[100] it is reasonable to conclude from this that magic and miracles (including exorcism) were not seen to be issues in the way that outsiders viewed Christianity in Athens or Rome.

Nevertheless, along the way, in answering the charge of atheism, the subject of demons arises. Thales is credited with being the first to distinguish between God, demons, and heroes (*Leg.* 23.5). Athenagoras notes that some poets consider demons as gods, others as matter, and still others as people who once lived (24.1). Giving his perspective, he says that Christians recognize that, besides God, and created free by him, "there are other powers; . . . one of them is opposed to God" (24.2). Echoing the Genesis 6 story, he says that some of these powers or angels fell from heaven while lusting after maidens from whom the so-called giants were born (25.5–6). It is the souls of these giants who are the demons (25.1). Man is a well-ordered creature to the extent that he depends on the One who made him; otherwise, depending on the activity of the ruling prince and his attendant demons, he is swept along this way and that (25.4) and dragged to the idols (26.1). Athenagoras says that these people engross themselves in the blood from the sacrifice and cut themselves. But, he says, "I shall not discuss those who mutilate themselves with knives and knuckle-bones and what form of demons they have" (26.2). Perhaps we can assume that these are people whom some writers would have considered demonized (cf. Mark 5:5).

In answer to his own question, "What then?" (Τί οὖν; *Leg.* 27.1), he says that a soul experiences such trouble "when it attaches itself to the spirit of

97. His authorship of *On the Resurrection* remains in dispute. See Miroslav Marcovich, ed., *Athenagorae qui fertur De resurrectione mortuorum* (VCSup 53; Leiden: Brill, 2000), 1–19, esp. 1–3.

98. See Timothy D. Barnes, "The Embassy of Athenagoras," *JTS* 26 (1975): 111–14. The mention of "profound peace" (*Leg.* 1) may be a literary device rather than a reference to 177 CE, when Marcus Aurelius was between two great military campaigns. See Athenagoras, *Embassy for the Christians; The Resurrection of the Dead* (trans. and ed. Joseph H. Crehan; ACW 23; Westminster, MD: Newman; London: Green, 1956), 10–11.

99. See the discussion by Leslie W. Barnard, "Athenagoras, Galen, Marcus Aurelius, and Celsus," *CQR* 168 (1967): 176–77.

100. Cf. Robin Lane Fox, *Pagans and Christians* (New York: Knopf, 1987), 328.

matter and blends with it, when it does not look up to heavenly things and their Maker" (27.1). He goes on to give more detail: "When a soul is weak and docile, ignorant and unacquainted with sound teaching, unable to contemplate the truth, unable to understand who the Father and Maker of all things is, . . . the demons associated with matter . . . take hold of these deceitful moments . . . and by invading their thoughts flood them with illusory images" (27.2). Here there is no talk of exorcism. Instead, freedom from the demons comes from the worship of God and the truth, or right thinking.

In this approach Athenagoras is in company with Johannine theology. Although Athenagoras shows evidence of having read the Fourth Gospel,[101] he does not quote it and, in relation to the problem of demonic influence on people, he does not seem to be dependent on the text of the Fourth Gospel. Rather, Athenagoras and the Fourth Gospel share the same thought world, where the solution to the delusion of the demonic involves a choice to contemplate the truth rather than error.

11.6 Irenaeus of Lyons

The importance of Irenaeus is agreed on all sides. Long ago Desiderius Erasmus (ca. 1466–1536) was impressed with the strength of his mind and the freshness and vigor of his writing,[102] a style that suggests he received considerable education.[103] More recently, Robert Grant said: "Irenaeus of Lyons was the most important Christian controversialist and theologian between the apostles and the third-century genius Origen."[104] Despite the importance of this theologian, who is sometimes difficult to read, we know little about his life.[105]

Estimations on the date of his birth range from 98 to 147, though the most probable time is between 130 and 140 CE.[106] Although he is celebrated as such, there is slight and unconvincing evidence that he suffered a martyr's death[107]

---

101. Athenagoras, *Leg.* 10.2–3; cf. John 1:1, 3, 14; 10:30, 38; 14:10–11; 17:21. See the discussion by Hill, *Johannine Corpus*, 81–83.

102. See Osborn, *Irenaeus*, 7.

103. Denis Minns, *Irenaeus* (Washington, DC: Georgetown University Press, 1994), 1, who also notes that Pierre Nautin, *Lettres et écrivains chrétiens, des IIe et IIIe siècles* (Patristica 2; Paris: Cerf, 1961), suggests that Irenaeus may have pursued a career in rhetoric.

104. Grant, *Irenaeus*, 1.

105. For a brief life of Irenaeus, see Grant, *Irenaeus*, chap. 1.

106. See the discussion in Osborn, *Irenaeus*, 2. See also François M. M. Sagnard, *La gnose valentinienne et le témoignage de saint Irénée* (Paris: J. Vrin, 1947), 56; André Benoît, *Saint Irénée: Introduction à l'étude de sa théologie* (Paris: Presses universitaires de France, 1960), 49.

107. It was not until Pseudo-Justin (*Quaestiones et responsiones ad orthodoxos* 115, in PG 6, col. 1364) and Gregory of Tours (*Hist. Franc.* 1.752) that Irenaeus was called a martyr. See Jan T. Nielsen, *Adam and Christ in the Theology of Irenaeus of Lyons* (Assen: Royal Van Gorcum, 1968), 1n2.

in 202 or 203.[108] In any case, there is no evidence that he lived beyond Pope Victor, who was in office until 198. As is well known, Irenaeus is reported as saying that in his early years he saw Polycarp, the bishop of Smyrna (now Izmir in Turkey; Eusebius, *Hist. eccl.* 4.14.4), giving rise to the view that Irenaeus was a native of Asia Minor, possibly even born in Smyrna.[109]

Perhaps after spending some time in Rome (Irenaeus, *Haer.* 4.30.3), Irenaeus was in Lyons in 177; then after a delegation to Rome (Eusebius, *Hist. eccl.* 5.4.1–2), from about 178 he was bishop of Lyons (5.5.8). Lyons was a cultured city and important for the Roman public service as well as Gallic life. The small church reflected all social ranks, though not the dominance of the city over Gaul.[110] In the last twenty years of the century, Irenaeus wrote his *Adversus haereses*,[111] in Greek, against a battery of opponents, notably the Valentinians (*Haer.*, preface), but also Simon and Carpocrates (*Haer.* 2.31–35).[112] In this work he gives us evidence of what was happening concerning miracles in both the orthodox church as well as among those he was criticizing. In two places he has something to say about miracles—curing the weak, the lame, the blind, the deaf, the paralyzed, those distressed in any part of the body, as well as exorcism and raising the dead—taking place in his own time (*Haer.* 2.31.2, 3).

First, in the second book of *Adversus haereses*, Irenaeus refers to supposed miracles of those who follow, among other Gnostics, Simon Magus and Carpocrates of Alexandria.[113] He accuses the miracles of being magical deceptions: "For they can neither confer sight on the blind, nor hearing on the deaf" (*Haer.* 2.31.2). What is of interest to us is that he acknowledges that the Gnostics perform exorcism. Irenaeus says that they cannot "chase away [*effugo*] all sorts of demons except those that are sent into others by themselves, if they can even do so much as this" (*Haer.* 2.31.2). Thus, all he says the Gnostics can do—if anything—is transfer demons from one person to another. By implication Irenaeus is claiming that Christians are able to chase or drive away (*effugo*) demons. In this vocabulary we may

108. See discussions in Minns, *Irenaeus*, 8n11; and Osborn, *Irenaeus*, 2n3.

109. So Nautin, *Lettres*, 92, cited by Minns, *Irenaeus*, 1n3.

110. Osborn, *Irenaeus*, 2–3; citing Benoît, *Saint Irénée*, 52–55; and James S. Reid, *The Municipalities of the Roman Empire* (Cambridge: Cambridge University Press, 1913), 179.

111. What fragments we have of the work of Irenaeus in Greek have been salvaged from the works of others. For a thorough discussion of the manuscript history, including the Latin manuscripts, see Dominic J. Unger and John J. Dillon, *St. Irenaeus of Lyons: Against the Heresies* (ACW 55; New York / Mahwah, NJ: Paulist Press, 1992), 11–15. For studies on the Latin text, which is slavishly literal and, therefore, useful in establishing the original text of Irenaeus, see Unger and Dillon, *Irenaeus*, 14, 120n64, 121n70.

112. Cf. Nielsen, *Adam and Christ*, chap. 2.

113. Heinz Kraft, "Gab es einen Gnostiker Karpokrates?" *TZ* 8 (1952): 434–43, doubts the existence of Carpocrates; to the contrary see Kurt Rudolph, *Gnosis: The Nature and History of an Ancient Religion* (Edinburgh: T&T Clark, 1983), 299.

have hints of the methods by which Irenaeus understood exorcism to take place. That is, the exorcist used such language that was thought to send the demons scurrying.

In the way Irenaeus sets up the contrast between the miracles of the church and his opponents, he shows not only that the exorcisms of proto-orthodox Christianity were seen as similar to the "magical" exorcisms, but also why he thinks the church is more successful in its exorcisms. He says that his opponents "do not perform what they do either through the power of God, or in connection with the truth, nor for the well-being of people, but for the sake of misleading them by means of magical deceptions" (*Haer.* 2.31.2–3). In other words, the exorcisms performed by the church are done in the power of God or in connection with the truth. Also, in contrast to the healings of his opponents, in the healing that takes place in the church, there is "sympathy, and compassion, and steadfastness, and truth, for the aid and encouragement of mankind, are not only displayed without fee or reward, but we ourselves lay out for the benefit of others our own means" (*Haer.* 2.31.3).

Prayer and fasting is mentioned as a method of healing by Irenaeus, but it is associated only with raising the dead, which is seen as a difficult task (*Haer.* 2.31.2). In relation to Mark 9:29 we have seen that prayer and fasting was used in exorcism by those who were responsible for the interpolation at Mark 9:29 (see chap. 5, n. 132). Nevertheless, what the author of Mark 9:29 and Irenaeus have in common is that prayer and fasting is reserved for what were considered difficult cases, Irenaeus adding that the entire church in the particular area was involved "with much fasting and prayer" (*Haer.* 2.31.2).

The second place where Irenaeus mentions exorcism is in the following chapter of the same book, where he accuses the Gnostics of conferring "no real benefit or blessing on those over whom they declare that they exert power, but, bringing forward mere boys, and deceiving their sight, while they exhibit phantasms that instantly cease, and do not endure even a moment of time" (*Haer.* 2.32.3). Further, Irenaeus accuses them of maintaining "that the Lord, too, performed such works simply in appearance" only (*Haer.* 2.32.4).

In refuting their phantasms, he appeals first to predictions in the prophetical writing regarding Jesus. Then, interesting for us, he appeals to the reality of miracles taking place in his own time as support for the reality of the miracles of Jesus. In doing so, Irenaeus echoes Paul's list of charismata in 1 Corinthians 12:8–10:

> His real disciples have received grace from him and use it in his name for the benefit of other men, as each has received the gift from him. Some really and truly drive out demons, so that often those who have been cleansed of evil spirits believe and are in the church, and some have foreknowledge of the future, and visions and prophetic speech, and others lay their hands on the sick and make

them well, and as we have said [2.31.2], even the dead have been raised and have remained among us for many years. (*Haer.* 2.32.4)[114]

In a list of miracles that resembles—but is not dependent on—Paul's lists of charismata, the inclusion of exorcism by Irenaeus is striking. For, as we have seen, exorcism was probably not part of Paul's lists (§3.5 above) because he understood the charismata to be for the common or internal good of the church (1 Cor. 12:7). By the very inclusion of exorcism in Irenaeus' list, as well as him going on to say that miracles are "for the benefit of the Gentiles" (*Haer.* 2.23.4), he transforms the charismata, including exorcism, into part of the evangelistic process. That is, exorcism, along with the other miracles, enables people to believe and join the church. Concomitantly, exorcism is seen to be part of the means of being joined to the church, though there is no hint of a special rite of exorcism in itself or as part of the conversion-initiation process.

It is also striking that the list of miracles for evangelism is headed by exorcism. From this it is more than reasonable to conclude that Irenaeus took freedom from the demonic (in the form of evil spiritual beings needing to be expelled) to be not only the most important and common form of healing but also the greatest need of the Gentiles.

This passage is also illuminating because it tells us what Irenaeus considered to be the reason for success in exorcism. He says that those performing miracles "are in truth his disciples, receiving grace from him," and do so "in his name" (*Haer.* 2.32.4). That is, the success of a healing is understood to depend on the healer being a disciple or believer, receiving grace, and operating "in his name." A little later in the same paragraph Irenaeus goes on to say:

It is impossible to tell the number of the gifts which the church throughout the world received from God in the name of Jesus Christ, crucified under Pontius Pilate, and uses each day for the benefit of the Gentiles, neither deceiving nor making profit. For as it freely received from God, so it freely ministers. (*Haer.* 2.32.4)[115]

In this we see again that Irenaeus understands exorcism to be one of the gifts from God that the church has for the benefit of the Gentiles, and that, unlike their opponents, no fee is sought for the healings. Also, again (see §11.3 above), that Jesus is identified as having been "crucified under Pontius Pilate" suggests that this phrase was used in the words of exorcism.

Also, distinct from Paul, the contrast Irenaeus draws between the church and his opponents shows that he thinks the success of the miracles, including exorcism, depends on not only the gift (of the Spirit), but also on the healers

114. Translations from Grant, *Irenaeus*, 121.
115. Translations from Grant, *Irenaeus*, 121–22.

being truly followers of Jesus, receiving grace from God as well as promoting the welfare of others rather than, by implication, their own interests. In contrast to his opponents, the church does not require payment for exorcism: "As she [the church] has received freely from God, freely also does she minister [to others]" (*Haer.* 2.32.4). That all the gifts, including exorcism, are said to be "from God, in the name of Jesus Christ" (*Haer.* 2.32.4) likely indicates that the practice of exorcism involved using "the name of Jesus Christ." That the sick, and not those needing exorcism, have hands laid on them suggests that the laying on of hands was not used for exorcism and that, as in the Synoptic Gospels, there was understood to be a distinction between exorcism and healing the sick.

Irenaeus asserts that, in contrast to his adversaries, the church does not "perform anything by means of angelic invocations, or by incantations, or by any other wicked curious art; but, directing her prayers to the Lord, who made all things, in a pure, sincere, and straightforward spirit, and calling upon the name of our Lord Jesus Christ, she has been accustomed to work miracles for the advantage of mankind, and not to lead them into error" (*Haer.* 2.32.5). This serves Irenaeus' case: the miracles show that God was and by implication is directly involved in his creation through these miracles. The understanding of exorcism can be detected in Irenaeus saying that the devils are "driven out" and that people are "cleansed."

From what we are seeing, the value to us of Irenaeus is not exhausted in noting what he tells us about exorcism among the orthodox Christians. He also gives us glimpses into exorcism among those whom he attacks. Indeed, in book 1 of *Adversus haereses* he says he set out to provide ways of confuting gnostic heretics (*Haer.*, preface). In chapter 23 he deals with the Simon of Acts 8, whom he calls "the Samaritan" and accuses of being the one from whom all heresies got their start (*Haer.* 1.23.1–2). Irenaeus says that these "Simonians" have mystic priests who make use of exorcisms and incantations. While not denying the success of these priests, his criticism of them is that they live licentious lives and practice magic in whatever way they can. The nature of this magic is not clear beyond saying, "They make use of exorcisms and incantations, love-potions too and philters, and the so-called familiars, and dream-senders" (*Haer.* 1.23.4). When we compare this description with the orthodox healings, including exorcisms, mentioned in book 2 (see above), we can suppose that Irenaeus probably understood the difference to be the simplicity of the orthodox method, on the one hand, and, on the other hand, the complex healing methods of the heretics involving incantations and potions. We can also note that the lifestyle of the heretical exorcists is of importance to Irenaeus. We have already noted that, in book 2 of *Adversus haereses* (see above), Irenaeus accuses those who follow the Gnostics Simon Magus and Carpocrates of Alexandria of magical deceptions because all they can do, if anything, is transfer demons from one person to another (*Haer.* 2.31.2). Once

again, Irenaeus accuses his opponents of magical illusions. He also accuses
them of charging fees and, rather than helping people, seeking to destroy and
mislead them with their apostate inspirations and demonical working (*Haer.*
2.31.3). As we have noted, that Irenaeus felt the need to engage in this debate
shows how close Christian exorcism, of which he approved, was perceived
to be to the magical exorcism he sought to denigrate.

11.7 Theophilus of Antioch

Eusebius says that Theophilus was sixth from the apostles in the diocese
of Antioch and that he "was eminent" (*Hist. eccl.* 4.20). From his own writing
it is possible to deduce that he was a native of Mesopotamia (*Autol.* 2.24)
and that he became a Christian as an adult, perhaps through reading the
Old Testament (2.14).[116] Eusebius lists a number of books by this apologist
(Eusebius, *Hist. eccl.* 4.24), but only *To Autolycus* survives.[117] Since Theophilus ends what he considers to be a complete chronology with the death of
Marcus Aurelius, his apology must have been written in or soon after 180
CE. The work is what Rick Rogers calls a protreptic theology, intended "to
recruit converts to a moral life consistent with biblical law."[118] One of the
intriguing aspects of the work is that it does not mention Christ so that it
has been called a "Christianity without Christ" and, not least for that reason,
remains the focus of considerable debate.[119]

There is one passage that is of particular interest to us. After a list of
statements from the philosophers to show that they contradicted each other,
Theophilus says: "Being inspired by demons and puffed up by them, . . . they
spoke from a deceptive fancy, and not with a pure but an erring spirit. And
this, indeed, clearly appears from the fact that even to this day the demonized are sometimes exorcised in the name of the true God and these spirits
of error themselves confess that they are demons who also formerly inspired
these writers."[120] A number of aspects of exorcism known to Theophilus are
immediately obvious. First, demonization or possession is not thought to be

---

116. Cf. Rick Rogers, *Theophilus of Antioch: The Life and Thought of a Second-Century Bishop*
(Lanham, MD: Lexington, 2000), 3–14.

117. Theophilus, e.g., *Autol.* 2.30, mentions his own *History*. Eusebius, *Hist. eccl.* 4.24, mentions his works on Hermogenes and Marcion, as well as some catechetical manuals. To this we can
add, from Jerome, *Vir. ill.* 25, a commentary on the Gospel and one on the proverbs of Solomon
and, from Jerome's *Epist. 121* (*Ad Algasiam*), a Gospel harmony.

118. Rogers, *Theophilus*, 21.

119. See, e.g., J. Bentivegna, "A Christianity without Christ by Theophilus of Antioch," *StPatr*
13 (1975): 107–30.

120. Δαιμόνων δὲ ἐμπνευσθέντες καὶ ὑπ' αὐτῶν φυσιωθέντες, . . . φαντασίᾳ καὶ πλάνῃ
ἐλάλησαν, καὶ οὐ καθαρῷ πνεύματι ἀλλὰ πλάνῳ. ἐκ τούτου δὲ σαφῶς δείκνυται, εἰ καὶ οἱ
δαιμονῶντες ἐνίοτε καὶ μέχρι τοῦ δεῦρο ἐξορκίζονται κατὰ τοῦ ὀνόματος τοῦ ὄντως θεοῦ,

expressed as an illness with physical symptoms but in false religious statements that would mislead hearers. Secondly, the statement that exorcism continued "even to this day" is reasonably taken to allude to the history of exorcism in the church from the time of Jesus until the present. However, thirdly, saying that the demonized are "sometimes . . . exorcised" gives the first impression that not all the demonized are exorcised. Indeed, the last sentence of this chapter—"But sometimes some of them wakened up in soul, and, that they might be for a witness both to themselves and to all men, spoke things in harmony with the prophets regarding the monarchy of God, and the judgment and such like"—suggests that exorcism was not always needed to change the person. In any case, mentioning that "sometimes" the demonized were exorcised does indicate that exorcism was not common or frequently used against those leading people astray. Fourthly, in light of Theophilus saying that the spirits confess to have inspired these writings, it is reasonable to suggest that, during an exorcism, the demon(iacs) and exorcists interacted in a way that is familiar to us from the Gospels (e.g., Mark 5:7–13). Finally, and most interestingly, the exorcisms are said to take place or be empowered not by Jesus but "by the name of the true God" (κατὰ τοῦ ὀνόματος τοῦ ὄντως θεοῦ). Here we have reflected what we also saw in James: exorcism in the name of God (cf. §8.3–4 above). We have also seen that Justin admits that when Jews exorcised in the name of God, they were successful (*Dial.* 85.3; cf. §2.1f above). In turn, it is reasonable to conclude that the exorcisms of the Jews and some Christians continued to use the name of God and would have been difficult to distinguish from each other, though the exorcisms reflected in Theophilus are not of the deranged but of the deceived.

11.8 Montanism

Montanism[121] is of particular interest to us because it was an ecstatic movement—so that we could expect involvement in miracles and exorcism—and also because Tertullian (ca. 160–ca. 225) was its most renowned associate and defender.[122] Its founder, Montanus, who had two prophetesses as associates, Priscilla and Maximilla, is said to have begun prophesying in the small

---

καὶ ὁμολογεῖ αὐτὰ τὰ πλάνα πνεύματα εἶναι δαίμονες, οἱ καὶ τότε εἰς ἐκείνους ἐνεργήσαντες (Theophilus, *Autol.* 2.8).

121. The term was first applied in the fourth century by Cyril of Jerusalem (*Cat.* 16.8). They were also known by a number of terms: "Phrygians," "Pepuzites," "Priscillianists," "Quintillianists," as well as "Tertullianists." At least in the early stages they referred to themselves as "The New Prophecy" or perhaps "The Prophecy." See Christine Trevett, *Montanism: Gender, Authority and the New Prophecy* (Cambridge: Cambridge University Press, 1996), 2.

122. For a discussion of Tertullian's relationship with what came to be called Montanism, see David Rankin, *Tertullian and the Church* (Cambridge: Cambridge University Press, 1995), 27–31, 38, 41–51.

Phrygian towns of Pepuza and Tymion in the third quarter of the second century.[123] He encouraged his followers to gather in these towns to await the heavenly Jerusalem.[124] The movement, which spread to include Africa, where Tertullian joined it (ca. 206 CE), was not perceived to be doctrinally aberrant (at least initially), though it adopted a stricter lifestyle than most other branches of Christianity.[125]

Although our sources for Montanism include "the remarkable and idio-syncratic apologist Tertullian" (as Christine Trevett described him),[126] the *Passio Perpetuae et Felicitatis*,[127] as well as Montanist epigraphy,[128] most of our knowledge comes from outside and sometimes hostile opponents.[129] Our interest is in what these sources tell us about exorcism among Montanists in the first few decades of their existence. However, scouring the sources, all that we find is a note in Eusebius saying that, besides the prophecy in Phrygia by Montanus and his followers, there were "many other wonderful works [παραδοξοποιίαι[130]] of the grace of God," leading many to believe they were prophets (*Hist. eccl.* 5.3.4). In all likelihood these wonderful works or miracles could have included exorcism. More we cannot say.

However, interestingly, a little later Eusebius quotes an unidentified con-temporary[131] of Claudius Apolinarius of Hierapolis (second century) who described Montanus, the new convert, as giving access to the adversary (ἀντικειμένῳ). He is said to become obsessed (πνευματοφορηθῆναι) and to

---

123. Cf., e.g., Eusebius, *Chronicon*; *Hist. eccl.* 4.27; Epiphanius, *Pan.* 48.1. On the dating of Montanism, see Timothy D. Barnes, "The Chronology of Montanism," *JTS* 21 (1970): 403–8; and Trevett, *Montanism*, 26–45. On the debate on the founding of Montanism, see Anne Jensen, *Gottes selbstbewusste Töchter: Frauenemanzipation im frühen Christentum?* (Freiburg, Basel, Vienna: Herder, 1992); and the response by Trevett, *Montanism*, 159–62. More recently, see Laura Nasrallah, *An Ecstasy of Folly: Prophecy and Authority in Early Christianity* (HTS 52; Cambridge, MA: Harvard University Press, 2003), 156–62.

124. See the discussion by Daniel H. Williams, "The Origins of the Montanist Movement: A Sociological Analysis," *Religion* 19 (1989): 343; and Trevett, *Montanism*, 77.

125. See Ronald E. Heine, *The Montanist Oracles and Testimonia* (NAPSPMS 14; Macon, GA: Mercer University Press, 1989), ix; Trevett, *Montanism*, chap. 3; cf., e.g., 214–19, on the Monarchian error of some Montanists in Rome. However, note the caution by, e.g., David F. Wright, "Why Were the Montanists Condemned?" *Them* 2 (1970): 15–21.

126. Trevett, *Montanism*, 4.

127. See Jacqueline Amat, *Passion de Perpétue et de Félicité: Suivi des Actes* (SC 417; Paris: Cerf, 1996).

128. E.g., William Tabbernee, *Montanist Inscriptions and Testimonia: Epigraphic Sources Illustrating the History of Montanism* (NAPSPMS 16; Macon, GA: Mercer University Press, 1997). For older studies see Trevett, *Montanism*, 4.

129. See the collections of material by Pierre C. de Labriolle, *Les sources de l'histoire du Montanisme: Textes grecs, latins, syriaques* (Collectanea Friburgensia 24 = n.s., 15; Fribourg: Librairie de l'Université / Gschwend; Paris: Leroux, 1913); and Heine, *Montanist Oracles*.

130. See Lampe; BDAG.

131. Cf. Eusebius, *Histoire ecclésiastique: Livres V–VII* (trans. and annotated by Gustave Bardy; 4th ed.; SC 41; Paris: Cerf, 1994), 46n3.

rave, chatter, and talk strangely (ξενοφωνεῖν[132]), prophesying in a manner contrary to the practice of the church from the beginning. Eusebius' source says that while some were elated, others described Montanus "as possessed, a demoniac [δαιμονῶντι] in the grip of a spirit of error" (Hist. eccl. 5.16.7–8). Notably, not only are they said to try to stop him, but Eusebius quotes them as rebuking (ἐπετίμων) him (5.16.8). Although this could mean simply to rebuke or censure,[133] given the context—in which Montanus is thought to be possessed by Satan—and that later Montanists were subjected to exorcism,[134] as well as ἐπιτιμάω otherwise being used for exorcism,[135] we most probably have here evidence of Christian exorcism (of another Christian!) in Asia Minor. In view of the use of ἐπιτιμάω, it is reasonable to speculate that the method of exorcism was not unlike that familiar in the New Testament: firm words addressed to the demon, ordering it to leave the person. Thus, both here in attempting to silence Montanus and from Theophilus (see above), we learn that in Asia Minor and Antioch exorcism was sometimes used to correct those leading Christians astray. From the available sources we do not learn anything about the Montanists' involvement in exorcism. We could only guess concerning any possible practice of exorcism among these pneumatics, for whom it would seem a natural interest.

11.9 Clement of Alexandria

Had it not been for his assumed teaching of Origen,[136] as well as being overshadowed by him, Clement of Alexandria, one of the most educated early fathers,[137] might have gone on being called "blessed" and "saint," as he was in early Christianity.[138] We know next to nothing about his life, which probably began in Athens about 150 (cf. Clement, Strom. 1.1.11). He says he was taught by remarkable men. "Of these one was in Greece (the Ionian), a second in south Italy, a third in the Lebanon, a fourth in Egypt" (Eusebius, Hist. eccl. 5.11.3–4). His last teacher, tracked down he says, in Egypt, was Pantaenus, whom Eusebius calls "one of the most eminent teachers of

132. On which see LSJ and Lampe.
133. See LSJ and Lampe.
134. Cf. Cyprian, Epistulae 74.10; and the discussion by Trevett, Montanism, 156–58.
135. Howard C. Kee, "The Terminology of Mark's Exorcism Stories," NTS 14 (1968): 232–46.
136. See the discussion in Johannes Munck, Untersuchungen über Klemens von Alexandria (Stuttgart: Kohlhammer, 1933), 224–29.
137. Rudolph, Gnosis, 16; also, Salvatore R. C. Lilla, Clement of Alexandria: A Study in Christian Platonism and Gnosticism (Oxford: Oxford University Press, 1971), 226–34; and John Ferguson, Clement of Alexandria (New York: Twayne, 1974), 17–20.
138. Cf. Eusebius, Hist. eccl. 6.14.9. On the fluctuations of Clement's reputation, see Ferguson, Clement of Alexandria, 17.

his day."[139] After his conversion to Christianity, Pantaenus, a Sicilian Stoic philosopher, made a missionary journey east to India before becoming the first known head of what, in the early years of the third century, became the catechetical school in Alexandria (Eusebius, *Hist. eccl.* 5.10.1–4). The members of the school were, if not from the upper echelons of society certainly wealthy.[140] On the death of Pantaenus in about 180, Clement took over as head of the school until persecution forced him to flee the city in 202. Clement saw his mission as the defense of Christianity against philosophical attacks and the charge of atheism, and to facilitate the conversion of educated Greeks.

In the first chapter of his *Exhortation to the Greeks* (*Protrepticus*), he says he set out to convince readers to turn from their worthless beliefs to Christ who fills people with enthusiasm for the only true philosophy.[141] As part of this objective he mentions the alluring power of music known to the Greeks through the minstrels Amphion of Thebes and Arion of Methymna. In contrast to these deceivers with their destructive poetry he announces a new song "which has come to loose—and that speedily—the bitter bondage of tyrannizing demons." This song, he says, is about and embodies Truth who darts her light and stretches out her hand—that is, Wisdom—so as to deliver people from delusion for their salvation. In developing his analogy of Truth being a new song, which is the manifestation of the Word that was in and before the beginning, he says that whereas David who once embodied this Truth used the lyre, harp, and music to drive away demons, the Word of God, the new song, who now embodying this Truth, drives away demons, opens the eyes of the blind, and unstops the ears of the deaf (*Prot.* 1.1).

Clement's point is not that music is able to drive away demons, though he clearly considered that it could. Rather, he was illustrating the point through an analogy that it is Truth, along with Wisdom—sometimes expressed in music, but supremely embodied in Jesus—that drives away the demonic. Thus, it is not that Clement is describing or proposing exorcisms in which music is played to the demonized. Instead, he is making the point that demons are put to flight when God takes up his abode in people. In other words, the driving away or expelling of demons is not seen as taking place because a demon is commanded to leave or because music is played to them, but because the person has received the Truth embodied in Jesus. We see this made clear near the end of the *Exhortation to the Greeks* where Clement says, "I urge you to

---

139. Eusebius, *Hist. eccl.* 5.10.2; cf. 5.11.1–5; 6.13.1. See also Clement, *Strom.* 1.11.1.

140. See L. W. Countryman, *The Rich Christians in the Church of the Early Empire: Contradictions and Accommodations* (Texts and Studies in Religion 7; New York and Toronto: Edwin Mellen, 1980), 48–49, citing, in particular, Gustave Bardy, *Clément d'Alexandrie* (Paris: Gabalda, 1926), 15–16; Rebecca H. Weaver, "Wealth and Poverty in the Early Church," *Int* 41 (1987): 369–71.

141. Cf. Quasten, *Patrology*, 2:7.

be saved. This Christ desires. . . . And who is He? Briefly learn. The Word of truth . . . that regenerates a person by bringing that person back to the truth . . . expels destruction and pursues death . . . that he may cause God to take up his abode in people" (*Prot.* 11.117.3–4). Thus, for Clement, it is when Truth embodied in Jesus takes up residence in a person—the process of conversion—that the destructive demonic is displaced or driven away. Or, as he says elsewhere in echoing Valentinus, salvation or the presence of the Son in a person brings purity "by the expulsion of every evil spirit from the heart" (*Strom.* 2.20).[142] Although familiar with traditions now known in all four Gospels,[143] this approach to the demonic is clearly reminiscent of that of the Fourth Gospel.

11.10 *Apostolic Tradition*

This document is of interest to us not only because of the reference to exorcism but also, in particular, because exorcism is linked to baptism in mainstream Christianity, possibly before the end of the second century.[144] This text, which is invaluable for information concerning church liturgy and life, deals with the ordination of bishops, the catechumenate, and then baptism. An epilogue in chapter 21 is followed by material on the duties of deacons (*Trad. ap.* 22, 24, 34, 39), fasting (23, 33, 36), the communal supper (25–30), offerings of fruit (31, 32), private prayer (35, 41, 42), care of the consecrated elements (37, 38), cemeteries (40), and when to pray (41–43).[145] It was not until 1906 that Eduard von der Goltz suggested what became widely accepted, that Hippolytus was responsible for the *Apostolic Tradition*, once thought to have been lost but known as *The Egyptian Church Order*.[146] In turn, therefore, in its present form, the *Apostolic Tradition* has been dated around 235 CE, the time of the death of Hippolytus.[147] However, because of its lack of unity and frequent incoherence, as well as doublets, in recent times there

142. The point here at which Clement maintains his distance from mainstream Gnosticism is in his setting false or heretical gnosis over against the true gnosis of the Christian. See Rudolph, *Gnosis*, 16.

143. François M. M. Sagnard, *Clément d'Alexandrie: Extraits de Théodote* (SC 23; Paris: Cerf, 1970), 250–53.

144. Cf. Henry Ansgar Kelly, *The Devil at Baptism: Ritual, Theology, and Drama* (Ithaca, NY: Cornell University Press, 1985), 138–39, 192–94.

145. Cf. Geoffrey J. Cumming, *Hippolytus: A Text for Students: With Introduction, Translation, Commentary and Notes* (Bramcote, UK: Grove, 1976), 5.

146. On the identification of and textual witnesses to the *Apostolic Tradition*, see Paul F. Bradshaw, Maxwell E. Johnson, and L. Edward Phillips, *The Apostolic Tradition* (Hermeneia; Minneapolis: Fortress, 2002), 1–11.

147. See Alistair Stewart-Sykes, *On the Apostolic Tradition: An English Version with Introduction and Commentary* (Crestwood, NY: St. Vladimir's Seminary, 2001), 12.

has been increasing interest in seeing the text not as having a single author but, like the *Didache* (see §10.3 above), as having been a "living" composite work, compiled over a number of years.[148] The strength of this view obliges us to investigate its dating and geographical origins, as well as the nature of the material relating to exorcism.

In the section giving directions concerning those who will receive baptism, the *Apostolic Tradition* says, in the context of examining the candidates: "From the time they are set apart a hand is laid on them daily whilst they are exorcised. When the day of their baptism draws near, the bishop should exorcise each of them so that they may be sure that they are pure" (*Trad. ap.* 20.3).[149] Given Tertullian tells us that, in Africa, the bishop exorcised baptismal candidates a week prior to baptism,[150] and that the *Apostolic Tradition* goes on to say that candidates are to wash themselves on the fifth day of the week (20.5), we can probably assume the bishop was conducting daily exorcisms on the candidates for a week. Then, on the Sabbath, when they are to be baptized, the bishop lays his hand on them and exorcises or adjures "them of every foreign spirit and they shall flee away from them and shall not return to them" (20.8). Beyond the laying on of the bishop's hand[151] (a new development in exorcism), we are not told how the exorcism is conducted. However, the resemblance of this direction to the direct speech of Jesus in Mark 9:25,[152] as well as other similar approaches to exorcism known to us,[153] suggests that the bishop was probably expected to use such or similar words.

The text goes on to say, "When he has finished exorcising them, he should blow on their faces; and when he has sealed their forehead, their ears, and their noses he should make them stand up" from their kneeling position (*Trad. ap.* 20.8; cf. 20.7). In this context, the blowing probably represents a

148. See Paul F. Bradshaw, "Redating the Apostolic Tradition: Some Preliminary Steps," in *Rule of Prayer, Rule of Faith: Essays in Honor of Aidan Kavanagh, O.S.B.* (ed. Nathan Mitchell and John F. Baldovin; Collegeville, MN: Pueblo / Liturgical Press, 1996), 3–17.

149. There are probably allusions to exorcism in what are likely later additions to *Trad. ap.* 3.5: "And let him have the power of high priesthood . . . to loose every tie according to the power which you gave to the apostles"; and, "He [Jesus] was handed over . . . in order to . . . break the chains of the devil" (4.8). See Bradshaw, Johnson, and Phillips, *Apostolic Tradition,* 34, 37; and the discussion in John E. Stam, *Episcopacy in the Apostolic Tradition of Hippolytus* (Theologische Dissertationen 3; Basel: Reinhardt, 1969), 88–89. English translations of *Trad. ap.* here are those of Stewart-Sykes, *Apostolic Tradition.*

150. See Stewart-Sykes, *Apostolic Tradition,* 107–8; and Alistair Stewart-Sykes, "Manumission and Baptism in Tertullian's Africa: A Search for the Origin of Confirmation," *StLit* 31 (2001): 129–49. For a brief discussion of the possibility that baptisms took place at Easter, see Stewart-Sykes, *Apostolic Tradition,* 108–9.

151. The Arabic and Ethiopic has the plural, "hands." See Bradshaw, Johnson, and Phillips, *Apostolic Tradition,* 106.

152. Noted by Cumming, *Hippolytus,* 17.

153. See Josephus, *Ant.* 8.47; *PGM* IV. 1254; cf. 3024–3025.

sealing.[154] However, the simpler and therefore likely earlier[155] Ethiopic text only says, "And if he has completed anathematizing them, he is to breathe on them" (20.8).[156] Here the breathing on the candidates is more obviously subsequent to and not part of the exorcism. Although this breathing was later understood, by Ambrose, for example (*Sacr.* 1.2; cf. 3.11–15), to be an opening (*apertio*) in order for the candidate to understand,[157] it is just as likely to represent infusing the candidates with the Holy Spirit (cf. John 20:22).[158] In the next chapter the bishop is directed to perform an exorcism over some oil which a deacon places on the left hand of the presbyter who, on taking hold of a person to be baptized, bids the person to renounce Satan (*Trad. ap.* 21.6–9). The text goes on to say, "And when he has renounced all this, he should anoint him with the oil of exorcism, saying to him: 'Let all evil spirits depart from you'" (21.10). However, we probably need to discount this in attempting to understand second-century exorcism. For not only is such use of prebaptismal "exorcised oil" otherwise unknown until the mid- to late fourth century,[159] but also, in the Egyptian liturgical tradition, prebaptismal anointing was not exorcistic until the fourth century.[160]

We are left, then, to consider the place and date of the simple prebaptismal exorcism first mentioned in 20.3 and then mentioned in association with the bishop laying on his hand(s) and adjuring the demons to flee and not return (*Trad. ap.* 20.8). Stripping away what seem to be later additions, this chapter is likely to be one of the core components of the *Apostolic Tradition*.[161] Further, in view of the simple and general directions in the first three verses giving way to specific and repeated instructions (20.3) involving the bishop, there is good reason to suppose that the latter material on the bishop performing exorcisms has been added later.[162] If this is correct we probably have evidence of exorcism being conducted as a preliminary to baptism at least by the late second century.

154. Bradshaw, Johnson, and Phillips, *Apostolic Tradition*, 111.

155. So also Bradshaw, Johnson, and Phillips, *Apostolic Tradition*, 111.

156. Translation from Bradshaw, Johnson, and Phillips, *Apostolic Tradition*, 106.

157. See Edward Yarnold, *The Awe-Inspiring Rites of Initiation: Baptismal Homilies of the Fourth Century* (Slough, UK: St Paul, 1971), 16.

158. See the discussion of Jesus breathing on his followers in John 20:22 by Craig S. Keener, *The Gospel of John: A Commentary* (2 vols.; Peabody, MA: Hendrickson, 2003), 2:1204–6.

159. Bradshaw, Johnson, and Phillips, *Apostolic Tradition*, 131 and n. 50.

160. See Paul F. Bradshaw, "Baptismal Practice in the Alexandrian Tradition: Eastern or Western?" in *Living Water, Sealing Spirit: Readings on Christian Initiation* (ed. Maxwell E. Johnson; Collegeville, MN: Pueblo / Liturgical Press, 1995), 92–95; Maxwell E. Johnson, *Liturgy in Early Christian Egypt* (JLS 33; Nottingham, UK: Grove, 1995), 7–16; Bradshaw, Johnson, and Phillips, *Apostolic Tradition*, 131–32.

161. See Bradshaw, Johnson, and Phillips, *Apostolic Tradition*, 14–15; and independently, Stewart-Sykes, *Apostolic Tradition*, esp. 51.

162. Cf. Bradshaw, Johnson, and Phillips, *Apostolic Tradition*, 108.

From the evidence we have, nothing can be said about the details of such exorcism other than that it is likely to have been simple, since no instructions are given. It is unlikely that a special class of exorcists would have been in mind.[163] Rather, those who were considered able to do so probably conducted them (see *Trad. ap.* 14.1). Unfortunately, I am not sure that it is possible to say with much confidence which geographical region of Christianity is being represented by this text. In its final form this chapter may well resemble what was known in the later Roman system of scrutinies.[164] However, the week of preparation assumed in the earlier strata (cf. 20.3, 5) may reflect a North African tradition,[165] supporting the Alexandrian origin of the baptismal liturgies of chapters 15–21.[166] Slightly favoring this provenance is the practice in Alexandria among Valentinian Gnostics of equating exorcism and baptism.[167] In short, we have in the *Apostolic Tradition* the first association of exorcism with baptism in mainstream Christianity, late in the second century, perhaps in Alexandria and, perhaps, adapted from practices reflected in Theodotus of Alexandria.[168]

11.11 Christian Magical Exorcisms

I have already argued that what we can call magical exorcisms—those exorcisms that were thought to be successful because of what was said and done rather than because of who performed them—were probably the most commonly known form of exorcism at the time of the emergence of Christianity (see §2.1 above). That Luke thought early Christians were also involved in such exorcisms is likely from the end of his story of the sons of Sceva, where he says that believers confessed their practices and burned their books publicly (see §6.3d above).

Assembling evidence that could tell us about magical exorcism among Christians up to the end of the second century is frustrated not only by the paucity of evidence but also by the difficulty of dating the material which is, frequently, composite in nature.[169] Notwithstanding, in general it is reasonable

163. The earliest reference to the office of exorcist is by Pope Cornelius (d. 253) in a letter to Fabius, bishop of Antioch (Eusebius, *Hist. eccl.* 6.43.3, 11).

164. See Stewart-Sykes, *Apostolic Tradition*, 109–110.

165. See Stewart-Sykes, "Manumission and Baptism in Tertullian's Africa," 129–49, esp. 132.

166. See A. Salles, "La 'Tradition apostolique' est-elle un témoin de la liturgie romaine?" *RHR* 148 (1955): 181–213; and the discussion by Stewart-Sykes, *Apostolic Tradition*, 17–19.

167. See Clement, *Exc.* 77–78, 80, 82–83, 86; and the discussion by Elizabeth A. Leeper, "From Alexandria to Rome: The Valentinian Connection to the Incorporation of Exorcism as a Prebaptismal Rite," *VC* 44 (1990): 7–9.

168. Cf. Leeper, "Alexandria," 6–24. Stewart-Sykes, *Apostolic Tradition*, 108, admits that although the connection with Theodotus is tenuous, it is not impossible.

169. See the discussion in Graham H. Twelftree, "Jesus the Exorcist and Ancient Magic," in *A Kind of Magic: Understanding Magic in the New Testament and Its Religious Environment* (ed.

to say that, in view of what we see from Luke's story of the sons of Sceva from the first century, and from magical exorcisms among Christians in the third and fourth centuries,[170] it is highly likely that, during the period of our interest, Christians were involved in such exorcisms.

Unfortunately, the only text that arguably warrants consideration is a section of *PGM* IV.[171] Although it is generally agreed that this papyrus dates from the fourth century CE, its contents are more likely to come from the second century CE.[172] In *PGM* IV. 1227–1264 some Coptic text is embedded in the extant prescription for exorcism, which reads:

> Hail, God of Abraham; hail, God of Isaac; hail, God of Jacob; Jesus Chrestos, the Holy Spirit, the Son of the Father, who is above the Seven, who is within the Seven. Bring Iao Sabaoth; may your power issue forth from NN, until you drive away this unclean demon satan, who is in him. (*PGM* IV. 1231–1239)

However, this is probably not a Christian text. First, although the names "Christos" (Christ) and "Chrēstos" (excellent) were pronounced the same and not generally confused in Coptic manuscripts of the classical period,[173] they are confused here. The confusion may have arisen from pagan Copts taking up the name of Jesus Christ into their text. For the words, "Jesus Chrestos, the Holy Spirit, the Son of the Father," not only interrupt the pattern of invoca-

---

Michael Labahn and Bert Jan Lietaert Peerbolte; European Studies on Christian Origins; LNTS 306; London and New York: T&T Clark, 2007), 57–86.

170. In this period the following are to be considered: (a) a text having extensive contact with New Testament vocabulary and published by David R. Jordan and Roy D. Kotansky, "A Solomonic Exorcism," in *Kölner Papyri (P. Köln)* (ed. Bärbel Kramer et al.; Abhandlungen der Nordrhein-Westfälischen Akademie der Wissenschaften: Sonderreihe, Papyrologica Coloniensia 7.8; Opladen: Westdeutscher Verlag, 1997), 53–69, which is dated from the third or fourth century CE; (b) the Greek exorcistic phylacteries discussed in David R. Jordan and Roy D. Kotansky, "Two Phylacteries from Xanthos," *RAr* (1996): 161–71, are also Christian and from just beyond the second century; (c) *GMA*, part 1, §68 (p. 387) is a fourth century fragment of a Christian liturgical exorcism from Cyprus; (d) the third century J. Paul Getty Museum 4.2 x 2.0 cm gold-foil amulet (Acc. no. 80.AI.53) for deliverance "from every evil spirit and from every epileptic fit and seizure" (lines 4–7) is possibly Christian, on which see Roy D. Kotansky, "Two Amulets in the Getty Museum and a Gold Amulet for Aurelia's Epilepsy: An Inscribed Magical-Stone for Fever, 'Chills,' and Headache," *J. Paul Getty Museum Journal* 8 (1980): 181; and *PGM* IV. 1231–1239, on which see Twelftree, "Ancient Magic."

171. E.g., Marvin W. Meyer and Richard Smith, eds., *Ancient Christian Magic: Coptic Texts of Ritual Power* (Princeton, NJ: Princeton University Press, 1999), offer no example of a datable exorcistic text from before the end of the second century.

172. See André Jean Festugière, *La révélation d'Hermès Trismégiste* (4 vols.; Paris: Gabalda, 1949–1954), 1:303n1. In light of taking μηνοτύραννε (line 2664) to refer to the Attis Meno-tyrannus inscriptions, which are dated between 374 and 390 CE, more recently Eugene N. Lane, "On the Date of *PGM* IV," *SecCent* 4 (1984): 25–27, sets the terminus post quem for the compilation of *PGM* IV as ca. 380 CE.

173. Bentley Layton, *The Gnostic Treatise on Resurrection from Nag Hammadi* (HDR 12; Missoula, MT: Scholars Press, 1979), 44–45.

tion established in the foregoing line, but, from a Christian perspective, the order and combination of these names is not what we would expect from a Christian. It is as if there has been an unsuccessful attempt to incorporate a corrupted trinitarian formula.

Secondly, the use of the phrase "unclean demon satan" as an individual class of demon, rather than the Christian archdemon, suggests that these words were borrowed or adapted from outside Christian sources.[174] At best, then, we could speculate that, on noting that Christians were exorcising unclean spirits in the name of Jesus Christ or even using a trinitarian formula, pagan Copts borrowed their key vocabulary. Therefore, we are left with only our very general suggestion that it is highly likely that during our period of interest Christians were involved in magical exorcisms. (This rather speculative conclusion will receive considerable support from what we learn from Celsus; see §12.2 below.) If this is correct, it seems reasonable to infer from what we have seen in this chapter that proto-orthodox Christianity sought to distinguish its exorcisms from other Christian as well as non-Christian ones that were similar but seen as text-based or incantational rather than Jesus-based.

Although we have covered a great deal of material in these last two chapters, it is important that we delay summarizing and drawing conclusions from this material until we have taken into account information from outsiders.

---

174. A similar use of "satan" is found in 4Q213a 1.17 and 11Q5 19.15–16; see Michael E. Stone and Jonas C. Greenfield, "The Prayer of Levi," *JBL* 112 (1993): 262–65.

12

Critics of Christianity

To THIS POINT, the third part of our study has involved passing under review Christian writers of the second century who may provide us with interpretive tools—we have been using the image of a lens—to understand more fully what the New Testament has to say about exorcism among early Christians. In refining our lens with which to look back on the writings of the New Testament, we turn to the literary remains of the early critics of Christianity—outsiders—to see what they can contribute to our understanding of exorcism among early Christians. The earliest critics—Pliny the Younger, Tacitus, Suetonius, Epictetus, Crescens, Phlegon of Tralles, Marcus Cornelius Fronto, Lucius Apuleius, Aelius Aristides, and Marcus Aurelius—prove less helpful than we might wish. Insight from critics from the later part of the second century—Celsus, Lucian of Samosata, and Galen—prove more fruitful.

12.1 Early Critics

The earliest mention of Christianity in pagan literature is by Pliny the Younger, who served as governor of Bithynia Pontus from September 111 until his death in 113 CE. In writing to the emperor, Trajan, for advice concerning trials of Christians, Pliny describes Christians as, for example, stubborn and inflexible and says: "They had met regularly before dawn on a fixed day to chant verses alternately among themselves in honor of Christ as if to a god, and also to bind themselves by an oath . . . to abstain from theft, robbery, and adultery, to commit no breach of trust. . . ." He sums up this description by saying that Christianity was nothing but a degenerate or depraved and excessive "superstition" (*superstitio*; *Epistulae* 10.96). In this there is nothing to suggest that Pliny was aware that miracles, or exorcism in particular, was associated with Christianity in Bithynia Pontus.

Similarly, in discussing the fire of Rome in 64 CE, Tacitus (ca. 56–after 118) describes the Christians there as "hated because of their crimes," as being a "destructive superstition," and as having a "hatred of the human race [*odio humani generis*]" (*Ann.* 15.44).[1] Again, there is nothing here to suggest that Tacitus thought Christianity involved miracles or exorcism in particular. Even his understanding that Christianity had Palestinian roots (15.44) does not alter his impression of it being socially disruptive;[2] his description of Judaism focuses on their theology and their separateness (cf. *Hist.* 5.5), not on any activity that could be construed as related to miracles or exorcism.

Writing after 122 CE, Suetonius (born ca. 69) says that Claudius expelled the Jews from Rome (in 49 CE) because they "constantly made disturbances at the instigation of Chrestus" (*Claud.* 5.25).[3] In *Nero* 16.2 Suetonius approves of the emperor inflicting punishment "on the Christians, a class of men given to a new and mischievous superstition (*superstitionis novae ac maleficae*). *Maleficus* can be used to specify a charm or means of enchantment (see Tacitus, *Ann.* 2.69). However, in the transferred sense as used here, it describes something hurtful, mischievous, or wicked.[4] In short, Suetonius has nothing to tell us about Christians and miracles.

The same result is reached in reading the (sometimes uncertain) references to Christianity in a number of other authors:[5]

a. Regarding Epictetus (ca. 50–ca. 130), all we can be certain of is that, in *Discourses* 4.7.1–6, he mentions the lack of fear as characteristic of Galileans (Christians).[6]

1. That is, perhaps, seeming to hate others by withdrawal from society. See Harald Fuchs, "Tacitus über die Christen," *VC* 4 (1950): 86.

2. Stephen Benko, "Pagan Criticism of Christianity during the First Two Centuries A.D.," *ANRW* II.23.2 (1980): 1065.

3. *Chrestus* is usually taken to be a variant spelling of *Christus*. However, see the discussion by Benko, "Pagan Criticism," 1057–62, in which he makes a convincing case that Suetonius would not "confuse the Christian movement with a local troublemaker, Chrestus" (1059), so that this passage is not referring to Christianity.

4. See P. G. W. Glare, *Oxford Latin Dictionary* (Oxford: Clarendon, 1982), 1067.

5. On what follows, see Benko, "Pagan Criticism," 1055–1118.

6. Against William A. Oldfather, *Epictetus* (2 vols.; LCL; Cambridge, MA: Harvard University Press; London: Heinemann, 1966–1967), 1:272–73n1, that at *Diatr.* 2.9.19–22 Epictetus refers to Christians. Benko, "Pagan Criticism," 1078, rightly argues that Jews are in mind.

b. Crescens (mid-second century)[7] only says that Christians are "atheists" and "impious" (Justin Martyr, 2 *Apol.* 3).

c. Hadrian (76–138 CE),[8] as now cited in Eusebius, only tells us that Christians needed to be given a fair trial.[9]

d. A spurious letter of Hadrian's, published after 140 CE by Phlegon of Tralles,[10] gives insight into the early Christians in Egypt.[11] Along with the Jews they are considered astrologers and soothsayers, for example, but there is no consideration of them as miracle-workers or exorcists.[12]

e. Perhaps responsible for what is now found in the work of Minucius Felix (late second to early third century CE), the Roman orator, Marcus Cornelius Fronto (ca. 100–166), describes Christians as, for example, unskilled, atheists, fearless of death, and credulous. They know each other by secret signs and are involved in cannibalism and abominable acts of lust. However, there is no hint of the Christians being involved in healing or exorcism; even the charge of being credulous is not linked to such activity (Minucius, *Oct.* 8; 9).[13]

f. There may be a reference to Jesus being a magician in the *Apologia* by Lucius Apuleius (born ca. 125). As part of his defense against being charged with magic, he says, "I am ready to be any magician you please—the great Carmendas himself or Damigeron or *his* . . . Moses of whom you have heard, or Jannes or Apollobeches or Dardanus himself or any sorcerer of note from the time of Zoroaster and Ostanes till now" (*Apologia* 90). The letters *his* could be a reference to Jesus (*ihs*). However, the text does not permit a decision either way.[14]

g. Similarly, Aelius Aristides (117–after 181 CE) describes a group of Palestinian people who could equally be Cynics or Christians.[15]

h. It is possible that Marcus Aurelius (121–180 CE) mentions the Christians in his *Meditations*. In talking about their readiness to die he says: "This readiness must be the result of a specific decision; not, as with the

7. Cf. Tacitus, *Dialogus de oratoribus* 19.1; Eusebius, *Hist eccl.* 4.16.3.

8. See Werner Eck, "Hadrianus," in *Brill's New Pauly: Encyclopaedia of the Ancient World* (ed. Hubert Cancik and Helmuth Schneider; Leiden and Boston: Brill, 2002–), 5:1083–88.

9. Eusebius, *Hist. eccl.* 4.9.1–3; cf. 4.8.6; 4.26.10.

10. See David Magie, *Scriptores historiae Augustae* (3 vols.; LCL; 1921–1932; repr., London: Heinemann; Cambridge, MA: Harvard University Press, 1979–1982), 3:397–40.

11. Benko, "Pagan Criticism," 1081.

12. Flavius Vopiscus of Syracuse, *Saturninus* 7 and 8.

13. Cf. W. H. C. Frend, *Martyrdom and Persecution in the Early Church* (New York: New York University Press, 1967), 187–88; Graeme W. Clarke, "Four Passages in Minucius Felix," in *Kyriakon: Festschrift Johannes Quasten* (ed. Patrick Granfield and Josef A. Jungmann; 2 vols.; Münster: Aschendorff, 1970), 2:499–504; Albert Henrichs, "Pagan Ritual and the Alleged Crimes of the Early Christians: Some New Evidence," in Granfield and Jungmann, *Kyriakon*, 1:18–35.

14. See the discussion by Benko, "Pagan Criticism," 1091.

15. See the discussion by Benko, "Pagan Criticism," 1098.

Christians, of obstinate opposition, but of a reasoned and dignified decision" (*Med.* 11.3).[16] In relation to our subject, as we have already noted
(§11.5 above), although he expressed his dislike of wonder-workers
with their stories of spells and exorcisms (1.6), he says nothing about
it in relation to the Christians. Again we note from this that Christians cannot have been particularly known for their miracle-working
or exorcisms.

The conclusion to draw here is obvious and can be succinct: from what
we can glimpse from the surviving fragments of its outside critics, up until
the end of the third quarter of the second century, Christianity had made no
impact on society in terms of being seen as a religion of miracles and miracle-
workers, including exorcism, either the kind we see portrayed in the Gospels
or the magical exorcism of the period. Although these texts permit only the
thinnest of conclusions in relation to exorcism among early Christians, there
are three critics of Christianity that are particularly helpful to us. For the
last quarter of the century we have three important critics who may help
us to see how significant exorcism was seen to be among the Christians. For,
coming to Celsus, Lucian, and Galen, the three great second-century critics
of Christianity, even though still not extensive, we reach more substantial
insights into the way outsiders viewed this new religion. Again, we will take
them in chronological order, beginning with Celsus.

12.2 Celsus

The general value of Celsus to our inquiry is that he is our best independent
witness to Christianity in the second century.[17] From the evidence available,
from his pen around 177–180 came the first comprehensive philosophical
polemic against Christianity.[18] Fortunately for our purposes, in this *True Doctrine* (ἀληθὴς λόγος), known to us only through being quoted almost in its
entirety by Origen (ca. 185–ca. 254), Celsus gives us insights into exorcism
among early Christians. Sadly, we know nothing of Celsus apart from what we
learn from Origen, who was writing three quarters of a century removed, in

16. For discussion of the reference to Christians being a gloss, see P. A. Brunt, "Marcus Aurelius and the Christians," in *Studies in Latin Literature and Roman History* (ed. Carl Derox; vol.
1; Collection Latomus 164; Brussels: Latomus, 1979), 483–520. To be left aside because of its
uncertain origin is a text ascribed to Marcus Aurelius, preserved in Eusebius, *Hist. eccl.* 4.13.1–7.
See the discussion by Benko, "Pagan Criticism," 1093.

. 17. Gary T. Burke, "Walter Bauer and Celsus: The Shape of Late Second-Century Christianity," *SecCent* 4 (1984): 3.

18. For a discussion on the date of Celsus, see Henry Chadwick, *Origen: Contra Celsum*
(1953; repr., Cambridge: Cambridge University Press, 1965), xxvi–xxviii.

the middle of the third century (Eusebius, *Hist. eccl.* 6.36.2).[19] This distance in time, as well as in objectives, between Celsus and Origen means that we must distinguish carefully between what each says in order to understand Celsus as clearly as possible.

Origen's only certain knowledge of Celsus is that he had been dead a long time (*Cels.*, preface 4), and that he often spoke of Plato with great respect (*Cels.* 6.47).[20] Taking into account his interest in Egyptian lore (3.19; 8.58) and his quoting an Egyptian magician (6.41), it is reasonable to suppose that Celsus is to be placed in Alexandria. There is further support for this conclusion in that Celsus refers to the *Dispute between Papiscus and Jason* (*Cels.* 4.52), for Papiscus is a Jew of Alexandria, and Jason a Hebrew Christian of Pella.[21] Yet, since Celsus says that he has traveled through Phoenicia and Palestine, we must take into account that his information about Christianity, though likely to be dominated by Egypt, would not be restricted to it (7.3–11).[22]

Our particular interest in Celsus is that he knew not only of Jesus being considered a miracle-worker,[23] but also that Christians performed miracles: "Christians get the power which they seem to possess by pronouncing the names of certain demons and incantations." Origen takes this to be exorcism for he comments: "[Celsus is] hinting, I suppose, at those who subdue demons by enchantments and drive them out" (*Cels.* 1.6; cf. 6.39).

A little further on Origen quotes Celsus as saying, "Why need I enumerate all those who have taught rites of purification, or spells which bring deliverance [ἀποπομπίμους], or formulas that avert evil [δαιμονίους]" (*Cels.* 6.39).[24]

---

19. Christopher P. Jones, *Culture and Society in Lucian* (Cambridge, MA; London: Harvard University Press, 1986), 20: "The Celsus to whom Lucian dedicates the *Alexander* is generally agreed to be, not the Platonist against whom Origen wrote his defense of Christianity, but a man with whom Origen at first confused his opponent, an Epicurean who also received an open letter from Galen." For the contrary view, see Jacques Schwartz, *Biographie de Lucien de Samosate* (Collection Latomus 83; Brussels: Latomus / Bruxelles-Berchem, 1965), 23–24.

20. For a discussion on the identity of Celsus, see Chadwick, *Origen*, xxiv–xxvi.

21. See the discussion by Chadwick, *Origen*, 227n1. Chadwick, *Origen*, xxix, citing Walter Bauer, *Orthodoxy and Heresy in Earliest Christianity* (London: SCM, 1972), chap. 2, suggests that Celsus is to be situated in Alexandria because he confuses orthodox and gnostic Christianity, and it was especially at Alexandria that the lines between Gnosticism and orthodoxy had not been clearly drawn. However, against Bauer and claiming that Celsus could distinguish between "orthodoxy" or the "great church" and the sects, see Robert L. Wilken, "Diversity and Unity in Early Christianity," *SecCent* 1 (1981): 107; and Burke, "Walter Bauer," 4–7.

22. Cf. Burke, "Walter Bauer," 3. Burke notes that the link with Rome is circumstantial at best from the reference in *Cels.* 5.62 to the Marcellian sect derived from a Marcellina. Irenaeus mentions a Marcellina who came to Rome, leading many astray (*Haer.* 1.25.6). However, Burke says, we cannot be sure of the identity of the Marcellina(s) and that she did not have an expression of her sect in the East that was known to Celsus; he concludes, "Nothing in the *TD* can definitely place Celsus in Rome at all" (7).

23. *Cels.* 1.28, 38, 68; 2.48, 49.

24. See Chadwick, *Origen*, 355; cf. *ANCL* 4:591. For Origen on exorcism in his own time, see, e.g., *Cels.* 1.6, 25; 7.4.

A few lines later Celsus is quoted as saying that he had seen among Christian elders "books containing barbarian names of demons and magical formulas" (6.40). Celsus sees Christian and other exorcisms similarly for he draws a parallel between the Christians and magicians who, "for a few obols make known their sacred lore in the middle of the marketplace and drive demons out of people and blow away disease" (1.69). There is corroborating evidence for this kind of exorcism in that there is a similar description of exorcism in the magical papyri. Thus *PGM* IV. 3081–3083 directs the exorcist: "While conjuring, blow once, blowing air from the tips of the feet up to the face, and it will be assigned." In other words, to Celsus, Christian and other exorcisms seemed indistinguishable.

In taking into account Celsus' description of Christian exorcism we need to note that it is quite likely he is not describing a small "heretical" group of Christians but what he saw as mainstream—"orthodox"—Christianity. For it is only late in book 5 that Origen begins to show that Celsus distinguishes other competing Christian groups, and even there the orthodox are regarded as numerically superior (*Cels.* 5.61) and likely to be the ones of interest to Celsus. Also, when Celsus finally deals with the sects he does so principally in two self-contained sections (5.61–64; 6.24–52).[25] Therefore, it is reasonable to conclude that Celsus has been in contact with and is describing the majority of Christians—whom he associates with the uneducated and morally depraved (cf. 1.9, 50; 6.41),[26] perhaps primarily in Alexandria—conducting exorcisms that are indistinguishable from what we see reflected in the magical papyri.

12.3 Lucian of Samosata

This Greek writer[27] and philosopher-satirist[28] is of interest to us for, in *The Death of Peregrinus*, he makes some passing comments about Christianity that touch on our subject.[29] Attempts at outlining the life of Lucian have proved

25. Following Burke, "Walter Bauer," 6.

26. Cf. C. T. H. R. Ehrhardt, "Eusebius and Celsus," *JAC* 22 (1979): 41. Origen will only admit to a minority of Christians being so described; *Cels.* 1.9.

27. On the manuscripts and text of Lucian, see Jacques Bompaire, ed., trans., *Lucien: Œuvres*, vol. 1, *Introduction générale*, opuscules 1–10 (Collection des universités de France, Série grecque 360; Paris: Les Belles Lettres, 1993), chaps. 2–4.

28. However, Lucian did write serious work. See Hubert Cancik, "Lucian on Conversion: Remarks on Lucian's Dialogue *Nigrinos*," in *Ancient and Modern Perspectives on the Bible and Culture: Essays in Honor of Hans Dieter Betz* (ed. Adela Yarbro Collins; Atlanta: Scholars Press, 1998), 48, citing Eunapius, *Vitae sophistarum* (introduction): "Lucian of Samosata is a man who tries seriously to provoke laughter; he recorded the life of Demonax, a philosopher of his times; in that book and in very few others was he completely serious."

29. Lucian makes passing references to Christians also in *Alex.* 25 and 38, on which see Marcel Caster, *Lucien et la pensée religieuse de son temps* (Paris: Les Belles Lettres, 1937), 349; and Jennifer A. Hall, *Lucian's Satire* (New York: Arno, 1981), 212–13.

difficult.[30] We probably cannot be more precise than to say that he was born in Samosata between 115 and 125, though the latter date may be preferred if we depend on Lucian saying he was about forty when he wrote *Doubly Indicted* in 165.[31] From what he says in the *Dream*, he was apprenticed to his uncle as a sculptor, soon giving it up in disgust for rhetoric. Rather than adopt the usual role of using his skills in courts of law, Lucian followed the later sophists in traveling as a speaker, spending time in Ionia, Italy, Antioch, Samosata, and Greece, where he probably lived in Athens for some years. As a rhetor and as his works confirm, his mission in life was to entertain rather than to teach or change society. Perhaps more than once he was in Egypt, where he may have died some time after the death of Marcus Aurelius in 180 (*Alex.* 48).[32]

The Death of Peregrinus is an attack on Peregrinus, a well-known contemporary, written in the form of a letter, addressed to Cronius, a lesser known Platonist.[33] The work tells of the life and immolation of Peregrinus, whom, Lucian says, liked to call himself Proteus[34] and was, for part of his early life, a Christian. He is depicted as becoming a local church leader and suffering imprisonment as a Christian.

In interpreting what Lucian has to say about Christianity we need to give attention to two issues. The first concerns how we should read what Lucian writes in relationship to his contemporary events. It has been thought that his writing is disconnected from life around him, his objective being to produce a literary diversion, declaiming on Greek cultural traditions, rather than reflecting his own society.[35] However, more recently it has been convincingly argued that Lucian's writing is closely involved in and reflects his own society.[36] In

---

30. Schwartz, *Biographie*, chap. 6; Graham Anderson, *Lucian: Theme and Variation in the Second Sophistic* (Leiden: Brill, 1976), appendix 1; Jones, *Culture*, appendix B. Barry Baldwin, *Studies in Lucian* (Toronto: Hakkert, 1973), reminds us that "there is virtually nothing in the evidence, internal and external, for Lucianic chronology that deserves the status of fact" (18). Even if Galen refers to Lucian in his commentary on Hippocrates' *Epidemics* at 2.6.29, nothing about the life of our subject is revealed. See G. Strohmaier, "Übersehenes zur Biographie Lukians," *Philologus* 120 (1976): 117–22; and the discussion in Hall, *Lucian's Satire*, 4–6 and 436n5.

31. See the discussion by Hall, *Lucian's Satire*, 6–16, esp. 16. See also Baldwin, *Lucian*, 10–11; and Jones, *Culture*, 8.

32. Hall, *Lucian's Satire*, 41–44.

33. Jacob Bernays, *Lucian und die Kyniker* (Berlin: Wilhelm Hertz, 1879), 3–4; and John Dillon, *The Middle Platonists: 80 B.C. to A.D. 220* (Ithaca, NY: Cornell University Press, 1996), 362, 379–80.

34. Lucian, *Peregr.* 1: "Unlucky Peregrinus, or, as he delighted to style himself, Proteus, has done exactly what Proteus in Homer did." The sarcasm is obvious for Homer, *Od.* 4.349–570, has Proteus, a minor sea god, take on various shapes to escape capture.

35. So, e.g., Rudolf Helm, *Lucian und Menipp* (Leipzig and Berlin: Teubner, 1906), esp. 1–16; on whom see Barbara P. McCarthy, "Lucian and Menippus," *YClS* 4 (1934): 3–58; and Jacques Bompaire, *Lucien écrivain: Imitation et création* (Paris: E. de Boccard, 1958), esp. parts 2 and 3.

36. So Jones, *Culture*, 6–23. Baldwin, *Lucian*, 118, concludes: "Virtually all that he wrote is relevant to, and was inspired by, his own age."

particular, Peregrinus is probably not a figment of Lucian's imagination for Athenagoras and Aulus Gellius both probably refer to the same person.[37] In light of the way Lucian treats the magician Pancrates as a real person—though altered and used to represent more than his own activities[38]—we can suppose that the real Peregrinus has been used to represent more than his own life. He probably carries the burden of Lucian's satire and mockery against such "poor wretches" who are deluded and, in turn, delude others more wretched than themselves—in this case the Christians (*Peregr.* 11–13).[39]

A second issue in relation to interpreting *The Death of Peregrinus* is not so much the questions of when and where it was written, but whether or not these questions are important in understanding what Lucian has to say. Lucian gives the impression that he is writing not long after the death of Peregrinus, which took place at the end of the Olympic games in 165.[40] However, sufficient time must have passed for there to exist a cult of Peregrinus and for the death of his disciple, Theagenes, to have taken place in Rome.[41] Also, since Lucian is writing this work after having been in Olympia, and in that he went from Greece to Egypt, rather than place the writing of this work soon after the death of Peregrinus,[42] it is most likely that *The Death of Peregrinus* was written later in his life while he was in Egypt. Notwithstanding, in that Lucian has gained wide experience through his travels, and is writing for a wide audience, as well as reworking themes in his different writings, the place and date of his writings is of little significance in interpreting what he has to say.[43] Instead, what he writes can be taken to reflect more than the events about which he writes. For us these two conclusions mean that what Lucian is writing about Christianity is likely to reflect what he knew of the movement across the world of his experience.

In *The Death of Peregrinus* 11 Lucian cheekily says that it was in Palestine that Peregrinus "learned the wondrous lore of the Christians." Although he does not say it in so many words, Lucian probably considered that Peregrinus was a miracle-worker. For at a point in his story when Peregrinus is no longer a Christian, he says, "By Zeus, it would be nothing unnatural if, among all those dolts [who witness his death] that there are, some should be found to assert that they were relieved of quartan fevers by him" (*Peregr.* 28).

37. Athenagoras, *Leg.* 26.3; Aulus Gellius, *Noct. att.* 12.11.1. See W. H. C. Frend, *The Rise of Christianity* (Philadelphia: Fortress, 1984), 175–76.

38. Jones, *Culture*, 49–50.

39. To the contrary, Hans Dieter Betz, *Lukian von Samosata und das Neue Testament* (1961), 5–13, thinks that Lucian is satirizing only Peregrinus rather than Christians.

40. Schwartz, *Biographie*, "Tableau chronologique," facing page 148; cf. Jones, *Culture*, 120 (and n. 14), 169.

41. Lucian tends not to mention the living, though, as Jones suggests, he may not have been so scrupulous with a person he did not like. Jones, *Culture*, 120.

42. So Schwartz, *Biographie*, 19; Anderson, *Lucian*, 178 and n. 3.

43. See Anderson, *Lucian*, appendix 1.

As sarcastically as he speaks of Peregrinus (cf. *Peregr.* 1), he describes the Christians as even worse—as "poor wretches"—for "in a trice he made them all look like children" (11). Lucian says that Peregrinus was a prophet, law-giver, cult leader, "the new Socrates" (12)[44] and even god for the Christians, second only in their worship of "the man who was crucified in Palestine" (11). In going on to tell of the imprisonment of Peregrinus as a Christian, Lucian also describes their charitable works and the good communication and strong bonds between Christians of different places, as well as their despising of death (12). He also says that the Christians deny the Greek gods but worship "that crucified sophist himself and live under his laws" (13). Further, he says that they will receive new doctrines without any definite evidence so that "if any charlatan and trickster [γόης καὶ τεχνίτης], able to profit by occasions, come among them, he quickly acquires sudden wealth by imposing upon simple folk" (13). Given that he probably understood Peregrinus as a miracle-worker, it is also probable that this is a sarcastic reference to the susceptibility of Christians to the miraculous.[45] Further, given that in other places Lucian pokes fun at the miraculous, particularly exorcism,[46] we can suppose that the charlatans and tricksters (13) would perhaps be understood to include exorcism in their repertoire.

From this it is reasonable to conclude that, including not least in Egypt around the third quarter of the second century, Lucian probably viewed Christians as having a particular interest in miracles, perhaps including exorcism. Despite gaps in his knowledge,[47] since Lucian has considerable and sometimes precise knowledge of Christianity,[48] we can further conclude only that the Egyptian Christianity known to Lucian had perhaps made an impact on the community through its involvement in exorcism.

12.4 Galen

Galen was born into an important cultured family at Pergamum in Asia in September 129 CE.[49] He received a broad education, traveled widely in furthering his study of medicine, and spent most of the last thirty years of his

44. On Lucian borrowing from Plato here, see Anderson, *Lucian*, 75 and n. 81.

45. On Lucian's satire of religion, see Hall, *Lucian's Satire*, 194–207.

46. E.g., Lucian, *Philops.* 16, 31–32.

47. Gilbert Bagnani, "Peregrinus Proteus and the Christians," *Historia* 4 (1955): 111: "Lucian's ignorance of Christianity and Christian doctrine is really monumental." On Lucian's knowledge of Christianity, also see Hall, *Lucian's Satire*, 214–15; and Frend, *Rise*, 175–76.

48. See Hans Dieter Betz, "Lukian von Samosata und das Christentum," *NovT* 3 (1959): 226–37.

49. For an introduction to Galen, see David E. Eichholz, "Galen and His Environment," *GR* 20 (1951): 60–71; and Glen Warren Bowersock, *Greek Sophists in the Roman Empire* (Oxford: Clarendon, 1969), 66–68.

life in Rome. There he enjoyed friendship with Marcus Aurelius, successfully attending to the health of his son Commodus, as well as increasing his reputation not only in medicine but also as a philosopher.[50] Galen died in Rome in about 199. In his extensive work, much of it written after 169, when he was in Rome, there are four brief references to the Christians.[51]

Two of the references appear in his *De pulsuum differentiis*, perhaps written in the last years of Marcus Aurelius, between 176 and 180. They betray Galen's low view of Christians (and Jews) in their uncritical faith and easy acceptance of novelties.[52] In one place he says, "One might more easily teach novelties to the followers of Moses and Christ than to the physicians and philosophers who cling fast to their schools."[53] In a second place, criticizing Jews and Christians for learning by authorities alone and having their beliefs prescribed for them, he says, "If one had come into the school of Moses and Christ, [one would] hear talk of undemonstrated laws."[54] The third reference, which may have been written anytime before 192[55] and occurs in an otherwise lost work against Aristotle, also denigrates the Christians for their faulty thinking: "If I had in mind people who taught their pupils in the same way as the followers of Moses and Christ teach theirs—for they order them to accept everything on faith—I should not have given you a definition."[56]

Previous criticisms of Christianity had deemed it a superstition.[57] However, though he is critical of it, Galen is the first pagan author who places Christianity on the same footing as Greek philosophy.[58] This is probably because the Christianity with which Galen was familiar in upper-class Roman society had begun to spread among the higher strata of society. Eusebius tells us that it was not until the reign of Commodus that the educated, wealthy, and wellborn were drawn to Christianity (Eusebius, *Hist. eccl.* 5.21.1–3). However, Galen is critical of the Christian philosophy because it has no rational basis: Christians are "philosophers without a philosophy."[59] This helps us understand Galen's fourth reference to Christianity, which follows a similar theme and is of particular interest to us. The passage appears in

50. On the link between medicine and philosophy, see Bowersock, *Greek Sophists*, 66–68.

51. Galen, *Puls.* 3.3; 2. 4; and two references that survive only in Arabic. See Richard Walzer, *Galen on Jews and Christians* (London: Oxford University Press, 1949), 10–16.

52. See the discussion in Benko, "Pagan Criticism," 1100.

53. Galen, *Puls.* 3.3, cited in Walzer, *Galen*, 14.

54. Galen, *Puls.* 2.4, cited in Walzer, *Galen*, 14; cf. 49–56 for a discussion of the passage.

55. Walzer, *Galen*, 15.

56. The passage survives only as a quotation in an Arabic *Life of Galen*. See Walzer, *Galen*, 14–15, 87–98.

57. E.g., Pliny the Younger, *Epistulae* 10.96.8: "*superstitionem pravam et immodicam.*"

58. Walzer, *Galen*, 43.

59. So Adolf von Harnack, *History of Dogma* (from 3rd German ed., 1894–1898; trans. Neil Buchanan; 1894–1899; repr. as 7 vols. in 4, New York: Dover, 1961), 1:237.

Galen's lost summary of Plato's *Republic*, written in about 180 and surviving only in Arabic.[60] Galen says: "The people called Christians [are] drawing their faith from parables [and miracles], and yet sometimes acting in the same way" as those who philosophize.[61] He goes on to speak highly of Christian morality. Richard Walzer tells us that the word "miracle" here is only found in one branch of the tradition. While, as Walzer says, Galen could have spoken of miracles,[62] the addition of the word is more easily explained than its absence, not least since Galen's work in Arabic translation was transmitted by Christians. Therefore, it is likely that "miracle" was added to the text later by Christian copyists.[63]

In attempting to reconstruct Galen's attitude toward miracles we have to keep in mind that in the period there was a renaissance of the cult of Asclepius, god of the whole range of the healing arts. Although there was no competition between the healings associated directly with Asclepius and those from the hands of the doctors, their methods were quite separate and sometimes the former were not accepted by the doctors.[64] Therefore, although Galen sees Christianity as a philosophy and is sympathetic to its morals, his criticism of Christians as superstitious suggests that if he knew of such practices as miracles and exorcism, he would have taken advantage of mentioning them.

In turn, therefore, we have further evidence of Christianity—known at least by outsiders in educated Greco-Roman society—as having no obvious interest in miracles or exorcism. Indeed, Eusebius tells us that there was a group of philosophical Christians in Rome who "do not inquire what the divine Scriptures say," but study "Euclid and admire Aristotle and Theophrastus and some of them even worship Galen" (*Hist. eccl.* 5.28.13–14).[65] Although the evidence from Eusebius probably does not allow us to follow Walzer in suggesting that this group of Christians in Rome was dependent on the logic of Galen in building up a Christian philosophy independent of and anterior to the Alexandrian school or Clement and Origen,[66] there remains at least corroborating evidence of a Christianity in Rome in the late second century that was seen by one outsider as a philosophy and not known for its interest in miracles or exorcism.

60. For dating see Walzer, *Galen*, 16.
61. A statement referred to in works of Arabic universal history, Christian theology, and the history of medicine. See Walzer, *Galen*, 15, 89–90.
62. Walzer, *Galen*, 69.
63. On the transmission of Galen's works in Arabic, see Walzer, *Galen*, 4.
64. Bowersock, *Greek Sophists*, 69–70.
65. See the discussion by Leslie W. Barnard, "Athenagoras, Galen, Marcus Aurelius, and Celsus," CQR 168 (1967): 169–71.
66. Barnard, "Athenagoras," 170–71, discussing Walzer, *Galen*, 75–86.

12.5 A Summary

Judging from the snippets of information we have from the early critics, Christianity had not made sufficient impact in terms of its miracles, including exorcism, to warrant their mention. The three more substantial later critics are particularly helpful in seeing how late second-century Christianity was viewed in relation to exorcism. In light of what we learn from Celsus, whose information is likely to be dominated by his experience in Alexandria, we have to take seriously that in the late second century, exorcism among Christians in that city was indistinguishable from other kinds of exorcisms: books of spells, barbarian names, and rites that included at least the act of blowing in conducting exorcisms for profit. From Lucian we have learned that he probably viewed Christians as having a particular interest in miracles, perhaps including exorcism, so that, in turn we can only say that perhaps the Egyptian Christianity known to him had made an impression on those around them through involvement in exorcism. We have just seen that, from Galen's perspective, Christianity—at least those in the upper echelons of society—is likely to have had no obvious interest in miracles or exorcism.

Part 4

Exorcism among Early Christians

13

Conclusions
and Contemporary Coda

E VEN THOUGH LUCIAN, for example, ridiculed it, and whatever we make of it, exorcism was an obvious and well-known practice in the world of the early Christians. However, this study has been undertaken because, when reviewing the literary remains of the early Christians, it is not immediately obvious how they viewed the role of or practiced this form of healing. Indeed, there is a complexity to the interest in and place of exorcism among early Christians that has so far eluded present theorists. It has been alleged that exorcism not only "found an extraordinary flowering" in Christianity, as MacMullen put it (see p. 27), but also that it was part of the evangelistic engine of the early church, explaining its extraordinary and unparalleled success. On the other hand, pressed by the lack of overt reference to exorcism by Paul and the glaring and puzzling absence of reference to exorcism in the Fourth Gospel, it has been supposed that the early church showed a great reluctance to become involved in exorcism.

Alternatively, noting particularly the contrasting perspectives of Mark and the Fourth Gospel, it could be that interest in exorcism among early Christians diminished over time. Or, perhaps it is socio-economic factors or cultural variations across time and between places that explain what we see in the New Testament evidence. However one attempts to solve the various aspects of the problem of exorcism among early Christians, I recognize that the results cannot be held too firmly. For it is to be acknowledged that we are dealing with the mere fragmentary remains of the once much larger body of literature that was produced. Further, the literature is, at times, only tangentially related to our interests. Notwithstanding, it seems to me that we are in a position to draw some significant conclusions.

In attempting to understand how early Christians saw the place and practice of exorcism, two further points have taken our attention along the way and require some concluding comments: the association of the rite of baptism with exorcism and, given the central place of exorcism in the ministry of Jesus, there is the question of his perceived role as a model for the early Christians as we attempt to describe their interest in and practice of exorcism.

13.1 Options for Exorcism

The place we chose to begin solving these problems and differences of opinion was through setting out the options and models for exorcism available to early Christians. From our review of Jesus and the other exorcists of his time, some important results emerge. One is that Jesus did not have a monopoly on exorcism for, contrary to what MacMullen would have us believe, the practice flourished with other individuals and in other movements and traditions. In turn, this means that the early Christians had a choice of models in conducting exorcisms, ranging from what we have termed the magical to the magico-charismatic (which believers saw in their traditions about Jesus), and later in the second century, to the charismatic approach.

Contrary to what we might expect, the method adopted by the followers of Jesus was not his magico-charismatic approach. Nor did we find evidence of the adoption of the charismatic approach that became available later in our period. Instead, the early Christians resorted to a more magical method, which depended not so much on their own personal force as on explicitly engaging an outside power-authority to evict the demons. However, we noted that the most significant differences between the magical exorcisms of the early Christians and their contemporaries was both the reported Christians' high level of confidence and the extreme brevity of their method.

Given the preponderance of magical exorcisms and the early Christians' sense of dependence on Jesus, the adoption of this magical approach is not surprising and leads to noting another important result of our examination of Jesus and other exorcists. That is, we have seen that there is little direct incentive in the very early Jesus traditions for his followers to be involved in exorcism. Indeed, we have no direct evidence that Jesus charged his followers with performing exorcisms before Easter, nor that he would have expected them to be exorcists after his death. Nevertheless, in that we have good evidence that Jesus sent his followers out on a pre-Easter mission and that the early Christians—before and after Easter—probably, like Jesus, considered they were living in a similar situation (with the kingdom of God only partially realized), exorcism is likely to have been seen as of ongoing significance to them.

However, with Jesus removed they no longer had his tangible model before them. Further, if and when exorcism was taken up—by later followers who probably saw themselves as less spiritually authoritative, as well as dependent on Jesus—as we have just noted, we can understand why they resorted to what would have been considered the more appropriate, and the more familiar, magical method. Already, therefore, we probably have some explanation for the varying interest in exorcism among early Christians. That is, while it could be, and was, seen as a natural extension and expression of the ministry of Jesus, the very early traditions about him did not contain any injunction from him to do so. This leads us to our major conclusions from studying the texts of the New Testament.

13.2 The Varying Importance of Exorcism

It is obvious that the New Testament should take pride of place in our desire to understand the role and practice of exorcism among early Christians. From this evidence we are in a position to set out some conclusions.

First, exorcism varied in importance among early Christians from being of central importance to being inappropriate and, therefore, irrelevant. On the one hand, most striking is that, for Mark's Gospel, exorcism was profoundly significant and could be described as the most important part of the evangelistic engine; it was seen as the major work of Christian ministry, even surpassing the importance of the verbal proclamation of the kingdom. Our results from Paul and Q are less certain. Paul says nothing overt about exorcism. However, we suggested that Paul's silence has more to do with his letters' dealing with the internal life of his churches rather than with their mission or, like the Gospels, with the story of Jesus than it does with Paul's alleged disinterest in exorcism. In any case, reading between the lines of his letters and from noting that he likely modeled his ministry on Jesus, it is more than reasonable to conclude that exorcism was at least a part of his ministry. We also noted that 1 Corinthians 4:20 is possible evidence that exorcism was an established part of Christianity as Paul knew it.

Even though Q—a document of uncertain status—did not attempt to give exorcism a high priority, in light of readers' being criticized for their simplistic exorcisms that were supposedly empowered by Satan, the author encouraged the readers in their mission, which was to involve exorcism. Then, Hebrews likely carries hints of exorcism being part of the message of salvation, and James probably reflects exorcistic practice familiar from the Synoptics and Jewish traditions. However, in 1 Peter, Jesus' dominion over the demonic is linked with Easter. As these are only hints from letters dealing with other matters, we cannot be certain of our reading of these texts. This is not the case with the Fourth Gospel.

Nothing has prepared us for the ground change we find in reading the Fourth Gospel. In relation to sickness and healing, Jesus and, by implication, the church operated without recourse to the categories of "demon possession" and "exorcism." Not only has the Fourth Gospel left behind the commonplace, prevalent, and ambiguous exorcisms of the ministry of Jesus, and all the groups of Christians we have so far encountered in the Synoptic Gospels; the writer has radically and obviously reinterpreted the ministry of Jesus and its significance. Rather than exorcism being part of the defeat of Satan, the cross functions as the focus of the complete defeat of the evil ruler of this world (John 12:31; 14:30; 16:11). This defeat becomes existential as Jesus draws all people to himself (12:32). In other words, Satan is not confronted in the form of sickness caused by demons but in the form of unbelief inspired by the father of lies. So exorcism is not the response to the demon possession; truth is its antidote. Also, rather than concentrating on sickness and its causes, or even its cures, the Fourth Gospel highlights and focuses on the Healer (note, e.g., 9:1–41). Thus Johannine theology felt that it was possible to fulfill its obligations to the Jesus tradition without acknowledging either that Jesus was an exorcist or that Christians should be involved in exorcism.

Secondly, in response to the suggestion that the early church was reluctant to be involved in exorcism, a number of points can be made. To begin with, there is the very clear evidence from Mark's Gospel that there was anything but reluctance among some Christians to be involved in exorcism. He shows that more than one group of Christians in Rome was involved in exorcism. Then, even though so many of our results from reading Paul remain speculative, perhaps, we can at least say that it is unlikely that Paul could be used as evidence that early Christians were reluctant to become involved in exorcism. However, it is the possible perspective of the readers of Q that come nearest to supporting the view that some early Christians were reluctant to become involved in exorcism. Yet, this reluctance was not fueled by theological conviction. Rather, painful practical experience of criticism from outsiders, bad experience from insiders, and lack of success wore away the resolve of those who were thought to need reminding of the model of Jesus and his supposed intention for his followers to be involved in exorcism. Also, in Matthew we discovered neither a suspicion nor a reluctance in relation to exorcism but, because of adverse experience, perhaps a caution and certainly a lowering of its priority. On coming to the Fourth Gospel, we find not so much a reluctance to be involved in exorcism as a finding it to be inappropriate or an inadequate response to evil. Since demonization in the Fourth Gospel is not the mere affliction of individuals with evil entities but the inability of all to apprehend the truth because of the influence of the father of lies, the demonic is confronted not by exorcism but by truth.

Our third conclusion from examining the New Testament data is that, over time, there appears to have been a diminution of interest in exorcism.[1] From what we can recover about the initial followers of Jesus they were heavily involved in exorcism. We have already noted the similarly strong interest in exorcism in Mark, our earliest Gospel. For Luke, a little later, exorcism was part of a balanced approach to ministry involving both word and deed that continued the ministry of Jesus. Perhaps slightly later still, in the last twenty years of the century, Matthew vests contemporary exorcisms with the same significance as did Jesus and proposes them as part of the evangelistic endeavor; but they are less important than the spoken word. Then, in what is agreed to be the last written, in the Fourth Gospel exorcism is of no interest. However, our conclusion on the diminution of interest in exorcism is rendered uncertain when we take Q into account. Arising in the mid-60s, before Mark, we find a document that reflects a more circumspect approach to exorcism among its readers than Mark. Our information from Paul, 1 Peter, Hebrews, and James is too slight to give us clear insight. It is, therefore, to the second-century material that we will turn in the hope of clarification.

Fourthly, so far as it is possible to tell from the New Testament texts, it does not seem that there is a cultural or socio-economic factor involved in the variation of interest in exorcism.[2] For example, on the one hand, we have Luke from among the cultured and at home with the wealthy who is very interested in exorcism. On the other hand, Johannine Christianity, also with its financial and social security, is not interested in exorcism. Similarly, 1 Peter who writes for poor rural people shows no interest in linking exorcism with defeat of the demonic, while James, also writing for the poor, probably does reflect an interest in exorcism. We will have to rely on the second-century material to help us see if this conclusion can be sustained.

Fifthly, with Paul writing to people in Asia and Greece, Q perhaps originating in the north and west of the sea of Galilee, Mark writing to Roman Christians, Luke and Matthew being from Syrian Antioch, and the Fourth Gospel coming from Ephesus, we do not have enough consistent evidence to suggest that the variation in interest in exorcism is a function of geography. Again, the lens of the second century may be able to help us.

Before turning to the second-century material we can, sixthly, draw together what we have discovered about the function and practice of exorcism where

1. So Maurice F. Wiles, "Miracles in the Early Church," in *Miracles: Cambridge Studies in Their Philosophy and History* (ed. C. F. D. Moule; London: Mowbray, 1965), 221–34, esp. 221–25. Cf. John Dominic Crossan, *The Historical Jesus: The Life of a Mediterranean Jewish Peasant* (North Blackburn, Victoria: Collins Dove / HarperCollins, 1993), 310.

2. Against Eric Sorensen, *Possession and Exorcism in the New Testament and Early Christianity* (WUNT 2.157; Tübingen: Mohr Siebeck, 2002), 9.

it was used among the early Christians reflected in the New Testament documents. In that we have already summarized each of the chapters on the New Testament data,[3] here we only need to bring forward a bare minimum of data in order to gain a sense of perspective on the range of evidence, as well as have representative material for scrutiny with our second-century lens.

Given Paul's language of "signs and wonders," he would probably have seen exorcisms as functioning as salvific experiences through which God brought freedom to people. We have no direct evidence as to how Paul would have performed an exorcism. If he saw himself as dependent on Jesus, and if Luke is to be relied upon, it is likely he would not have imitated Jesus but used the name of Jesus in a magical sense. Q presents Jesus as a model for exorcism, and the readers were to see exorcism as visible expressions of the coming of the kingdom of God and that it involved "gathering" people into the followers of Jesus. Like the community of Q, in the face of criticism that had likely caused them fear and perhaps failure—though not (so far as we can ascertain) reluctance, the readers of Mark are encouraged to model Jesus in being empowered by the Spirit and to see failure as the result of a lack of faith or being "with Jesus." Mark also provides Jesus as a model for the practice of exorcism. However, this is nuanced in advocating prayer—a faith-filled statement dependent on the Holy Spirit directed to the demon—and also in endorsing exorcising "in the name of Jesus," as if it were being performed by Jesus. Thus, put another way, what we see, not only in Mark but also in the other Synoptics, is that in taking up exorcism the early Christians saw themselves depending on Jesus rather than emulating him.

In Luke, as in Q, exorcism was the realization of the coming of God's powerful presence. For Luke, the mere presence of Holy Spirit–empowered Christians was sufficient to perform an exorcism. Once again, exorcisms were seen to depend on rather than copy Jesus. Concomitantly, Luke condemns text-based exorcism or seeking payment for bringing this expression of salvation. Although apparently like other exorcisms, the Christian practice as Luke understands it is distinguished by the sheer number of exorcisms and seeming effortless success because of their direct Spirit empowerment. We can also note that, for Luke, word and deed—including exorcism—are balanced, though the deed can become word. Again, as for Q, Matthew understood exorcism to be the tangible coming of the kingdom or powerful presence of God. From Matthew's Gospel it is clear that exorcism had not been a successful aspect of the activity of the readers. Part of the reticence we noted in Matthew concerning exorcism probably stems from there being peripatetic ecstatic Christians visiting Antioch conducting exorcism (likely among the Christians), whom he thought were "savaging" the community with their perceived libertine lifestyle. In the snippets of information available in the

3. See §§2.8; 3.6; 4.11; 5.10; 6.4; 7.8; 8.4; and 9.11 above.

letter of James, we probably have evidence that Christians were performing exorcisms in the name not only of Jesus but also, like others around them, in the name of God. These exorcisms were not, as we might suppose in a church reflecting either Matthew or Paul's perspective, conducted by members of the community. Rather, like the exorcisms of the Qumran community, they were probably conducted by the "elders."

13.3 The Lens of the Second Century

I have referred a number of times to the image of a lens as a useful metaphor for the way we can use the literature of the second century to help us see aspects of earlier material that might otherwise not be obvious to us. Drawing together the results of our discussion of exorcism among early Christians of the second century (chaps. 10 and 11), it is now possible to assemble our lens, including some polishing available from the second-century critics of Christianity (chap. 12). In doing so, a number of elements emerge.

1. *Early second century: No interests in exorcism.* The vicissitudes of history have left us with a limited and fragmentary witness to the life of the early Christians in the proto-orthodox church of the second century. Notwithstanding, a clear result of our examination of this material is that none of the Apostolic Fathers—the earlier writers—expressed any interest in the subject of exorcism. Of course, none of their pieces of literature of this period had purposes that would require exorcism to be a central theme. Their concern was not so much with the outside world (in relation to which an interest in exorcism could be expected) as with consolidating the little Christian communities around the rim of the Mediterranean. Their interests were the internal matters of, for example, division (*1 Clement*), teaching for baptismal candidates (*Didache*), repentance (*Shepherd of Hermas*), unity (Ignatius), and how the Old Testament was to be interpreted (*Barnabas*).[4] Yet, in that some of them make passing reference to Jesus' ministry or mention demons, for example, and also especially since they were most probably aware of Synoptic traditions, it remains surprising, if not a little short of astounding, that the subject found no explicit treatment—sometimes where we could have expected it—in any of the Apostolic Fathers.

With varying degrees of certainty, we can say this is also true of the early apologists, Quadratus, Aristides, and Diognetus. It might be argued that, in some cases, for example with Quadratus, we may have been arguing from silence. Notwithstanding, there are some texts that give us sufficient information to see that they were not interested in exorcism. In at least the case of the

---

4. So Leslie W. Barnard, *Justin Martyr: His Life and Thought* (London: Cambridge University Press, 1967), 1.

Didache, the absence of any interest in the miracles, including exorcism, was probably part of a deliberate distancing of Christianity from the miraculous. Along with the implication being that Jesus was the only miracle-worker, miracles are associated with false messiahs, false Christians, and false Christianity. The Didachist is promoting a miracles-free Christianity, ruling out an interest in exorcism. From the *Preaching of Peter* we can see that exorcism was not important, probably because Jesus was seen as a covenant maker, and that the mission of the church was understood to amount to speaking. From what we have seen of exorcism in the early second century, it could not be concluded that it was important in the mission and expansion of the church.

2. *The demonic is otherwise defeated.* Often influenced by the Fourth Gospel or at least breathing the same air, other material spread across the period deals with the demonic in ways other than by exorcism. In *Barnabas*, from Alexandria toward the end of the first century, there is possibly a desire to downplay miracles similar to that seen in the *Didache*. For Barnabas restricts miracles to the exodus and Jesus' ministry. Nevertheless, the demonic is mentioned, but it is the notion of salvation as God coming to dwell in a person that rids a person of the demonic. There is no mention of exorcism; miracles are not at all significant in relation to mission, save perhaps to be a distraction (cf. *Barn.* 4.14). The *Shepherd*, coming from around the turn of the first and second centuries, uses the category of demon possession but never considers exorcism. Instead, perhaps sharing the same pool of dualistic ideas as the Fourth Gospel, this writer sees the demonic defeated not through a power-encounter but through what could be called self-applied moral or intellectual exorcism involving behavioral and cognitive exercises of faith and repentance.

What is notable from Athenagoras later in the century is that the church with which he was familiar may not have been known for its miracles or exorcisms for he did not see the need to defend miracles before the skeptical Marcus Aurelius. At least in relation to dealing with demons we saw that freedom from them comes about through worship of God and truth or right thinking. Again, from Clement of Alexandria, the perspective is that demons are driven away not by exorcism, which is not mentioned, but in the process of conversion—when Jesus, the Word of God, takes up residence in a person, or the person receives the Truth, displacing the demonic.

3. *Mid-second century: Renewed interest begins in Rome.* One of the most significant results of our study of the second century is that, with the longer ending of Mark (dependent on all four Gospels), we came to the first document of proto-mainstream second-century Christianity to express considerable interest in exorcism, both in relation to Jesus and his immediate, as well as later, followers. The miracles are proofs of belief and are evidence of a unity between Jesus and his followers so that it is as if Jesus (perhaps understood to be his Spirit) were performing the miracles. Thus the exorcisms could be said to be regarded as the result of, or even inherent in, the message.

Then, a decade or so later in Rome, with Justin Martyr we have a demonology and an approach to exorcism reminiscent of the Synoptic Gospels. Indeed, Justin probably considered exorcism to be the most common and important form of Christian healing and the most important evangelistic weapon in a demon-infested world. Notwithstanding, even though exorcism was important to Justin, reflecting Johannine theology, he also offers truth as the antidote to demons inspiring error. Perhaps, then, in Justin we see the notions that the deranged can be exorcised and the deceived challenged with the truth in happy coexistence.

Justin also alludes to baptism-conversion as the general defeat of, or protection from, the demonic for an individual. Nevertheless, it is to be noted that, in giving evidence for the defeat of demons, he points not to baptism but to exorcism "in the name of Jesus Christ." Thus we see that, while baptism is being associated with exorcism—perhaps even inadvertently—the nature of that relationship is not clear and will not find explicit treatment, until after our period.[5] For it is not until the very end of our period, perhaps in Alexandria, that the *Apostolic Tradition* provides evidence of exorcisms being conducted as a preliminary to baptism.

Tatian, in the beginning of the third quarter of the second century, is particularly interesting. His experience was probably that demons were dispatched from a person when they encountered the power of the "word of God" or Christian truth. Given that Jesus is said to have conducted exorcisms by "the word," we can suppose that Tatian saw Christian exorcism as modeled on that of Jesus.

In Irenaeus, also writing in the last quarter of the second century, we come to considerable evidence of a high point of interest in exorcism among early Christians in the period. That is, like Justin Martyr, and reminiscent of the Synoptic Gospels, he gives evidence that both mainline as well as other Christians conducted exorcism—probably consisting of at least a verbal threat to the offending demon that involved no potions but used the name of Jesus, as well as prayer and fasting in difficult cases. However, Irenaeus claims the use of the power of God and the association with truth as the unique feature of the exorcisms of which he approves. They were also conducted free of charge with sympathy and compassion and, along with other miracles, perhaps were the most important aspect of evangelism. There is no hint of a special rite of exorcism associated with initiation into Christianity. It is of particular interest to note that Irenaeus, taking up discussion of exorcism, shows that the

5. Elizabeth A. Leeper, "From Alexandria to Rome: The Valentinian Connection to the Incorporation of Exorcism as a Prebaptismal Rite," *VC* 44 (1990): 6–24; and Elizabeth A. Leeper, "Exorcism in Early Christianity" (PhD diss., Duke University, 1991), 59–62. Cf. Hippolytus, *Trad. ap.*, 20.7; Cyril of Jerusalem, *Procat.* 9; *Cat.* 16.19; Augustine, *Pecc. merit.* 1.34. See also Christine Trevett, *Montanism: Gender, Authority and the New Prophecy* (Cambridge: Cambridge University Press, 1996), 157.

proto-orthodox Christian exorcisms he represents were seen to be much like those conducted by others.

4. *Problems at Antioch.* If, as is generally thought, Matthew is to be located in late first-century Antioch, we have seen that his adverse experience with the miracles of false Christians there caused him to lower the importance of exorcism. Around the turn of the century, the Didachist, also probably in Antioch and with the same experience, went as far as relegating exorcism to false Christianity. Early in the second century, the letters of Ignatius give us little information other than that the work of Satan is associated with false doctrine and that there was an approach to the defeat of the demonic reminiscent of Johannine theology. Late in the second century, Theophilus of Antioch also associates demonization with false belief. Sometimes, in a dialogue with those deceived, there was an exorcism using "the name of the true God." (Along with James, this is evidence that both Jews as well as Christians successfully carried out exorcism in this way.) More often, according to Theophilus, the deceived were "awakened" in other unspecified ways. In line with this treatment of the deceived, we can note that the critical opponents of the Montanists in the mainline church saw their "Christianity" as demonic and used exorcism against them rather than as part of their mission to the outsiders.

5. *The critical element.* To these major elements of our lens, another can be added from the critics of Christianity. These outside critics are particularly helpful in seeing how late second-century Christianity was viewed in relation to exorcism. From the surviving fragments of criticism up until the end of the third quarter of the second century we gain the impression that Christianity was not known for any involvement in exorcism. This conclusion correlates with one of our conclusions from Christian writers: that it was not until well into the second century that Christian writers express an interest in exorcism. Then, in light of what we learn from Celsus, writing about his knowledge from Alexandria, it is reasonable to conclude that, in the latter part of the second century, exorcism among "orthodox" Christians in that city was indistinguishable from other exorcisms: spell texts, foreign names, and rites including the act of blowing, to perform exorcisms for financial gain. We could add here that, keeping in mind the aversion to text-based exorcism we noted in Luke, it is likely there was an ongoing interest among some Christians in such exorcisms not represented in the literature we have been surveying. From Lucian, we have learned that, though described in terms of being susceptible to charlatans and tricksters, the Egyptian Christianity known to Lucian had probably made itself known to outsiders at least for its involvement in exorcism. However, we have just seen from Galen's perspective, the late second-century Christianity he knew in Rome is likely to have had no obvious interest in miracles or exorcism.

Considering the material of this part of our study from another perspective, we see no socio-economic correlations that would explain the varying interest in exorcism. For example, neither the *Shepherd*, coming from the lower levels of society; nor the *Didache*, coming from a relatively wealthy community; nor the highly educated writer of the *Letter to Diognetus*; nor Clement of Alexandria, one of the most educated early fathers working in a wealthy setting, showed any interest in exorcism, even though Clement, for example, deals with the problem of spirits in a person. On the other hand, Irenaeus, a well-educated person in a cultured city, is particularly interested in exorcism, and the educated philosopher Justin Martyr thought exorcism was the most important weapon Christians possessed against the demon-infested world.

Rather than a socio-economic factor being related to an interest in exorcism, there seems to be a geographical pattern in which Rome features as the place of interest in the subject. It can even be reasonably argued that Tatian and Irenaeus gained their interest in exorcism from when they were in the city. Keeping chronology in mind, the time when the longer ending of Mark became established, probably in Rome, marks the beginning of the obvious renewed interest in exorcism in the second century, which may first be seen in Justin. Can we not speculate, then, that on the rediscovery of Mark with its longer ending, there was a renaissance of interest in exorcism in that city, an interest that found its way to Lyons in the West and Syria in the East?[6] However, by late in the second century, Galen's knowledge of Christianity in Rome apparently did not include miracles or exorcism.

13.4 A View through the Lens

The conclusions to which we have come in the previous section have value in themselves in helping us understand exorcism in the second-century proto-orthodox church. Nevertheless, our particular interest in this material is that it provides us with a literary lens through which, with sensitivity, we can look back with greater insight to note not only what we might have missed but also to have other aspects confirmed concerning exorcism in the first-century churches represented by the New Testament documents. Looking back through this lens of second-century literature the following points appear most significant in nuancing and adding to our conclusions so far.

To begin with, a number of aspects of what we saw in the New Testament documents are confirmed.

- We have found no evidence to change our view that exorcism did not see an "extraordinary flowering" in early Christianity. Beyond the Synoptic

6. This conclusion matches the view of Arthur J. Bellinzoni, "The Gospel of Matthew in the Second Century," *SecCent* 9 (1992): 197–258, esp. 254–56, that only from the middle of the second century did the Gospel of Matthew come to be used instead of pre-Synoptic traditions.

Gospels, the dearth of Christian material on exorcism up until the early part of the second century prevents us from affirming any particular flourishing of exorcism in the proto-orthodox church.

- It is not possible to say that exorcism was the primary engine of evangelism, "a very powerful method of mission and propaganda."[7] Only in some churches was exorcism used and in fewer was it seen to be of such significance.

- The reluctance or caution regarding exorcism that we saw in some traditions in the New Testament—the first readers of Q and Matthew—is also reflected in the later literature, as in, for example, the *Didache*. The second-century lens confirms this reluctance to be part of an endeavor to express a distance from a false Christianity and such associated phenomena. What evidence we have suggests that this was particularly evident at Antioch. However, we must not lose sight of the considerable interest in exorcism that is reflected in the Synoptic traditions where, at least in Mark, there was anything but reluctance regarding exorcism.

- Our discussion of exorcism in Justin Martyr and Irenaeus showed that Christian and non-Christian exorcism could be taken as much the same. This, along with our discussion of the debate between Celsus and Origen, brings into sharper relief Luke's struggle with borderline clashes between approaches to exorcism that appeared similar—those that were text and incantational based and those that depended in some way on the direct presence of Jesus.[8]

- We can see more clearly that there were other ways in which the demonic was confronted. Thus, through the lens of the literature of the second century, the great anomaly of the Fourth Gospel's avoidance of exorcism is less startling and more readily explicable. For many Christians, demonic encounters were not confined to individual maladies but, alternatively, involved theological error as, for example, also in Ignatius. In turn, the demonic was not confronted by an exorcist but by an encounter with God in Jesus through conversion or, more generally expressed, with the Truth. It is not that there was a reluctance to become involved in exorcism, perhaps because of an increasing intellectual sophistication, but an understanding that the demonic could be doctrinal and dealt with and defeated other than through exorcism. In this approach to exorcism, we can see more clearly that, while Jesus may have been considered of profound and central importance to Christianity, the modeling of his ministry was not seen to be important by large sections of the church.

7. Adolf von Harnack, *The Expansion of Christianity in the First Three Centuries* (2 vols.; 1904–1905; repr., New York: Arno, 1972), 1:160.

8. Stephen Benko, *Pagan Rome and the Early Christians* (Bloomington: Indiana University Press, 1986), chap. 5, "Magic and Early Christianity."

- Concerning the practice of exorcism itself, using the lens of the second-century literature, we are able to affirm that there was a variety of approaches that, like the Jews and even the pagans, involved using the name of God, as in James (cf. Theophilus) as well as "in the name of Jesus."

One of the notable results of our using the second-century lens can be the revision of the impression from the New Testament literature that the interest in exorcism was diminishing. For, although writers of the early part of the second century showed no interest in exorcism, a revival of interest, centered on Rome, seems to have taken place in the middle of the century with the rediscovery of the Gospel of Mark with its recently produced new ending. Taking a longer-term perspective to include the first two centuries of the Christian church, it seems reasonable to conclude that what we see in the New Testament as a diminution of interest is likely to be a witness to the fluctuating fortunes of exorcism, much in the same way that over the centuries since there has been a varying interest in such phenomena. In turn, from the second-century Christian literature, as well as that from the critics, we have seen that it is highly likely that the church was, at times, and in different places, not known for its interest in miracles and exorcism. Again, this confirms what we see in the Fourth Gospel, that it was thought possible for a church to have no interest in a ministry of exorcism.

Keeping in mind the narrow base of this study, our second-century lens also helps us see how different streams of the church treated the Jesus traditions in shaping their theology and practice. We have seen that one section of the church (Mark) gave great attention to Jesus being an exorcist as well as to the importance of exorcism in the ministry of the church, while another (the Fourth Gospel) felt able to ignore exorcism completely. In the second century we see this even more clearly. In *1 Clement*, for example, even though there is obvious knowledge of Synoptic traditions, interest in miracles (including exorcism) has all but disappeared, mission being seen as preaching without any appeal to miracle. Similarly, the *Preaching of Peter* shows interest in neither Jesus as a miracle-worker or exorcist nor in the mission of the church being other than proclamation.

Thus, our second-century lens has shown us that the function of Jesus in early Christianity was much more varied than we might conclude from the New Testament, which is headed and dominated by biography-like texts that place the life of Jesus and his ministry at the heart of understanding the nature and practice of Christianity. What may be adumbrated in Paul—a relatively low interest in the life and ministry of Jesus—finds obvious expression and treatment in the second century: Gospel narrative traditions did not exert a very strong influence on the early Christians. That is, the early church found itself able to be highly selective, emphasizing or ignoring not only various aspects of the Jesus tradition in its life and ministry but also, in the case of Theophilus of Antioch, failing even to mention him. This observation enables us to see more clearly that the nature of the ministry of the historical Jesus was far less determinative—was not everywhere the imperative—for early Christian ministry than some of the Gospels writers would lead us to suppose. Thus, while Mark, Luke, and (more cautiously) Matthew exhorted their readers to use Jesus as a model for exorcism, Johannine theology did not. Moreover, where Jesus was a model for exorcism it was not his precise technique that was axiomatic.[9]

Perhaps, after all, Rudolf Bultmann was not far wide of the mark in suggesting that it was the existence of Jesus that was of fundamental importance to Christianity, not what he did or even said. In *Jesus and the Word* he may well have captured the essence of what we have seen in this study. That is, Jesus—and we have seen this reflected in considerable sections of the early church—was not interested in his work but concerned with the end or purpose of that work.[10] Then, from what we have seen of the treatment of the theme of exorcism by various writers in the first two centuries of the proto-orthodox church, while Jesus remained important, they felt they could reflect this not by reproducing his words or works, but in applying such aspects of their received traditions reflecting him that enabled them to be faithful to their seeing and proclaiming him as Savior.

13.5 Contemporary Coda

This has been an historical study—an attempt to understand the obviously conflicting data regarding the place and practice of exorcism among early Christians represented by the New Testament documents. If I have been successful in allowing readers to view the apparently disordered material from the appropriate vantage points, it will have become inescapably clear that some early Christians, such as those reflected in Mark's Gospel, took exorcism to be of profound importance in understanding Jesus, as well his and their own mission. Others, such as those reflected in the Fourth Gospel, did not. Though retaining demon possession as a category to describe the presence of evil in

9. In relation to the words of Jesus, see Leon E. Wright, *Alterations of the Words of Jesus, as Quoted in the Literature of the Second Century* (HHM 25; Cambridge, MA: Harvard University Press, 1952), 116–17: "The words of Jesus were for the early Christians 'Spirit' and they were 'life.' These words were freely drawn upon and adapted, without literal restraints, in their uniquely authoritative ministry to the 'felt needs' of the Christian community." See also the conclusions of E. P. Sanders, *The Tendencies of the Synoptic Tradition* (SNTSMS 9; Cambridge: Cambridge University Press, 1969), esp. 274–75.

10. Rudolf Bultmann, *Jesus and the Word* (1926; trans. Louise Pettibone Smith and Erminie Huntress Lantero from 2nd German ed., 1934; London and Glasgow: Collins / Fontana; New York: Charles Scribner's Sons, 1958), 15.

a person, exorcism was not seen as the appropriate response. What our sec-ond-century literary lens brought into sharper focus was that the Markan-like perspective—later privileged by the position given to the Synoptic Gospels in the New Testament canon—was set aside by some early Christians. They felt able to respond to the demonic and traditions about Jesus in a quite different way from the initial followers and earliest interpreters of Jesus. In broad terms, rather than emulating Jesus and confronting the demonic either as he did or "in the name of Jesus" (as if he were the exorcist), the demonic (understood as error) was challenged by the Truth. Between these two poles were those early Christians who, like those represented by Matthew, were more cautious.

Counting myself among those who see the canon of Scripture, especially the New Testament, as one—though not the only—informant of contemporary Christian theology,[11] and also having a personal concern for the theological and pastoral implications of any New Testament study, I take it to be a happy obligation to consider briefly some contemporary corollaries of what we have seen in the texts.

I remain convinced by the testimony of credible witnesses and reasonable arguments,[12] as well as personal experience, that it is judicious to entertain the idea of the existence of some form of destructive spiritual entities not unreasonably designated "evil spirits."[13] Before undertaking this study, I was convinced that "if the contemporary church is to bring healing to the whole person, and be able to confront the great varieties of manifestations of evil in the world, . . . it must be prepared to become involved in exorcism; exorcism has its rightful place as part of the whole ministry given to the Church to push back the frontiers of evil."[14]

In light of this study, I am no longer able to hold this view. It is not, I need to make clear, that I wish to dispense with exorcism, nor do I wish to discourage its use. Rather, insofar as I allow the whole New Testament canon to inform my views on exorcism and the demonic, I am obliged to recognize that it has provided the church with a range of options for understanding and dealing with the demonic. I concede that the church may confront the demonic in the form of an exorcism *or* in the form of Truth.[15] Indeed, the point at which

11. E.g., John Macquarrie, *Principles of Christian Theology* (London: SCM, 1977), 4–18, lists experience, revelation, Scripture, tradition, culture, and reason as the formative factors of Christian theology.

12. E.g., Graham Dow, "The Case for the Existence of Demons," *Chm* 94 (1980): 199–208; Macquarrie, *Principles*, 237–38, 262–63. Cf. Phillip H. Wiebe, "Finite Spirits as Theoretical Entities," *Religious Studies*, 40 (2004): 341–50; and Phillip H. Wiebe, *God and Other Spirits: Intimations of Transcendence in Christian Experience* (New York: Oxford University Press, 2004).

13. More fully, see Graham H. Twelftree, *Christ Triumphant: Exorcism Then and Now* (London: Hodder & Stoughton, 1985), chap. 6, "Exorcism Now?"

14. Twelftree, *Christ Triumphant*, 191.

15. In a private communication, Mark Roberts drew my attention to the approach, e.g., of Neil Anderson, *Victory over the Darkness* (Ventura, CA: Regal, 1990), which encourages encounters with the truth instead of any form of exorcistic power-encounter.

we can stand and observe the greatest order in the data of the New Testament is in recognizing that early Christians would agree that evil, expressed in derangement or deceit, is to be confronted with the divine.

Besides this most important corollary, for those who consider that exorcism remains an important aspect of Christian ministry there are three other particular corollaries that follow from this study.[16] First, in contrast to some writers in the ancient world, New Testament writers are remarkably restrained in both their interest, and the imagery they use, in their demonology.[17] For example, Lucian's graphic description of a demon (*Philops.* 31; cf. 16) and the whole of the *Testament of Solomon* stand in stark contrast to the New Testament, where little interest is shown in demons and demonology except where it relates to soteriology. Instead, the focus of attention on God's salvation in Jesus redirects attention away from demons and speculation on the causes of various illnesses. This is particularly evident in the Fourth Gospel where the focus of attention is on the healer and not on the disease.

The contemporary church would do well to follow the example of the early church, not to ignore the demonic, but to focus attention on Jesus, who defeats the demonic. Undue concern and involvement with the demonic has often been seen as opening oneself up to its influence. The well-known passage of C. S. Lewis from his preface to *The Screwtape Letters* bears repeating here.

> There are two equal and opposite errors into which our race can fall about the devils. One is to disbelieve in their existence. The other is to believe, and to feel an excessive and unhealthy interest in them. They themselves are equally pleased by both errors and hail a materialist or a magician with the same delight.[18]

Karl Barth issued a similar warning that the Christian and the theologian "must not linger or become too deeply engrossed [in the demonic, as] . . . there is the imminent danger that in so doing we ourselves might become just a little or more than a little demonic."[19] In other words, we should pay as little attention to the demonic as is pastorally possible. Yet we should confront the demonic as much as is pastorally required.

Secondly, one of the noticeable, though not entirely unique, aspects of the exorcistic technique of Jesus and the early Christians was its extreme brevity. For Jesus, this probably arose out of his sense of power-authority over the demonic; for the early Christians it came from their sense of reliance on Jesus. In

---

16. More fully on contemporary implications arising out of the study of exorcism in the New Testament, see Twelftree, *Christ Triumphant*, 178–93.

17. On demonology in antiquity, see the essays in Lange.

18. C. S. Lewis, *The Screwtape Letters* (Rev. ed.; New York: Collier, 1982), 3.

19. Karl Barth, *Church Dogmatics*, III/3 (Edinburgh: T&T Clark, 1961), 519. See also, "Deliver Us from Evil": General Audience of Pope Paul VI, November, 15, 1972, reported in *L'Osservatore Romano*, November 23, 1972.

relation to the contemporary church we can probably conclude that verbosity is an indication of spiritual powerlessness and a lack of discernment.

Finally, in line with others in the period, we have seen that the New Testament writers held the conviction that *exorcism was a confrontation between the divine and the demonic* in which the demonic was defeated. In the exorcisms among early Christians the incantation, the words or prayers of the exorcist were important, not because of any inherent "power" to evict the demon, but because they brought about a confrontation between Jesus and the demonic. To pick up this trajectory today would be to conduct exorcisms so that the demon is confronted not by words, the exorcist, the sacraments, the Lord's Prayer, nor even the church—but by Jesus. As Tertullian, at the end of our period, put it: The demonic "is defeated by the pressure of divine grace."[20]

20. Tertullian, *An.* 57.5.

Select Bibliography

Adinolfi, Marco. "L'esorcismo di Gesù in Mc 1,21–28 e i quattro esorcismi di Apollonio riferiti da Filostrato." *SBFLA* 42 (1992): 49–65.

Aichinger, Hermann. "Zur Traditionsgeschichte der Epileptiker-Perikope Mk 9, 14–29 par, Mt 17, 14–21 par, Lk 9, 37–43a." In *Probleme der Forschung*, edited by Albert Fuchs, 114–23. Vienna: Herold, 1978. Also in *SNTSU* 1 (1978): 110–53.

Albl, Martin C. "'Are Any among You Sick?' The Health Care System in the Letter of James." *JBL* 121 (2002): 123–43.

Ambrozic, Aloysius M. "New Teaching with Power (Mk 1.27)." In *Word and Spirit: Essays in Honour of David Michael Stanley*, edited by J. Plenik, 113–49. Willowdale, ON: Regis College, 1975.

Anderson, Graham. *Sage, Saint and Sophist: Holy Men and Their Associates in the Early Roman Empire*. London and New York: Routledge, 1994.

Annen, Franz. "Die Dämonenaustreibungen Jesu in den synoptischen Evangelien." *Theologische Berichte* 5 (1976): 107–46.

———. *Heil für die Heiden: Zur Bedeutung und Geschichte der Tradition vom besessenen Gerasener (Mk 5,1–20 par.)*. Frankfurt: Knecht, 1976.

Arnold, Clinton E. *Ephesians: Power and Magic: The Concept of Power in Ephesians in Light of Its Historical Setting*. Cambridge: Cambridge University Press, 1989.

———. *Powers of Darkness: Principalities and Powers in Paul's Letters*. Downers Grove, IL: InterVarsity, 1992.

———. "Returning to the Domain of the Powers: *Stoicheia* as Evil Spirits in Galatians 4:3,9." *NovT* 38 (1996): 55–76.

Asahu-Ejere, Kingsley. *The Kingdom of God and Healing-Exorcism (Mt 4:17–5:12)*. Frankfurt am Main: P. Lang, 2003.

Aune, David E. "Magic in Early Christianity." *ANRW* II.23.2 (1980): 1507–57.

Avemarie, Friedrich. "Warum treibt Paulus einen Dämon aus, der die Wahrheit sagt? Geschichte und Bedeutung des Exorzismus zu Philippi (Act 16, 16–18)." In Lange, 550–76.

Bächli, Otto. "'Was habe ich mit Dir zu schaffen?' Eine formelhafte Frage im A.T. und N.T." *TZ* 33 (1977): 69–80.

Baltensweiler, Heinrich. "'Wer nicht gegen uns (euch) ist, ist für uns (euch)': Bemerkungen zu Mk 9,40 und Lk 9,50." *TZ* 40 (1984): 130–36.

Barnard, Leslie W. "Athenagoras, Galen, Marcus Aurelius, and Celsus." *CQR* 168 (1967): 168–81.

Barrett-Lennard, R. J. S. *Christian Healing after the New Testament: Some Approaches to Illness in the Second, Third, and Fourth Centuries.* Lanham, MD: University Press of America, 1994.

Bartlett, David Lyon. "Exorcism Stories in the Gospel of Mark." PhD diss., Yale University, 1972.

Bauernfeind, Otto. *Die Worte der Dämonen im Markusevangelium.* BWANT 44. Stuttgart: Kohlhammer, 1927.

Bell, Catherine. *Ritual: Perspective and Dimensions.* New York and Oxford: Oxford University Press, 1997.

Benko, Stephen. "Early Christian Magical Practices." SBLSP 21 (1982): 9–14.

———. "Pagan Criticism of Christianity during the First Two Centuries A.D." *ANRW* II.23.2 (1980): 1055–118.

Benoit, Pierre. "Pauline Angelology and Demonology: Reflexions on the Designations of the Heavenly Powers and on the Origin of Angelic Evil according to Paul." *RelSBul* 3 (1983): 1–18.

Berger, Klaus. *Die Auferstehung des Propheten und die Erhöhung des Menschensohns: Traditionsgeschichtliche Untersuchungen zur Deutung des Geschickes Jesu in frühchristlichen Texte.* SUNT 13. Göttingen: Vandenhoeck & Ruprecht, 1976.

Berkhof, Hendrikus. *Christ and the Powers.* Scottdale, PA: Herald, 1962.

Best, Ernest. "Exorcism in the New Testament and Today." *Biblical Theology* [Belfast] 27 (1977): 1–9.

Betz, Hans Dieter. "Eine Episode im Jüngsten Gericht (Mt 7,21–23)." *ZTK* 78 (1981): 1–30.

———. "Jewish Magic in the Greek Magical Papyri (PGM VII. 260–271)." In *Envisioning Magic: A Princeton Seminar and Symposium,* edited by Peter Schäfer and Hans G. Kippenberg, 45–63. Leiden: Brill, 1997. Repr., pages 187–205 in Betz, *Gesammelte Aufsätze,* part 4, *Antike und Christentum.* Tübingen: Mohr Siebeck, 1998.

Bieringer, Reimund, D. Pollefeyt, and F. Vandecasteele-Vanneuville, eds. *Anti-Judaism and the Fourth Gospel: Papers of the Leuven Colloquium, 2000.* Jewish and Christian Heritage Series 1. Assen: Royal Van Gorcum, 2001.

Black, Matthew. "*Pasai exousiai autō hypotagēsontai.*" In *Paul and Paulinism: Essays in Honour of C. K. Barrett,* edited by M. D. Hooker and S. G. Wilson, 74–82. London: SPCK, 1982.

Blackburn, Barry L. *Theios Anēr and the Markan Miracle Traditions.* WUNT 2.40. Tübingen: Mohr Siebeck, 1991.

Böcher, Otto. *Christus Exorcista: Dämonismus und Taufe im Neuen Testament.* BWANT 16. Stuttgart: Kohlhammer, 1972.

———. *Dämonenfurht und Dämonenabwehr: Ein Beitrag zur Vorgeschichte der christlichen Taufe.* BWANT 10. Stuttgart: Kohlhammer, 1970.

———. *Das Neue Testament und die dämonischen Mächte.* SBS 58. Stuttgart: KBW, 1972.

———. "Wölfe in Schafspelzen: Zum religionsgeschichtlichen Hintergrund von Matth. 7, 15." *TZ* 24 (1968): 405–26.

Bokser, Baruch M. "Wonder-Working and the Rabbinic Tradition: The Case of Hanina ben Dosa." *JSJ* 61 (1985): 42–92.

Bolt, Peter G. *Jesus' Defeat of Death: Persuading Mark's Early Readers.* SNTSMS 125. Cambridge and New York: Cambridge University Press, 2003.

———. "Jesus, the Daimons and the Dead." In *The Unseen World: Christian Reflections on Angels, Demons and the Heavenly Realm*, edited by Anthony N. S. Lane, 75–102. Grand Rapids: Baker, 1996.

Bonner, Campbell. "The Technique of Exorcism." *HTR* 36 (1943): 39–49.

———. "The Violence of Departing Demons." *HTR* 37 (1944): 334–36.

Bowersock, Glen Warren. *Greek Sophists in the Roman Empire.* Oxford: Clarendon, 1969.

Bowman, John. "Exorcism and Baptism." In *A Tribute to Arthur Vööbus: Studies in Early Christian Literature and Its Environment, Primarily in the Syrian East*, edited by Robert H. Fischer, 249–63. Chicago: Lutheran School of Theology at Chicago, 1977.

Bradshaw, Paul F. "Baptismal Practice in the Alexandrian Tradition: Eastern or Western?" In *Living Water, Sealing Spirit: Readings on Christian Initiation*, edited by Maxwell E. Johnson, 82–100. Collegeville, MN: Pueblo / Liturgical Press, 1995).

Brashear, William M. "The Greek Magical Papyri: An Introduction and Survey; Annotated Bibliography (1928–1994)." *ANRW* II.18.5 (1995): 3380–684.

Bream, Howard N. "By the Finger of God: Demon Possession and Exorcism in Early Christianity in Light of Modern Views of Mental Illness." *JR* 34 (1954): 63–64.

Brenk, Frederick E. "The Exorcism at Philippoi in Acts 16.11–40: Divine Possession or Diabolic Inspiration?" *Filología Neotestamentaria* 13 (2000): 3–21.

———. "In the Light of the Moon: Demonology in the Early Imperial Period." *ANRW* II.16.3 (1986): 2068–145.

Bridges, Carl B. "Jesus and Paul on Tolerance: The Strange Exorcist and the Strange Concession." *Stone-Campbell Journal* 1 (1998): 59–66.

Broadhead, Edwin K. "Echoes of an Exorcism in the Fourth Gospel?" *ZNW* 86 (1995): 111–19.

Brown, Peter. "Sorcery, Demons and the Rise of Christianity from Late Antiquity into the Middle Ages." In *Witchcraft, Confession and Accusations*, edited by M. Douglas, 119–46. London: Tavistock, 1970.

Brown, Peter. "The Rise and Function of the Holy Man in Late Antiquity." *JRS* 81 (1971): 80–101.

————. "Sorcery, Demons and the Rise of Christianity: From Late Antiquity into the Middle Ages." In *Religion and Society in the Age of Saint Augustine*, 119–46. London: Faber & Faber, 1972.

Brox, Norbert. "Magie und Aberglaube an den Anfängen des Christentums." *TTZ* 83 (1974): 157–80.

Brucker, Ralph. "Die Wunder der Apostel." *ZNT* 4 (2001): 32–45.

Bühner, Jan.-A. "Jesus und die Antike Magie: Bemerkungen zu M. Smith." *EvT* 43 (1983): 156–75.

Burke, Gary T. "Walter Bauer and Celsus: The Shape of Late Second-Century Christianity." *SecCent* 4 (1984): 1–7.

Burkill, T. A. "Historical Development of the Story of the Syrophoenician Woman." *NovT* 9 (1967): 161–77.

————. "The Syrophoenician Woman: The Congruence of Mk 7 24–31." *ZNW* 57 (1966): 22–37.

Bursey, Ernest James. "Exorcism in Matthew." PhD diss., Yale University, 1992.

Busse, Ulrich. *Die Wunder Propheten Jesus: Die Rezeption, Komposition und Interpretation der Wundertradition im Evangelium des Lukas.* Stuttgart: KBW, 1977.

Caird, George B. *Principalities and Powers: A Study in Pauline Theology.* Oxford: Clarendon, 1956.

Carr, Wesley. *Angels and Principalities: The Background, Meaning, and Development of the Pauline Phrase "hai archai kai hai exousiai."* SNTSMS 42. Cambridge: Cambridge University Press, 1981.

Cavadini, John C. *Miracles in Jewish and Christian Antiquity: Imagining Truth.* Notre Dame, IN: University of Notre Dame Press, 1999.

Cave, C. H. "The Obedience of Unclean Spirits." *NTS* 11 (1964–1965): 93–97.

Collins, Adela Yarbro. "The Origin of Christian Baptism." In *Living Water, Sealing Spirit: Readings on Christian Initiation*, edited by Maxwell E. Johnson, 35–57. Collegeville, MN: Liturgical Press, 1995.

Cook, John G. "In Defence of Ambiguity: Is There a Hidden Demon in Mark 1.29–31?" *NTS* 43 (1997): 184–208.

————. "Some Hellenistic Responses to the Gospels and Gospel Traditions." *ZNW* 84 (1993): 233–54.

Crouzel, Henri. "Celse et Origène à propos des 'démons.'" In *Frontières terrestres, frontières célestes dans l'antiquité*, edited by Aline Rousselle, 331–55. Perpignan: Presses Universitaires de Perpignan, 1995.

Danove, Paul L. *The End of Mark's Story: A Methodological Study.* Leiden: Brill, 1993.

Davies, Stevan L. *Jesus the Healer: Possession, Trance, and the Origins of Christianity.* New York: Continuum, 1995.

Dermience, Alice. "Tradition et rédaction dans la péricope de la Syrophénicienne: Marc 7,24–30." *RTL* 8 (1977): 15–29.

Derrett, J. Duncan M. "Contributions to the Study of the Gerasene Demoniac." *JSNT* 3 (1979): 2–17.

———. "Getting on Top of a Demon (Luke 4:39)." *EvQ* 65 (1993): 99–109.

———. "Law in the New Testament: The Syrophoenician Woman and the Centurion of Capernaum." *NovT* 15 (1973): 161–86.

———. "Legend and Event: The Gerasene Demoniac; An Inquest into History and Liturgical Projection." In *Studia biblica 1978*, part 2, *Papers on the Gospels*, edited by Elizabeth Anne Livingstone, 63–73. JSNTSup 2. Sheffield: JSOT Press, 1980.

Dibelius, Martin. *Die Geisterwelt im Glauben des Paulus*. Göttingen: Vandenhoeck & Ruprecht, 1909.

Dickie, Matthew. *Magic and Magicians in the Greco-Roman World*. New York: Routledge, 2001.

Dillon, Richard J. "'As One Having Authority' (Mark 1:22): The Controversial Distinction of Jesus' Teaching." *CBQ* 57 (1995): 92–113.

Dölger, Franz Joseph. *Der Exorzismus im altchristlichen Taufritual: Eine religionsgeschichtliche Studie*. Studien zur Geschichte und Kultur des Altertums 3:1–2. Paderborn: Ferdinand Schöningh, 1909.

Dondelinger, Patrick. "The Practice of Exorcism in the Church." In *Illness and Healing*, edited by Louis-Marie Chauvet and Miklós Tomka, 58–67. London: SCM; Maryknoll, NY: Orbis Books, 1998.

Dormandy, Richard. "The Expulsion of Legion: A Political Reading of Mark 5:1–20." *ExpTim* 111 (1999–2000): 335–37.

Downing, F. Gerald. "Magic and Scepticism in and around the First Christian Century." In *Magic in the Biblical World: From the Rod of Aaron to the Ring of Solomon*, edited by Todd E. Klutz, 86–99. JSNTSup 245. London and New York: T&T Clark, 2003.

Draper, Jonathan A. "The Jesus Tradition in the Didache." In *The Miracles of Jesus*, edited by David Wenham and Craig Blomberg, 269–87. Gospel Perspectives 5. Sheffield: JSOT Press, 1985.

———. "Torah and Troublesome Apostles in the Didache Community." In *The Didache in Modern Research*, edited by Jonathan A. Draper, 340–63. AGJU 37. Leiden: Brill, 1996.

———. "Weber, Theissen, and 'Wandering Charismatics' in the Didache." *JECS* 6 (1998): 541–76.

Duling, Dennis C. "Solomon, Exorcism, and the Son of David." *HTR* 68 (1975): 235–52.

Dunn, James D. G., and Graham H. Twelftree. "Demon-Possession and Exorcism in the New Testament." *Chm* 94 (1980): 210–25.

Dupont-Sommer, André. "Exorcismes et guérisons dans les écrits de Qumran." In *Congress Volume: Oxford 1959*, edited by G. W. Anderson, 246–61. VTSup 7. Leiden: Brill, 1960.

Eck, Ernst van, and Andries G. van Aarde. "Sickness and Healing in Mark: A Social Scientific Interpretation." *Neot* 27 (1993): 27–54.

Edwards, Mark J. "Three Exorcisms and the New Testament World." *Eranos* 87 (1989): 117–26.

Emmrich, Martin. "The Lucan Account of the Beelzebul Controversy." *WTJ* 62 (2000): 267–79.

Eshel, Esther. "Genres of Magical Texts in the Dead Sea Scrolls." In Lange, 395–415.

Eve, Eric. *The Jewish Context of Jesus' Miracles*. JSNTSup 231. London and New York: Sheffield Academic, 2002.

Farmer, William R. *The Last Twelve Verses of Mark*. SNTSMS 25. Cambridge: Cambridge University Press, 1974.

Fenton, John. "The Order of the Miracles Performed by Peter and Paul in Acts." *ExpTim* 77 (1966): 381–83.

Ferguson, Everett. *Demonology of the Early Christian World*. Symposium Series 12. New York: Edwin Mellen, 1984.

Fiederlein, Friedrich Martin. *Die Wunder Jesu und die Wundererzählungen der Urkirche*. Munich: Don Bosco, 1988.

Fischer, Robert H., ed. *Tribute to Arthur Vööbus: Studies in Early Christian Literature and Its Environment, Primarily in the Syrian East*. Chicago: Lutheran School of Theology at Chicago, 1977. With plates.

Forbes, Chris A. "Pauline Demonology and/or Cosmology? Principalities, Powers and the Elements of the World in their Hellenistic Context." *JSNT* 85 (2002): 51–73.

———. "Paul's Principalities and Powers: Demythologizing Apocalyptic?" *JSNT* 82 (2001): 61–88.

Fox, Robin Lane. *Pagans and Christians*. New York: Knopf, 1987.

Frankfurter, David. "Narrating Power: The Theory and Practice of the Magical *Historiola* in Ritual Spells." In *Ancient Magic and Ritual Power*, edited by Marvin W. Meyer and Paul Mirecki, 457–76. RGRW 129. New York and Leiden: Brill, 1995.

Frend, W. H. C. "Christianity in the Second Century: Orthodoxy and Diversity." *JEH* 48 (1997): 302–13.

Fridrichsen, Anton. *The Problem of Miracle in Primitive Christianity*. Minneapolis: Augsburg, 1972.

Fuchs, Albert. *Die Entwicklung der Beelzebulkontroverse bei den Synoptikern*. SNTSU 5. Linz: Fuchs, 1980.

Gabriel, A. "The Gerasene Demoniac (Mk 5:1–20): A Socio-Political Reading." *BiBh* 22 (1996): 167–74.

Garland, David E. "'I Am the Lord Your Healer': Mark 1:21–2:12." *RevExp* 85 (1988): 327–43.

Garrett, Susan R. *The Demise of the Devil: Magic and the Demonic in Luke's Writings*. Philadelphia: Fortress, 1989.

———. "Light on a Dark Subject and Vice Versa: Magic and Magicians in the New Testament." In *Religion, Science, and Magic: In Concert and in Conflict*, edited by Jacob Neusner, Ernest S. Frerichs, and Paul Virgil McCracken Flesher, 142–65. New York and Oxford: Oxford University Press, 1989.

Gathercole, Simon. "Jesus' Eschatological Vision of the Fall of Satan: Luke 10,18 Reconsidered." *ZNW* 94 (2003): 143–63.

Geller, M. J. "Jesus' Theurgic Powers: Parallels in the Talmud and Incantation Bowls." *JJS* 28 (1977): 141–55.

Gerhardsson, Birger. *The Mighty Acts of Jesus according to Matthew*. Lund: C. W. K. Gleerup, 1979.

Gero, Stephen. "Galen on the Christians: A Reappraisal of the Arabic Evidence." OCP 56 (1990): 371–411.

———. "The So-called Ointment Prayer in the Coptic Version of the Didache: A Re-evaluation." *HTR* 70 (1977): 67–84.

Giesen, Heinz. "Dämonenaustreibungen—Erweis der Nahe der Herrschaft Gottes: Zu Mk 1,21–28." *Theologie der Gegenwart* 32 (1989): 24–37.

Glasswell, Mark E. "The Use of Miracle in the Markan Gospel." In *Miracles: Cambridge Studies in Their Philosophy and History*, edited by Charles F. D. Moule, 149–62. London: Mowbray, 1965.

Gokey, Francis X. *The Terminology for the Devil and Evil Spirits in the Apostolic Fathers*. Patristic Studies 93. Washington, DC: Catholic University of America Press, 1961.

Graf, Fritz. *Magic in the Ancient World*. Revealing Antiquity 10. Cambridge, MA: Harvard University Press, 1997.

———. "Theories of Magic in Antiquity." In *Ancient Magic and Ritual Power*, edited by Marvin W. Meyer and Paul Mirecki, 93–104. RGRW 129. New York and Leiden: Brill, 1995.

Grant, Robert M. *Miracle and Natural Law in Graeco-Roman and Early Christian Thought*. Amsterdam: North-Holland, 1952.

———. "Paul, Galen, and Origen," *JTS* 34 (1983): 533–36.

Grappe, Christian. "Jésus exorciste à la lumière des pratiques et des attentes de son temps." *RB* 110 (2003): 178–96.

Grayston, Kenneth. "Exorcism in the NT." *Epworth Review* 2 (1975): 90–94.

Green, William Scott. "Palestinian Holy Men: Charismatic Leadership and Rabbinic Tradition." *ANRW* II.19.2 (1979): 619–47.

Guijarro, Santiago Oporto. "La dimensión política de los exorcismos de Jesús: La controversia de Belcebú desde la perspective de las ciencias socials." *EstBíb* 58 (2000): 51–77.

———. "The Politics of Exorcism." In *The Social Setting of Jesus and the Gospels*, edited by Wolfgang Stegemann, Bruce J. Malina, and Gerd Theissen, 159–74. Minneapolis: Fortress, 2002.

———. "The Politics of Exorcism: Jesus' Reaction to Negative Labels in the Beelzebul Controversy." *BTB* 29 (1999): 118–29.

Guillemette, Pierre. "La forme des récits d'exorcisme de Bultmann: Un dogme à reconsidérer." *ÉgT* 11 (1980): 177–93.

———. "Mc 1, 24 est-il une formule de défense magique?" *ScEs* 30 (1978): 81–96.

Harnack, Adolf von. *The Expansion of Christianity in the First Three Centuries*. 2 vols. 1904–1905. Repr., New York: Arno, 1972.

Hayden, Daniel R. "Calling the Elders to Pray." *BSac* 138 (1981): 258–66.

Herrmann, Leon. "Les premiers exorcismes juifs et judéo-chrétiens." *Revue de l'Université de Bruxelles*, n.s., 7 (1954): 305–8.

Hiers, Richard H. "Satan, Demons, and the Kingdom of God." *SJT* 27 (1974): 35–47.

Hill, David. "False Prophets and Charismatics: Structure and Interpretation in Matthew 7,15–23." *Bib* 57 (1976): 327–48.

Hills, Julian V. "Luke 10.18—Who Saw Satan Fall?" *JSNT* 46 (1992): 25–40.

Hollenbach, Paul W. "Help for Interpreting Jesus' Exorcisms." SBLSP 32 (1993): 119–28.

———. "Jesus, Demoniacs, and Public Authorities: A Socio-Historical Study." *JAAR* 49 (1981): 567–88.

Howard, J. Keir. *Disease and Healing in the New Testament: An Analysis and Interpretation.* Lanham, MD; New York; and Oxford, UK: University Press of America, 2001.

———. "New Testament Exorcism and Its Significance Today." *ExpTim* 96 (1984–85): 105–9.

Hull, John M. *Hellenistic Magic and the Synoptic Tradition.* SBT 2.28. London: SCM, 1974.

Hüneburg, Martin. *Jesus als Wundertäter in der Logienquelle: Ein Beitrag zur Christologie von Q.* Arbeiten zur Bibel und ihrer Geschichte 4. Leipzig: Evangelische Verlagsanstalt, 2001.

———. "Jesus als Wundertäter: Zu einem vernachlässigtem Aspekt des Jesusbildes von Q." In *The Sayings Source Q and the Historical Jesus,* edited by Andreas Lindemann, 635–48. BETL 158. Louvain: Leuven University Press / Peeters, 2001.

Iwe, John C. *Jesus in the Synagogue of Capernaum: The Pericope and Its Programmatic Character for the Gospel of Mark; An Exegetico-Theological Study of Mark 1:21–28.* Tesi Gregoriana, Serie Teologia 57. Rome: Editrice Pontificia Università Gregoriana, 1999.

Janowitz, Naomi. *Magic in the Roman World: Pagans, Jews, and Christians.* New York and London: Routledge, 2001.

Jefford, Clayton N. *The Sayings of Jesus in the Teaching of the Twelve Apostles.* VCSup 11. Leiden: Brill, 1989.

Jervell, Jacob. "The Signs of an Apostle: Paul's Miracles." In *The Unknown Paul,* 77–95. Minneapolis: Augsburg, 1984.

Johnson, George. "'Kingdom of God' Sayings in Paul's Letters." In *From Jesus to Paul: Studies in Honour of Francis Wright Beare,* edited by Peter Richardson and John C. Hurd, 143–56. Waterloo, ON: Wilfrid Laurier University Press, 1984.

Johnson, Sherman E. "Parallels between the Letters of Ignatius and the Johannine Epistles." In *Perspectives on Language and Text: Essays and Poems in Honor of Francis I. Andersen's Sixtieth Birthday, July 28, 1985,* edited by Edgar W. Conrad and Edward G. Newing, 327–38. Winona Lake, IN: Eisenbrauns, 1987.

Johnston, Wendell G. "Does James Give Believers a Pattern for Dealing with Sickness and Healing?" In *Integrity of Heart, Skillfulness of Hands: Biblical and Leadership Studies in Honor of Donald K. Campbell,* edited by Charles H. Dyer and Roy B. Zuck, 168–74. Grand Rapids: Baker, 1994.

Jonge, Marinus de. "Light on Paul from the *Testaments of the Twelve Patriarchs*." In *The Social World of the First Christians: Essays in Honor of Wayne A. Meeks*, edited by L. Michael White and O. Larry Yarborough, 100–115. Minneapolis: Fortress, 1995.

Kahl, Werner. *New Testament Miracle Stories in Their Religious-Historical Setting: A Religionsgeschichtliche Comparison from a Structural Perspective*. Göttingen: Vandenhoeck & Ruprecht, 1994.

Kampling, Rainer. "Jesus von Nazaret—Lehrer und Exorzist." *BZ* 30 (1986): 237–48.

Käsemann, Ernst. "Die Heilung der Besessenen." *Reformatio* 28 (1979): 7–18.

———. "Die Legitimität des Apostels: Eine Untersuchung zu II Korinther 10–13." *ZNW* 41 (1942): 33–71.

———. "Lukas 11, 14–28." In vol. 1 of *Exegetische Versuche und Besinnungen*, 242–48. Göttingen: Vandenhoeck & Ruprecht, 1960.

Kee, Howard C. "Magic and Messiah." In *Religion, Science, and Magic: In Concert and in Conflict*, edited by Jacob Neusner, Ernest S. Frerichs, and Paul Virgil McCracken Flesher, 121–41. New York and Oxford: Oxford University Press, 1989.

———. *Medicine, Miracle, and Magic in New Testament Times*. SNTSMS 55: Cambridge: Cambridge University Press, 1986.

———. "The Terminology of Mark's Exorcism Stories." *NTS* 14 (1967–68): 232–46.

Kelhoffer, James A. *Miracle and Mission: The Authentication of Missionaries and Their Message in the Longer Ending of Mark*. WUNT 2.112. Tübingen: Mohr Siebeck, 2000.

Kelly, Henry Ansgar. *The Devil at Baptism: Ritual, Theology, and Drama*. Ithaca, NY: Cornell University Press, 1985.

Kelsey, Morton T. *Healing and Christianity: In Ancient Thought and Modern Times*. New York and London: Harper & Row, 1973.

Kertelge, Karl. "Jesus, seine Wundertaten und der Satan." *Conc* 1 (1975): 168–73.

———. *Die Wunder Jesu im Markusevangelium: Eine redaktionsgeschichtliche Untersuchung*. SANT 23. Munich: Kösel, 1970.

Kilgallen, John J. "The Return of the Unclean Spirit (Luke 11,24–26)." *Bib* 74 (1993): 45–59.

Kingsbury, Jack Dean. "Observations on the 'Miracle Chapters' of Matthew 8–9." *CBQ* 40 (1978): 559–73.

Kirchschläger, Walter. "Exorzismus in Qumran?" *Kairos* 18 (1976): 135–53.

———. *Jesu exorzistisches Wirken aus der Sicht des Lukas: Ein Beitrag zur lukanischen Redaktion*. ÖBS 3. Klosterneuburg: Österreichisches KBW, 1981.

Klauck, Hans-Josef. *Magic and Paganism in Early Christianity: The World of the Acts of the Apostles*. Edinburgh: T&T Clark, 2000.

Kleist, J. A. "The Gadarene Demoniacs." *CBQ* 9 (1947): 101–5.

Klutz, Todd E. *The Exorcism Stories in Luke-Acts: A Sociostylistic Reading*. SNTSMS 129. Cambridge: Cambridge University Press, 2004.

———. "The Grammar of Exorcism in the Ancient Mediterranean World: Some Cosmological, Semantic, and Pragmatic Reflections on How Exorcistic Prowess Contributed to the Worship of Jesus." In *Jewish Roots of Christological Monotheism*:

Papers from the St. Andrews Conference on the Historical Origins of the Worship of Jesus, edited by Carey C. Newman, James R. Davila, and Gladys S. Lewis, 156–65. JSJSup 63. Leiden: Brill, 1999.

———. "Reinterpreting 'Magic' in the World of Jewish and Christian Scripture: An Introduction." In *Magic in the Biblical World: From the Rod of Aaron to the Ring of Solomon*, edited by Todd E. Klutz, 1–9. JSNTSup 245. London and New York: T&T Clark, 2003.

Knoch, Otto. *Dem, der glaubt, ist alles möglich: Die Botschaft der Wundererzählungen der Evangelien*. Stuttgart: KBW, 1986.

Knöppler, Thomas. "Paulus als Verkünder fremder δαιμόνια: Religiongeschichtlicher Hintergrund und theologische Aussage von Act 17,18." In Lange, 577–83.

Knox, Wilfred L. "Jewish Liturgical Exorcisms." *HTR* 31 (1938): 191–203.

———. "ΠΕΡΙΚΑΘΑΙΡΩΝ (*Didache* iii 4)." *JTS* 40 (1939): 146–49.

Kollmann, Bernd. *Jesus und die Christen als Wundertäter: Studien zu Magie, Medizin und Schamanismus in Antike und Christentum*. FRLANT 170. Göttingen: Vandenhoeck & Ruprecht, 1996.

Kovacs, Judith L. "Now Shall the Ruler of This World Be Driven Out: Jesus' Death as Cosmic Battle in John 12:20–36." *JBL* 114 (1995): 227–47.

Kruse, Heinz. "Das Reich Satans." *Bib* 58 (1977): 29–61.

Labahn, Michael. "Jesu Exorzismen (Q 11, 19–20) und die Erkenntnis der ägyptischen Magier (Ex 8, 15)." In *The Sayings Source Q and the Historical Jesus*, edited by Andreas Lindemann, 617–33. BETL 158. Louvain: Leuven University Press / Peeters, 2001.

LaGrand, James. "The First of the Miracle Stories according to Mark (1:21–28)." *CurTM* 20 (1993): 479–84.

Lahurd, Carol Schersten. "Biblical Exorcism and Reader Response to Ritual in Narrative." In *The Daemonic Imagination: Biblical Text and Sacred Story*, edited by Robert Detweiler and William G. Doty, 53–63. SR 60. Atlanta: Scholars Press, 1990.

Lamarche, Paul. "Le possédé de Gérasa (Mt 8, 28–34; Mk 5, 1–20; Lc 8, 26–39)." *NRTh* 90 (1968): 581–97.

Lampe, Peter. "Die dämonologischen Implikation von 1 Korinther 8 und 10 vor dem Hintergrund paganer Zeugnisse." In Lange, 584–99.

———. *From Paul to Valentinus: Christians at Rome in the First Two Centuries*. Minneapolis: Fortress, 2003.

———. "Miracles and Early Christian Apologetic." In *Miracles: Cambridge Studies in Their Philosophy and History*, edited by Charles F. D. Moule, 205–18. London: Mowbray, 1965.

———. "Miracles in the Acts of the Apostles." In *Miracles: Cambridge Studies in Their Philosophy and History*, edited by Charles F. D. Moule, 163–78. London: Mowbray, 1965.

Landmann, Salcia. "Exorzismen in der jüdischen Tradition." *ZRGG* 28 (1976): 357–66.

Lang, Friedrich Gustav. "*Sola Gratia* im Markusevangelium: Die Soteriologie des Markus nach 9,14–29 und 10,17–31." In *Rechtfertigung: Festschrift für Ernst Käsemann zum 70. Geburtstag*, edited by Johannes Friedrich, Wolfgang Pöhlmann, and Peter Stuhlmacher, 321–38. Tübingen: Mohr Siebeck; Göttingen: Vandenhoeck & Ruprecht, 1976.

Lange, Armin, Hermann Lichtenberger, and K. F. Diethard Römheld, eds. *Die Dämonen: Die Dämonologie der israelitisch-jüdischen und frühchristlichen Literatur im Kontext ihrer Umwelt / Demons = The Demonology of Israelite-Jewish and Early Christian Literature in the Context of Their Environment*. Tübingen: Mohr Siebeck, 2003.

Langton, Edward. *Essentials of Demonology: A Study of Jewish and Christian Doctrine, Its Origin and Development*. London: Epworth, 1949.

Lanpher, James E. "The Miraculous in Mark: Its Eschatological Background and Christological Function." PhD diss., University of Notre Dame, 1994.

Laus, Therry. "Paul and 'Magic.'" In *Magic in the Biblical World: From the Rod of Aaron to the Ring of Solomon*, edited by Todd E. Klutz, 140–56. JSNTSup 245. London and New York: T&T Clark, 2003.

Lee, Jung Young. "Interpreting the Powers in Pauline Thought." *NovT* 12 (1970): 54–69.

Légasse, Simon. "Les faux prophètes: Matthieu 7, 15–20." *ÉtudFranc* 18 (1968): 205–18.

Leeper, Elizabeth Ann. "Exorcism in Early Christianity." PhD diss., Duke University, 1991.

———. "From Alexandria to Rome: The Valentinian Connection to the Incorporation of Exorcism as a Prebaptismal Rite." *VC* 44 (1990): 6–24.

———. "The Role of Exorcism in Early Christianity." *StPatr* 26 (1993): 59–62.

Léon-Dufour, Xavier. "L'épisode de l'enfant épileptique." In *Études d'évangile*, 183–227. Paris: Seuil, 1965.

Leivestad, Ragnar. *Christ the Conqueror: Ideas of Conflict and Victory in the New Testament*. New York: Macmillan, 1954.

Limbeck, Meinrad. "Jesus und die Dämonen: Der exegetische Befund." *BK* 30 (1975): 7–11.

Lindars, Barnabas. "Rebuking the Spirit." *NTS* 38 (1992): 84–104.

Lips, Hermann von. "Anthropologie und Wunder im Johannesevangelium: Die Wunder Jesu im Johannesevangelium im Unterschied zu den synoptischen Evangelien auf dem Hintergrund johanneischen Menschenverständnisses." *EvT* 50 (1990): 296–311.

Loader, William R. G. "Son of David, Blindness, Possession, and Duality in Matthew." *CBQ* 44 (1982): 570–85.

Love, Stuart L. "Jesus, Healer of the Canaanite Woman's Daughter in Matthew's Gospel: A Social-Scientific Inquiry." *BTB* 32 (2002): 11–20.

Lührmann, Dieter. "Neutestamentliche Wundergeschichten und Antike Medizin." In *Religious Propaganda and Missionary Competition in the New Testament World: Essays Honoring Dieter Georgi*, edited by Lukas Bormann, 195–204. Leiden: Brill, 1994.

MacGregor, George H. C. "Principalities and Powers: The Cosmic Background of Paul's Thought." *NTS* 1 (1954–1955): 17–28.

MacMullen, Ramsay. *Christianizing the Roman Empire (A.D. 100–400)*. New Haven and London: Yale University Press, 1984.

———. *Enemies of the Roman Order: Treason, Unrest, and Alienation in the Empire*. Cambridge, MA: Harvard University Press, 1966.

Mainville, Odette. "Jésus et l'Esprit dans l'oeuvre de Luc: Éclairage à partir d'Ac 2, 33." *ScEs* 42 (1990): 193–208.

Manson, William. "Principalities and Powers: The Spiritual Background of the Work of Jesus in the Synoptic Gospels." *BSNTS* 3 (1952): 7–17.

Manus, Chris U. "Healing and Exorcism: The Scriptural Viewpoint." In *Healing and Exorcism: The Nigerian Experience*, edited by Chris U. Manus, Luke N. Mbefo, and E. E. Uzukwu, 84–104. SISTSym 1. Enugu, Nigeria: Snapp, 1992.

Maquart, F. X. "Exorcism." In *Soundings in Satanism*, assembled by S. J. Sheed, 72–91. New York: Sheed & Ward; London: Mobrays, 1972.

Marcus, Joel. "The Beelzebul Controversy and the Eschatologies of Jesus." In *Authenticating the Activities of Jesus*, edited by Bruce D. Chilton and Craig A. Evans, 247–77. Leiden: Brill, 1999.

———. "The Evil Inclination in the Epistle of James." *CBQ* 44 (1982): 606–21.

Marguerat, Daniel. "Magic and Miracle in the Acts of the Apostles." In *Magic in the Biblical World: From the Rod of Aaron to the Ring of Solomon*, edited by Todd E. Klutz, 100–24. JSNTSup 245. London and New York: T&T Clark, 2003.

Marlé, René. "Victoire du Christ sur les forces du mal." *Esprit et Vie* 104 (1994): 465–79.

Mastin, Brian Arthur. "Scaeva the Chief Priest." *JTS* 27 (1976): 405–12.

McCasland, S. Vernon. *By the Finger of God: Demon Possession and Exorcism in Early Christianity in the Light of Modern Views of Mental Illness*. New York: Macmillan, 1951.

———. "The Demonic Confessions of Jesus." *JR* 24 (1944): 33–36.

———. "Signs and Wonders." *JBL* 76 (1957): 149–52.

McCullar, Scott. "The Path of Membership in the Early Church." *Faith and Mission* 19 (2002): 19–25.

Mees, Michael. "Die Heilung des Kranken vom Bethesdateich aus Joh 5:1–18 in frühchristlicher Sicht." *NTS* 32 (1986): 596–608.

Metzger, Bruce M. "St. Paul and the Magicians." *PSB* 38 (1944): 27–30.

Meyer, Marvin W., and Richard Smith, eds. *Ancient Christian Magic: Coptic Texts of Ritual Power*. Princeton, NJ: Princeton University Press, 1999.

Meyer, Paul D. "The Gentile Mission in Q." *JBL* 89 (1970): 405–17.

Milavec, Aaron. "Distinguishing True and False Prophets: The Protective Wisdom of the Didache." *JECS* 2 (1994): 117–36.

Milik, Józef Tadeusz. "'Prière de Nabonide' et autres écrits d'un cycle de David: Fragments araméens de Qumrân 4." *RB* 63 (1956): 407–15.

Mills, Mary E. *Human Agents of Cosmic Power in Hellenistic Judaism and the Synoptic Tradition*. JSNTSup 41. Sheffield: Sheffield Academic, 1990.

Mitchell, Nathan. "Baptism in the *Didache*." In *The Didache in Context: Essays on Its Text, History, and Transmission*, edited by Clayton N. Jefford, 226–55. NovTSup 77. Leiden and New York: Brill, 1995.

Morrison, Clinton D. *The Powers That Be: Earthly Rulers and Demonic Powers in Romans 13.1–7*. SBT 29. London: SCM, 1960.

Motyer, Stephen. *Your Father the Devil? A New Approach to John and "the Jews."* Carlisle, UK: Paternoster, 1997.

Moule, Charles F. D., ed. *Miracles: Cambridge Studies in Their Philosophy and History*. London: Mowbray, 1965.

Myers, Ched. *Binding the Strong Man: A Political Reading of Mark's Story of Jesus*. Maryknoll, NY: Orbis, 1994.

Nauman, St. Elmo, Jr., ed. *Exorcism through the Ages*. New York: Philosophical Library, 1974.

Neirynck, Frans. "The Miracle Stories in the Acts of the Apostles: An Introduction." In *Les Actes des Apôtres: Traditions, rédaction, théologie*, edited by Jacob Kremer, 169–213. Gembloux: Duculot, 1979.

Neusner, Jacob, Ernest S. Frerichs, and Paul Virgil McCracken Flesher, eds. *Religion, Science, and Magic: In Concert and in Conflict*. New York and Oxford: Oxford University Press, 1989.

Niederwimmer, Kurt. "An Examination of the Development of Itinerant Radicalism in the Environment and Tradition of the Didache." In *The Didache in Modern Research*, edited by Jonathan A. Draper, 321–39. AGJU 37. Leiden and New York: Brill, 1996.

Nielsen, Helge Kjaer. *Heilung und Verkündigung: Das Verständnis der Heilung und ihres Verhältnisses zur Verkündigung bei Jesus und in der ältesten Kirche*. Leiden: Brill, 1987.

Nock, Arthur D. "Greek Magical Papyri." *JEA* 15 (1929): 219–35.

———. "Paul and the Magus." In *The Beginnings of Christianity*, part 1, *The Acts of the Apostles*, edited by F. J. Foakes-Jackson and Kirsopp Lake, 5:164–88. 1933. Repr., Grand Rapids: Baker, 1979.

Obijole, Bayo. "St. Paul's Concept of Principalities and Powers." *BiBh* 15 (1989): 25–39.

Obijole, Olubayo O. "Principalities and Powers in St. Paul's Gospel of Reconciliation." *African Journal of Biblical Studies* 1 (1986): 113–25.

O'Brien, Peter T. "Principalities and Powers: Opponents of the Church." *Evangelical Review of Theology* 16 (1992): 353–84.

Oegema, Gerbern S. "Jesus' Casting Out of Demons in the Gospel of Mark against Its Greco-Roman Background." In Lange, 505–18.

Page, Sydney H. T. *Powers of Evil: A Biblical Study of Satan and Demons*. Grand Rapids: Baker; Leicester: Apollos, 1995.

Park, Eung Chun. *The Mission Discourse in Matthew's Interpretation*. WUNT 2.81. Tübingen: Mohr Siebeck, 1995.

Penney, Douglas L., and Michael O. Wise. "By the Power of Beelzebub: An Aramaic Incantation Formula from Qumran (4Q560)." *JBL* 113 (1994): 627–50.

Perkins, Larry. "'Greater than Solomon' (Matt 12:42)." *TJ* 19 (1998): 207–17.

Pesch, Rudolf. "'Eine neue Lehre aus Macht': Eine Studie zu Mk 1,21–28." In *Evangelienforschung: Ausgewählte Aufsätze deutscher Exegeten*, edited by Johannes Baptist Bauer, 241–76. Graz: Styria, 1968.

———. "The Markan Version of the Healing of the Gerasene Demoniac." *Ecumenical Review* 23 (1971): 349–76.

———. "Zur theologischen Bedeutung der 'Machttaten' Jesu: Reflexionen eines Exegeten." *TQ* 152 (1972): 203–13.

Piepkorn, Arthur C. "Baptism according to the Didache." In *The Didache in Modern Research*, edited by Jonathan A. Draper, 212–22. AGJU 37. Leiden and New York: Brill, 1996.

———. "Charisma in the New Testament and the Apostolic Fathers." *CTM* 42 (1971): 369–89.

Pikaza Ibarrondo, Xabier. "Exorcismo, poder y Evangelio: Trasfondo histórico y eclesial de Mc 9,38–40." *EstBíb* 57 (1999): 539–64.

Pilch, John J. *Healing in the New Testament: Insights from Medical and Mediterranean Anthropology*. Minneapolis: Fortress, 2000.

———. "Sickness and Healing in Luke-Acts." In *The Social World of Luke-Acts: Models for Interpretation*, edited by Jerome H. Neyrey, 182–209. Peabody, MA: Hendrickson, 1991.

Pimentel, Peter. "The 'Unclean Spirits' of St Mark's Gospel." *ExpTim* 99 (1987–88): 173–75.

Piper, Ronald A. "Jesus and the Conflict of Powers in Q: Two Q Miracle Stories." In *The Sayings Source Q and the Historical Jesus*, edited by Andreas Lindemann, 317–49. BETL 158. Louvain: Leuven University Press / Peeters, 2001.

———. "Satan, Demons, and the Absence of Exorcisms in the Fourth Gospel." In *Christology, Controversy, and Community*, edited by David G. Horrell and Christopher M. Tuckett, 253–78. NovTSup 99. Leiden and Boston: Brill, 2000.

Plumer, Eric. "The Absence of Exorcisms in the Fourth Gospel." *Bib* 78 (1997): 350–68.

Praeder, Susan Marie. "Miracle Worker and Missionary: Paul in the Acts of the Apostles." SBLSP 22 (1983): 107–29.

Pulleyn, Simon. "The Power of Names in Classical Greek Religion." *CQ* 44 (1994): 17–25.

Remus, Harold. "Does Terminology Distinguish Early Christian from Pagan Miracles?" *JBL* 101 (1982): 531–51.

———. "Magic or Miracle? Some Second-Century Instances." *SecCent* 2 (1982): 127–56.

────. *Pagan-Christian Conflict over Miracle in the Second Century.* Cambridge, MA: Philadelphia Patristic Foundation, 1983.

Rese, Martin. "Jesus und die Dämonen im Matthäusevengelium." In Lange, 463–75.

Robbins, Vernon K. "Beelzebul Controversy in Mark and Luke: Rhetorical and Social Analysis." *Forum* 7 (1991): 261–77.

Robinson, James M. "The Mission and Beelzebul: Pap. Q 10:2–16; 11:14–23." SBLSP 24 (1985): 97–99.

Roosa, William V. "The Significance of Exorcism in the Gospel of Mark." PhD diss., University of Chicago, 1934.

Rordorf, Willy. "Baptism according to the Didache." In *The Didache in Modern Research*, edited by Jonathan A. Draper, 212–22. AGJU 37. Leiden and New York: Brill, 1996.

Rousseau, John J. "Jesus, an Exorcist of a Kind." SBLSP 32 (1993): 129–53.

Russell, E. A. "The Canaanite Woman and the Gospels (Mt 15:21–28; cf. Mk 7:24–30)." In *Studia biblica 1978*, part 2, *Papers on the Gospels*, edited by Elizabeth Anne Livingstone, 263–300. JSNTSup 2. Sheffield: JSOT Press, 1980.

Russell, Jeffrey Burton. *The Devil: Perceptions of Evil from Antiquity to Primitive Christianity.* Ithaca, NY: Cornell University Press, 1977.

Sanders, James A. "A Liturgy for Healing the Stricken." In *The Dead Sea Scrolls: Hebrew, Aramaic, and Greek Texts with the English Translations*, edited by James H. Charlesworth, vol. 4A, *Pseudepigraphic and Non-Masoretic Psalms and Prayers*, 155–57. PTSDSSP. Tübingen: Mohr Siebeck; Louisville: Westminster John Knox, 1997.

Schenk, Wolfgang. "Tradition und Redaktion in der Epileptiker-Perikope Mk 9 14–29." *ZNW* 63 (1972): 76–94.

Schenke, Ludger. *Die Wundererzählungen des Markusevangeliums.* Stuttgart: KBW, 1974.

Schille, Gottfried. *Die urchristliche Wundertradition: Ein Beitrag zur Frage nach dem irdischen Jesus.* Stuttgart: Calwer, 1967.

Schlier, Heinrich. *Principalities and Powers in the New Testament.* QD 3. Freiburg and New York: Herder; Edinburgh: Nelson, 1961.

Schlosser, J. "L'exorciste étranger (Mc 9.38–39)." *RevScRel* 56 (1982): 229–39.

Schmithals, Walter. "Der Markusschluss, die Verklärungsgeschichte und die Aussendung der Zwölf." *ZTK* 69 (1972): 379–411.

Segal, Alan F. "Hellenistic Magic: Some Questions of Definition." In *Studies in Gnosticism and Hellenistic Religions: Presented to Gilles Quispel on the Occasion of his 65th Birthday*, edited by R. van den Broek and M. J. Vermaseren, 349–75. Leiden: Brill, 1981.

Seitz, Oscar J. F. "Two Spirits in Man: An Essay in Biblical Exegesis." *NTS* 6 (1959–1960): 82–95.

Smith, Jonathan Z. "Towards Interpreting Demonic Powers." *ANRW* II.16.1 (1978): 425–39.

Smith, Morton. *Jesus the Magician.* San Francisco: Harper & Row, 1978.

Smith, Robert H. "Matthew's Message for Insiders: Charisma and Commandment in a First-Century Community." *Int* 46 (1992): 229–39.

Smith, Wesley D. "So-called Possession in Pre-Christian Greece." *TAPA* 96 (1965): 403–26.

Söding, Thomas. "'Wenn ich mit dem Finger Gottes die Dämonen austriebe . . .' (Lk 11,20): Die Exorzismen im Rahmen der Basileia-Verkinündigung Jesu," in Lange, 519–49.

Sommerville, John E. "The Gadarene Demoniac." *ExpTim* 25 (1914): 548–51.

Sorensen, Eric. *Possession and Exorcism in the New Testament and Early Christianity.* WUNT 2.157. Tübingen: Mohr Siebeck, 2002.

Stanton, Graham N. "Jesus of Nazareth: A False Prophet Who Deceived God's People?" In *Jesus of Nazareth: Lord and Christ; Essays on the Historical Jesus and New Testament Christology*, edited by Joel B. Green and Max Turner, 164–80. Grand Rapids: Eerdmans; Carlisle, UK: Paternoster, 1994.

Starobinski, Jean. "The Gerasene Demoniac: A Literary Analysis of Mark 5:1–20." In Roland Barthes et al., *Structural Analysis and Biblical Exegesis: Interpretational Essays*, translated by Alfred M. Johnson Jr., 57–84. Pittsburgh: Pickwick, 1974.

Sterling, Gregory E. "Jesus as Exorcist: An Analysis of Matthew 17:14–20; Mark 9:14–29; Luke 9:37–43a." *CBQ* 55 (1993): 467–93.

Stock, A. "Jesus and the Lady from Tyre: Encounter in the Border District." *Emmanuel* 93 (1987): 336–39, 358.

Strange, William A. "The Sons of Sceva and the Text of Acts 19:14." *JTS* 38 (1987): 97–106.

Stuhlmacher, Peter. "Matthew 28: 16–20 and the Course of Mission in the Apostolic and Postapostolic Age." In *The Mission of the Early Church to Jews and Gentiles*, edited by Jostein Ådna and Hans Kvalbein, 17–43. WUNT 1.127. Tübingen: Mohr Siebeck, 2000.

Tassin, Claude. "Jésus, exorciste et guérisseur." *Spiritus* [Paris] 120 (1990): 285–303.

Taylor, B. E. "Acts 19:14." *ExpTim* 57 (1946): 222.

Theissen, Gerd. *Miracle Stories of the Early Christian Tradition.* Edinburgh: T&T Clark, 1983.

Thevon, Jacques. "A Critical Overview of the Church's Ministry of Deliverance from Evil Spirits." *Pneuma* 18 (1996): 79–92.

Thomas, John Christopher. "The Devil, Disease and Deliverance: James 5.14–16." *JPT* 2 (1993): 25–50.

———. *The Devil, Disease and Deliverance: Origins of Illness in New Testament Thought.* JPTSup 13. Sheffield: Sheffield Academic, 1998.

Toorn, Karel van der. "The Theology of Demons in Mesopotamia and Israel: Popular Belief and Scholarly Speculation," in Lange, 61–83.

Trebilco, Paul R. "Paul and Silas—'Servants of the Most High God' (Acts 16.16–18)." *JSNT* 36 (1989): 51–73.

Trunk, Dieter. *Der messianische Heiler: Eine redaktions- und religionsgeschichtliche Studie zu den Exorzismen im Matthäusevangelium.* HBS 3. Freiburg: Herder, 1994.

Twelftree, Graham H. *Christ Triumphant: Exorcism Then and Now*. London: Hodder & Stoughton, 1985.

———. "ΕΙ ΔΕ . . . ΕΓΩ . . . ΕΚΒΑΛΛΩ ΤΑ ΔΑΙΜΟΝΙΑ . . ." In *The Miracles of Jesus*, edited by David Wenham and Craig Blomberg, 361–400. Gospel Perspectives 6. Sheffield: JSOT Press, 1986.

———. "Exorcism in the Fourth Gospel and the Synoptics." In *Jesus in Johannine Tradition*, edited by Robert T. Fortna and Tom Thatcher, 135–43. Louisville: Westminster John Knox, 2001.

———. *Jesus the Exorcist: A Contribution to the Study of the Historical Jesus*. WUNT 2.54. Tübingen: Mohr Siebeck, 1993.

———. "Jesus the Exorcist and Ancient Magic." In *A Kind of Magic: Understanding Magic in the New Testament and Its Religious Environment*, edited by Michael Labahn and Bert Jan Lietaert Peerbolte, 57–86. European Studies on Christian Origins. LNTS 306. London and New York: T&T Clark, 2007.

———. *Jesus the Miracle Worker: A Historical and Theological Study*. Downers Grove, IL: InverVarsity, 1999.

Valantasis, Richard. "Demons, Adversaries, Devils, Fishermen: The Asceticism of *Authoritative Teaching* (*NHL*, VI,3) in the Context of Roman Asceticism." *JR* 81 (2001): 549–65.

Vencovsky, Jan. "Der gadarenische Exorzismus: Mt 8, 28–34 und Parallelen." *CV* 14 (1971): 13–29.

Versnel, Hendrik S. "Some Reflections on the Relationship Magic—Religion." *Numen* 38 (1991): 177–97.

Verweyen, Hansjürgen. "Die historische Rückfrage nach den Wundern Jesu." *TTZ* 90 (1981): 41–58.

Vogler, Werner. "Dämonen und Exorzismen im Neuen Testament." *Theologische Versuche* 15 (Berlin: Evangelische Verlagsanstalt, 1985): 9–20.

Vögtle, Anton. "The Miracles of Jesus against Their Contemporary Background." In *Jesus in His Time*, edited by Hans Jürgen Schultz, 96–105. London: SPCK, 1971.

Wahlen, Clinton. *Jesus and the Impurity of Spirits in the Synoptic Gospels*. WUNT 2.185. Tübingen: Mohr Siebeck, 2004.

Wall, Robert W. "'The Finger of God': Deuteronomy 9.10 and Luke 11.20." *NTS* 33 (1987): 144–50.

Walzer, Richard. *Galen on Jews and Christians*. London: Oxford University Press, 1949.

Warrington, Keith. *Jesus the Healer: Paradigm or Unique Phenomenon?* Carlisle, UK, and Waynesboro, GA: Paternoster, 2000.

———. "Some Observations on James 5:13–18." *EPTABul* 8 (1989): 160–77.

Weaver, Dorothy Jean. *Matthew's Missionary Discourse: A Literary Critical Analysis*. JSNTSup 38. Sheffield: JSOT Press, 1990.

Welbourn, F. B. "Exorcism." *Theology* 75 (1972): 593–96.

White, L. Michael. "Scaling the Strongman's 'Court' (Luke 11.21)." *Forum* 3 (1987): 3–28.

Whittaker, Molly. "'Signs and Wonders': The Pagan Background." *SE* 5 (TU 103; Berlin: Akademie-Verlag, 1968): 155–58.

Wild, Robert A. "'Put on the Armor of God.'" *TBT* 36 (1998): 365–70.

Wiles, Maurice F. "Miracles in the Early Church." In *Miracles: Cambridge Studies in Their Philosophy and History*, edited by Charles F. D. Moule, 221–34. London: Mowbray, 1965.

Wilhelms, E. "Der fremde Exorzist: Eine Studie über Mark 9.38." *ST* 3 (1949): 162–71.

Wilkinson, John. "The Case of the Bent Woman in Luke 13:10–17." *EvQ* 49 (1977): 195–205.

———. "The Case of the Epileptic Boy." *ExpTim* 79 (1967–68): 39–42.

———. "Healing in the Epistle of James." *SJT* 24 (1971): 326–45.

Williams, Benjamin E. *Miracle Stories in the Biblical Book Acts of the Apostles.* Lewiston, NY: Mellen, 2001.

Willoughby, Harold R. "By the Finger of God: Demon Possession and Exorcism in Early Christianity in Light of Modern Views of Mental Illness." *CH* 20 (1951): 91–92.

Wink, Walter. "Jesus as Magician." *USQR* 30 (1974): 3–14.

———. *Naming the Powers: The Language of Power in the New Testament.* Philadelphia: Fortress, 1984.

Woods, Edward J. *The "Finger of God" and Pneumatology in Luke-Acts.* JSNTSup 205. Sheffield: Sheffield Academic, 2001.

Woodward, Kenneth L. *The Book of Miracles: The Meaning of the Miracle Stories in Christianity, Judaism, Buddhism, Hinduism, Islam.* New York: Simon & Schuster, 2000.

Wróbel, Miroslaw Stanislaw. *Who Are the Father and His Children in JN 8:44 and Its Context?* CahRB 63. Paris: Gabalda, 2005.

Yamauchi, Edwin M. "Magic in the Biblical World." *TynBul* 34 (1983): 169–200.

———. "Magic or Miracle? Disease, Demons and Exorcisms." In *The Miracles of Jesus*, edited by David Wenham and Craig Blomberg, 89–183. Gospel Perspectives 6. Sheffield: JSOT Press, 1986.

Yates, Roy. "Jesus and the Demonic in the Synoptic Gospels." *ITQ* 44 (1977): 39–57.

Young, Frances. "Paul and the Kingdom of God." In *The Kingdom of God and Human Society: Essays by Members of the Scripture, Theology and Society Group*, edited by Robin Barbour, 242–55. Edinburgh: T&T Clark, 1993.

Young, William. "Miracles in Church History." *Chm* 102 (1988): 102–21.

Zerwick, Maximilian. "In Beelzebul principe daemoniorum (Lc.11, 14–28)." *VD* 29 (1951): 44–48.

Ziesler, John A. "The Name of Jesus in the Acts of the Apostles." *JSNT* 4 (1979): 28–41.

Ancient Writings Index

Name Index

Subject Index

343

error, theological, and demonization. *See* heresy and demonization

eschatology and exorcism. *See* exorcism: and eschatology

Eusebius, 26, 27n12, 219, 220, 226, 234, 239, 254, 256, 257, 267, 274, 275

exorcism

as battle, 46, 49, 96, 98, 99, 108, 110, 114, 115, 119, 127, 140, 182n48, 196, 197, 198

to bind or muzzle, 46, 119

and blowing, 260–61, 270, 276, 288

of buildings or places, 48

"cast out" (ἐκβάλλω), 93–94, 135, 235, 236

Christian, 52–54, 73–77, 98–99, 127–28, 154–55, 171–73, 268, 276, 279–95

fluctuating fortunes, 291

similar to others, 241–43, 250–54, 290

varying importance, 281–85

of Christians, 257

chronological variation, 30, 36, 164, 208, 279, 283, 289

and conversion, 26, 252, 259, 286, 290

cultural and social variation, 30, 130, 145n98, 209, 279, 283

contemporary church, 9, 292–95

defined, 25n2

diminishing interest in, 30, 209, 279, 283, 291

as divorce bill (see *geṭ* [magical])

engine for evangelism, 26, 27, 279, 281, 290

and eschatology, 48, 89, 92, 93, 94, 96, 98, 99, 114, 128, 134, 135, 154, 167, 169, 172, 197, 217

and evangelism or mission, 26, 27, 28, 29, 49, 50, 51, 53, 76, 77, 85, 87–89, 98–99, 112, 115–16, 118, 137–41, 154, 160–61, 164–68, 170–73, 207, 211, 212, 221, 242, 247, 252, 280–81, 286, 287, 288, 290, 291, 292 (*see also* miracles: and mission [or evangelism])

flowering in Christianity, 27, 53, 279, 289

geographic variation, 30, 36, 164, 165, 208, 209, 279, 283, 289, 291

head-focused, 39, 181n42

magical, 36–42, 44, 53, 153, 208, 210, 280

Christian, 141, 155, 231, 262–64, 280

See also exorcism: text-based

magico-charismatic, 44, 52, 53, 280

and mission. *See* exorcism: and evangelism or mission

in the New Testament, 25

range of kinds, 35, 36–45, 53

reluctance towards, 28, 83, 98, 279, 282, 284, 290

rite of, 35, 40, 225, 243, 252, 276, 287, 288

significance for early Church, 26n12, 52–53, 289–92

over a sufferer, 39, 181–82

text-based, 38, 39, 40, 43, 152–55, 179, 264, 284, 288, 290

threats involved, 40, 45, 287

violent, 40n15, 47, 115

See also smell or odor and exorcism

exorcist(s)

of ancient magic, 36–42, 42–44, 46

apprentices, 43

bilingual, 43

charismatic, 44–45, 52, 53, 280

"elders" (πρεσβύτεροι), 182

"exorcist" (ἐξορκιστής), 25n2

followers of Jesus as, 49–54, 76, 216, 227, 295

Jewish, 92

lifestyle of, 253

office of, 262n163

peripatetic, 38, 42–43, 83, 151, 161–64, 166–67, 172, 187n19, 216, 217, 218, 284 (*see also* prophets: traveling)

Qumran texts and, 182

Syrian, 45

the unknown, 36, 38, 51, 63n22, 118n100, 125–27, 128, 129n2, 132, 153

See also Apollonius of Tyana; exorcism: range of kinds; Jesus; Paul; Qumran and texts; Sceva, sons of

"exorcize" (ἐξορκίζω), 25n2, 40

fasting, 216, 251

and baptism, 219

See also prayer: and fasting

finger (of God), 47, 48, 87, 89, 90, 91, 93, 94, 134, 135, 141, 193, 194

fish in exorcism, 37

Fronto, Marcus Cornelius, 265, 267

fumigation. *See* smell or odor and exorcism

Galen, 33, 208, 265, 268, 269n19, 271n30, 273–75, 276, 288, 289

Gellius, Aulus, 272